Also in the Variorum Collected Studies Series:

R.B. SERJEANT
Studies in Arabian History and Civilisation

LUCIE BOLENS
L'Andalousie du quotidien au sacré (XIe–XIIIe siècles)

GEORGE MAKDISI
History and Politics in Eleventh-Century Baghdad

FRANZ ROSENTHAL
Science and Medicine in Islam

FRANZ ROSENTHAL
Muslim Intellectual and Social History

C.F. BECKINGHAM
Between Islam and Christendom

WILFERD MADELUNG
Religious Schools and Sects in Medieval Islam

M.J. KISTER
Society and Religion from Jāhiliyya to Islam

M.J. KISTER
Studies in Jāhiliyya and Early Islam

NICHOLAS LOWICK
Islamic Coins and Trade in the Medieval World

NICHOLAS LOWICK
Coinage and History of the Islamic World

S.M. STERN
Coins and Documents from the Medieval Middle East

JEAN MAURICE FIEY
Communautés syriaques en Iran et Irak des origines à 1552

ROBERT MANTRAN
L'Empire ottoman du XVIe au XVIIIe siècle

GEORGES VAJDA
Etudes de théologie et de philosophie arabo-islamique à l'époque classique

Customary and Shari'ah Law in Arabian Society

R. B. Serjeant

Customary and Shari'ah Law in Arabian Society

Routledge
Taylor & Francis Group
LONDON AND NEW YORK

First published 1991 by Ashgate Publishing

Published 2016 by Routledge
2 Park Square, Milton Park, Abingdon, Oxon OX14 4RN
711 Third Avenue, New York, NY 10017, USA

Routledge is an imprint of the Taylor & Francis Group, an informa business

ISBN 9780860782995 (hbk)

A CIP catalogue record for this book is available
from the British Library.

A CIP catalogue record for this book is available
from the US Library of Congress.

Transfered to Digital Printing in 2012

COLLECTED STUDIES SERIES CS349

CONTENTS

This book consists of ix + 340 pages

PUBLISHER'S NOTE

The articles in this volume, as in all others in the Collected Studies Series, have not been given a new, continuous pagination. In order to avoid confusion, and to facilitate their use where these same studies have been referred to elsewhere, the original pagination has been maintained wherever possible.

Each article has been given a Roman number in order of appearance, as listed in the Contents. This number is repeated on each page and quoted in the index entries.

PREFACE

This second collection of eighteen studies is concerned with Arabian society, ancient and contemporary, with emphasis on its law, especially customary law in southern Arabia. The author regards *sharīʿah* as developed from pre-Islamic customary law, mainly outside Arabia, which it modified, sometimes to a quite considerable extent. Customary law which is no mere semi-random assemblage of precedents, is based on certain principles and procedures, sometimes embodied in maxims. I am inclined to think that such maxims simply continued on into Islam in a number of cases. Customary law and practice as they exist today do seem, taken as a whole, to be a continuation of pre-Islamic law with minor modifications whereas *sharīʿah* diverges in many important respects from it. A case in point is the change in procedure made by the "improved" letter to Abū Mūsā the authenticity of which is disputed by the celebrated Ibn Ḥazm. Acquaintance with Arabian custom and customary law is helpful in interpreting the pre-Islamic inscriptions and it can also contribute to understanding of the Qur'ān, the Sīrah of the Prophet and early Islamic history. Quite recently it has come to my notice that an authority drawn upon by one of the customary law documents I am editing would have written in Ṣanʿā' about 500 H. and doubtless he drew on much older traditional law.

In the texts corrections have been made to printers' slips which these days are far commoner than formerly, now that printing costs mean that an author rarely is accorded a second proof – in one article they were exceptionally many.

The author is happy to have the opportunity to express his thanks to Arab friends and other scholars who have accorded him such generous help and who still continue to do so. This has been much more than it has been possible to acknowledge in the articles themselves. He also gratefully acknowledges the kindness of the editors of the various journals, conference proceedings and Festschrifts in graciously permitting him to reproduce the articles of his which they published. He again expresses his thanks to Variorum in the person of Dr John Smedley who has again seen this volume through the press with unfailing patience.

St. Andrews, Scotland
January, 1991

R.B. SERJEANT

I

The Ḍa‘īf and the Mustaḍ‘af and the status accorded them in the Qur’ān

Let me commence this paper with the prosaic statement that the Qur’ân concordance lists nine places where the word *ḍa^{c}īf* occurs (in its singular or plural forms) and the word *istaḍ^{c}afa* or *mustaḍ^{c}af* also nine times.

Commenting on *Sûrat al-Baqarah* (Qur’ân, II:282), Ibn ^{c}Abbâs[1] explains *ḍa^{c}īf* in the phrase *ḍa^{c}īf-an safīh-an* as "*aḥmaq*[2], stupid!", and *safīh* as "*jâhil*, unlettered", both in Kinânah dialect. Rippin quotes a 6th century author as rendering *safīh* as "unlettered, a child, women and children, or squanderers of money and corrupters of religion". I do not intend to deal with *safīh* here but it seems to me to mean ’foolish, unsteady, irresponsible’, a combination of all these ideas – as far as one can find an equivalent for this word in

1 Quoted in A. Rippin, ’Ibn ^{c}Abbâs’s Al-lughât fī ’l-Qur’ân’, *BSOAS*, London, 1981, XLIV,I,23.

2 Lane, *Lexicon*, gives the senses, ’foolish, unsound in intellect or understanding’. *The Sabaic dictionary*, ed. Beeston et alii, Leiden, 1982, reports a root *sfh* but not *ḍ^{c}f*.

English. The explanations of *ḍa*ᶜ*īf* attributed to Ibn ᶜAbbâs however are interpretative and secondary meanings of the word. Translators of the Qur'ân into English, relying on such secondary interpretations of *ḍa*ᶜ*īf* and *mustaḍ*ᶜ*af*, have, in my view, failed to comprehend the full significance of the two words, rendering *ḍa*ᶜ*īf* simply as 'weak' and *mustaḍ*ᶜ*af* as 'weak' also, or 'oppressed'.

My contention is that in certain Quranic contexts the sense of *ḍa*ᶜ*īf* should be understood in the light of its usage in the *Ḥadîth* which concurs with that of Arabian society, without interruption, right up to our present age. *Ḍa*ᶜ*īf*, weak, is a term applied by the Arabians to persons without the capacity to fight for and defend themselves, therefore to those classes which do not bear arms[1], the majority being peasants, perhaps also shepherds, but including craftsmen, petty tradesmen and others. Women and children are also considered to be *ḍa*ᶜ*īf*.[2] I have defined the *ḍa*ᶜ*īf* as 'the opposite of a strong (*qawî*)

---

1 See my 'South Arabia' in C.A.O. van Nieuwenhuijze, *Commoners, climbers and notables*, Leiden, 1977, reprint in my *Studies in Arabian history and civilisation*, London, 1981, IX, 232.

2 *Ibid., loc. cit.*, described to me in Ḥaḍramawt as workers in clay, builders, potters, field-workers.

tribesman or person of noble birth called *sharîf* '. In the *Ḥadîth* which provides the incontrovertible evidence of this sense of *ḍaᶜîf* it is also the opposite of *qawî* and *kabîr*. A tradition quoted by Muslim[1] states that '*al-mu'min al-qawî khayr ... min al-mu'min al-ḍaᶜîf*, the strong/powerful believer is better ... than the weak believer. The Prophet commanded support (*naṣr*) of the *ḍaᶜîf*.[2] Muslim *ḍaᶜafah*, perhaps in this sense, are mentioned as being present at the battle of Badr and Wâqidî[3] reports that the Prophet gave equal shares of the booty to the '*fâris al-qawm alladhî yaḥmî-him*' and to the *ahl al-ḍaᶜîf*). On both sides at Badr the *Sîrah* records the names of *mawlâs* who took some part in the battle or were present at it though I think they would be accounted *ḍaᶜîf* in the social order.

Ṭabarî[4] describes the Prophet's followers as *al-ḍuᶜafâ' wa-'l-masâkîn wa-'l-aḥdâth min al-ghilmân wa-'l-nisâ'*, the weak,

---

1 Muslim, *Ṣaḥîḥ*, Cairo, 1374-75/1955-56, IV,2052.

2 Bukhârî, *Ṣaḥîḥ*, Cairo, 1345 H., VIII, 65. Illustrative of the standing of the *ḍaᶜîf* is a *ḥadîth* (Muslim, *op. cit.*, III,1457) reported on the authority of Abû Dharr. 'I [Abû Dharr] said: "O Apostle of Allah, why do you not appoint me governor *(tastaᶜmilu-nî)*?" (He said) And he clapped his hand on my shoulder, then he said: "O Abû Dharr, you are a *ḍaᶜîf*, and it is a trust/charge *(amânah)*"'. The plain sense of this would seem to be that his lowly status made this out of the question, however worthy he might be in other respects.

3 *Kitâb al-Maghâzî*, ed. Marsden Jones, Oxford, 1966, I,99.

4 *Ta'rîkh*, ed. de Goeje et alii, Leiden, 1879-90, I,III,1563.

poor[1], young lads and women. Whereas of 'the elder and persons of honour of his people not one followed him (*ammâ dhawu 'l-asnân wa-'l-sharaf min qawmi-hi falam yattabi*ᶜ*-hu min-hum aḥad-un*)'. This of course was in the early stages of his mission. The *ḍa*ᶜ*îf* then is not a person *physically* weak in these contexts, but one of inferior status in society.

The contrast between the two categories is apparent in the interesting *ḥadîth* of the Caliph ᶜUmar who is reported as saying: 'The people of al-Kûfah have got the better of me (*ghalaba-nî*). I make the *mu'min* governor over them and he is reckoned weak (*yuḍa*ᶜᶜ*afu*) [and therefore it is behaved insolently towards him][2] and I make the strong (*qawî*) governor over them and he is accused of wrong-doing (*yufajjar*)'. The *mu'min* reckoned weak is ᶜAmmâr b. Yâsir and the other governor is Abû Mûsâ al-Ashᶜarî.[3]

*Mustaḍ*ᶜ*af* has been rather loosely rendered by the translators who usually follow such definitions as that given by Ibn al-Athîr[4] who considers *taḍa*ᶜᶜ*aftu* equivalent to *istaḍ*ᶜ*aftu-hu*,

---

1 I am inclined to think that *masâkîn* in this context does not mean 'poor', but the settled artisan groups described in my *Studies in Arabian history*, *op. cit.*, IX,230.

2 So in Lane, *Lexicon*. The *ḥadîth* is quoted by Ibn Al-Athîr, *Nihâyah*, Cairo, 1311/1893-94, III,20.

3 See my 'The Caliph ᶜUmar's letters to Abû Mûsâ al-Ashᶜarî and Muᶜâwiya', *Journal of Semitic Studies*, Manchester, 1984, XXIX,73 *seq*.

4 Loc. cit. Cf. Ibn Sîdah, *al-Mukhaṣṣaṣ*, 11, 97, *al-ḍa*ᶜ*f*, XII,201, *istiḍâf*.

adding that, because of a man's neediness and mean state, people treat him insolently/haughtily. One would expect however that *istaḍ^{c}afa* would convey something of the sense 'to consider weak', even, 'to make weak'. Balâdhurî[1] provides an important definition of the *mustaḍ^{c}afs* as 'those who have no tribe (^{c}*ashîrah*)[2] and no *man^{c}ah'*. *Man^{c}ah* is not easy to define, but it may be taken here as the protection which a man enjoys as a member of an arms-bearing group. Balâdhurî's *mustaḍ^{c}af* has, then, a status identical with that of the *ḍa^{c}îf*. The *mustaḍ^{c}afûn* who were included in the circle of the Prophet's early adherents were ^{c}Ammâr b. Yâsir, Bilâl a slave later freed, Khabbâb a *mawlâ* a freed slave, ^{c}Āmir b. Fuhayrah who became a Muslim while *mamlûk* (owned), Abû Fakayhah a *mawlâ* of the Banû ^{c}Abd al-Dâr.

Ibn Isḥâq/Ḥishâm[3] indicates that Abû Jahl, a chief of Makhzûm ,[4] was the individual who used to rouse Quraysh against the followers of the Prophet and he describes his policy in his treatment of the various social classes in Mecca. 'When he heard that a man who had honour and protection (*sharaf wa-man^{c}ah*) had accepted Islam (*aslam*) he severely rebuked and shamed him, saying: "You have abandoned the religion of your father, a better man than you are. We shall indeed declare you to be unsteady/foolish/irresponsible (*la-nusaffihanna ḥilma-ka*), declare your judgement to be poor

---

1 *Kitâb Ansâb al-Ashrâf*, I, ed. Muḥammad Ḥamîdullâh, Cairo, 1959, 156.

2 For the various definitions of ^{c}*ashîrah* see Lane, *Lexicon*; it seems to be a small sub-tribe, family even.

3 *Al-Sîrat al-Nabawiyyah*, ed. al-Saqqâ et alii, Cairo, 1375/1955, I,320.

4 Banû Makhzûm had sided with the ^{c}Abd al-Dâr when the Prophet's ancestors, ^{c}Abd Manâf, fell out with them in the Jâhiliyyah.

and detract from your honour (*sharaf*)". If he was a merchant he would say: "Indeed, by Allah, we shall bring about a slump in your trading and put an end to your wealth". If he was a *ḍaᶜīf* he would beat him and incite [people] against him'. It is evident from this passage that there were three main classes in Mecca, the independent possessors of *sharaf*, a probably intermediate class of merchants, and the *ḍaᶜīfs* who were not fighting men and obviously lacked sharaf. It seems to have been the objective of the powerful arms-bearing groups in pre-Islamic Arabia to reduce their opponents to the status of *ṣaghâr wa-dhillah*, i.e. humiliation - as the Yathrib tribes had at least partly done to the Jewish tribes before Islam, and the Prophet's opponents sought to do to him when they concluded a pact to cut off intermarriage with the Banû Hâshim and ban trading with them.

It might have been expected that the emigrants to Abyssinia would have been described as *mustaḍᶜafûn* - if we understand the term *istaḍᶜafa* as to seek to make *ḍaᶜīf*, but this is not used of them. Many, indeed most, were of noble birth, but a poem does speak of them escaping from humiliation (*al-dhull wa-'l-makhzâh wa-'l-hûn*). The Prophet himself did not accompany them to Abyssinia because of his position with Allah (*bi-makâni-hi min Allâh*)[1] and his paternal uncle Abû Ṭâlib, but he was unable to protect (*yamnaᶜ*) them.

---

1 This, I presume, refers to the Prophet's standing as a member of the ᶜAbd Manâf house which held certain offices and functions by right at Mecca, linked to the shrine.

Qur'ân passages

The most significant passage containing the word *ḍa*^{c}*îf* in the sense which has been discussed above is Sûrah II:282, cited below:[1]

يٰٓاَيُّهَا الَّذِيْنَ اٰمَنُوْٓا اِذَا
تَدَايَنْتُمْ بِدَيْنٍ اِلٰٓى اَجَلٍ مُّسَمًّى فَاكْتُبُوْهُ ۭ
وَلْيَكْتُبْ بَّيْنَكُمْ كَاتِبٌۢ بِالْعَدْلِ ۠ وَلَا يَاْبَ
كَاتِبٌ اَنْ يَّكْتُبَ كَمَا عَلَّمَهُ اللّٰهُ فَلْيَكْتُبْ ۚ وَلْيُمْلِلِ
الَّذِيْ عَلَيْهِ الْحَقُّ وَلْيَتَّقِ اللّٰهَ رَبَّهٗ وَلَا يَبْخَسْ
مِنْهُ شَيْـًٔا ۭ فَاِنْ كَانَ الَّذِيْ عَلَيْهِ الْحَقُّ سَفِيْهًا
اَوْ ضَعِيْفًا اَوْ لَا يَسْتَطِيْعُ اَنْ يُّمِلَّ هُوَ فَلْيُمْلِلْ
وَلِيُّهٗ بِالْعَدْلِ ۭ

The translation into English would run:

1. 'O you who have believed, when you contract a debt, one to the other, for a stated/named term/period, write it down.

2. And let a writer/someone who is able to write [Bell] write between you justly; and let not a writer refuse to write as

---

1 See Ṭabarî, *Tafsîr*, ed Maḥmûd & Aḥmad Shâkir, Cairo n.d., VI,43; Richard Bell, *The Qur'an translated*, Edinburgh, 1937-39,I,41.

Allah has taught him.

3. And let him write and let him who owes the due dictate and let him act honestly [1] to Allah, his Lord, and not omit any [part] of it.

4. And if he who owes the due is a *safīh*/foolish/irresponsible person or *ḍa*ᶜ*īf* unable to dictate he [himself], let his protector/supporter/lord dictate justly'.

Arrangements for witnesses follow. Small or large amounts and their term are to be written down, 'unless it be *tijârah ḥâḍirah* which you are circulating among you'. This latter phrase Ṭabarî interprets as ready money transactions.

Ibn ᶜAbbâs[2] interprets this clause 1 as applying to *al-salam fî 'l-ḥinṭah, fî kayl ma*ᶜ*lûm ilâ ajal ma*ᶜ*lûm*, an advance for wheat, for a known measure up to a known period/term. However earlier in this sûrah (verse 261) it is stated that: "The like of those who spend their properties in the way of Allah is the like of a grain that produced/put forth seven heads of corn (*sanâbil*), there being a hundred grains in each head'. This is suggestive more of the millet family than of wheat. It is however clause 4 which concerns us here. *Walî* is rendered by Rippin as 'legal guardian' but this appears to me to be a developed idea unlikely to be appropriate in the society of Medina/Yathrib. One has only to consult the arrangements for security in the city[3] to see that the protector or supporter of a *ḍa*ᶜ*īf* is likely to have been a tribesman, perhaps even a *naqîb*.

---

1 *Yattaqî*, to act with clean hands. I have discussed this root in *Studies in Arabian history*, articles V & VI,21.

2 Ṭabarî, loc. cit.

3 *Studies in Arabian history*, VI,10.

In the Medinan community the *ḍa^{c}īf* to whom clause 4 refers would, in the majority of cases, most likely be a cultivator, a suggestion which is supported by the view of Ibn ^{c}Abbâs that the due or debt is in respect of grain, though the actual transaction itself is a little vague. If it relates to a share-cropping contract the advance might be of the kind that the capitalist makes to the cultivator. This need not concern us here. If the *ḍa^{c}īf* is indeed a cultivator and one unable to write, it could well be that the city *mufassirs* of the Qurân would consider him dull stupid (*'aḥmaq*), but this is not the basic sense of *ḍa^{c}īf*. It is of course very unlikely that a *ḍa^{c}īf* would be able to dictate sufficiently coherently for a document of law, or even a written document in general, and I have myself seen illiterates in Arabia explaining their case to a 'writer' who would formulate their words into language appropriate to it.

Sûrah II, 266, considers the case in a kind of parable of a man overcome by old age who has *dhurriyyatun ḍu^{c}afâ'u*, rendered by Bell, 'an offspring of weaklings' and in the same sense by Rodwell and the earlier translator Sale. In my view it means 'offspring unable to defend themselves', i.e., 'unprotected'. Ibn ^{c}Abbâs[1] comes near this sense when he explains the passage as 'His offspring were unable to defend their garden [against the fiery wind] because of their youth'. *Sûrat al-Nisâ'* (IV,9) alludes to 'Those who, should they leave behind them *dhurriyyatan ḍi^{c}âfan*, would fear on their account', and this I would certainly understand as 'unprotected' rather than physically weak.

---

1 Ṭabarî, *Tafsîr, 546.*

Sûrat Hûd (XI, 91), in the account of the mission of the prophet Shu^{c}ayb to Madyan, tells that the tribe of Madyan said: 'O Shu^{c}ayb we do not understand (*nafqahu*, rendered by the commentary[1] 'recognise the truth of') much of what you say and we consider you among us a *ḍa^{c}îf* and but for your sept (*rahṭ*)[2] we should stone you, and you are not at all noble/honourable/esteemed over us/more than we are (*wa-mâ anta* ^{c}alay-nâ bi-^{c}*azîzin*)'. Shu^{c}ayb replies: 'O my tribe (*qawmi*) is my sept more noble/honourable/esteemed over you than Allah?' The Qur'ânic passage clearly reflects Muḥammad's own situation with regard to Quraysh in Mecca, protected by his own small sept of the clan. Shu^{c}ayb's rejoinder means that he is under the protection of Allah whose power to defend him is surely infinitely greater than that of his own sept or sub-clan. The commentators appear to be puzzled by *ḍa^{c}îf* here and maintain that Shu^{c}ayb was blind, but the word *ḍa^{c}îf* in the context here can only refer to his social status, and clearly the intention is to lower it - to *'istaḍ^{c}af'* it, in fact. The Prophet possessed both *sharaf*, honour, and protection through his family as already stated above.

Sûrat Ibrâhîm (XIV, 21), says: 'The *ḍu^{c}afâ'* said to those who considered themselves to be chiefs[3]: "We were followers of you (*kunnâ la-kum taba^{c}an*). Can you protect us/avail us at

1 Ṭabarî, op. cit., XV,457.

2 Ibn al-Athîr, op. cit., II, defines the *rahṭ* as the ^{c}*ashîrah* of a man and his family, making it variously less than ten men, or up to forty men. This would seem to fit in with the numbers of the Abû Ṭâlib house.

3 The commentator explains *istakbarû* as referring to the leaders (*qâdah*) and it can mean 'to be full of pride'. The *ḍu^{c}afâ'* are defined as *al-tubbâ' min-hum li-'l-matbû'in*, the followers of them of the followed.

all against the punishment of Allah?" They said: "Were Allah to guide us we should certainly guide you"'. This context leaves us in little doubt of the situation of the *ḍuʿafâ'* as coming under the protection of the *kabîrs*, the latter word meaning, in ancient and contemporary Arabia, a tribal chief, who of course were unable to protect them against Allah.

Sûrat Ghâfir (XL, 47) envisages the wrangling and reproaches of the unbelievers when consigned to Hell. 'The *ḍuʿafâ'* say to those who considered themselves to be chiefs: "We were followers of you. Can you protect/avail us against a share/portion of Hell-fire?" Those who considered themselves to be chiefs said: "We are all in it. Allah has already judged (*ḥakama*) between the servants [of Allah *ʿibâd*]"'. There is a kind of imagery here of God as a tribal arbiter and the tribe and its followers sharing in suffering any penalty the arbiter awards.

The responsibility of the tribal leaders for turning the *ḍaʿîf* group away is repeated in *Sûrat Saba'* (XXXIV, 31): 'Those who were considered weak say to those who considered themselves chiefs: "But for you we would have been believers"'. Again the Qur'ân pictures the recriminations that follow their accusations, with the chiefs rejecting the accusations of the *mustaḍʿafûn*.

The Prophet's situation in Mecca and the social order that existed there is also reflected in *Sûrat al-Aʿrâf* (VII, 75) in the story of Ṣâliḥ. 'The *Mala'*[1] of his people who considered

---

1 The *Mala'* was a sort of council of leading men exercising authority. The Prophet also had a *Mala'* in Medina. Ibn al-Athîr, op. cit., IV, 104, defines the *Mala'* as *Ashrâf al-nâs wa-ru'asâ'u-hum wa-muqaddamû-hum alladhîna urjaʿu ilâ qawli-him.*

themselves to be chiefs said to those who were considered to be *ḍa*ᶜ*îfs* – to those of them who believed: "Do you know that Ṣâliḥ was sent from his Lord?" They said: "We believe in that with which he was sent". Those who considered themselves to be chiefs said: "We do not believe in that with which you were sent"'.

In *Sûrat al-Tawbah* (IX, 89) it is possible that the *ḍu*ᶜ*afâ'* might be interpreted as 'physically weak'. The midsummer being hot the Aᶜrâb, tribesmen, the Banû Ghifâr being named by Ibn Isḥâq, proffer excuses for not joing an expedition, no doubt that made to Tabûk. These were unacceptable to the Prophet, but he exempted the *ḍu*ᶜ*afâ'*, the sick (*marḍâ*) and those without the wherewithal to provide for it. It seems to me however that here again the *ḍu*ᶜ*afâ'* were those of the non-arms-bearing class, not 'physically weak' persons, and in any case the latter would probably be covered by the term *marḍâ*. The Aᶜrâb tribesmen, fighters and others who *qa*ᶜ*ada*, the word is still used in this sense today in Ḥaḍramawt, 'stayed still' and did not go to war are promised painful punishment by the Qur'ân. The *Musnad* of Ibn Ḥanbal[1] has a tradition that 'the *jihâd* of the old man (*kabîr*), the *ḍa*ᶜ*îf* and the woman is the *Ḥajj* and ᶜ*Umrah*'. Ṭabarî[2] categorizes those whose duty it was to join the expedition as either a *mujtahid ṭâ'i*ᶜ or *munâfiq fâsiq*. A *ṭâ'i*ᶜ is an individual or group responding to the sum-

---

1 *Musnad*, Cairo, 1313 H., II,421. Ibn Hanbal, I,212 340 speaks of *amara ḍa*ᶜ*afata Banî Hâshim*, he ordered the *ḍa*ᶜ*îfs* of the Banû Hâshim.

2 Tafsir, XIV,418.

mons to come out and fight, as embodied in the phrase, *al-sam*[c] *wa-'l-ṭâ*[c]*ah*, to hear and obey, a cliché still used in tribal Arabia to our own day.

In *Sûrat al-Qaṣaṣ* (XXVIII, 4) it is recounted that 'Pharaoh became exalted in the land and he made the people of it into parties (*shiya*[c]*an)* seeking to degrade *(yastaḍ*[c]*ifu)* a section (*ṭâ'ifah)*[1] of them, slaughtering their sons and sparing their women ... We wish to show favour to those who were degraded/treated as *ḍa*[c]*îf* in the land and make them *imâms* and make them the heritors'. Bell maintains that the passage is Medinan but largely based on earlier versions. The redactors of the Qur'ân however assign the sûrah to the Meccan period and the parable of Pharaoh's treatment of Moses seems to reflect conditions for the Prophet and his followers at Mecca rather than Medina. *'Imâms'* is often understood as 'leaders in religion', 'spiritual leaders', but the sense of 'models, examples' may well be better suited to the context. It looks however as if the passage had been expanded at this

1 *Ṭâ'ifah* is the term employed to denote a tribe of the *Anṣâr*, section or group, in Document A of the 'Eight documents' (so-called '*Constitution of Medina*').

point.

In a passage of *Sûrat al-Nisâ'* (IV,75) which Bell places 'some considerable time after Uḥud'[1] the Qur'ân harangues *'alladhîna âmanû'*[2]: 'What is the matter with you that you do not fight in the way of Allah and [for] the *mustaḍᶜaf* (Bell, 'oppressed') of men, women and children who say: "Lord of ours, take us out of this city (*qaryah*) the people of which are unjust, and assign us a protector (*walî*) from with you, and assign us a supporter (*naṣîr-an*) from with you"'. Further on (IV,97) those who say: 'We were *mustaḍᶜaf* in the land' are exhorted: 'Is not the land of Allah wide so that you can make the *hijrah* in it?' The sûrah goes on however to state that men, women and children who can find no way to make the *hijrah* may be pardoned by Allah.[3] *Sûrat al-Anfâl* (VIII,26) exhorts (the believers)[4]: 'Remember when you were few, *mustaḍᶜafûn* in the land, fearing that the people would carry you

1 Bell, op.cit., I,78.

2 It is to be remarked that *âmanû* not *aslamû* is used. For my discussion of the two categories of *Mu'minûn*, which could mean 'those who grant security', and the *Muslimûn*, see *Studies in Arabian history*, VI,12 seq. The two terms become more or less synonymous.

3 It seems logical to suppose this passage was composed before the *ṣulḥ* at al-Ḥudaybiyah, after which the Prophet would not accept *mustaḍᶜaf* in Medina. Verse 75 ends in *naṣîran* and verse 97 in *maṣîran*. It occurs to mind that these verses may have followed directly, one after the other, before the final redaction of the Qur'ân.

4 An earlier verse (24) asks *alladhîna âmanû* to respond to God and His Apostle when He/he summons you.

off by force[1], and He found you refuge (in Medina) and aided you with His support (*naṣr*)'.

****

On examination of the Qur'ânic passages cited above, it does seem clear that the term *ḍaᶜîf* as employed in them does mean a person of inferior social status who requires protection by those who hold the power to defend him - if necessary by aggressive action against those who molest him. The powerful arms-bearing tribesfolk take great pride in protecting their *ḍaᶜîf*s and exacting compensation or retaliation for any injury done to them.

Whether the term *mustaḍᶜaf* was applied also to those of the Prophet's adherents enjoying high social status who endured insult and detraction of their honour at the hands of their fellow tribesmen in Mecca is uncertain. In the *Sîrah* and other early writings it is possible that the use of *mustaḍᶜaf*[2] may have consciously been avoided - as being uncomplimentary to persons of high social standing and of religious eminence at the same time. But there is no evidence known to me that this was so.

The question arises as to whether or not it was the policy of the Prophet to abolish the distinction between the *qawî* and

---

1 I have followed Ṭabarî in translating *yatakhaṭṭafa-kumu* but this seems to me an unlikely sense. Dozy, *Supplément*, "arracher à quelqu'un ce qu' il possède", "to tear away from someone that which he possesses", seems more suitable to the situation.

2 It is the case however that Bukhârî reports a Tradition that Ibn ᶜAbbâs and his mother were of the *mustaḍᶜaf*s. The term *ḍaᶜîf mustaḍᶜaf* is found in Ibn Mâjah, *zuhd*,4. Ibn al-Athîr, *Nihâyah*,III,20, defines al-*ḍuᶜafâ'* as *alladhîna yubarri'ûna anfusa-hum min al-ḥawl wa-'l-quwwah.*

the *ḍa*ᶜ*īf*. *Sûrat al-Qaṣaṣ* (XXVIII, 6), classified as 'Meccan', promises the people whom Pharaoh *'yastaḍ*ᶜ*if'* that 'We shall establish firmly/strengthen them in the land (*numakkina lahum fi 'l-arḍ*)'. It should be remarked that *makkana* can also mean 'to give power/authority to'. Assuming that this verse describing Pharaoh's treatment of the Banû Isrâ'îl reflects the parallel situation of the Prophet at Mecca, it nonetheless seems to me that the intention is to do no more than to settle and ameliorate the condition of the *ḍa*ᶜ*īf*. In the passage from *Sûrat al-Baqarah* quoted above, it is evident that the existence of *ḍa*ᶜ*īf* status is recognized as a plain fact of the social structure – the clear intention of this passage is to ensure equitable and honest treatment for the *ḍa*ᶜ*īf*. It does not envisage an alteration in the social system. (Whether it is to be deduced from other Qur'ânic passages that such a change was envisaged, I leave an open question.) Indeed, as history relates, the Prophet came to terms with his erstwhile opponents, the aristocrats of Quraysh, once he had gained control of Mecca; after the reconciliation they even made common cause against the Prophet's foes.

Supplementary note

Abû Sufyân, in reproaching the Hâshimites for inaction when Abû Bakr was elected *khalîfah*, says: 'What has Abû Bakr to do with your affairs? Where are the two *mustaḍ*ᶜ*af*s, where are the two humiliated ones (*al-adhallân*), ᶜAlî and al-ᶜAbbâs?' (Ṭabarî, *Ta'rîkh*, I,IV,1827) They had, in his view as reported by Ṭabarî, lost status to a member of one of the least considered of the clans of Quraysh.

* * * * *

Addenda

P.35/15 ʿUmar's dictum to meet this situation is that only the flexible (*layyin*) without weakness (*ḍaʿf*) and the strong (*qawiyy*) without violence/severity (*ʿunf*) is suitable for this (governorship, *wilāyah*) Ibn ʿAbd Rabbihi, *al-ʿIqd*, Cairo, 1359/1940, I, 28.

P.36/6 An *ʿashīrah* is said to be a group whose ancestor is known to be ten generations back. Muḥammad asked the tribes to *yamnaʿū-hu*, Ṭabarī, *Tārīkh*, I, 1204. On his deathbed Umayyah b. al-Ṣalt says: *Lā ʿashīrati taḥmī-nī wa-lā mālī yafdī-nī* (Ibn Qutaybah, *ʿUyūn al-akhbār*, Cairo, 1383/1963, II, 310.

II

THE CALIPH 'UMAR'S LETTERS TO ABŪ MŪSĀ AL-ASH'ARĪ AND MU'ĀWIYA

The authenticity of 'Umar's well known letter to Abū Mūsā al-Ash'arī on the conduct of the *qāḍī* has long been suspect to western scholars; Emile Tyan has shown conclusively, with an excellent coverage of sources that, as we now have it, the letter cannot be accounted genuinely to 'Umar.[1] Major early Muslim authorities do not as much as refer to it, and the Andalusian Ibn Ḥazm (d. 456/1064) rejects it positively as spurious.[2] This is naturally disturbing to Muslim scholars for, as Ibn Qayyim al-Jawziyya says, "This is a highly esteemed letter (*kitāb*) which the ulema accepted and upon which they constructed the bases of judgement (*uṣūl al-ḥukm*) and testimony, and the *ḥākim* and *muftī* most greatly require it".[3] While Margoliouth remarks that it "whether genuine or not, is of great importance for the history of Muslim judicial institutions",[4] Dr Muḥammad Ḥamīdullāh has made considerable researches in the effort to prove the letter genuine.[5] He has published not 'Umar's other much briefer letter to Abū Mūsā, but another virtually identical letter which the Caliph sent to Mu'āwiya; but the possibility that the shorter letter (Abū Mūsā 2) may be connected with the famous letter (Abū Mūsā 1), as I have suggested in the *Cambridge history of Arabic literature*, I,[6] finds no place in his valuable collection of basic Islamic documents. Yet the

1 *Histoire de l'organisation judiciaire en pays d'Islam*, Leiden 1960, 77-80.

2 *al-Muḥallā*, Cairo 1347, I, 59. He calls it *al-risāla al-makdhūba al-mawḍū'a 'alā 'Umar*, "the false, lying letter imposed on 'Umar."

3 *I'lām al-muwaqqi'īn 'an Rabb al-'Ālamīn*, Cairo n.d., 72.

4 "Omar's instructions to the Kadi", *JRAS* (1910), 307 ff.

5 *Majmū'at al-wathā'iq al-siyāsiyya li 'l-'ahd al-nabawī wa 'l-khilāfa al-rāshida*, 2nd ed. Beirut 1389/1969, 343 f. It is curious that the text of the famous letter is missing in several mss. consulted by him. Cf. *J. Pak. Hist. Soc.* (1971).

6 Cambridge 1983, 148-9. *Qaḍā'* was apparently not a pre-Islamic practice.

"improved" letter, as I regard Abū Mūsā I, if it must lose the authority of the second Caliph, has nonetheless the validity of representing the attitudes of the Islamic ulema as they evolved in the early second century – to which it undoubtedly belongs – and to recognise it as such seems in no way to impugn the faith.

The Arabic text of Abū Mūsā I is well enough known not to require to be reproduced here, but concerning Margoliouth's rendering of it, Ḥamīdullāh says with some justice that "it is hopelessly unsuccessful and scarcely gives a correct idea of the contents[7]." His own translation, however, inserts or omits material or else supplies senses not in the original. The following is an essay at a close literal translation without pretensions to elegance. The text followed is that of Margoliouth.[8]

1. Pronouncing judgement (*qaḍā'*) is an established/unequivocal ordinance and followed practice (*sunna*).

2. You must understand, when a case is contested before[9] you, that the pronouncement of a judgement (*ḥaqq*) which cannot be put into effect is no use.

3. Act impartially between the people in your audience-room (*majlis*) and before you,[10] so that the man of noble status (*sharīf*) be not greedy for your partiality and the man of inferior status (*ḍa'īf*[11]) despair of justice from you.

4. The onus of the proof is on the plaintiff and the oath on him who denies [the charge].

5. Conciliation (*ṣulḥ*) is permissible between people, except a conciliation which make licit what is forbidden or forbids what is licit.

7 "Administration of justice in early Islam", *IC*, XI (1937), 169.

8 *Loc. cit.* Many variant readings are given by Margoliouth; further variants may occur in texts published since his time and noted by Ḥamīdullāh. These do not, however, affect the main propositions of the text to any significant extent. Lesser variants are disregarded here. On the whole, these seem to arise from defects in the script rather than oral transmission.

9 al-Ṭabarī, *Tafsīr*, ed. Maḥmūd and Aḥmad Shākir, Cairo 1374/1954-5 ff; III, 548-9, commenting on sūra II, 188, *tudlū bi-hā ila 'l-ḥukkām*, says it means *tukhāṣimū bi-hā*. The Qur'ān is warning against taking property cases before *ḥākims* on account of the waste involved. This seems to indicate that this form of litigation was still practised in Medina.

10 *Fī wajhi-ka* is the common south Arabian expression today for "under your protection" and the sense would certainly fit this context well.

11 For my discussion of this term, see *Studies in Arabian history and civilisation*, London 1981, IX, 232. I have collected classical references which show that this sense is ancient as well as contemporary.

6. Let not a judgement (*qaḍā'*) which you judged yesterday, but over which you re-consulted yourself and were guided to your rectitude, prevent you from retracting to justice/right (*al-ḥaqq*), for nothing can invalidate justice/right. You must realise that retraction to justice/right is better than long persistence in a thing invalid.

7. Pay attention to comprehending what revolves disturbingly in your mind (lit. breast), that has no Qur'ān or practice (*sunna*) applicable to it, and become acquainted with similarities and analogies. Then after that compare the matters. Then have recourse to that which is most preferable to God and most in conformity of them to justice/right (*ḥaqq*) as you see it.

8. Set a term for a person who advances a plea, not being [himself] present, up to which he may come [to present his case].[12] If he produces a proof he will receive his due,[13] but if not, you can deem it permissible to issue a judgement (*qaḍā'*) against him.

9. The Muslims are persons whose testimony is admissible (*'udūl*), with the exception of a person who has received a whipping for [an offence against morality] involving a fixed penalty (*ḥadd*), or from whom false testimony has been experienced, or one suspect on account of client relationship (*walā'*[14]) or kinship (*qarāba*) [to a litigant].

10. God is concerned with your secret hearts and averts [punishment] from you in accordance with outward characters.[15]

11. Have a care to avoid flurriedness, vexation and annoyance with the litigants (*khuṣūm*)[16] in the battlefields (*mawāṭin*[17]) of justice in which God confers reward and makes goodly store. For whosoever's secret heart is right in what lies between him

[12] Margoliouth's rendering here seems to me to be incorrect.

[13] *Akhadha bi-ḥaqqi-hi.*

[14] A *mawlā.*

[15] While Margoliouth's rendering has been accepted here, it still seems to me possible that, for "outward characters", "proofs" could be a valid translation for *bayyināt*. The sense would then be that if a man be proven innocent he will not be punished as a matter of course, but his motives, etc., are a matter between him and God for God to judge.

[16] According to Ḥamīdullāh, *loc. cit.*, Ibn 'Abd Rabbihi, *al-'Iqd al-farīd*, Būlāq ed., reads *iyyā-ka wa'l-tanāfur bi 'l-nās wa'l-tanakkur li 'l-khuṣūm fī 'l-ḥuqūq*, as does al-Balādhurī (in an unpublished ms.) but the Cairo 1359/1940 edn., I, 102,-reads *al-ta'adhdhā*.

[17] *Mawāṭin* simply seems to be "the courts".

and God, God will make right/reconcile[18] what lies between him and the people; and whosoever decks himself out for the world with something other than what God knows of him, God will bring shame upon him.

The letter Abū Mūsā 2 is to be found in Ibn Abi 'l-Ḥadīd's commentary on the *Nahj al-balāgha*.[19] It falls into two parts, a long introduction, mostly aphoristic, differing stylistically from the second part which contains four terse instructions from the Caliph. There can be little doubt that part 1 has been tagged on to part 2 at a considerably later date. I do not think any of part 1 can have emanated from 'Umar; but part 2, which conforms to the language and circumstances of Abū Mūsā's time, I see no reason to think was not addressed to him, and this is the assumption for the moment. The Arabic text of part 2 is given for comparison with Abū Mūsā 1 and 'Umar's letter to Mu'āwiya below.

الزم أربع خصال يسلم لك دينك وتحيط بأفضل حظك.

١ إذا حضر[لك] الخصمان فعليك بالبينات العدول والأيمان القاطعة.

٢ ثم ائذن للضعيف حتى ينبسط لسانه ويجترئ قلبه.

٣ وتعاهد الغريب فإنه إذا طال حبسه ترك حقه وانصرف الى أهله.

٤ واحرص على الصلح مالم يبن القضاء.

والسلام عليك.

The translation of the full version as given by Ibn Abi 'l-Ḥadīd follows.

Part 1

He ('Umar) wrote to Abū Mūsā while he was governor of al-Baṣra, "I have heard that you admit people, all and sundry, all together. So when this letter of mine reaches you, admit those of honourable status (*ahl al-sharaf*), those concerned with the

[18] *Aṣlaḥ Allāh mā bayna-hu wa-bayna 'l-nās*. Perhaps this is also a reference to conciliation (*ṣulḥ*) of clause 5.

[19] The passage is quoted by Ḥasan al-Sandūbī in his edition of al-Jāḥiẓ, *al-Bayān wa 'l-tabyīn*, Cairo 1375/1956, II, 171, in a footnote from the *Nahj*, but I have not traced it in the edition available to me. Ḥamīdullāh, *Majmū'at al-wathā'iq*, 357, quotes the letter without the preamble of Ibn Abi 'l-Ḥadīd, from al-Sarakhsī, *al-Mabsūṭ*, and Wakī', *Akhbār al-quḍāt*, see, below, p. 70 n. 26.

Qur'ān (*ahl al-Qur'ān*) and men of piety and religion (*al-taqwā wa 'l-dīn*). When they have taken their seats[20] admit the commoners (*al-'āmma*). Do not defer today's business till tomorrow so that affairs press on you and get neglected. Beware of those who follow [their] fancies[21], for people have fancies which are pursued, preferred worldly things and hidden rancours. Call yourself to account in [time of] ease before the reckoning of [time of] hardship, for he who calls himself to account in [time of] ease before the reckoning of [time of] hardship will return to content and happiness, whereas he who lets his life distract him and his fancies engross him will revert to repentance and regret. None save a man of firm judgement, extreme patience, bearing no rancour or malice against his subjects[22] applies God's command to the people, Do not let[23] people get to know a fault (*'awra*) of yours and fear not a critic's censure in what is right/just (*al-ḥaqq*).

Part 2.

Stick to four practices/customs, and your conduct (*dīn*) will be sound and you will attain your most abounding fortune.
1. When two opposing parties present themselves, you are responsible [for seeing to the production of] proofs, witnesses of probity[24] and decisive oaths.
2. Then admit the man of inferior status (*ḍa'īf*) so that his tongue may be loosened and his heart emboldened.
3. Look after the stranger, for when he is long detained he will abandon his suit and go back to his people.
4. Take pains to arrive at conciliation so long as judgement (*qaḍā'*) is not clear.
Peace upon you.

Commentary

Dīn, religion, also means *ḥukm* = *qaḍā'*, law, regulation of

20 Lane's *majlas* (pl. *majālis*), places of honour upon which it is forbidden to sit without permission, could well apply here.

21 *Ahwā'*, passions, inclinations, heresies, etc.

22 Ibn al-Athīr, *Nihāya*, citing 'Umar's letter to Abū 'Ubayda (cf. below, p. 73), defines *ḥaṣīf al-'uqda* as *al-muḥkam al-'aql*, and *al-'uqda* here means *al-ra'y wa 'l-tadbīr*.

23 Reading *tuṭli'* for *yuṭli'* of the text.

24 *al-'udūl*, cf. below, p. 71.

affairs, etc. *Ḥaẓẓ*, fortune, is doubtless to be intended in its Qur'ānic senses.[25] *Ḍa'īf* is rendered as "man of inferior status", but though this is applicable to its use in Abū Mūsā I, in the circumstances of this letter it might mean the weaker of two tribal opposing parties.

The text of 'Umar's parallel letter to Mu'āwiya follows, taken from Wakī' (d. 393/1003),[26] evidently an earlier version than that of al-Jāḥiẓ (150-255/767-869)[27] and al-Sarakhsī (d. about the last decade of the 5th/11th century). Al-Jāḥiẓ's authority for the letter is 'Āmir al-Sha'bī (who heard from the Caliph 'Umar's son):

أما بعد فإنى كتبت اليك فى القضاء بكتاب لم آلُك فيه ونفسى خيرًا، فالزم خصالاً يسلم دينك وتأخذ بأفضل حظك عليك.

١ إذا حضر[28] الخصمان فالبينة العدول[29] والأيمان القاطعة.

٢ أَدْنِ الضعيف حتى يجترئ قلبه و ينبسط لسانه.

٣ وتعاهد الغريب فإنه إن طال حبسه ترك حقه[30] وانطلق إلى اهله، وإنما أبطل حقه من لم يرفع به رأسًا.

٤ واحرِص على الصلح بين الناس مالم يستَبِنْ لك القضاء.[31]

Commentary

The al-Jāḥiẓ-al-Sarakhsī texts, virtually the same, contain certain alterations from and additions to the primitive text of Wakī', intended to clarify the sense. Both mention "five practices" (*khiṣāl*) in the preamble – compare with the "four" in the letter to Mu'āwiya – but there are not "five". Where

[25] al-Sarakhsī, *al-Mabsūṭ*, Cairo 1324/1906-7, XVI, 65-6, who quotes the letter to Mu'āwiya, also gives a commentary on the sense. He says it means a thing for which one is praiseworthy in the World and for which one obtains reward in the Hereafter.

[26] *Akhbār al-quḍāt*, Cairo 1366/1947, I, 74-5.

[27] *al-Bayān wa 'l-tabyīn*, ed. al-Sandūbī, II, 171.

[28] al-Jāḥiẓ, al-Sarakhsī, *taqaddama ilay-ka/la-ka*.

[29] *Ibid.*, *fa-'alay-ka bi 'l-bayyina al-'ādila wa 'l-yamīn al-qāṭi'a*.

[30] *Ibid.*, *fa-inna-ka in lam tu'ahhid-hu/tu'āhid-hu wa-inna-mā/wa-rubba-mā ḍayya'a ḥaqqa-hu*.

[31] *Ibid.*, *'alay-ka bi 'l-ṣulḥi bayna 'l-nāsi mā lam yastabin la-ka faṣlu 'l-qaḍā'*.

Wakī''s text has *man lam yarfa'*[32] *bi-hi rās-an* they read *wa-āsi bayn al-nās fī lafẓi-ka wa-ṭarfi-ka* at the end of clause 3. *Wa-āsi* is unmistakably a misreading for *wa-rās-an*, and an additional clause has been created by lifting the sense from clause 3 of letter Abū Mūsā 1. It is not likely that any figure was mentioned in the originals of either of 'Umar's letters.

As the phrase *al-bayyina* (Abū Mūsā 2, *bayyināt*) *al-'udūl wa 'l-aymān al-qāṭi'a* stands, *al-'udūl* is to be understood in apposition to *al-bayyina/āt*,but al-Jāḥiẓ has misunderstood this and substitutes *al-bayyina al-'ādila*, just proof, which has little meaning. The sense in both the earlier letters is that proofs are to be produced, i.e. persons of probity as witnesses and decisive oaths. This looks like the maxim quoted in Abū Mūsā I, but which I believe to be far more ancient, *al-bayyina 'alā man idda'ā wa 'l-yamīn 'alā man ankara.*

The use of the plural "oaths" is also significant, for, in 'Umar's time, *qasāma*, the fifty-fold oath taken by a tribe producing fifty men to swear, would be current practice, as it still is in southern Arabia. *Qasāma* was disliked by the urban *fuqahā'*, and al-Jāḥiẓ may have consciously made the alteration to the singular for this reason, or, familiar with courts where plaintiff and defendant were single individuals, he may have done so thinking to clarify the sense. But al-Jāḥiẓ did not hesitate to tamper with earlier texts.[33]

There is probably more to clause 3 than the simple desire for justice to the stranger, for if he goes back to his tribe, then the latter will seek to obtain justice for him by taking action of an aggressive nature against his opponent, thus by-passing the central authority and threatening the security established by the Sunna Jāmi'a.[34]

Similarly, 'Umar sees that it is dangerous to leave a dispute unsettled and urges that such cases be settled by negotiation. He refers to an earlier letter sent to Mu'āwiya.

Comparison of Abū Mūsā I with Abū Mūsā 2

The clauses of Abū Mūsā I modify Abū Mūsā 2 or are added to it, often to introduce the more developed procedure of the 2nd century A.H.

32 Variant, *yarfuq*.

33 See my remarks in *Cambridge history of Arabic literature*, I, 143.

34 See my "The *Sunnah Jāmi'ah* ...", *BSOAS* (1978), XLI, 17f., repr. in *Studies in Arabian history*.

Clause 1 is a strong asseveration that the function of *qāḍī* is an established institution. It has no place in Abū Mūsā 2, and is intended to justify its existence against any opposing view.

Clause 2 may imply that the *qāḍī* should not issue a judgement which the authorities will overrule.

Clause 3 corresponds to Abū Mūsā 2, no. 2, but gives it a wider application.

Clause 4 corresponds to the content of Abū Mūsā 2, no. 1, but is a maxim perhaps already long established.

Clause 5 corresponds to Abū Mūsā 2, no. 4, but it plays down conciliation as a method of settling cases – this might not be in the interests of the *qāḍī* and seems not to be much approved.[35]

Clause 6 has no parallel in Abū Mūsā 2.

Clause 7 is a statement of the doctrine which was evolving in the 2nd century A.H. and has no place in Abū Mūsā 2.

Clause 8 corresponds to Abū Mūsā 2, no. 3, but completely modifies its attitude and purpose.

Clause 9 deals with *'udūl*, persons of probity whose testimony is acceptable, mentioned in Abū Mūsā 2, no. 1, but takes a radically egalitarian attitude over those qualified to act as such. In tribal society, kinship would be anything but an obstacle in swearing the fifty-fold oath in *qasāma*.

Clauses 10 and 11 have no parallel in 'Umar's original letter and are moralising in tone.

Abū Mūsā al-Ash'arī and the question of qaḍā'

Abū Mūsā was an Ash'arī of the Wādī Rima' tribes, and I recently visited his tomb, reputed by local tradition to be in al-Ḥimā[36] village just east of Zabīd; but he is said to have died in Mecca or al-Kūfa, in which latter place al-Balādhurī places his tomb at *munqaṭa' al-buyūt*, i.e. where the houses stop.[37] He was

[35] Wakī', *op. cit.*, I, 75, quotes a tradition from 'Aṭā', "It is not fitting for the *qāḍī* when the judgement (*qaḍā'*) is clear (*tabayyan*) to arrange conciliation between them (*yuṣliḥ bayna-hum*)". Another tradition (al-Dārimī, *Adab*, 50; al-Tirmidhī, *Birr*, 26) runs, "He who arranges conciliation between people is not a liar (*laysa bi 'l-kādhib man aṣlaḥ bayn al-nās*)".

[36] The name of this place in itself may indicate that it had a certain sacred quality about it. Uways al-Qarnī is also reputed to be buried here, but this too seems incorrect.

[37] *Ansāb al-ashrāf*, IV A, ed. M. Schloessinger and M. J. Kister, Jerusalem 1971, 243. His grave was at a shop (*dukkān*), the owner of which is mentioned.

Abū Bakr's *'āmil*, governor, of Zabīd, Rima', Aden and al-Sāḥil, the coast.[38] His son remained in al-Kūfa and his grandson became Amīr of al-Baṣra. He seems originally to have come to the Ḥijāz with a band of tribal blades seeking service as soldiers, like tribal bands used to come to the Zaydī Imāms. In 17/638 'Umar appointed him to al-Baṣra and a little after this 'Umar sent him a letter, probably Abū Mūsā 2. The corresponding letter that went to Mu'āwiya is likely to have been sent at the same time, on his appointment to Syria in 18/639, and the fact that some reports state that the letter was sent to Abū 'Ubayda b. al-Jarrāḥ,[39] his immediate predecessor, would seem to fix the despatch of the letter in that year.

It has been pointed out that Abū Mūsā was *not* sent as *qāḍī* to al-Baṣra, but as governor.[40] It is inconceivable that the proud and unruly, independent tribes at so early a period were settling their disputes by anything but tribal *'urf* under their hereditary tribal arbiters and headmen (*'arīf*, *naqīb*),[41] without regard or reference to the central authority except as the arbiter of ultimate appeal. These circumstances in themselves negate the possibility of so sophisticated a letter as Abū Mūsā 1 having been sent by 'Umar. The situation is well illustrated by the circumstances under which Abū Mūsā was briefly transferred in 22/642-3 from al-Baṣra to al-Kūfa.[42] 'Umar had appointed as governor there 'Ammār b. Yāsir, whose father was Madhḥijī, 'Ansī, of the Yemen, a *ḥalīf* of the Banū Makhzūm. He married

[38] Muḥammad b. Ḥabīb, *al-Muḥabbar*, Ḥaydarābād 1361/1942,126. *Ibid.*, 305, describes his facial hair, which is typically Yemeni. For a general note on him, see *Ansāb al-ashrāf*, I, 201, ed. Ḥamīdullāh, Cairo 1959. Cf. al-Ṭabarī, *Tārīkh*, ed. de Goeje *et alii*, Leiden 1879-1901, I, 2136; Ibn al-Athīr, *Usd al-ghāba*, Cairo 1284-5, V, 246. For the Ash'arīs, see 'Umar b. Yūsuf b. Rasūl, *Ṭurfat al-aṣḥāb*, ed. K. W. Zettersteen, Damascus 1369/1949, 38.

[39] So Abū Yūsuf, *Kitāb al-Kharāj*, Cairo 1346/1927, 140.

[40] al-Ṭabarī, *Tārīkh*, I, 2693, 'Umar's "governor (*'āmil*) over Kūfa and incidents (*aḥdāth*) was al-Mughīra b. Shu'ba, and over Baṣra, Abū Mūsā al-Ash'arī". His function was administrative rather than judicial.

[41] al-Ḥajjāj made 'Āmir al-Sha'bī (see below, p. 75) *'arīf* for his tribe (*qawm*) and *mankib* (= *rās al-'urafā'*, Ibn al-Athīr, *al-Nihāya*) over all Hamdān. He must have been a man of tribal standing to act in this capacity. For *naqīb*, see my "The *Sunnah Jāmi'ah*...", 10-11. See 'Āmir's biography in al-Dhahabī, *Tadhkirat al-ḥuffāẓ*, Ḥaydarābād 1375-6/1955-6, I, 79.

[42] Ibn Khaldūn, *The Muqaddimah*, tr. F. Rosenthal, New York 1958, I, 453, implies that letter, Abū Mūsā I, was sent to him on his appointment to Kūfa. This seems an error, but as an instruction when replacing the incompetent 'Ammār b. Yāsir in 22/642-3 it would at least be appropriate.

an *ama*, usually meaning a black slave-girl, of a Makhzūm lord, who freed her when she became pregnant with 'Ammār – thus 'Ammār became a client (*mawlā*) of the Banū Makhzūm.[43] The leader of the Banū Tamīm wrote to 'Umar concerning 'Ammār, "He is no *amīr* and the way he acts is insupportable (*mā huwa fī-hi mā yaḥtamil*)".[44] Another chief (*sayyid qawmi-hi*),[45] Jarīr al-Bajalī, told 'Umar to 'Ammār's face that his *amīr* was "inadequate, not giving satisfaction, with no knowledge of how properly to conduct affairs".[46] Yet another chief called him a crop-eared slave (*'abd*). Socially and administratively, 'Ammār was unequal to a task that only a tribal arbiter could perform – perhaps 'Umar had chosen him in pursuance of his known precautionary policy of keeping Quraysh in the Ḥijāz, to be interpreted as a curb on their ambitions which might be furthered by the standing they enjoyed with the tribes. In contrast to 'Ammār, "the judgement (*kalām*) of Abū Mūsā was just like a butcher who never misses the joint/point".[47]

'Umar's letter addressed to the two governors of the only major territories under Muslim control at that time is to be understood as a political guideline for them. Clause 1 is only really a reaffirmation of traditional Arabian legal procedure. 'Umar b. al-Khaṭṭāb, Ibn Qutayba recounts, "recited the verse of Zuhayr b. Abī Sulmā[48] and when he came to his words,

Three are the ways whereby a case/justice is decided,[49] Oath-taking, summoning before a judge (*nifār*), or proof. [To decide in any case, these ways lie before you, Three (in all), each of the bringing you appeasement (*shifā'*)].

'Umar began admiring his knowledge of cases (*'ilma-hu bi 'l-ḥuqūq*) and his distinguishing (*tafṣīl*) between them, saying, 'Justice (*al-ḥaqq*) does not go beyond one of three (things), either an oath, or summoning before an arbiter (*muḥākama*), or proof that rebuts (*ḥujja*)'".[50] This in no way tallies with the opening clause of Abū Mūsā 1, which would have 'Umar declare that *qāḍī*-ship was an established ordinance.

43 *Usd al-ghāba*, IV, 43.
44 al-Ṭabarī, *Tārīkh*, I, 2676.
45 *Usd*, I, 279.
46 al-Ṭabarī, *Tārīkh*, I, 2677.
47 I.e. when chopping up meat. *Mafṣil* (also related to *faṣl*, deciding a case) has both senses – hence the pun.
48 *Dīwān*, Cairo 1944, repr. 1964, 75.
49 Cf. *Cambridge history of Arabic Literature*, I, 123.
50 *'Uyūn al-akhbār*, Cairo 1383/1963, I, 67.

It is significant that Ibn Ḥazm remarks, "In this letter (*risāla*) are things on which they disagree with 'Umar, among them being '*al-Muslimūn 'udūl*... (The Muslims are persons whose testimony is admissible...)'".[51] In the tribal society of the first decades of Islam, the egalitarian attitude that any Muslim's testimony is admissible is not likely to have been current. In Yemeni tribal law documents which I am editing, under *Bāb al-shahāda* it is stated that in *man'a* the testimony of the tax-collector (*jabbā*), merchants and those engaged in demeaning occupations (*mihra daniyya*) is not acceptable. Though these documents are not early, the attitude they take is what would be current in the first century A.H.

This scrutiny of the documents assumes that the simple genuine letter of 'Umar, Abū Mūsā 2, was preserved by his descendants, and ultimately formed a basis for "improved" letter Abū Mūsā 1. Nonetheless, I can recall seeing no positive statement that the family did keep 'Umar's letters before the statement in Wakī''s history that "Abū Mūsā made Abū Burda his executor and produced to him a writing (*kitāb*)".[52] This is said to have contained the text of Abū Mūsā 2 which is quoted – an assertion which arouses suspicion of the reliability of the statement as evidence. Mysteriously, Qatāda is not credited with obtaining the famous expanded letter from any member of Abū Mūsā's descendants, though receiving *ḥadīth* from several of them. Perhaps, if he received it from Bilāl, the latter's bad character would eliminate him as a *thiqa* in the eyes of the traditionists, and to quote it on his authority would not validate it.

The sources of 'Umar's letters to Abū Mūsā and Mu'āwiya

It is simplest to turn first to the letter to Mu'āwiya – this is quoted by al-Jāḥiẓ on the authority of 'Āmir al-Sha'bī, the Sha'bīs being of Hamdān in the Yemen. He was at one time in charge of *al-qaḍā'* in Kūfa under the Umayyads. 'Āmir is

[51] *al-Muḥallā*, I, 59. al-Ṭabarī, *Tārīkh*, I, 2135, says that Abū Bakr made 'Umar a *qāḍī* during his term as Caliph "and he remained a year without anyone bringing a case before him (*yukhāṣim ilay-hi*)". This seems inconsistent with other reports such as al-Ṭabarī, *Tārīkh*, I, 2212, "It is said that in his days 'Umar had no *qāḍī*". Tyan, *op. cit.*, 76, quotes al-Mas'ūdī, *Tanbīh*, tr. Carra de Vaux, 254, as reporting that neither Muḥammad nor the four Rāshidūn Caliphs nominated any *qāḍīs*.

[52] *Op. cit.*, I, 70 f.

regarded as a reliable authority who claimed to commit *ḥadīths* solely to memory and not to write them down.[53] He was a man of integrity and honour. When he was in Medina he heard [traditions] from Ibn 'Umar, the Caliph's son, and could have discussed the letter with him. A version not touched up by al-Jāḥiẓ, nor by those who transmitted to him from 'Āmir al-Sha'bī, is also given by Wakī' (see above, p. 68 n. 19). There is no apparent reason why it cannot be accepted as genuine.

It has been shown that the earliest authority in the *isnāds* for Abū Mūsā I is Qatāda b. Di'āma (60-118/679-736),[54] but it has not been noticed that he related on the authority of Abū Burda b. Abī Mūsā and his son Sa'īd b. Abī Burda[55] "who was one of his contemporaries" and regarded as a *thiqa*.[56] Qatāda, however, also related on the authority of a much better-known member of the house, Bilāl b. Abī Burda b. Abī Mūsā.[57] There are also *isnāds* remounting to 'Abdallāh b. Abī Burda, but the situation is somewhat confused and some of the authorities suspect.[58] Qatāda is an authority who is known for his verbatim narration of *ḥadīth* as he received it. Nowhere is it stated that Qatāda received 'Umar's letter, Abū Mūsā I, from the latter's descendants, but unquestionably he could have done, and it is reasonable to presume that he did. Sufyān b. 'Uyayna (107-98/725-814), al-Jāḥiẓ's authority for Abū Mūsā I,[59] was

53 al-Dhahabī, *op. cit.*, I, 79, quotes an early traditionist as saying that *mursal al-Sha'bī ṣaḥīḥ*, i.e. "traditions not traced up interruptedly to their author quoted by al-Sha'bī are sound".

54 Ibn Ḥajar al-'Asqalānī, *Tahdhīb al-tahdhīb*, Ḥaydarābād 1325-7, VIII, 351 f.

55 Ibn Ḥazm, *Mulakhkhaṣ ibṭāl al-qiyās wa 'l-ra'y wa 'l-istiḥsān wa 'l-taqlīd wa 'l-ta'līl*, ed. Sa'īd al-Afghānī, Damascus 1379/1960, rejects clause 7 of Abū Mūsā I on *qiyās* and *ra'y*, stating that this letter is not genuine and attacking the *isnād* "by way of 'Abdallāh b. Abī Sa'īd, he being unknown (*majhūl*)", but in this latter statement Ibn Ḥazm is in error, for Abū Sa'īd is Abū Burda, who had a son 'Abdallāh whose name follows below. On the margin of the ms of this work a note appears, "On the authority of Idrīs al-Awdī who said, 'Sa'īd produced to us on the authority of Abū Burda a writing (*kitāb*) and said, "This is the *kitāb* of 'Umar to Abū Mūsā," and he mentioned the letter (*risāla*)'. This refers to letter Abū Mūsā I and unequivocally implicates Sa'īd as supporting the "improved" text, but one is left in doubt as to the reliability of this statement.

56 *Tahdhīb*, III, 8.

57 *Ibid.*, I, 500; *Akhbār al-quḍāt*, II, 25.

58 *al-Muḥallā*, IX, 393.

59 al-Dhahabī, *op. cit.*, I, 264, Cf. *'Uyūn al-akhbār*, III, 174.

generally agreed to be a trustworthy narrator of *ḥadīth*, and assuming that the *rijāl* of the *isnād* linking him to Qatāda were also honest men, the redrafting of letter Abū Mūsā 2 into the "improved" Abū Mūsā 1 would have been done and conveyed to Qatāda during the latter's life-time, i.e. prior to 118/736. The evidence points in the direction of Abū Mūsā's descendants as possible composers of letter Abū Mūsā 1.

The descendants of Abū Mūsā al-Ash'arī

Abū Mūsā died in 52/672 or 42/662-3, leaving sons, one of whom was Abū Burda, 'Āmir b. 'Abdallāh, who died, aged 80, in 103/721-2. Abū Burda's mother was Jewish, but though Wakī'[60] cites a poem satirising the Jewish element which thereby entered the line, Abū Burda was respected and one of the first *qāḍīs* of Kūfa. His son by a slave-girl emancipated after bearing her master a male child (*umm walad*), Bilāl (the name itself suggests he may have been black), rose to prominence as Amīr and Qāḍī of al-Baṣra. "Khālid al-Qasrī put him charge of the *qaḍā'* in the year 109/727-8, and he continued as Qāḍī until Yūsuf b. 'Umar came in the year 125/743 and deposed him".[61]

Bilāl, however able he may have been, was not a man of integrity like his father, as is evident from the tale that Abū Burda informed al-Ḥajjāj, "My son has taken bribes (*irtashā*), so depose me". Al-Ḥajjāj, however, reinstated him, but along with a colleague. "Bilāl was extremely unjust (*ẓalūm*), not caring what he did in judging (*ḥukm*) and other matters". He was, however, highly critical of incorrect Arabic and is reported to have said "That this case (*ḥaqq*) should go (away, be lost?) is preferable to me than that he should commit faults of speech (*yalḥan*)".[62] Al-Mubarrad says that the first of the *qāḍīs* to show injustice (*jawr*) in judgement was Bilāl: "Bilāl used to say, 'Two men will present themselves before me and I find one of them more engaging to me (*akhaff 'alā qalbī*) so I decide in his favour'".[63]

Bilāl also displayed a certain arrogance,[64] saying *anā qāḍ^in ibn*

60 *Op. cit.*, I, 33.
61 *Tahdhīb*, I, 1325.
62 *Akhbār al-quḍāt*, II, 408; cf. *Tahdhīb*, *loc. cit.*
63 *al-Kāmil*, Cairo 1356/1937, I, 395.
64 *Akhbār al-quḍāt*, I, 28.

qāḍin "I am a *qāḍī*, son of a *qāḍī*",[65] and he seems to have been known for snide remarks about contemporary figures. With all his cleverness, it would seem that he showed a feeling of social inferiority which, one surmises, may stem from his mother's low birth. The mingling of Arabian tribal blood with that of townsfolk of Iraq doubtless meant that a different outlook and code of conduct had developed in the house of Abū Mūsā from that of tribal arbiters.

So when one looks for the author of the letter Abū Mūsā I, attributed to 'Umar, Bilāl's character and circumstances make him a suitable candidate – an unscrupulous man who might not hesitate to improve on 'Umar's style in order to bring letter Abū Mūsā 2 into line with the more sophisticated style current in his day, and certainly a man with the competence in language to do so. The letter opens with a challenging statement on the *qāḍī*'s office of which Bilāl was so proud, but which many other Muslim scholars of repute throughout the ages have regarded with distaste.[66] A sense of social inferiority could explain his egalitarian attitude on witnesses (*'udūl*) in clause 9. His attitude to conciliation (*ṣulḥ*), one of tolerance merely, may further reflect his pride in the office of *qāḍī*. It must be recognised, however, that the letter is an excellent piece of work and the code drawn up in it admirable.

If Bilāl is indeed the author of the letter, and not another member of the house of Abū Mūsā in contact with Qatāda, the rider that all the family were party to the deception is hardly escapable. A further conclusion to be drawn is that the letter is to be dated prior to Qatāda's death (118/736) or, if the *isnād* to Qatāda is rejected – and there is no reason to do so – prior to Bilāl's deposition in 125/743, or when he died, which does not seem known. This would date existence of the theory on Qur'ān-*sunna-qiyās-ra'y* (clause 7) to early in the second century A.H.

No proof is forthcoming of course that Bilāl was responsible for re-casting 'Umar's original laconic letter to his grandfather to suit the circumstances of his own day – it might have been

[65] For flattering verses of Ru'ba b. al-'Ajjāj on Bilāl, see *Akhbār al-quḍāt*, I, 33, *wa-anta ya 'bna 'l-qāḍiyayn qāḍin*, etc. Cf. Charles Pellat, "Risālat 'Amr b. Baḥr al-Jāḥiẓ fi 'l-ḥakamayn wa-taṣwīb Amīr al-Mu'minīn 'Alī b. Abī Ṭālib fī fi'li-hi", *al-Machriq* (1958), LII, 431. By this time, Abū Mūsā has become recognised as a *qāḍī*.

[66] al-Sarakhsī, *op. cit.*, XVI, 68, quotes Ibn Mas'ūd as saying *fa-man ibtalā bi 'l-qaḍā' fa 'l-yaqḍi bi-mā fī Kitāb Allāh.*

Sa'īd or 'Abdallāh, other sons of Abū Burda, for the expanded letter is transmitted on their authority. But because Bilāl was a bad character, this does not mean that he could not draft good rules of procedure.

The patent link between the two letters is undeniable, though their purpose is different, for whereas 'Umar's genuine letter is concerned with a tribal society, the "improved" letter appears to have been framed rather for a centralised government to deal with a predominantly urban situation. The shift of emphasis between the earlier and later documents is in itself indicative of the way in which early Islamic society in Iraq was evolving and of the modification of its law process to suit that society.

The above is offered as a token of respect for an old friend, Professor Charles Beckingham.

Addenda

P.72/fn.36 Uways al-Qarnī/Qaranī's mother was from Kudādah of Murād (*Iklīl II*, ed. Akwa', 41).

P.75/12 An authority quoted in one of the tribal law treatises, I have now established, would have written ca. 500 H. but a long tradition lies behind this law – which it may eventually be possible to trace back to the pre-Islamic era.

P.79 To Professor M.J.Kister I am indebted for several references to authors of the late 4th to early 6th centuries H. – al-Dāraquṭnī, *Sunan*, Medina, 1386/1966, IV, 206; Abū Isḥāq Ibrāhīm al-Shīrāzī *al-Luma' fī uṣūl al-fiqh*, Beirut, 1405/1984, 2789; Ibn al-Jawzī *Manāqib Amīr al-Mu'minīn 'Umar b. al-Khaṭṭāb*, Beirut, 1402/1982, 129–35 & Ibn Ḥazm, *al-Iḥkām fī uṣūl al-aḥkām*, Cairo, 1398/1978, 1296–1301. All refer to or quote the "improved" letter on the authority of Sa'īd b. Abī Burdah, some also citing weak authorities. Ibn al-Jawzī also quotes the brief letter to Abū 'Ubaydah b. al-Jarrāḥ (see p.73 supra). In this treatise of his Ibn Ḥazm again rejects the "improved" letter. Ibn al-Jawzī reports the statement of al-Shāfi'ī: "I went to Sa'īd b. Abī Burdah and asked him about 'Umar's *rasā'il* which he used to write to Abū Mūsā and which Abū Mūsā had bequeathed to Abū Burdah", Sa'īd produced the "improved" letter. While the evidence pins the *transmission* on Sa'īd I still favour Bilāl as *author* of the "improved" version. Note the probably spurious tradition cited by Ibn al-Jawzī, that 'Umar wrote to Abū Mūsā: "Your secretary who wrote to me committed solecisms (*laḥana*), so whip him." This sounds like invention by the pedantic Bilāl b. Abī Burdah (see p.77 supra).

III

THE INTERPLAY BETWEEN TRIBAL AFFINITIES AND RELIGIOUS (ZAYDĪ) AUTHORITY IN THE YEMEN

TRADITIONAL ARABIA is dominated politically and socially by the arms-bearing tribal class and its chiefs. All other classes come under its protection, be they families of hereditary arbiters between them, who share in with the tribes the quality of *sharaf,* honour, or the non-arms-bearing classes of artisans, agricultural labourers who are accounted by them «weak» *(ḍaʿīf)* and sometimes also «defective in honour» *(nāqiṣ al-sharaf).* In the past social mobility upwards was next to impossible, unless, and this was probably not frequent, through the possession or acquisition of «spiritual power», *(sulṭa rūḥiyya),* though this too is an hereditary quality with which certain families are endowed. The order described is naturally susceptible to some modification in accordance with circumstances, and social mobility downwards, especially loss of tribal standing, not uncommon, but on the whole it appears to have hardly changed over, say, two thousand years.

The important Yemeni tribes in the main are settled, and live in villages, though a few may have nomadic pastoral sections as well. Tribes and families recognise different degrees of social standing as between one and the other; they are not always equal; they are certainly not egalitarian. In not only tribal society but more generally, a family will not consent to marry its girls into a family it regards as lower in the social scale – this can happen when both families have tribal status – and a tribesman marrying into a menial family loses his own standing.

The power and honour of a tribe can be gauged by its ability to defend itself and to extend its protection to other groups. When unable to defend itself a tribe loses in status. A tribe, or section within a tribe, with large numbers therefore tends to have a higher status thananotherofthe group – the books of genealogies will say of such and such a sub-tribe, *fī-him al-bayt waʾl-ʿadad,* in them is the house (the shaykhly house) and number (of men). Tribes are fiercely intent to preserve their honour unblackened,unsullied – indeed not only is this closely connected with their standing as a tribe, but it affects their security, for a group too weak or inactive to preserve its honour by, for example, defending its protected clients or not avenging a murder, is in danger of exposure to attack by more powerful tribes and might even be reduced to client status itself. For this reason a tribe with diminished numbers seeks to ally itself with a strong tribe and may even break away from the confederation to which it belongs if for one reason or another the tribes of that confederation fail to come to their aid. As Jāḥiẓ says, the expression of weakness of a tribe leads to the downfall of the mighty/noble (*ᶜazīz*). *Man qalla fulla wa-man fulla ukila.. wa-man ẓafara qatala,* Those who are few are defeated and those who are defeated are consumed.. and he who conquers slays.[1]

As each tribe, itself sub-divided into various sections and houses, is an independent unit, tribal Arabia is to be conceived of as normally in a state of anarchy. A tribesman is secure in his own tribal territory, but without some arrangement for protection outside it his life and property are at the mercy of others. Hence, the tribal law corpus collected by the late Ettore Rossi and me[2] is concerned with protection, truces, the payment of blood-monies and damages, all of which involve the essential function of an arbiter. Where personal or tribal honour is affronted, fines by way of restitution are at least doubled or even heavier penalties exacted. This tribal anarchy in fact is a system that works to maintain security since the sanctions which must inevitably be applied sooner or later for offences are heavy.

Tribes must therefore look for arbiters to settle differences and they must also establish a secure centre where for political, economic and, arising out of this, religious reasons, they may meet on neutral ground. Tribal honour among the shaykhly houses is so sensitive that no shaykh or tribal lord can brook submission to the authority of another, unless possibly temporarily to a *muqaddam ḥarb,* a war chief. They therefore tend to look to an outsider to act as arbiter in their disputes – this tendency indeed runs all through Arabian society. No potential arbiter is more acceptable than the member of a house upon which Allah has conferred some superior and supernatural quality – for who can quarrel with God's authority? Secular arbiters there are, but the theocratic approach to the function of arbitration which brings the arbiter political power seems to suit social conditions better. There are indications that in the south such pre-Islamic rulers as the *mukarribs* were theocratic in type. The arbiter may use his influence to bind together a group of tribes as did the Prophet's ancestor Quṣayy and of course the Prophet himself; in such case they may be described as *mujammiᶜ*, uniter or creator of a group *(jamāᶜa)* - but it is only an arbiter of outstanding personality who manages to achieve this.

As I have stated elsewhere, office in Arabia is at the same time both heredit-

1. «Risāla fi ʾl-ḥakamayn», ed. C. Pellat, *al-Mashriq/Machriq,* Beirut, 1958, lii, Cf. al-Maydānī's *Man qalla dhalla.*
2. E. Rossi, «Il diritto consuetudinario delle tribù arabe del Yemen», *Rivista degli Studi Orientali,* XXIII, Roma, 1948, and my unpublished edition of *K. al-Lawāzim fi-ʾl-manᶜa.*

ary and elective, be that office secular or religious. A shaykh, sulṭān, imam or *manṣab,*[3] etcetera, is elected from the members of a family which has traditionally held this office. It is recognised that an office-holder requires contributions from the tribe, even if he be a man of means, to enable him to fulfil the duties thereof adequately. One of the most important of these is entertainment of guests and, under one name or another, the tribes pay him fixed duties for this purpose.

There is little love lost between tribes and townsmen in the Yemen. Al-Zubayrī the poet of the Yemeni Liberals in his polemic against the Imams tells us that «when... we examine the sentiments of the greatest force among the populace, i.e., the tribes, those of them who farm — and those who do not, then indeed we find them harbouring a general sense of bitterness against the inhabitants of the towns as a whole, considering the townsfolk, as they maintain, to be sharing with the Imams in the benefits and gains of government, and responsible for its outrages and misdeeds».[4] Al-Zubayrī has given a propagandist anti-Imamic twist to tribal resentment of townsfolk that doubtless long pre-dates Zaydī rule. Nor do city folk love the tribes. «Ṣanᶜāʾ folk are brethren, but not the tribesman».[5] So the Ṣanᶜānī proverb runs, and there are memories of past tribal sackings. The Imams must repair for support to the tribesmen of the high mountains and castled strongholds, but once in power they have to administer from a centre and the towns are centres from which revenue is most easily obtained and to which the tribesman must go for his needs. The tribesman in his *ṭamᶜ*, cupidity, would like himself to plunder the cities, so the Imam becomes the defender of the cities and his first preoccupation is to maintain public security, thus he may turn against the very tribes which helped him to power and he has to treat them lightly in the matter of taxation.

The role of the Zaydī Imams in dealing with the Yemeni tribes is in the continuing tradition of their great ancestor the Prophet Muḥammad in his relation with the Arabian tribes of his own time. Indeed the Prophet in his political role was clearly following established tradition and method, going back, no doubt, to centuries before, but which in any case can be demonstrated, from the Arabic sources themselves, to have been that of Quraysh of Mecca. So, to consider the policies of the Zaydī Imams in perspective it is directly relevant to survey in brief some of the salient features of the political scene in sixth and early seventh century Ḥijāz.

Muḥammad's ancestor Quṣayy had united the tribes of Quraysh and settled them in the sacred enclave, the Ḥaram, of Mecca where they were secure from

3. Lord of a *ḥawṭa*.
4. «The Yemeni poet al-Zubayrī and his polemic against the Zaydī Imams», *Arabian Studies*, Cambridge-London, 1978, 108.
5. *Ṣanᶜāʾ; an Arabian Islamic City*, London, 1983, 168a.

attacks by the tribes. These tribes, known as *muḥrimūn,* one can only assume, gave Quraysh some guarantee that they would respect the inviolability of Mecca. The house of Quṣayy kept the guardianship of the Kaᶜba in their hands and formed a sort of religious aristocracy – Muḥammad was a scion of this house, an inheritor of a religious function, but the branch to which he belonged, Hāshim, also had a function as arbiters *(ḥakam).* Quraysh were settled tribes but they managed to establish a secure caravan system along the main Arabian trade routes so that the Meccans were linked to the celebrated annual trade cycle moving around the Arabian Peninsula,[6] and at the same time they had this special status as Quraysh Allāh, their title even in the pre-Islamic age as custodians of the Kaᶜba. There are indications that tribes paid the Ḥaram some kind of contribution and the sanctuary of course received votive offerings.

Muḥammad's action in breaking with his tribe Quraysh and taking protection with the tribes of Yathrib/Medina is known as *hijra,* usually rendered «migration», and the parallel action of the first Zaydī Imam al-Hādī is sometimes described as his *hijra.* Quraysh regarded the Prophet as a breaker of the unity established by his ancestor Quṣayy, a *mufarriq,* but in setting up a new confederation he became a uniter, a *mujammiᶜ* just as Quṣayy had been. The tribes appear to have regarded the quarrel in which Muḥammad eventually became victorious almost as a dynastic dispute, and it is significant that the members of the house of Quṣayy, his relatives, who had opposed him, joined him and received office.

On his arrival in Yathrib the Prophet had made agreements with the headmen *(naqībs)* of its tribes to set up this new confederation *(umma)* and he was constituted the final arbiter *(maradd)* between the various subtribes there. The *naqīb* is described by Ṭabarī as *al-amīn al-ḍāminᶜala ᵓl-qawm,* he who is entrusted/trustworthy, who takes the responsibility for/guarantees (the blood-monies) on behalf of the tribe.[7] One may compare what the poet Zuhayr says,[8]

Ḍaminnā māla-hu fa-ghadā salīm-an
ᶜAlay-nā naqṣu-hu wa-lahu ᵓl-namāᵓu
I stood surety for/protected his property, so he went away safe.
I bear his loss but he has what it produces.

Zuhayr is here taking pride in his rank rather than boasting of wealth or lofty moral purpose.

The *naqībs* in general represented and were responsible for the tribes of which they were chiefs and they acted in accordance with the customary law of the particular group to which they belonged.[9] It was in conjunction with them that

6. Muḥammad b. Ḥabīb, *Kitāb al-Muḥabbar,* Ḥaydarābād, 1942, 263 seq.
7. *Tafsīr,* ed. Maḥmūd & Aḥmad Shākir, Cairo 1374/1954-5, x, 110. Cf. al-Wāqidī, *Kitāb al-Maghāzī,* ed. Marsden Jones, London, 1966, 547 for definition of actions and duties of a *naqīb;* Al-Suhaylī, *al-Rawḍ al-unuf,* Cairo, 1332/1914, ii, 16-17.
8. *Sharḥ Dīwān Zuhayr,* Cairo, 1384/1964, 77.
9. Cf. my «The *Sunnah Jāmiᶜah...*» *BSOAS,* xli, London, 1978, 21 passim.

the Prophet administered Yathrib, but though protected by Aws and Khazraj he lacked any ready-made power base there and as Ibn Isḥāq candidly shows he would turn their perpetual rivalry to his own advantage. These two tribes of the Aws and Khazraj, he says, «when with the Apostle of Allah used to spring up at one another like a couple of stallions, the Aws not doing anything on behalf of the Apostle of Allah in which there was difficulty but the Khazraj said, «They shall not through this carry off greater esteem with the Apostle of Allah in Islam.» (He said) And they would not stop until they achieved something the same as it. Whenever the Khazraj did anything the Aws said the same as it.»[10]

Ibn Isḥāq[11] tells us clearly that, in deciding their attitude to Islam «the ᶜArab [probably the settled Muḥrimūn tribes] were only waiting to see what happened to this tribe *(ḥayy)* of Quraysh and the Apostle of Allah. For Quraysh were the imam (Example) and guide *(hādī)* of men, and *Ahl al-Bayt wa-ʾl-Ḥaram,* the People of the Temple and Sacred Enclave and pure stock *(ṣarīḥ)* of Ismāᶜīl son of Ibrāhīm and the leaders *(qāda)* of the ᶜArab did not deny this... When Mecca was taken and Quraysh became subject to him and he subdued it to Islam and the ᶜArab knew that they had no power to fight the Apostle or display enmity towards him they entered Allah's religion... 'in batches'».

Sometimes the Prophet seems to have supported one tribal group against another as in the case of Farwa b. Musayk of the south Arabian Murād, but history here is still obscure. Where he found it impolitic or unpractical to bring a tribe into the new confederation by persuasion or force, he resorted to the use of part of his revenue to provide a subsidy for its leaders. Qurʾān ix,60 states that *ṣadaqāt* are for *fuqarāʾ masākīn, al-ᶜāmilīn ᶜalay-hā, al-muʾallafa qulūbu-hum, riqāb, ghārimūn* and the *sabīl Allāh,* i.e. the poor, those in charge of collecting the *ṣadaqat,* slaves, debtors and for campaigning. Of the *muʾallafūn,* those whose hearts are composed, Ṭabarī[12] says, «The Apostle used to give them a little *(yarḍakh la-hum)* of the *ṣadaqāt,* and when he gave them (anything) from the *ṣadaqāt* and they obtained benefit from it they said, 'This is a good religion *(dīn ṣāliḥ)!'* And if it was otherwise they abused him *(ᶜābū-hu)* and abandoned him.» In fact the Prophet, as his power and consequently his revenues grew, quite often gave munificent gifts, as when he presented a hundred camels to Mālik b. ᶜAwf.[13] The cynical tribal attitude remarked upon by Ṭabarī has not changed.

On the other hand the Arabians at large believed firmly in the power of the Prophet deriving from a supernatural source, to do them good or ill. I have remarked elsewhere on his making rain and it is recorded that one of the tribes came to ask him to lift a ban and pray for rain for them. Contact with the Prophet

10. Ibn Isḥāq/Ibn Hishām, *Sīrat Rasūl Allāh,* ed. F. Wüstenfeld, Göttingen, 1858-60, 714.

11. Ibid., 933.

12. Op.cit., xiv, 313. *Khayr,* translated «benefit» can mean «wealth» in the Qurʾān.

13. Ibn Isḥāq, op.cit., 881.

could bring *baraka*[14] and his curse was greatly feared. The curse of God is invoked against the aggressor in the «Eight Documents», 3b (the «Constitution of Medina») and was pronounced by ᶜAlī and Muᶜāwiya against the other after the abortive arbitration. Arabians still credit their saints and holy men with powers similar to those of the Prophet.

The adherents of the Prophet took the oath of allegiance to him and, to take a case in point, the poet al-ᶜAbbās b. Mirdās al-Sulāmī[15] boasts of keeping to it. Personal devotion to the Prophet and to the *Ahl al-Bayt,* the People of the House, the Prophet's posterity, is a constantly recurring theme in Islamic history and an inspiration for both Sunnīs and Shīʿa. Not only have the *Ahl al-Bayt* a claim to exercise authority as successors to the Prophet, but they have produced many an outstanding personality and they so often possess winning qualities that charm the hearts of men.

Pagan or monotheistic pre-Islamic Arabia had a tradition of theocratic as well as secular government – this form of organisation was followed by the Prophet Muḥammad when he set up his confederation *(umma)* at Yathrib/Medina, and it expanded vastly with the adherence of one Arabian tribe after another. A few centuries later the Zaydī Imams sought to establish a theocratic state in the Yemen on broadly similar lines in a society of basically the same type as that of 6th/7th century Ḥijāz.

Hamdān; Ḥāshid and Bakīl

The two great tribal groupings, both of Hamdān, Ḥāshid and Bakīl, sometimes called al-Janāḥayn, the two wings of support for the Zaydī Imams (though as often as not they have been in conflict with them), have a long history. In the pre-Islamic age they figure for example in the Ḥaram Bilqīs inscriptions.[16] Ḥāshid at Khaywān and other localities were supporters of Ilīsharaḥ Yaḥḍab, king at the *maḥram* of Ṣanᶜā'about the third century;[17] The city of Ḥrmtm is mentioned in connection with the Bakīl tribe[18] and one of the two monarchs called Ilīsharaḥ Yaḥḍab of Marthad was of Bakīl.[19] Maḥram and Ḥrmtm are names suggestive in themselves of sacred enclaves.

When the Prophet was seeking a man to present him to his tribe since his own people Quraysh were preventing him from conveying «the word of my Lord», a man of Hamdān came to him.[20] The Prophet asked if his tribe had the power to protect *(manᶜa)* and the Hamdānī replied that it had, telling the

14. It is difficult to translate the range of meaning of this term - good fortune, etc.
15. *Dīwān,* ed. Yaḥyā al-Jubūrī, Baghdad, 1388/1968, 59.
16. A. Jamme, *Sabaean inscriptions from Maḥram Bilqīs (Mârib),* Publications of the American Foundation for the Study of Man, iii, Baltimore, 1962, index.
17. Ibid., 322. Cf. *Ṣanᶜāʾ,* op.cit., 37.
18. Ibid., 301.
19. Ibid., 308.
20. Abū Nuᶜaym al-Iṣbahānī, *Dalāʾil al-nubuwwa,* 2nd ed., Haydarābād, 1950, 246.

Prophet that he would present him to his tribe, then return to him – clearly with acceptance to take him under their wing. Meanwhile, however deputations of the Supporters (Anṣār) arrived from Yathrib and no more is heard of the Hamdānī's proposal.

As to how Hamdān eventually came to adhere to the Prophet, traditional accounts vary but a document quoted by Ibn Saᶜd[21] was brought back to the Yemen by Qays b. Mālik al-Arḥabī from Mecca to which he had gone to join the Prophet. This document Qays wrote on behalf of the Uḥmūr (Ḥimyar) tribes, Qudam, Dhū Marrān, Dhū Laᶜwa, and the Adhwāʾ of Ḥamdān and their Arabs (or, the Arabs of them (reading ᶜArab for Gharb)), Arḥab, Nihm, Shākir, Wādiᶜa, Yām, Murhiba, Dālān (of Jawf), Khārif, ᶜUdhar, Ḥajūr and their associates *(Khalāʾiṭ)*[22] and clients *(mawālī)*. These tribes were to «hear and obey»[23] and the only other stipulations were that they should perform the prayer and pay the *zakāt*. The Prophet made the Arḥabī, Qays, governor over «your tribes the Uḥmūr (Ḥimyar), the Arabs of them and their *mawālī*. Qays was allotted in perpetuity by the Prophet what later would be called a *marjūᶜ* or return from the *māl Allāh*, a portion of the tax which works out at 200 *ṣāᶜ* of *dhura* on 900 *ṣāᶜ* collected from Nisār, and a like quantity of raisins from Khaywān.

Most, if not all of these ᶜArab tribes belong to the Ḥāshid or Bakīl groups. Qudam b. Qādim is an Islamic saint[24] with a shrine that has pre-Islamic inscriptions, and Marrān a village in the area – I visited both, but not Laᶜwa which is however mentioned in the *Ṣifa*.[25] All these ᶜArab tribes are settled and cultivate their lands and are not migratory or pastoral.

21. *Al-Ṭabaqāt al-kubrā*, Beirut, 1380-88/1960-68, i, 340-1. The document looks authentic.

22. For *khalāʾiṭ* cf. C. de Landberg, *Arabica V*, Leiden, 1898, 116. They seem to be free associates with parity, not protected like a *jār*, distinct from *mawālī*, the latter rendered as «clients» rather than «allies».

23. *Al-samᶜ wa-ʾl-ṭāᶜa*. Abū ᶜUbayda, *Kitāb al-Amwāl*, Cairo, n.d., 219, «As for the *hijra* of the *bādī* it is his duty to respond when he is summoned *(duᶜiya)* and that he should obey *(yuṭīᶜ)* when ordered». This use of *hijra* comes very near that sense used in the Yemen. The *bādī* is the tribal country dweller. A distinction is made between the *bādī* and the *Aᶜrāb*, the Tradition being found in al-Nasāʾī and Ibn Ḥanbal. ᶜĀʾisha mentioned the Aᶜrāb in the Prophet's presence and he said, «O ᶜĀʾisha, they are not Aᶜrāb. They are the people of our *bādiya* (steppe) and we are the people of their *ḥāḍira* (cultivated land and villages). When they are summoned they respond, and they are not Aᶜrāb».
Al-Ḥajjāj called the Syrians *ahl al-samᶜ wa-ʾl-ṭāᶜa*. See Nabia Abbott, *Studies in Arabic literary papyri*, III, *Language and literature*, Chicago, 1972, 82, quoting Ṭabarī's *Tārīkh*, especially, ii, 1134, which says the Syrians *lam yukhālifū ṭāᶜata*. She also quotes Masᶜūdī, *Murūj*, v, 454, as stating that the South Arabians had a low opinion of the Syrians as arbiters and people of the lower classes.

24. See E. Griffini, «Il poemetto di Qudam Ben Qādim», *Rivista degli Studi Orientali*, vii, Roma, 1916-18. Qudam is the eponymous ancestor of a Ḥāshid group and the poem attributed to him of some importance.

25. Al-Hamdānī, *Ṣifat Jazīrat al-ᶜArab*, Leiden, 1884-91, 66. Cf. *Iklīl X*, ed. Muḥibb al-Dīn al-Khaṭīb, Cairo, 1368, index, and for Hamdān in general.

ᶜAlī b. Abī Ṭālib, al-Masᶜūdī[26] informs us, had in one day induced Hamdān to accept Islam at his hands and the rest of the Yemen followed. It does not however seem to have been so simple as this! Yet at Ṣiffīn a Hamdān shaykh testifies that the Yemeni tribes of southern Iraq support ᶜAlī against Muᶜāwiya, declaiming extempore,

O come to Bakīl's aid, Lakhm of it and Ḥāshid,
My soul be your ransom, thrust with spear, slash with sword[27].

So also in the 3rd century it is with a tribe of Hamdān that the first Zaydī Imam, al-Hādī, based himself at Ṣaᶜda, and Duᶜām[28] his most prominent supporter, was a Hamdānī of the Arhābī tribe.

Al-Hādī ila ʾl-Ḥaqq Yaḥyā b. al-Ḥusayn; the first Zaydī Imām

Al-Hādī Yaḥyā, a descendant of the Prophet Muḥammad through the union of his daughter Fāṭima with his cousin ᶜAlī b. Abī Ṭālib was the founder of the Zaydī imamate of the Yemen destined to endure over a thousand years, though with greatly varying fortunes. He belonged to that branch of the House of ᶜAlī descended from the latter's son al-Ḥasan, whereas the ᶜAlawīs in Ḥaḍramawt are descended from his other son Ḥusayn. They are known as Sayyids or Ashrāf, these titles used more or less interchangeably for either of the two branches. Al-Hādī was evidently a sayyid of outstanding quality. Physically strong and courageous, he was furthermore, as the histories and works of *fiqh* affirm, competent in the fields of politics and administration. The Zaydī rite derives its name from a descendant of ᶜAlī b. Zayd b. ᶜAlī, who came out in rebellion against the Umayyad caliphs, demand «enjoining what is right and forbidding what is wrong, *al-amr bi-ʾl-maᶜrūf wa-ʾl-nahy ᶜani ʾl-munkar*». The Zaydī rite, with the positive attitude which this imposes, was suited to society in warlike Yemen in a way in which the quietism and religious dissimulation *(taqiyya)* of the main Shīᶜa sects was not. Al-Hādī visited Zaydī Ṭabaristān but found it politic to leave and first came to the Yemen in 280/893/4 «until disobedience was shown by them to his orders which were in consonance with pure *sharīᶜa*»[29] - a punishment he gave for wine-drinking seems to have displeased the Yemenis and led to his departure.

The *Sayyids* and *Ashrāf,* and not least the Zaydī Imāms, are the bearers of *sharīᶜa* law as formulated by the jurists in the Holy Cities, Iraq and Syria. Born in Medina, al-Hādī, founder of the Hādawī school of Zaydī *fiqh,* was well placed to absorb family traditions on the Prophet's political practice and the law he exercised - he relied on his own opinion *(ijtihād)* to a large extent, a characteristic of

26. *Al-Tanbīh,* BGA viii, ed. M.J. de Goeje, Leiden, 1894, 274.

27. A. J. Arberry & C.F. Beckingham, *Religion in the Middle East,* ii, Cambridge, 1969, «The Zaydīs», 286. Cf. ᶜAlī b. Muḥammad al-ᶜAbbāsī al-ᶜAlawī, *Sīrat al-Hādī ila ʾl-Ḥaqq,* ed. Suhayl Zakkār, Beirut, 1392/1972, 184.

28. This seems the better reading than Daᶜᶜām.

29. Cf. «A Zaidī manual of *ḥisba* of the 3rd century (H.)»,*RSO,* ccviii, 1957, 1-34.

the Zaydī school. (It is the writer's view that the law and practice of the Prophet and his four immediate successors were basically Arabian custom, though they with little modifications underwent significant re-interpretation, not to say alteration, in the 2nd and 3rd centuries).

In the Arabian Peninsula law, custom and morals among the tribes and country districts undoubtedly continued much as they were before the appearance of Muḥammad, and the northern Yemen in which al-Hādī arrived had scarcely changed from the days of paganism - indeed this has remained much the case in parts of southern Arabia till our own time. This is expressed by van Arendonk[30] in reverse, as it were. «L'Islam de la population paraît avoir été très défectueux». Actually it was scarcely islamized at all! As already seen the Prophet only stipulated that Hamdān perform the prayer and pay the *zakāt* tax — they had also of course to break politically with those who would not accept Allāh's authority, i.e. as exercised by the Prophet, and in the latter case, as his power grew, the Prophet would grant them security. The tribal leaders were often the collectors of tax, and it is significant that the question of tax was often the motive for the «Apostacy» after the Prophet's death. The cities were the centres of islamization and Ṣanᶜāʾ even participated at least to some extent in the formulation of Islam, having some notable early Traditionists,[31] but this can hardly have affected the countryside. Al-Hādī even had to instruct in how to perform the prayer - and I found my own soldiers when stationed in Ṣubayḥī tribal territory in 1940 showing the villagers the way to pray of which they had been ignorant.

The most flagrant contravention of the Islamic code lay in the attitude to sexual morality which appears to have remained as pagan as it was in the Jāhiliyya. It may be argued that al-Duᶜām's soldiers, «profligates drinking wine, mounting males and fornicating publicly with women» were only acting as troops before and after them have done, and that the catamite[32] indulging in orgies with men and women is not unknown elsewhere (al-Hādī had him decapitated and his corpse hung up), but the *Sīrat al-Hādī*[33] describes a situation apparently accepted as normal to Yemenite society at that time[34].

«Among al-Duᶜām's troops in Bayt Zūd[35] there were four hundred immoral *(fājira)* women fornicating publicly without concealing it. Indeed the soldiers would go to judgement about them to their sultans and governors *(ᶜummāl)*. They (the women) used to gather each evening at the door of their profligate Sultan

30. C. van Arendonk, *Les débuts de l'Imāmat Zaidite au Yémen*, trad. française J. Ryckmans, Leyde, 1960, 137. *Iklīl I*, ed. O. Löfgren, Leyden, 1965, 102, mentions a man with seven wives!
31. Cf. al-Rāzī, *Tārīkh madīnat Ṣanᶜāʾ* ed. Ḥusayn ᶜAbdullāh al-ᶜAmrī & ᶜAbd al-Jabbār Zakkār, Damascus, 1394/1974.
32. *Sīrat al-Hādī*, op.cit., 213.
33. Ibid., 94.
34. Ibid., 94, and for al-Hādī's tempering his actions, 227.
35. The text's *dhuʾd* corrected from al-Hamdānī, *Ṣifa*.

and would dance in front of him and weave[36] their hair, displaying their ornaments,[37] showing off the beautiful parts of their bodies and wearing the thinnest cloth they could get, to reveal the hidden parts of their bodies. The soldiers would come and when a man desired one he would pay her money (dirhams) in the presence of those there with them. Perhaps she might not go to him that night and in the morning he would go to the Sultan and tell him that his damned woman had not come to him that night, having accepted his money. Thereupon the Sultan would order her to be punished/fined and that she should go to her lover *(ṣāḥib)*». These dancing women recall to me the Maᶜn «gypsies» whom I saw in Dathīna thirty years ago[38].

Again[39] about a day's journey from Khaywān a host would bring his daughter or sister, all dressed up to his guest and she would be with him all day or night and he might even touch her *ᶜawra* while her father and others were present. Ibn al-Mujāwir records similar practices in the 7th/13th century - indeed *tawrīd* provision of a woman as part of the entertainment of a guest has continued in parts of the south to our own time. Al-Hādī was extremely strict and[40] and a Yām man punished for wine-drinking died under eighty lashes awarded by one of his governors. A man of Yuᶜfiṛ and another of Hamdān even came out in revolt against him because he had forbidden them to drink wine and behave immorally.[41] Al-Hādī's severity in regard to customs the tribes did not regard as immoral was a factor contributing to his limited success in the Yemen, though by no means the only one. I have long felt that the notorious poem permitting wine, woman and song, attributed to one of Qarmaṭī poets of ᶜAlī b. al-Faḍl and recited by him on the *minbar* of the Jāmiᶜ of al-Janad with its rejection of Islam and its moral code, is not to be assumed an outright forgery[42]. It becomes understandable as a reaction against Islamic restrictions on practices upon which tribal society took a contrary view and which indeed in the remoter tribal areas still has a different moral outlook on them. In fact al-Hādī's son accuses the foes of the Imām of immorality in the following verses,[43]

We rose with the Book (Qurʾān) - they called it liar,

36. *Nashara,* probably the same as Ḥaḍramī *tanwīsh,* described in my *South Arabian hunt,* London, 1976, note 109. I have since seen tribal girls in Abu Dhabi dance weaving their loosened hair.
37. Cf. Qurʾān, xxiv, 60, *ghayra mutabarrijāt-in bi-zīnat-in.*
38. «The Maᶜn «Gypsies» of the West Aden Protectorate», *Anthropos,* Posieux (Fribourg), lvi, 1961, 737-49.
39. *Sīrat al-Hādī,* 125.
40. Ibid., 80.
41. Ibid., 19.
42. Quoted in Ibn Samurah, *Ṭabaqāt fuqahāʾ al-Yaman,* ed. Fuʾād Sayyid, Cairo, 1957, 75, listing sources and variants. *Khudhi ʾl-daff yā hādhihi wa-ʾlᶜabī, wa-ghannī hazārī-kī thumma ʾṭrabī.* The metre needs re-examination.
43. *Sīrat al-Hādī,* 261.

Turning to musical instruments and drink.[44]
They said, «We cannot do without wines
And sinning *(fisq)* with the secluded girl of swelling breasts.
You prevent folk against their will
From (enjoying) pleasures and desired delights.[45]

(Wine is still secretly made *by Muslims* in the tribal areas which grow grapes in the vicinity of Ṣanᶜāʾand drunk by them). The thin veneer of Islam among some tribes is illustrable from the practice of the group which choses one of its number to perform the Ramaḍān fast and he fasts only one day[46]! As an example of the different moral outlook on sexual matters I might cite the treatment of the girl with an illegitimate child and of her lover among the Nakhaᶜī tribe[47].

Obscure as the first few centuries of Yemeni history are, power in the northern Yemen tribal districts undoubtedly lay in the hands of the shaykhs, known as shuyūkh al-ḍamān,[48] in the 3rd Islamic century when al-Hādī arrived there. Like the Prophet Muḥammad he made his entrance as an arbiter endowed with authority from Allāh. The *Sīrat al-Hādī*[49] alludes to the Hāshimis of the early Zaydīs as inheriting the Prophet's position *(maqām)*.

Al-Hādī's biographer[50] tells us that in Ṣaᶜda tribal dissensions had led to losses of many men and the district was furthermore in the throes of a drought. The Saᶜd and Rabīᶜa tribes of Ṣaᶜda[51] of Khawlān b. ᶜAmr came out to meet him where he had camped outside the town and greeted him and he greeted them.[52] He made a moving address *(khuṭba)* so that they wept at his words, unable to contain their emotion, like pilgrims to the Bayt Allāh. Al-Hādī then ordered a Qurʾān *(muṣḥaf)*[53] to be brought and made them swear to one another to leave off dissension and hostility *(fitna wa-ᶜadāwa)* - which they did. He then made them swear to himself obedience and support *(ṭāᶜa wa-munāṣara)*, and they paid allegiance to him on the spot. They also undertook to carry out God's command

44. Al-Hādī was also opposed to musical instruments *(Sīra*, 114), *al-iᶜtikāf ᶜala ʾl-lahw wa-ʾl-mazāmīr wa-ʾl-ḍarb bi-ʾ l-maᶜāzif wa-ʾ l-ṭanābīr*, as of course were the Ḥamīd al-Dīn in the 20th century.
45. Further immoralities are in *Sīra*, 114, 119, 125, 213; Arendonk, op.cit., 137. A.S. Tritton, *Rise of the Imāms of Ṣanaa*, Madras-London, 1925, 83, notes that there was no marriage rite among some tribes, but co-habitation and when a woman was with child a dowry was fixed; the guest was also provided with a woman. Cf. Landberg, *Arabica IV*, Leiden, 1897, 25 seq.
46. *Ṣanᶜāʾ*, 310a.
47. «The «White Dune» at Abyan», *Journal of Semitic Studies*, Manchester, xvi,i, 1971, 80 seq.
48. See pp. 14, 25, 27.
49. *Sīra*, 174.
50. Ibid., 41.
51. Al-Ḥamdānī, *Ṣifa*, 247, describes Yursam as *muṣnada daᶜwatu-hum ilā Banī Saᶜd b. Saᶜd.* Nowadays Khawlān is called Khawlān b. ᶜĀmir
52. In the Aden Protectorate when one tribe greeted another, each would each form a long line facing the other and the chief men issue from the rank to greet the chiefs of the other.
53. Unbound sheets?

and (give) assistance[54]. Al-Hādī now had a power base in Ṣaᶜda and its tribes, for he had arrived with only about fifty men of his own. He had also succeeded in making peace here where the leaders *(quwwād)* of Āl Yuᶜfir had failed. Thus began his *daᶜwā,* his summons[55] to the Book of Allāh and the *sunna* of His Prophet.

The two tribes were now reconciled and God sent down upon them abundant rain which rendered their land fertile, harvests abundant and prices low, their beasts healthy, and they kept the roads secure. These are signs of *baraka,* i.e. al-Hādī's political success was followed and justified by his success in acting as a rain-maker, a quality also belonging to his ancestor the Prophet[56]. As it is said, «*Idhā ẓahara ᵓl-ᶜadl nazala ᵓl-qaṭr,* When justice appears down comes rain». Al-Hādī then sent governors to each village *(miklāf)*[57] to collect the tax on cereals *(jibāyat al-ṭaᶜām).* So he now had some revenue with which to build up his Zaydī state, but it can hardly have been much, and he would have to rely on political manipulation. His own small group was composed of ᶜAlawīs and Ṭabarīs from the Zaydī state in Ṭabaristān.

Al-Hādī's subsequent career was one of hard fighting. The Yemeni tribes at large by no means accepted the Prophet's House as their rightful rulers and were guided by their own interests. Though al-Hādī took and courageously defended Ṣanᶜāᵓ he was obliged to evacuate it for Ṣaᶜda because he lacked money *(nafaqa)* to pay his supporters and was unable to persuade the citizens of Ṣanᶜāᵓ to contribute to his finances. On leaving the city he promised it disaster, rather after the manner of the Prophet himself with his enemies - and so it was, for in 292/905 Ṣanᶜāᵓ was much destroyed by the Qarmaṭī, Ibn al-Faḍl.

Despite the reverses al-Hādī suffered, there remained even a superstitious regard for the qualities possessed by the Prophet's House. When the governor of Najrān, Muḥammad b. ᶜUbayd Allāh, was slain an avenger cut off his head saying,

> I have appeased my heart of you, o son of ᶜAlī,
> And I care not after that what should befall me
> From the wrath of God and curse of the Prophet.[58]

54. *Sīra,* 126, Ibid., 48 seq. in his *daᶜwā* at Ṣaᶜda, al-Hādī made it conditional on his supporters to give him «obedience *(ṭāᶜa)* to my command in all your conditions as long as I give obedience to God. And if I do not obey God you are not obliged to obey me. And if I diverge or turn away from the Book of God and the *Sunna* of His Apostle then I have no plea against you».

55. The *ṣārikh,* the call for aid, and so presumably the carrier of the message, was the form the summons took, e.g. *arsal al-ṣārikh fī ᵓl-nās fa-ᵓjtamaᶜū ilayh,* He sent the herald among the people and they assembled before him *(Sīra,* 99). Perhaps even in those days the herald was a *muzayyin* (see p. 45). For other cases, *Sīra,* 107, 112, 128, 135, 163-4.

56. See «The Yemeni poet al-Zubayrī...», 119. Like the Prophet, al-Hādī used to be shaded from the sun by a cloud when he walked abroad *(Sīra,* 128).

57. *Makhālīf* are rendered as *qurā,* villages.

58. *Sīra,* 378.

The head was taken by a woman who had lost her brother fighting the Imām and she mutilated, roasted and ate it, in true pagan style.[59]

Though the founding of the infant Zaydī imāmate under al-Hādī naturally follows the pattern of the Prophet, unlike his great ancestor he was not able to extend protection in his later years to other powerful groups and attach them to the nucleus at Ṣaᶜda. During the centuries to follow, until the arrival of the Mamlūks who abruptly terminated the mediaeval age in the Yemen when they destroyed the Ṭāhirid sultanate, the Zaydī Imāms ruled their obscure little state of which Ṣaᶜda was a kind of capital. At times they were able to take Ṣanᶜāʾ and especially in the period of Rasūlid decline, to hold it. It was in heading the Yemeni upsurge against the first and second Ottoman occupations that they were destined to play a major role in the country's history.

At this point it seems appropriate to discuss the concept of *mawadda,* i.e. affection, for the Prophet's House, and the institution, peculiar to the Yemen, of *hijra.*

Mawadda

In Arabic the word *mawadda,* synonymous with *maḥabba,* means «love», and in the literature relating to the Prophet's house, the descendants of ᶜAlī and Fāṭima, allusions to the love for them are commonplace[60]. But a truer rendering of the term *ahl al-mawadda* would be «people affected to» the Ahl al-Bayt in, of course, greater or lesser degrees. Now in the pre-Islamic Sabaic inscriptions one finds the term *mwd* (= Arabic root *wdd* and its derivatives defined[61] as «friend» of the ruler (title in archaic texts) and the verb *s¹twddw,* to consent, agree, come to an agreement. Qurʾān iii,101 «How do you disbelieve when Allāh's signs have been recited to you and His Apostle is among you. And whosoever has recourse for protection *(yaᶜtaṣim)* to Allāh has been guided to the straight path», is said to refer to the *ulfa* and *mawadda* established between the Aws and Khazraj tribes (on an occasion when their ancient feuds seemed like to break out afresh). Ṭabarī[62] demonstrates that *mawadda* comes near to the terms *dhimma* and *amān,* treaty/bond and security. When one looks again at Qurʾān, xlii,23, asking for no reward *«illa ʾl-mawaddata fī ʾl-qurbā»,* lit., «except love for the relations» (of the Prophet), *mawadda* could have a much stronger implication, and might possibly

59. Ibid., 380.

60. Ḥaḍramī Sayyids are usually addressed as *«ḥabīb».* The poet Kumayt loved ᶜAlī, but does not blame Abū Bakr or ᶜUmar.

61. A.F.L. Beeston, J. Ryckmans, M. al-Ghul, W. Müller, *Sabaic dictionary,* Louvain-la-Neuve-Beirut, 1982, 155. Beeston informs me that the term also occurs in Minean but with no evidence to show that it has any special sense as indicated here.

62. *Tafsīr,* op.cit., vii, 62 seq.

be closer to «support» or «loyalty»[63]. It is pertinent therefore to scrutinise the use of *mawadda/maḥabba*[64] in the biography of the first Zaydī Imām in the Yemen, al-Hādī.

Al-Hādī in 286/899 went to Bayt Wathīᶜ whose notables had been in correspondence with him and declared themselves affected to him *aẓharū maḥabbata-hu)*[65]. What this implied emerges from the passage that follows. The notables came out to meet al-Hādī and accompanied him into the town *(balad)*.. They paid him allegiance, heard and obeyed *(bāyaᶜū-hu wa-samiᶜū wa-aṭāᶜū)*. «Hearing and obeying» means to respond to his *ṣārikh* — his herald sent out to cry for aid, and to follow his command in battle. Subsequently Abu ᵓl-ᶜAtāhiya, the governor *(wālī)* of Ṣanᶜāᵓ and its districts *(makhālīf)*, belonging to Āl Ṭarīf who invited al-Hādī to take over power in the city said to him,[66] «Ask me to swear *(istaḥlif-nī)*, oh Commander of the Faithful». This al-Hādī duly did accepting his allegiance *(ᶜala ᵓl-qiyām maᶜa-hu bi-ᵓl-ḥaqq wa-ᶜalā ᵓl-ḥaqq wa-ᵓl-amr bi-ᵓl-maᶜrūf wa-ᵓl-nahy ᶜani ᵓl-munkar)*. Group after group of soldiers (followers of Abu ᵓl-ᶜAtāhiya) then came to swear to «hear and obey» al-Hādī.[67] Al-Hādī was then able to enter Ṣanᶜā?

The obligations that are implicit in *mawadda* are well brought out in verses of Muḥammad b. Ṭarīf al-Wādiᶜī, the Wādiᶜa being a section of Kaᶜb Hamdān.[68] These were addressed to one of al-Hādī's governors after the latter had persuaded the tribe to take an oath to support the Imām.

63. Balādhurī, *Ansāb al-Ashrāf*, IVA, ed. M. Schloessinger & M.J. Kister, Jerusalem, 1971, 122, gives Ḥusayn's understanding of the verse, «The relationship *(qarāba)*, the right *(ḥaqq)* of which God magnified and ordered to be observed and [which God ordered], with the intention of reward to him [the Prophet]-that affection *(mawadda)* for the people of it (i.e. the relationship), is our relationship, [we] the Ahl al-Bayt».

64. The use of *mawadda* in the sense proposed for Sabaic seems to find confirmation in Qurᵓān, xxix, 25, *Innamā ᵓttakhadhtum min dūni ᵓllāhi awthān-an mawaddata bayni-kum*, You have taken, to the exclusion of Allāh, *awthān*, only in order to come to an agreement over differences. In this connection I would cite the important information of Landberg, *Arabica V*, 146 seq. Current among the tribes of South Arabia he shows that «*ᶜAlī wathan* (= *ᶜalayya)* est une formule sacramentale d'une grande solemnité. C'est une menace adressée à un autre». *ᶜAlay/nā bin*, with pronominal suffixes to the *bin*, he points out, means «I/we swear that...», and that the parallel expression among the Zaydīs and Muslims of the Yemen is *ᶜalayya qasam*. *Awthān* in the Qurᵓānic context above if rendered as «oaths» would certainly make the passage easier to understand. The pre-Islamic Arabs swore by their deities, as in the verse *Bi-Waddi-ki mā qawmī ᶜalā mā tarakti-him*, explained as *bi-ḥaqqi ṣanami-ki ᶜalay-ki (Tāj al-ᶜarūs*, Kuwait, 1385/1985-, i.282). One speculates as to whether the special function of the diety Wadd was connected wih the swearing of oaths of alliance etc. A further Qurᵓān passage, v,82, states that the Christians are *aqraba-hum mawaddat-an li-ᵓlladhīna āmanū*.

65. *Sīra*, 125.

66. Ibid., 207.

67. Ibid., 67, to compare.

68. Ibid., 287-8.

Then at evening he dismounted amid Ka^c^b in the place of honour brought and loved *(yuḥabb)*, among those affected to him, partisan *(awdād wa-ashyā^c^)*, supporters *(anṣār)* responding to the Ahl al-Bayt (the Prophet's House).

Banū Ka^c^b protectors *(ḥumā)*, ceaseless in preventing injustice, with swords flashing like meteors.

...

To al-Hādī they are protective support *(nuṣra ḥāmiya)* never disheartened, against his foes. Whenever he summons them they issue forth in close packed hosts, clamorous!

...

Thus were their forebears with his ancestor the Chosen (Muḥammad).

...

To rise with the sons of the Prophet is the most glorious boast and the pride of the Arabs.

The boast that the Wādi^c^a ancestors fought alongside the Prophet's House is supported by a verse attributed to ^c^Alī b. Abī Ṭālib quoted by Nashwān b. Sa^c^īd[69] but not found in *Nahj al-balāgha*.

During al-Hādī's troublous times Abu ^ɔ^l-^c^Atāhiya said to him that «I hope things will return to affection for you *(maḥabbati-ka)*» - here it would be fair to understand *maḥabba* as «loyalty». It seems then that *mawadda* had a technical sense both in the pre-Islamic period and carrying on into the time of al-Hādī, of fealty and support.[70]

Hijra (pl. hijar)

The institution known as *hijra* has been discussed in its various senses in *Ṣan^c^ā^ɔ^*;[71] it is related to the sacred enclaves, the *ḥaram* and the Lower Yemen and Ḥaḍramawt *ḥawṭa*. It functions indeed similarly in some ways to the Prophet's *ḥaram* at Yathrib/Medina. Ṣan^c^ā^ɔ^ is *muhajjara*, i.e. its inviolability is guaranteed by seven powerful Yemeni tribes in its vicinity though its inviolability has often been infringed upon in the past. Perhaps the *hijra* status of Ṣan^c^ā^ɔ^ should be related to its position as a *sūq* and the *ḍāmin al-sūq* or guarantor of the security of the market, tribe or individual lord/shaykh, to whom reference is made in Yemeni histories and in my corpus of tribal law documents. This inviolability may seem

69. *Die auf Südarabien bezüglichen Angaben Našwān's im Šams al-^c^ulūm*, ed. ^c^Aẓīmuddīn Aḥmad, *GMS.*, Leyden-London, 1916, 114.

70. Further examples of *mawadda* are *Sīra*, 200, a Banu ^ɔ^l-Ḥārith man of *ahl al-maḥabba wa-^ɔ^l-mawadda;* ibid., 286, Ibn Bisṭām writes that he is *bi-^ɔ^l-mawadda wa-^ɔ^l-maḥabba wa-anna-hu lahu ^c^alā ^c^ahd;* ibid., 133 the Fuṭaymiyyūn are *ahl al-mawadda* to al-Hādī; cf. 209, 306.

71. Op.cit., 40b seq.

inconsistent with the frequent tribal attacks made on the city accompanied by rapine and murder.

In tribal law in general, to violate the security of a place of which the security has been guaranteed by tribes, brings extra heavy penalties upon the offender.

Sayyids coming under the special protection of the tribe are called *hijrat al-qabīla* and the Sayyid is respected and protected *(muḥtaram wa-muhajjar)* even from insult. The tribes are at his behest and respond to his summons or cry *(al-qabā'il tulabbī ṣawt-ah)*. If the Sayyid should be attacked the Shaykh will assemble his tribesmen to defend him, and should he be insulted they will bring sacrificial beasts *(ᶜaqā'ir)* to conciliate him and these they will slaughter at his door. As a *hijra* does not fight or take part in any tribal responsibility if he does not wish to do so, he can mediate between tribes. Though I was informed that other classes can be *hijra*, Ḥabshūsh[72] seems to confine the term to those of high social standing only for he says, «the *hijar* have a special distinction and honour *(nāmūs)* with the tribes». Men of religion who are *hijra* are thus taken as *marjaᶜ*, reference, i.e. in matters of law, and become arbiters - the term is equivalent to *maradd* the function accorded to the Prophet at Yathrib by its tribes in the second of the two treaties he made in his first year at Yathrib.

The Sayyid *marjaᶜ* in the *hijra* is described also as *qudwa,* an example, paragon, which term is applied in Wādī Ḥaḍramawt, to take a case in point, to the Sayyid *manṣab* or lord of the *ḥawṭa* at Thibī village. This epithet for the Sayyid arbiter, or some synonymous word, is evidently pre-Islamic for in Labīd's *Muᶜallaqa* among verses on the theme of the protection and justice of which his tribe takes charge, we find,

Min maᶜshar-in sannat lahum ābā'u-hum
Wa-li-kulli qawm-in sunnat-un wa-imāmu-hā.[73]
Of a company for whom their ancestors laid down a way/custom,
For every tribe has a way/custom and example-paragon of it.

The commentator explains Imām as example/paragon *(mithāl)*.

Hjr is a word which figures relatively frequently in the pre-Islamic inscriptions of south Arabia, generally in the sense of «town», but Ry 508 alludes to «the tribes *(ashᶜāb)* of Hamdān and their *hjr* and Aᶜrāb. Coming between two names of tribal groups it seems better sense to read it as *hijar,* a distinct category on its own, perhaps like Labīd's Imām/paragon, arbiters protected and honoured by the tribe. Again, in CIH 541,1173 we find the phrase *bi-ashᶜābn w-hjr/hijar,* and in a Mārib inscription I think *hijar* may be read in at least one place for *hajar.*

The act of *hijra,* says Ṭabarī,[74] is a man's separating from his homeland and

72. Op.cit., 42a.
73. See my discussion of this verse in *Cambridge history of Arabic literature,* Cambridge, 1983, 123.
74. *Tafsīr,* ix, 113.

tribe *(farq waṭani-hi wa-ᶜashīratihi)*, but this does also mean in consequence the adhering to a new group when one breaks with the first group.

Hijra in the Yemen means also an inviolable enclave and there are a great many of these,[75] but the strange thing is that neither in its sense as an institution or a geographical term is it mentioned by al-Hamdānī or any other source known to me until the author of *Ghāyat al-amānī*[76] reports in the year 546/1151-2 that the Zaydī Imām al-Mutawakkil Aḥmad b. Sulaymān returned to his *hijra*, ᶜAmrān al-Khārid, at the head of al-Jawf and here the sultans of Āl al-Daᶜām came to him. There are quite frequent mentions of *hijras* by him after this date, and Yāqūt[77] refers to *hijrat* Buḥayḥ of the Ṣanᶜāʾ districts *(nawāḥī)* and Dhū Ghabab of the Dhamār districts, neither of these places known to the *Ṣifa* of al-Hamdānī. The two towns in their vicinities are the important northern centres. The author of the *Ghāya* assumes that the nature of a *hijra* is understood by his readers, as of course it would be when he was compiling his chronicles, but it looks as if it was already quite long established in its geographical sense by the 6th/12th century. Whether earlier writers chose to ignore *hijra* in either of its senses for ideological or other reasons, or whether it only acquired a geographical application some time after al-Hamdānī one cannot say - the institution is ancient and my feeling is that the term in both its senses is ancient also.

As, in the course of time, rivalries developed between the various Sayyid houses descended from al-Hādī individuals of them, either in fear of the Imām in office, or in rebellion against him, would flee to a tribal *hijra* for security and raise the tribe against him. This appears to have happened very frequently in the decline of the Zaydī Imāmate during the late 18th and early 19th centuries. As the Ḥamīd al-Dīn Imāms, Yaḥyā in particular, were able to achieve a large measure of centralization of power concentrated in themselves, the status of the *hijra* was naturally weakened and its organisation replaced by officials of the Imāmic government, so that in our time far fewer evidences remained of its functioning than in the past. A tribesman who had committed the heinous crime of murdering in the *hijra* would now be seized and handed over to the civil authority. In addition to paying the *diya* he would also have to pay a fine called *hajar* for having committed his murder there. It is to the tribal *hijra* that the Imāms send for soldiers *(junūd)*and for *zakawāt*-taxes, the tithes *(ᶜushūr)* on crops being assessed by the tribal Mashāyikh «on trust» *(bi-ʾl-amāna)* in the Zaydī districts, and the Shaykh receiving a «return» *(marjūᶜ)* for collecting them. It was also because these *hijras*, guaranteed by the *shuyūkh al-ḍamān* were potential centres of disaffection to the

75 . See Ismāᶜīl al-Akwaᶜ, *al-Madāris al-Islāmiyya fī ʾl-Yaman*, Damascus, 1980, discussing the *hijra* in its Islamic scholarly connection.

76 . Yaḥyā b. al-Ḥusayn b. al-Qāsim, *Ghāyat al-amānī fī akhbār al-quṭr al-Yamānī*, ed., Saᶜīd ᶜĀshūr, Cairo, 1388/1968, i, 306. Cf. *al-Simṭ al-ghālī*, in G. Rex Smith, The Ayyūbids and early *Rasūlids in the Yemen*, GMS, n.s., xxvi, London, 1974-78, ii,79.

77 . *Muᶜjam*, art. *hijra*.

régime that Imām Yaḥyā did all he could to diminish the influence of the *hijras* and their shaykhs, as also of the Hāshimite families themselves. This is played upon for propaganda purposes by the celebrated Yemeni poet al-Zubayrī[78] in his polemic against the Imāmate.

Ḥāshid *hijras* are mentioned below[79]. The *hijra* of Arḥab, which nowadays is counted a Bakīl tribe, is at Ṣirwāḥ[80] which I passed by in 1966 - I was told that «Ṣirwāḥ is hajar Arḥab, their *hijra*», and I have since wondered that as they seemed synonymous, or almost so, to my informant, whether the ancient *hajar* of the inscriptions was the same institution as the Islamic *hijra*. When al-Zubayrī broke away from the puppet government set up in Ṣanᶜāʾ by Nasser and formed the Party of God (Ḥizb Allāh) he wanted to assemble both the tribes following the Imām and those following the Republic in Ṣirwāḥ of Arḥab - the tribes are assembled by a beacon on Mount Riyām. The Arḥabīs speak of *ḥalīqat Arḥab* the assembly of the fighting men of Arḥab when they *iḥtalaqū*, assemble in response to a summons to war. It seems that in Ṣirwāḥ as a rule the tribes collect, Hamdān (Ḥāshid al-Kubrā), Arḥab, Nihm, Murhiba, Sufyān, Hamdān Ṣaᶜdah, Bakīl. It was commented to me that Zubayrī constituted a real danger to the Royalists, the supporters of the Ḥamīd al-Dīn, where the tribes were concerned, because his approach to them was religious, like that of the Sayyids. The Royalists were more apprehensive of him than of either the Egyptians or the Republicans because they felt the latter would ruin themselves by their actions. It is interesting that the Egyptians, ᶜAmrī and the Royalists are said all to have wished to get rid of Zubayrī, but the evidence is that the assassins were paid by the Royalists. They were captured however and held in detention by the Egyptians and Republicans who seem simply to have them go.

It is to be remarked that the Bakīl tribes, Sufyān, Arḥab, Bal-Ḥārith, Banī Ḥushaysh, Sanḥān, ᶜIyāl Sirayḥ, Nihm, ᶜIyāl Yazīd (of the Jabal), Dhū Muḥammad, Dhū Ḥusayn, and others though they correspond very nearly to the lists in *Ṭurfat al-aṣḥāb*,[81] do not always seem to be located in the same areas today as in the earlier centuries of Islam.

Ḥāshid and Bakīl and the Imāms of the Yemen

Throughout the centuries of political manoeuvre and strife from the days of al-Hādī during the ensuing medieval ages the tribes of Ḥāshid and Bakīl figure in the Yemeni chronicles, fighting now on one side, now on another, often sup-

78. Op.cit., 109.
79. See p. 29.
80. Arḥab, I was told in 1966, is called Arḥab al-Jawd because it was generous with its men *(liʾanna-hā jādat bi-rijāl-hā)* in the fighting with Nasser's troops.
81. Of al-Malik al-Ashraf ᶜUmar b. Yūsuf al-Rasūlī, ed. K.W Zetterstéen, Damascus, 1369/1949, index.

plying soldiers to the Zaydī Imāms, mostly, presumably, when the interests of both the parties happened to coincide or when the Imāms by playing on their sensitive code of tribal honour *(qabyala)* were able to pressure them to come out in their support. During the first Ottoman occupation they sometimes acted as auxiliaries to the Turks, but they mainly seem to have participated in the process of recovery of the Yemen from the Turks.

Prominent in Yemeni history for over two and a half centuries have been the Mashāyikh of the house of al-Aḥmar[82]. Al-Aḥmar were *fuqarāʾ ᶜilm,* scholars, though the term implies rather more than that, before they became Mashāyikh and Ḥāshid gave them their protection *(hajjarū-hum),* this being handed down by inheritance up to our present time. Ibn al-Aḥmar is the chief *(kabīr)* of Ḥāshid and Shaykh al-Ḍamān. The family are Mashāyikh of the ᶜUṣaymāt tribe of the Ḥāshid group and are known as hijrat Ḥāshid. Their *hijra* is located at Khamir and al-Qafla near al-Shahāra and they have extensive lands in Ḥabūr, Kuḥlān, etc. They have documents containing agreements that they be referred to in all disputes and that their decisions are to be implemented. It appears that the Imāms of the Ḥamīd al-Dīn had no special *hijra* of their own, but Ḥāshid *hajjarat al-Imām Yaḥyā,* accorded *hijra* status to Imām Yaḥyā, perhaps when his election was supported by the tough Ḥāshid chief, Nāṣir b. Mabkhūt al-Aḥmar. But though Yaḥyā married Nāṣir's foster-sister,[83] the Sharīfa Ḥūriyya, Nāṣir defected along with ᶜAbdullāh b. Juzaylān of Bakīl to the Idrīsī of ᶜAsīr, because, it is alleged, the 1912 Treaty of Daᶜᶜān, concluded by Imām Yaḥyā with the Turks, acknowledged that *Mīrī* tax was eventually to be paid to the Ottoman government. Opposed to Nāṣir were Ahnūm, traditionally loyal to the Ḥamīd al-Dīn and ᶜĀhim, Ẓulayma, Banī Surayḥ and Arḥab.

To hark back to an earlier period[84], the *naqīb* ᶜAlī b. Qāsim al-Aḥmar, along with Juzaylān of Bakīl and others, in the first half of the 12th/18th century, came out in support of the *daᶜwā* of Imām al-Nāṣir Muḥammad b. Isḥāq and clashed with Imām al-Manṣūr al-Ḥusayn b. al-Mutawakkil when they met at ᶜAṣir, just west of Ṣanᶜāʾ. The Imām contrived his assassination and had his head borne to Ṣanᶜāʾ impaled on a spear. Much fighting inevitably followed the murder and insult perpetrated on so prominent a tribal shaykh as al-Aḥmar. Imām Aḥmad Ḥamīd al-Dīn was to repeat the action two centuries later when he ordered the execution of the Shaykh of Ḥāshid after the troubles of 1959.

Describing the effects of Turkish rule on the northern tribes, Ḥāshid in par-

82. See my *Studies in Arabian history and civlisation,* London, 1981, (reprints of articles), 228.

83. Imāms would contract marriages with daughters of tribal shaykhs sometimes, to extend their influence; al-Badr I was told at al-Qāra in 1964 did so while I was there. The corpus of customary law treatises includes sections on the obligations set up as a result of contracting a marriage, including mutual defence etc.

84. *Ṣanᶜāʾ,* 84a-b; Muḥammad... Zabārah, *Nashr al-ᶜarf,* Cairo, 1359-76, i, 539.

ticular, during the second Ottoman occupation, Aḥmad al-Shāmī[85] maintains that, coupled with their chasing out the governors of the Prophet's House and their own inability to crush the tribes, it upset all order there. The result was divisive, he says, in that each tribe turned to reliance upon its tribal group feeling *(ᶜaṣabiyya qabaliyya)* to preserve its own identity against the Turk and also the tribal group feeling of the other tribes around it, aligning itself with its own Mashāyikh - which led to chaos and anarchy. Yet the love of the Ahl al-Bayt ran so strongly in their veins that while you might find them ignorant of the precepts and duties of Islam, yet no one would deny his tribe or comprise on the love of ᶜAlī and sons of ᶜAlī. The situation however had so deteriorated that, while they would make a show of obedience *(ṭāᶜa),* they would rule themselves according to the dictates of their *Ṭāghūt,* that is their traditional customary law.

After the Turkish withdrawal, «to keep down the heads of possible dissidents Yaḥyā's formidable warrior son Aḥmad was sent to Ḥajja of Ḥāshid country in 1338/1919-20. This town he took and fortified its castles, making it the base of his expeditions against other tribes. He wrested fiefs from the great Mashāyikh, broke the power of al-Aḥmar family, humiliated the tribes of the area and so kept them in subjection that Nāṣir b. Nāṣir Maḅkhūt fled to King ᶜAbd al-ᶜAzīz in Saᶜūdi Arabia»[86]. As Aḥmad al-Shāmī says, unjust customary law *(ᶜurf)* was abolished and replaced by *sharīᶜa,* women were enabled to inherit (which in tribal customary law they do not) and moreover the tribesfolk were not allowed to stumble about in their error and ignorance, but men and women instructors *(murshid)*[87] were sent to teach them the precepts and duties of the faith. Let it be said that the tribes themselves would see the case somewhat differently and customary law as practised can bring justice where a corrupt qāḍī will not, but on my travels in 1964, 1966 and since, I have often heard praised the security *(amn)* that prevailed in the days of Imām Aḥmad.

In the latter part of Imām Aḥmad's reign when his son al-Badr Muḥammad had been designated heir apparent and the Ḥamīd al-Dīn were divided among themselves, most seemingly favouring his uncle al-Ḥasan for the imāmate, Ḥāshid was with al-Badr, or at least so I am informed, and al-Ḥasan was favoured by Bakīl, Amīn Abū Rās being over hijrat Bakīl as Ibn al-Aḥmar was over hijrat Ḥāshid. It was to Ḥāshid that al-Badr turned in the unsettled conditions when his father was in Rome in 1959, unwisely releasing all political prisoners, including Ḥusayn al-Aḥmar.

85. Aḥmad al-Shāmī, *Imām al-Yaman Aḥmad Ḥamīd al-Dīn,* Beirut, 1965, 67 seq.
86. *Ṣanᶜāʾ,* 100a.
87. Al-Shawkānī states, «It was the duty of every judge *(ḥākim)* in every area to send reliable and competent men *(rijāl umanāʾ ᶜārifīn)* to teach the people their religion and duties towards God». Ḥusayn b. ᶜAbdullāh al-ᶜAmrī, *The Yemeni scholar Muḥammad b. ᶜAlī al-Shawkānī 1173-1250/1760-1834; his life, works and times...,* Durham University Ph.D. thesis, 1983, i.209. Imām Yaḥyā also sent them to the Ismāᶜīlī (Fāṭimī Ṭayyibī) districts for the same purpose, and he had Ismāᶜīlī writings destroyed where they were found.

It is to be kept in mind that the Mashāyikh are really each independent and the function of a paramount chief, apart from acting as chief arbiter, is only to call the whole tribal confederation out in time of war, and even then not all the tribes will necessarily respond.

When I was in the Yemen in late 1966 Dīrat Ḥāshid had agreed to try to drive out Nasserite troops, ᶜUṣaymāt at Mabyan, Khārif and Banī Ṣuraym at Kuḥlān and ᶜUdhar (ᶜIdhar) of al-Maḥābisha. ᶜUṣaymāt did not follow ᶜAbdullāh b. Ḥusayn al-Aḥmar in his support of the Republic but said that he was not to be molested and was to be allowed to remain in his place.

The Zaydī Imāms, 16th-20th Centuries

In facing the task of government an Imām must combine the qualities of a courageous and resolute warrior with those of a scholar, diplomat and administrator. He must be an arbiter of upright character, and he must have an almost encyclopedic knowledge of people, especially of tribes and families with the intricacies of their relationships... let it be said that an Imām, or even a prince, must also be an extremely hard worker, rarely able to devote time to relaxation - and he has constantly to be on the outlook for intrigues of one sort or another, against himself. The house of al-Qāsim the Great has produced some outstanding men who worked to the Yemen's advantage, despite having to act through officials rarely, to a greater or lesser degree, not corrupt, and to rely on military contingents furnished by the tribes whose loyalty may be described as permanently inconstant. There are a few exceptions. The soldiery themselves, as the writer has personally observed, are difficult to control, and largely inspired by a hope of subsidy from the Imām, or, failing that, extortion and plunder, often of their fellow-citizens. To keep his tribal soldiery happy an Imām must be able to pay them, sometimes to bribe them handsomely, so he cannot slacken in his efforts to raise money. An Imām is indeed aided by the tribesman's extraordinary credulity in his supernatural powers which include ability to slay by a curse or other such means. Yet, on occasion, I have heard tribesmen speak out in harshest frankness to princes of the revered House of the Prophet. It is a misfortune when a strong Imām is followed by a weak one. Sometimes there are several claimants from the House itself to the Imāmate - often the deceased Imām's sons. A scrutiny of Zaydī history reveals that, notwithstanding the theoretical principle that any holder with the appropriate qualifications may be elected to the office, it is most frequently a son who succeeds his father. Each pretender has a following from some tribal group he has cossetted - anyway it is not in tribal sectional interest to have a strong centralized government that will «clip their nails» and make them pay taxes. So brother fights brother, nephew fights uncle, order and security vanish, and the unarmed of the craftsmen and farmers suffer. There is no Imām who has not had to quell tribal lawlessness - often using one tribe to plunder another by way of reward[88].

It was the rift between Imām Sharaf al-Dīn in conjunction with his other sons, about the mid 10th/16th century, and his warrior son, al-Muṭahhar, that largely contributed to the first Ottoman occupation of the Yemen, as indeed it was the family squabbles that led to the anarchy in the 19th century and the second Ottoman occupation. In our own time the rivalry over the succession to Imām Aḥmad, brought about the loss of the Imāmate to the Ḥamīd al-Dīn in the events following the 1962 coup d'état..

The two phases of greatness of the Zaydī Imāmate both followed when the Imām of the age became the embodiment of the idea of liberation from the Ottomans and was able to manage the loose and undisciplined cohesion of the tribes. The first was al-Qāsim «the Great» who, in the first two decades of the 11th/17th century, succeeded in initiating the movement against the Ottomans, but it was his son al-Muʾayyad who drove them from the Yemen and he is as much the hero of the *Reconquista* as his father. Yet both Imāms had difficulty in controlling the tribes, their supporters, and getting them to honour agreements made by the Imām with the Turks The role of a *mujammiʿ*, uniter is no easy one.

When the Zaydīs took Zabīd, Mocha and Kamarān in 1045/1636 port revenues would become available from which to subsidize the tribes - perhaps this provided the economic sinews for the burst of military *élan* that sent Zaydī tribal armies on their career of conquest to the Oman borders during the splendid reign of al-Mutawakkil (ob. 1078/1676). Yet even so great a monarch as al-Mutawakkil had to pay subsidies to tribes like the Duhma and when he cut their stipends they responded by plundering a caravan of the Ṣaʿda merchants on the main route to Ṣanʿāʾ. The conquered territories, even the relatively remote Kathīrīs of Ḥaḍramawt had to contribute at least something to the Imām's exchequer but the ports, easily controllable by the Imām would doubtless be the most lucrative source of revenue.

The decline of the power of the Imāms can certainly be attributed to the fall in their revenues, especially when they lost the ports of their over-extended and unwieldy empire of mountains and tribes. A notable example of a tribal breakaway from the central government was the combination of tribes led by Yāfiʿ but including the Raṣṣāṣīs, Ḥawāshib, Dathīna, Āl Ḥumayqān, Murād, Bayḥān and al-Muṣʿabayn groups which took and plundered the city of Ibb, slaying men and women mercilessly. Though the Imām of the time was strong, he was unable to restore control over Yāfiʿ nor could his successors do so, but even the British never controlled the mountain tribes of Upper Yāfiʿ during the Protectorate period. By the mid 12th/18th century the Imāms had lost Lahej and Aden - Ḥāshid and Bakīl tribesmen were despatched against Faḍl al-ʿAbdalī who had

88. *Ṣanʿāʾ*, 78a.

murdered the Imām's agent in Lahej, but Faḍl slaughtered sacrificial animals *(ᶜaqāʾir)* in the markets of Yāfiᶜ - this is a form of appeal for help to tribal honour which may not be refused without loss of that honour - and Yāfiᶜ responded, driving the Imām's forces from Aden and Lahej.

Niebuhr remarks on the drop in revenues by the time of al-Mahdī ᶜAbbās, though accounted nearest to the Zaydī ideal of warrior monarch as he was, a follower of the *sharīᶜa,* generous giver and benefactor. Towards the close of the 12th/18th century the decline became more evident and the tribes so uncontrolled that the Imāms had to subsidize them to stop them plundering the country. In the early 19th century the tribes of Baraṭ, a high table-land in the north-east of the Yemen, Dhū Muḥammad and Dhū Ḥusayn had become so unruly as to plunder the suburb of Ṣanᶜāʾ, Bīr al-ᶜAzab. The Imam countered by putting these tribes to the ban in Ṣanᶜāʾ city and imprisoned their chiefs, tribesmen being taken in the streets and *sūqs* and murdered.

By the thirties of the 19th century the Zaydī Imāmate had fallen into such chaos and decay that in the Ṣanᶜāʾ region one puppet Imām succeeded another as described in *Ṣanᶜāʾ*[89] and the tribes did much as they liked. «Northern Yemen had reverted into an anarchy of tribal chiefdoms and little city states under various Imāms with tribal backing. Individual Imāms may have been men of quality and ability but they did not succeed in restoring stability». These circumstances enabled the Ottoman Turks once more expanding into Arabia, to enter Ṣanᶜāʾ in 1289/1872, but though they had initial successes against the northern tribes almost constant fighting was to follow - in my 1966 travels there time and again villages or castles destroyed by Turkish artillery were pointed out to me.

In 1307/1890 al-Manṣūr Muḥammad of the Ḥamīd al-Dīn house was recognised by the ulema as Imām and went to al-Madān of Ahnūm where he set to sending letters to rouse the tribes already impatient of the Turks - I visited the great fort he built at al-Ahnūm on my 1964 journey. A general rising broke out in 1309/1891-2, the tribesmen besieging Ṣanᶜāʾ whose unfortunate citizens were regarded by the Turks as implicated with the tribes while, if, under famine conditions, they left the city the tribesmen plundered them of all they had and «if they came across a woman they assaulted her honour». The Imām and chiefs of troops were helpless to check such excesses and so when a Turkish relieving force arrived it was welcomed in Ṣanᶜāʾ despite the oppression the Ṣanᶜānīs themselves endured at Turkish hands[90].

The part of Ḥāshid in support and opposition to Imām Yaḥyā during the Ottoman period and after has already been touched upon. Carried to power by the Zaydī tribes of the north, Imām Yaḥyā commenced on a reconquest of the

89. Ibid., 89a seq.

90. The Yemenis complained that the Turks regarded them as heretics which they deny, at the same time pointing to the immoral conduct of Turks in the Yemen.

Yemen after the departure of the Turks. «But for the wisdom *(ḥikma)* of Imām Yaḥyā and the *jihād* of his son al-Imām al-Nāṣir (Aḥmad)», says Aḥmad al-Shāmī, «this Mutawakkilite government could under no circumstances have been formed»[91]. This meant overcoming the Ismāᶜīlīs (Fāṭimī-Ṭayyibīs) of Jabal Ḥarāz who had been Turkish supporters in both occupations and the Zarānīq of the Tihāma whom the Turks and Tihāma merchants were forced to pay to keep the roads open. Sayf al-Islām Aḥmad had, as has been seen, turned Ḥajjah into a fortified base from which, after quelling Ḥāshid, he turned to the Zarānīq. He took the port of Ghulayfiqa and the vessels which used to supply the Zarānīq with arms from abroad, and after hard campaigning their capital Bayt al-Faqīh. His courage won their unwilling admiration so they nicknamed him Aḥmad al-Jinnī.

The Dahm of the Mashriq, the north eastern areas, would not submit to the Imām's rule but cut the roads and raided towns. So in 1351/1932-3 Aḥmad camped in Ḥarf Sufyān and set to bringing them to heel. At al-Jabal al-Aswad he built barracks, and he went to Midaqqa - the Ashrāf of the Jawf[92] and the chiefs of Dhū Ḥusayn came in and submitted to him, but Dhū Muḥammad of Baraṭ mountain plateau resisted until he went up by way of al-Kharāb and took al-ᶜInān, its capital, after fierce fighting. He also took hostages from the sons of the Dhī Nūf and Masāᶜīr who raided to Karab and Ṣayᶜar, as security for their good conduct - so that a man could go six days' travel from al-Jawf to Maʾrib in security and caravans pass freely. In 1947 I recall that Yemeni raisins and almonds used to come to Shibām in Ḥaḍramawt so these eastern routes must have been secure then.

Yaḥyā's expansion into the east and south brought him into confrontation with the British at Aden who had concluded a series of Protectorate treaties with independent tribes which for a brief period had been controlled by the Zaydī Imāms at the height of their power. These tribes are not Zaydīs but Shāfiᶜīs, though this was a distinction nominal rather than real because many Shāfiᶜī tribes on both sides of the Protectorate borders knew little more than the cults of saints that had replaced the gods of the pre-Islamic age. The Shāfiᶜī tribes wished to remain independent of the centralized government of the Imām with its taxes and Zaydī soldiers whose attitude, for instance to the ᶜAwdhalīs, was that they were Dhimmīs, i.e. protected persons of the Imām, like the Jews. Since the British left the Protectorate tribes much to their own devices and even paid them trifling

91. Al-Shāmī, op.cit., 69.

92. Shaykh ᶜAlī b. Mabkhūt al-ᶜIrāḍa told me that the Ashrāf al-Jawf were Āl Ṣāliḥ b. Ḥusayn, but there were also other groups. In Mārib they were Āl Khālid b. Ḥusayn, in Ḥarīb Āl Aḥmad b. Ḥusayn, and in Bayḥān Āl Muqbil b. Ḥusayn, this Muqbil being called al-Habīlī, ancestor of Sharīf Ḥusayn of Bayḥān who played so prominent a part in the politics of the fifties and sixties. His ancestor ᶜAbdullāh b. Ḥamza who was born in Barāqish was Imām from 591/1195 when he made his *daᶜwā* till 623/1226. These are the Ḥamazāt Imāms. See Zabāra, *Itḥāf al-mustarshidīn*, Ṣanᶜāʾ, 1343.

stipends,they preferred this to Imāmic rule, the Imām had to withdraw his soldiers from Protectorate territory he had occupied but he never abandoned his claim to these territories. Shāfiᶜī tribes on the Zaydī side of the border indeed were in touch with the British during World War I and, it seems, might have preferred Protectorate status to either the Turks or Imām. There was no national consciousness among them in those days.

In the days of the decline of the Zaydī imāmate during the late 18th and early 19th centuries, the Imāms had maintained a regular force of African soldiers, as incidentally did the Ḥaḍramī sultans, no doubt so as to have non-tribal troops more reliable than tribal contingents and as a counterpoise to the tribes. Their uniform was evidently based on that of the Turkish soldier, fez and red broadcloth. So also Imām Yaḥyā maintained a regular army at first with Turkish officers who had stayed on after the end of World War I. There was also a special bodyguard the *ᶜukfa* attached to members of the Ḥamīd al-Dīn House; it was composed of men of different tribes, and my impression is that they became attached to the particular prince they were serving and were loyal to him.[93] The ordinary soldier was poorly paid and when in a position to extort something from the ordinary citizen or peasant he would do so. The same of course was true of the slave troops of the Ḥaḍramī sultans until they were brought under control by the British administrators. In the Yemen corrupt officials and hard-hearted Zaydī soldiery pressed hard on the Shāfiᶜī districts which were directly administered and taxed, whereas in the Zaydī tribal districts taxes were collected by the Shuyūkh al-Ḍamān, who could obviously not oppress their tribesmen in the same way. *Ṣadaqa*, subsidies, of money and grain, used to be paid by the Imāms to the northern tribes and when a tribesman came in to Ṣanᶜāʾ or Taᶜizz he got an order from the Imām for some gift or subsidy. As already noted, this was how the Prophet dealt with powerful tribes.

In 1935 Yaḥyā sent ten young men to Iraq for training in various military skills and they returned to the Yemen as officers - those known to me who later became prominent figures were not tribesmen and they included at least one Sayyid. When they returned to the Yemen they were or became disaffected to the Imām's régime.

In winning back the Yemen from tribal anarchy and creating a centralized state Imām Yaḥyā had been greatly reliant on the powerful and able Āl Wazīr Sayyids but he began to place his own numerous sons in key positions and dislodge the Amīrs of the Āl Wazīr from their posts. A conspiracy was set afoot to murder Imām Yaḥyā and elect ᶜAbdullāh al-Wazīr Imām - the complicated plot is described in *Ṣanᶜāʾ*[94] in outline, but it was basically dynastic or, as Aḥmad al-

93. In 1964 when Sayf al-Islām ᶜAlī b. al-Ḥusayn was murdered at al-ᶜUḍla an *ᶜukfī* of his bodyguard went mad *(jinnin)* for grief and another said to me that rather my father or brother be killed than ᶜAlī.

94. Op.cit., 101a seq.

Shāmī says, it was a revolt of the ulema. Other elements were involved but all realised that the support of the Zaydī tribes could only be won by a Sayyid with tribal backing.

The conspirators had thought to assassinate the Heir-Apparent, Aḥmad, who had been aware of the plot through his spies, and who immediately showed his metal by moving from Taᶜizz to his *hijra* base at Ḥajja and summoning the tribes to his aid. They came in to him from every side with acclamations and threats against his foes. The way in which Aḥmad coerced or cajoled the tribes into action is in itself witness to his strength of character. One day he sent weapons and provisions to Jabal ᶜIyāl Yazīd, demanding that the tribe advance on Ṣanᶜāʾ, but their Mashāyikh hung back, prevaricating, seeking to profit by the situation to make excessive demands, even threatening to join the Āl Wazīr if he refused to accede to them. They assembled and marched with their tribal chants *(zawāmil)* to Saᶜdān. The Imām looked down on them from his window but as they persisted in their demands he quickly girt himself with his sword and dagger and came out to them, ordering the door of the courtyard to be locked. He then called out the shaykhs' names, one by one, and asked what they wanted. They persisted in their demands for money and new weapons until, in the confusion, the Imām was heard to shout, «You imagine I am weak and suppose I shall only win through you but your ideas have failed and your hopes are dashed. But I need no man - I am only through (the instrumentality of) God upon whom I rely and in whom I trust. I shall get all I want and I shall fill the face of the earth with blood and heads! I shall fight till I win or die a martyr! Be off with you if you want, to Ṣanᶜāʾ, with your false greed and you'll find money they are sharing out without counting, and weapons they'll hand out among you without reckoning». He then said, «But I shall n't let you go off with *my* weapons. So anyone who wants to leave this courtyard safe and sound, let him hand over his weapons or his corpse will be trampled underfoot». This he said alone, by himself, in a vast concourse. Then he went towards the mansion, the people falling back to make way for him, astounded. Then they recovered and shouted, «We shall die in front of you, Mawlā-nā, whatever way you wish». Turning to them like the experienced warrior he was, he said, «God bless you *(Bārak Allāh fī-kum)* - you are my trusty troops *(junūd mukhliṣūn)*. I cannot neglect you regarding what you need in respect of recompense, praise and benevolence».

The afternoon of that very day the men of the Jabal came with sacrificial animals *(ᶜaqāʾir)*, asking for pardon for what arisen from them[95].

The way in which Aḥmad brought out Arḥab and some other tribes was to send a certain ᶜAlī b. ᶜAlī al-Faqīh to slaughter four dogs in front of them. This was in order to put the shame on them *(yinakkif-hum)* so as to stir them up, as if he were saying to them, «The blood of people (of nobility) has, in your eyes,

95. Al-Shāmī, op.cit., 95.

become like that of dogs (unclean animals for whose blood, hunting dogs apart, no compensation is sought). It implied that ᶜAlī b. ᶜAlī was saying, *«Hādhā ᶜinda-kum yā Arḥab!»* «If you do not rise to avenge them You are as dogs». So they rose as one man to avenge the murder of Imām Yaḥyā.

Imām Aḥmad b. Yaḥyā Ḥamīd al-Dīn Nāṣir al-Dīn

«Imām Aḥmad Nāṣir al-Dīn was a ruler of tremendous personality, astute, brave, resolute, learned and witty, suspicious, unable to brook opposition, often terrifying, patient but swift to action»[96]. He had a *ṣawt jahwarī* stentorian voice. His rule was much stronger than that of his father[97], but the inimical forces working against him were many and varied - certain great Sayyid houses like the Sharaf al-Dīn, the tribal chiefs of Ḥāshid, Baraṭ and the Mashriq, certain Qāḍī houses, the young officers of the army and many Shāfiᶜīs, but in the aftermath of the 1962 changes there are still many who remember him with respect as maintaining law and order through the country. In 1948, Aḥmad al-Shāmī says[98], the towns were against him, but as already seen, he managed to call out the tribes, perhaps even those with whom he had fought in earlier years and brought to heel. He could and did deal severely with dissidents - he had his brothers who came out in rebellion against him executed - but all things considered he was reasonably clement in the Yemeni society in which he lived. He certainly won the unwilling admiration of the very enemies he had bested. Propagandists have dubbed him «the Tyrant (al-Ṭāghī)», but the well known politician «al-Ustādh» Aḥmad Nuᶜmān who so often opposed him and was imprisoned in Ḥajja after the dynastic coup of 1948, clearly respected him and perhaps, up to a point, was not unsympathetic to him.

Imām Aḥmad had a vast knowledge of tribes, families, and individual members of them which struck them as almost uncanny. He is said to have kept notes and he would not only know the names of those whom he met, but would astonish them by asking such questions as *«Kīf ᶜamm-ak filān, wa-ibnu-h filān»*. To this he might add some personal query in detail. The Prophet himself was well versed in this kind of lore for he is reported to have said, *«Lā saʾala-nī aḥad al-yawm ᶜan nasabi-hi illā alḥaqtu-hu bi-aṣli-hi,* May no-one ask me today about his genealogy but I shall trace him back to his origin»[99].

The forcefulness of Imām Aḥmad's character can hardly be better illustrated than in his famous fighting speech delivered at Hodeidah in 1959. This speech has been much misrepresented by propagandists against the régime, and al-Zubayrī's riposte is far better known than the speech itself.

The Imām had accidently become addicted to morphine supplied to him dur-

96. *Ṣanᶜāʾ*, 104b.
97. Al-Shāmī, 97.
98. Ibid., 11.
99. Al-Hamdānī, *al-Iklīl erstes Buch*, ed. O. Löfgren, Uppsala, 1954-65, 67.

ing a painful illness by his Italian physican, and he had to go to Italy for treatment, leaving his son al-Badr in charge. «With the cat away, the mice came out again. The Army in Taᶜizz and Ṣanᶜāᵓ was so restive that al-Badr called in the tribes, fearing the Army might attack him in Dār al-Bashāyir. Tapes of seditious speeches were made and sent with warning letters to the Imām in Rome. The Imām was also given to understand that his son intended to depose him. Aḥmad, now recovered, returned by sea... In Hodeidah he made his stern but rousing speech against those who had been creating disturbance in his absence - some fifty thousand tribesmen brought into Ṣanᶜāᵓ by al-Badr hurriedlyleft it on hearing the speech over the radio. *«Bawwaḥ al-shayba,* The old bull has bellowed», they said. Ḥusayn al-Aḥmar and other northern chiefs now came out in rebellion, but Aḥmad, by political means, including bribery, broke up support for him and he launched many northern tribes against them along with a force of the Regular Army commanded by two experienced Sayyid generals... The tribes and Army quelled the rebellion. Ḥusayn al-Aḥmar's supporters melted away. He and his son Ḥamīd had to surrender and were executed under circumstances not very creditable to the Imām»[100].

I am indebted to Sayyid Aḥmad al-Shāmī who supplied me with a recording of the speech at Beirut in 1969 which I transcribed and checked with him. It was delivered improptu in al-Ḥudayda on August 12th, 1959/Ṣafar 7th, 1379 before the crowds come to receive him on his return from Rome[101] (See Appendixes 1and2).

Imām Aḥmad's unswerving conviction that he acts with God's authority comes out strongly in the Hodeidah speech. Some years earlier indeed this conviction manifested itself when he was besieged in the ᶜUrḍī at Taᶜizz, but broke out of it sword in hand, challenging the besiegers to personal combat with the words, «Do you want to kill your Imām, the Commander of the Faithful? You can't do it! Your Imām is guarded by God». His escape from the intended assassination in the Hodeidah hospital also, when he feigned death, appeared near miraculous. The Imām's certainty undoubtedly impressed tribesfolk and in any case as a tribesman said to me in 1966, the tribes have *iᶜtiqād kāmil fī Āl Muḥammad,* complete belief in the House of Muḥammad. This belief in their House had however, I was told, weakened considerably among the young Ḥamīd al-Dīn princes who went to school in Cairo before 1962 for secondary education in the secularist political atmosphere of Nasserite Egypt and of course the whole position of the Sayyids was under attack from young Yemeni political writers like Muḥsin al-ᶜAynī as well as al-Zubayrī of the Yemeni Liberals[102].

100 *Ṣanᶜāᵓ*, 106. He is said to have executed them when under safe-conduct.

101 . In places the recording is unclear, the speech distorted by crowd background noise. Stars in the Arabic text indicate cheering.

102 . For instance Muḥsin al-ᶜAynī's *Maᶜārik wa-muᶜāmarāt ḍidd qaḍiyyat al-Yaman,* Cairo, n.d., but about 1957.

Imām Aḥmad in his tough policy with the Zaydī tribes naturally brought resentment from them and in the weakness of the Ḥamīd al-Dīn on his death they were at once prepared to raise their heads again, but the fear of him was so great that, it is said, tribesmen would at first visit his tomb in Ṣanᶜāʾ to make sure that these terrible eyes were dead and even that it was dug up for this reason.

Aḥmad had made a bid to take over the authority of Nājī al-Ghādir among the tribes of Khawlān east of Ṣanᶜāʾ for himself. This, al-Ghādir resisted, and the Imām sent his general, *(maqdamī)* Muḥammad al-Ḍumayn of the Ashrāf of al-Jawf, to fight against him and eventually al-Ghādir had to come to an agreement. I have noted the following *zāmils* (tribal chants) on the occasion - Imām Aḥmad used at times even to make a judgment in a *zāmil*. Nājī, who was apparently also something of a poet in colloquial Arabic, said

Yā salāmī shann yā nasl al-Ḥasan[103]
Min lisn ᶜawlah ṣādiqīn afᶜāla-hā.
Qad jīt li-ʾl-ṭāᶜa wa-tahmīd al-fitan
Wa-in ghalabtū bā nafukk aqfāla-hā (rajaz metre).
My greeting pours forth to you of al-Ḥasan's line[104]
From the tongues of gallant fighters with deeds so true.
I am come to obey, to settle the disputes,
But their locks we'll re-open if refuse you do!

To which al-Ḍumayn made the riposte,

Qāla ʾl-Sharīf, Ahlā bi-ṭāᶜat-kum li-man
Amri-h yaduqq suhūla-ha wa-jibāla-hā
Qad al-Habīlī bāᶜa-kum ba-rkhaṣ thaman
W-Iblīs qaffā wa-ʾkhtafā Dajjāla-hā.
Said the Sharif, «Welcome be your obeying him
Whose command strikes both the mountain and the plain.
The Habīlī, at the lowest price, has sold you,
Iblīs abandoned you, Dajjāl is hidden lain.»

Sharīf Ḍumayn's references to the Dajjāl and Iblīs mean the Sharīf Ḥusayn al-Habīlī of Bayḥān (of the same house as Ḍumayn though another branch) whom he stigmatizes as having left the Khawlānīs in the lurch after stirring them up against Imām Aḥmad, but when they sought help from him they did not receive it. Sharīf Ḥusayn certainly was in touch with the Ashrāf of the Jawf whom he even visited, and I think he must have been in touch with and sympathetic to Sayf al-Islām al-Ḥasan[105]. Sharīf Ḥusayn's influence and repute were high in the Jawf area as I learned for myself in 1966.

103. A *waw* at the beginning of this line would make the metre fit.
104. Ḍumayn as a Sharīf is descended from al-Ḥasan.
105. Sir Kennedy Trevaskis, *Shades of amber,* London, 1968, 180. Sharīf Ḥusayn probably expected the attack on al-Badr was by Sayf al-Islām Ḥasan's supporters.

Imām Aḥmad had also been tough with the Dahm in the Mashriq and took many hostages *(rahā'in)* from them and they were afraid of him. (When Nasser's troops found a way of entering the Jawf which was Royalist till then, the Dahm largely turned Republican *(tajamharū)*, but when they were compelled to evacuate the area Dahm became Royalist again *(tamaylakū)* and told me that their shaykhs would visit the camps during the day but fire on them at night). Taking hostages from tribes to ensure their good behaviour is a long established Yemeni practice - al-Hamdānī *(Iklīl* i,93) speaks of hostages *(ruhanāʾ)* from the notables of Rāziḥ. The Rasūlids held them in their northern castles and even budgeted for stipends for them. (The Aden Protectorate Sultans also held hostages and at Khawr al-ᶜUmayra fort the hostages of the ᶜAbdalī wore leg irons but were otherwise free to move about). I saw the quarters of the hostages in Imām Yaḥyā's magnificent castle at al-Sūda which he used a a base, and the little gardens they used to cultivate. These hostages were not kept in irons. The Protectorate hostages would be close relatives of tribal shaykhs and they would be changed for others when they had served a certain time. It is naturally not exactly a pleasure to act as a hostage, but in my experience it appeared not too much of a hardship either and a useful method of maintaining public security.

Imām al-Badr and the coup of 1962

It was the disunity of the Ḥamīd al-Dīn princes that led to the eclipse of the imāmate in the Yemen at a time when *kilma wāḥida* united action, was ever the more necessary in the face of external pressures, notably Nasser's ambitions to extend his power to the southern end of the Red Sea. Imām Aḥmad had, in his day, succeeded in foiling his brothers' ambitions, but al-Ḥasan, the eldest and most capable of them, was a far more acceptable candidate in the eyes of the Ḥamīd al-Dīn house for the throne than Aḥmad's son, Muḥammad al-Badr, whose personality and policies they deemed unsuitable to the Yemen. Al-Badr, though made heir-apparent, feared al-Ḥasan's ambitions and support by powerful northern tribes - so, as a young man of his times, he sought support in Nasser and the young officer group of the Yemeni army who became subverted by the Egyptian officers al-Badr introduced to train them at the Military Academy at Ṣanᶜāʾ. Though warned of their conspiracies he did not take the prompt action against them that characterised his father's deeds. Besieged by his disloyal young officers in his mansion in Ṣanᶜāʾ he escaped with a handful of loyal followers from Ṣanᶜāʾ and made for the north, intending to rally the tribes to his aid in the traditional manner.

In its early stages the Republic had a strong anti-Hāshimite strain, though there were Sayyids among the rebel officers. On the first Friday after the coup it was said to a man, actually of the Qāḍī class, «*Lā kanāwis baᶜd al-yawm,* There wont be any turbans after today». This was in allusion to the ulema «turbaned» class of Sayyids and Quḍāt. The Quḍāt families in the Yemen are distinguished by the hereditary designation of *qāḍī*, literally «judge», and form a group of Yemeni aristocracy the members of which are often Ulema filling administrative and sometimes military offices. About this time also the Jumhūrīs demanded Sayyids, especially officials, be handed over by Ahnūm. The Ahnūmīs refused, saying *«hijra la-nā fī-him»* and beat off Republican attacks. Certain of the extremist officers had already murdered many leading Sayyid high officials in Ṣanᶜāᵓ.

The many enemies Aḥmad's tough policies had made were now able to raise their heads - these included not a few of the great tribal lords. When al-Badr arrived at Ḍilaᶜ Hamdān, a little outside Ṣanᶜāᵓ, as he described to me in the cave at al-Qāra, the place of the Shaykh of Hamdān, ᶜĀṭif al-Muṣallī, he appealed to him for support, *bi-ḥaqq al-qabyala,* tribal honour, though ᶜĀṭif was described to me by others as a great *muthawwir,* pro-revolutionary. He sat with him an hour and ᶜĀṭif gave him mounts *(qurāsh),*equipment and thirty soldiers, and set him up to go on his way. Later ᶜĀṭif came to Ṣanᶜāᵓ and the officers asked him, «Why did you help al-Badr?» ᶜĀṭif replied that he was obliged to do so by *qabyala,* so they shot him in Liberation Street (Shāriᶜ al-Taḥrīr). This brought in his son Muḥammad (whom I met in Rimaᶜ in 1983) on al-Badr's side.

Sallāl, the non-tribal chief of al-Badr's staff, I am told, was in touch with him just before he left and advised him to go to Ḥajjah and rally support there with Ḥāshid, but he was unable to do so, being prevented by the Republicans with tanks. His appeal to ᶜAbdullāh al-Aḥmar of Ḥāshid whose father had backed him in 1959, was rejected in insulting terms - the execution of his father and brother when under Imām Aḥmad's safe-conduct rankled bitterly[106] and I suppose could be regarded as setting up a blood-feud with the Ḥamīd al-Dīn. Sinān Abū Luḥūm of Nihm and the Shāyif chief of Baraṭ were also hostile to the Ḥamīd al-Dīn. On the other hand, Nājī b. ᶜAlī al-Ghādir of Khawlān, though he had been put down by Imām Aḥmad, when he went to Ṣanᶜāᵓ to see what was happening there found the Sallāl-Bayḍānī régime so distasteful that he joined the Royalist side.

At first the tribes supporting the Imām seem to have fought without payment. The Royalists maintain that the Republicans started bribery and when the tribal Mashāyikh came in to Ṣanᶜāᵓ President Sallāl gave the tribes money and weapons - which many of them used against the Republic immediately after leaving the city. Sallāl invited the Mashāyikh to come to Ṣanᶜāᵓ and would hand them 2,000 to 3,000 riyals as a bribe, a large sum in those days - some would not even accept this. Nasser's political officers certainly distributed money and weapons to tribes. As the war dragged on and Saᶜūdī money as well poured into the country a tribe or sub-section would often *tamaylak* or *tajamhar* as it took a subsidy from one or the other side. Like the Ottomans, Nasserite forces could not maintain their hold of large areas of tribal country. When they withdrew most tribes

106. This was clear when I discussed his reply to al-Badr with him in Beirut.

tamaylak though not all. In my experience an internal division could split tribal allegiance into Royalist and Jumhūrī though they would not fight each other.

In 1964 tribesmen said to me that *«Bayt Ḥamīd al-Dīn hijra, bi-yad-hum al-ḥukm al-Nabawī,* The Ḥamīd al-Dīn House is *hijra* (which means they are bound to protect it), in their hand is the Prophet's rule/authority». We have complete belief in the Family of Muḥammad. To this was added that they either wanted a *ḥukm Nabawī Hāshimī,* Prophetic Hāshimite rule, or *kull qabīla taḥkum nafsa-hā,* each tribe should govern itself. The tribes, they said, dislike the government of individuals because they consider them (the Republican government in Ṣanᶜāᵓ was intended) *safala (= nāqiṣīn),* of low class. Tribes in the Ḥarīb area said they disliked *istiᶜmār al-Shawāfiᶜ,* Shāfiᶜī colonisation, alluding to the support given the Republic by the Shāfiᶜīs and perhaps to the settlement of numbers of Shāfiᶜīs in Ṣanᶜāᵓ after 1962. It is significant that Sallāl himself came from the Ṣanᶜāᵓ Sūq, the tribes despising *sūqīs.* They say *kalām ibn al-sūq* of a person whose word is not believed, but tribes pride themselves on not lying.

Nasser was obliged to withdraw his troops in 1967 and Royalist tribes invested Ṣanᶜāᵓ, but when victory seemed near, the dispute between al-Badr and most of the other Ḥamīd al-Dīn princes reasserted itself and the tribes grown accustomed to subsidies said with cynical humour that they wanted «half a victory» so that they might still enjoy bribes from both sides. On Jabal ᶜAybān west of Ṣanᶜāᵓ which they were occupying, Nājī b. ᶜAlī al-Ghādir, the war chief *(muqaddam ḥarb)* of Bakīl, told the energetic prince Muḥammad b. Ḥusayn that he would see Ṣanᶜāᵓ but never enter it, meaning he would support him no further than that. Perhaps the other tribal Mashāyikh may have felt they would not like to see a strong Imām return to power. Al-Badr was blamed by the princes for ignoring the threat posed by Nasser's intrigues in the Yemen and there was no united front. Finally the intervention of communist supported exernal forces, including Russian planes - a Russian pilot was brought down in Jaḥāna - against unenthusiastic tribes who had suffered much from YAR bombers and in whom the Saᶜūdīs had lost interest, meant that the Ḥamīd al-Dīn's opportunity was lost, though one of the princes held out near Ṣaᶜda till killed. The tribes could probably have checked the invaders in the mountain passes had the will been there.

Under the Republic the position of the Zaydī tribes is still strong and they receive subsidies as in the days of the Imāms - the Republic has to rely on Ḥāshid and Bakīl for its defence. What will happen in the greatly changing economic circumstances in the YAR is another chapter.

A great deal of fiction has been fabricated to show that the Imāms foster the belief in their supernatural powers. Hostile propaganda averred that at al-Qāra al-Badr used to fake miraculous appearances of himself. This, I am sure, is plain nonsense, as is the tale that Imām Aḥmad would tie a cord round his neck to make his eyes protrude - this is a physical feature I have remarked in his close relatives. The Sayyids in general are widely believed to have the power of summoning the

Jinn to serve them.[107] As the tribes believe in these supernatural powers of the Imāms, YAR planes bombed the tombs of past Imāms at Ẓafīr Ḥajja, Al-Mahdī Aḥmad b. Yaḥyā al-Murtaḍā and his son, but it was pointed out to me they had suffered little damage! A belief is, or was, current in the Yemen that one must have an Imām for when a man dies it will be said to him, «Now you are dead who was your Imām? *(mutt al-ān wa-man kān imām-ak)*»[108]. Imāms were believed to have power to heal humans or animals - this belief goes back a long way and the curious case is recorded of a sick man eating the seal on a letter from al-Hādī and being restored to health.[109]

Many believed that Imām Ahmad was *muṣarraf,* i.e. that bullets or swords would not penetrate his body[110] and perhaps Imām Aḥmad may have believed this himself. Educated persons however affirmed to me that neither the Imām nor the princes (Suyūf) were *muṣarraf*[111]. Imām Aḥmad's amazing escapes certainly encouraged the notion that he was *muṣarraf* and if he did nothing to dispel it, both he and al-Badr were surely too intelligent to fake wonders.

Customary law and the tribes

Though the Zaydī Imāms from al-Hādī onwards have endeavoured to replace tribal law by *sharīᶜa* the latter was only applied outside the towns when the Imāms were strong enough to enforce it. Ibn al-Mujāwir[112] writing in the 7th/12th century states that the Arabs of the Mountains and Tihāmas to the borders of the Hijaz do not accept the *sharᶜ* but *ḥukm al-manᶜ* which he recognizes as undoubtedly the law of the Jāhiliyya. It may be remarked that the term *sharᶜ* itself as commonly used in the countryside means a customary law, not *sharīᶜa.* The history *Ṭabaq al-ḥalwā*[113] writing in the 12th/18th century alludes to the laws of Baraṭ, presumably of Dhū Muḥammad and Dhū Ḥusayn of Bakīl. I have also been informed that in the hands of five groups of Bakīl there is a kind of written code called *al-Sabᶜa al-Qawānīn,* the Seven Canons, upon which their laws are based and that the whole area in the north is judged only by *ᶜurf* which, it was stated, is quicker and honester than the *(sharīᶜa)* courts. The Seven Canons are perhaps to be identified with the laws of Baraṭ already mentioned. Last century the Makramī Amīr of the Yām tribe gave the ᶜAlawī Sayyids of Ḥaḍramawt who,

107. Qāsim Ghālib et al., *Ibn al-Amīr wa-ᶜaṣru-ṣu,* Beirut, 1969, 139, speaks of the miracles *(karāmāt)* of each Imām through the services of the Jinn and the help of the angels. The hostility of this book to the Imāms is well known.

108. Cf. the belief among Ḥaḍramī Ṣūfīs that one must have a shaykh to find favour with the Almighty (The Saiyids of Ḥaḍramawt, in *Studies in Arabian history*... No. viii, 13).

109. *Sīrah,* 139.

110. Al-Shāmī, op.cit., 34, 74.

111. *Ṣurf* was defined to me as *taᶜwīḏ min al-Jinn.* A woman would say to her child, *Ṣarraf minnak kull shayṭān,* May every devil be averted from you.

112. *Tārīkh al-mustabṣīr, Descriptio Arabiae Meridionalis,* ed. O. Löfgren, Uppsala, 1951-54.

113. ᶜAbdullāh b. ᶜAlī al-Wazīr, *Ṭabaq al-ḥalwā wa-ṣiḥāf al-mann wa-ᵓl-salwā,* Chester Beatty Arabic Ms. 4097, 46b, 63b.

led by the ᶜAṭṭās, were attempting to establish a pilgrimage route to Mecca, an *ᶜahd*, pact, called *qāᶜida mujawwira* - this may provide a clue to the Seven Canons, since the *Kitāb Lawāzim al-manᶜa*[114] commences with a chapter on *jiwār*, and others deal with *rifāq, ḥalīf, ṣulḥ*, etc., and the Seven Canons are almost certain to cover this range of topics. Perhaps the *sijills* of the tribes to which al-Hamdānī alludes also deal with legal principles.

In Imām Yaḥyā's day, I am informed, the tribal law codes of the type found by Ettore Rossi, if found in a man's possession could bring about his execution - they were said also to exist in Khawlān and Kuḥlān. They give the impression of a society completely independent of the central power in its ethics and organisation, without *qāḍīs* but with arbiters and mediators. The extract from the corpus I am editing contains the following section

What is due to the masters/chiefs *(makhādīm)*

They are sultans, chiefs, those responsible for the payment of blood-money *(ghuramāʾ)*[115], those in authority over their tribes *(al-mālikūn li-ᶜashāᶜiri-him)*, those with whom a pact of security *(amāna)* has been contracted and who have been entrusted with authority[116], and what is allowable to him[117] and what is not. You must know that any tribe swearing *(yaḥlifūn)* to a man to hear and obey *(ᶜala ʾl-samᶜ waʾl-ṭāᶜa)*, and they commit an offence *(yakhtiyūn)*, are obliged to render amends[118].

A *ḥākim* must judge according to *sharᶜ* in the place of *sharᶜ* and *manᶜ* in what is appropriate in judging by *manᶜ*[119]. No one may judge by *manᶜ* unless he has *manᶜ*, *manᶜ* seeming basically to mean the power to protect and restrain. The testimony of men of religion *(ahl al-dīn)* is given precedence over that of others.

The celebrated scholar al-Shawkānī attacks the Dhū Ḥusayn and Dhū Muḥammad of Baraṭ for submitting «to the customary laws of their predecessors *(aḥkām al-ṭāghūt)*» but he applies this criticism to the Yemenis of the North (al-Qibla) and the East (al-Mashriq) who have not come under the control of the *dawla*. They are even worse than the subjects *(raᶜāyā)* under the control of the *dawla*, authority, «who cannot pray, or pray incorrectly». Following the *Ṭāghūt* these tribal areas deprive women of their inheritance, and if they follow *sharīᶜa* they do so reluctantly, or resisting it or acting unlawfully or show disdain for it[120].

114. Described in «Materials for South Arabian history» II, *BSOAS*, London, 1950, xiii, iii, 590 seq.

115. Seemingly the same as *ḍāmin*, sometimes one finds both used together, *gharīm ḍāmin*.

116. Reading *wulāt al-amr* or possibly *wallā-hu ʾl-amr*.

117. The Arabic of the text is not well constructed; «*hım*» may be rendered as «them».

118. This passage is taken from Yaḥyā b. Ḥabl (?) al-Qaḥṭānī of Arḍ al-Bayāḍ whom I have been unable to identify, but he may be of the Qaḥṭān between Najrān and ᶜAsīr. (Rossi, 26r). Aḥmad b. ᶜAlī b. Zinbāᶜ (Rossi coll.) says, *Man qad nuṣiba li-ʾl-amr wa-ʾl-nahy wa-ᶜuqida lahu dhālika aw akhadha-hu bi-ʾl-qudra - law kāna mālik-an li-ᶜashīrati-hi milk-an mashhūr-an fa-laysa li-aḥad-in an yajūr ᶜalay-hı* (understand with Lane, *fi ḥukmi-hi) wa-lā yaᶜtariḍ la-hu fī ᶜashīrati-hi*.

119. So al-Qaḥṭānī, who does include this in a section *Adab al-Qāḍī*, but perhaps this is simply with the intention of setting *manᶜ* in an Islamic framework.

120. Al-ᶜAmrī, op.cit., 211; cf. 146.

In the *man*ᶜ*a* element in *Ṭāghūt* there is little in the corpus positively un-Islamic, but practices like *bish*ᶜ*a,* trial by ordeal, are condemned by the ulema. The term itself does not seem to be opprobrious as used by the tribes and means both the arbiters who administer it and the law itself.[121] Disapproval of the ulema apart, recourse to the *Ṭāghūt* eats into the power of the centralizing authority of the Imāms, and Yaḥyā on the Turkish withdrawal in 1337/1918-19 immediately set about «cleansing the country of *ḥukm al-Ṭāghūt al-qabalī* dominating with its ignorance and error over minds and spirits». He delegated this to his son Aḥmad who to a large degree, there seems little doubt, did manage to suppress it openly at least, but Yemenis in Aden told me ordinary folk avoided the courts and had recourse to *muṣliḥs,* conciliators, as much as possible - *qāḍīs* in the Aden Protectorates had also the reputation for corruption as in the Yemen. So «clipping the nails of the *Ṭāghūt*» is the policy of the Imāms and of their centralization of power in the cities.

Summoning the tribes

A *ṣārikh,* or call for aid, will be sent to a tribe, perhaps with ᶜ*aqīras,* animals slaughtered to put a compulsion on the tribe to rise. Landberg[122] says they must be cows or camels. It is the *dawshān,* a sort of *maddāḥ*[123] who stirs up the tribes *(yuthawwir al-qabāʾil).* For this purpose *dawshāns* and *muzayyins* are sent to *rās al-*ᶜ*aqaba,*the head of the pass, and the *muzayyin* beats the drum while the *dawshān* calls *(yiṣīḥ), Ḥayyā-kum yā qabāyil qūmū li-ʾl-jihād - jāhidū* ᶜ*ala ʾl-sharaf wa-*ᶜ*ala ʾl-karāma wa-*ᶜ*ala ʾl-waṭan wa-*ᶜ*alā Amīr al-Muʾminīn wa-nuṣrat al-ḥaqq wa-iqāmat al-dīn min al-*ᶜ*aduww al-dākhil fī ʾl-waṭan.* (This particular ᶜ*aduww* was the Nasserite troops in 1964) Such lively addresses stir up the *nakhwa aṣīla,* noble pride of the tribes and the action is an ᶜ*āda mujarraba.* A proclamation will be made *(*ᶜ*amalū ẓāhira)* by a *dawshān* with the *muzayyin* at the drum, to assemble the tribe with a formula such as *«Yaqūl al-qabīla al-fulāniyya inna-hum bada*ᶜ*ū ba*ᶜ*ḍ al-ba*ᶜ*ḍ li-ʾl-ijtimā*ᶜ*».* When a proclamation of war is made in Khawlān they carry wood to the summit of al-Ṭiyāl mountains and light a beacon to raise all the Khawlān tribes. A *shaykh jihād* may be appointed to conduct the war, but he would not necessarily be a *shaykh qabīlah.* When the Imāms sent to the tribes for a levy for the army (not necessarily in time of war) the levy was termed *ḍarībat dam,* a blood tax, and a money contribution for the same purpose *buqshat al-bāṭil.* The *hijar* Sayyids were exempt from either. In tribal law a tribesman serving as a soldier with the government did not set up a blood-feud against his tribe if he

121 . Shaykh ᶜAbdullāh Khamīs told me in al-Riyāḍ some years ago that *Ṭāghūt* was a judge in tribal matters not drawn from special families, but chosen for impartiality and such like qualities. He would sometimes judge by *firāsa,* perspicacity, intuition. The term in Saᶜūdī Arabia did not seem to convey any pejorative attitude to the practice.

122 . *Ḥaḍramoût,* Leiden, 1901, 459 seq.

123 . He is of non-tribal status.

killed a man - the government was responsible and a tribesman might therefore avenge himself on any government official, high or low.

What surprises one in the Yemen is the quick switches of allegiances;a tribe might be fighting for the Imām one time, but be attacked or attacking him the next.

In Imām Aḥmad's day a small group of tribesmen with their leader, unable to maintain a livelihood in the Zaydī north would come to the Imām asking to be engaged as soldiers. The Imām might send them to a Shāfiᶜī district where they acted as a garrison and were used to enforce tax collection. In one sense this solved a problem but the Zaydī tribal soldier was not loved there.

★ ★ ★

In conclusion it may be observed that internally in the Yemen there is a seesawing tension between the tribes who desire *de facto* independence of the centralizing authority and the Imāms who exercise that authority - yet the tribes cannot dispense with the existence of such an authority. The centralised authority wishes to destroy or reduce local power and to replace the ancient customary law of the tribes by Islamic law. The literature on the other hand, while recording the interplay of tribe and Imām, the actual events, does not care much to examine the underlying reasons for tribal actions, and is much concerned with controversy among the sects and the ulema, supporting or criticizing the policies of the Imāms. It was of course the ulema who wrote the histories and their view of the tribes is unsympathetic, urban and sometimes aloof. The civilisation of the countryside and tribal society seems of minor interest to historians though in legal texts one finds material relating to custom, especially where it clashes with theories held by the ulema.

Bibliographical Note

The main written source has been the relevant chapters in R.B. Serjeant & Ronald Lewcock, *Ṣanᶜāʾ; an Arabian Islamic city,* which should be consulted for detailed information, and articles reprinted in my *Studies in Arabian history and civilisation,* London, 1982, notably «*Ḥaram* and *ḥawṭah:* the sacred enclave in Arabia», «South Arabia» which deals with the social structure of western Arabia, «The *Sunna Jāmiᶜa*... analysis and translation of the documents comprised in the so-called «Constitution of Medina»,» «The Saiyids of Ḥaḍramawt». Aḥmad al-Shāmī's *Imām al-Yaman, Aḥmad Hamīd al-Dīn* has been much relied upon, and *Dāmighat al-dawāmigh,* Hertford, 1967. My «The Yemeni poet al-Zubayrī and his polemic against the Zaydī Imāms» in *Arabian studies* is background for the modern period, and Ettore Rossi's invaluable «Il diritto consuetudinario...» and my own edition of *Kitāb Lawāzim al-manᶜa* have provided much of the tribal background, and of course Carl Rathjens, «Ṭāghūt gegen ʾscherīᶜa», *Jahrbuch des Linden-Museums,* Stuttgart, 1951. I have also consulted I. Goldfeld, *The tribal policy of the Prophet Muḥammad,* Cambridge Ph.D thesis, 1970, which is informative though I do not entirely concur in some of the conclusions.

Appendix I

خطبة الإمام أحمد في حديدة سنة ١٩٥٩

إخواني وأولادي سلمكم الله!

أحييكم تحيةً حارة منبعثةً من سويدآء القلب، إجلالاً لكم واعترافًا بما قُمتم بَه من الثبات على الموالاة والمودّة، وعدم الانصياع وتصديق الأشرار أهل الفساد الذين يريدون الإخلال بالأمن وإخافة الطريق والشَّوْفَة والفتنة والظلم والسير بلا حياء من الله ولا مراقَبه لَه.

وقد سبق في علم الله أنه سيكون خروج إمامكم إلى الخارج للمعالجة والاستشفآء. والآن قد عُدْتُ إليكم في صحّة جيّدة* وعافية كاملة ــ أحمد الله وأشكره على نِعَمه الوافية ــ وأحيّـي شعبي اليمني الباسل الثابت على الدين والولآء والمودّة، والسكون والاطمئنان، والتجنّب من النصارى وأعوانهم ــ أحيّـي شعبي العزيز الذي لاحقتني برقياته إلى حيث كنت يسألون عن صحتي وعافيتي. وما هذا إلاّ دليل رايع على صدق المحبّة والمودّة ــ والحمد لله رب العالمين. وقد كان ما كان من بعض السفهآء والأشرار المغرورين المخذولين، فأخافوا الأمن في تعزّ فقتلوا النفس الحرام، ونهبوا الأموال، وأخافوا السبيل، أخافوا بَيْضة الإسلام التي يلجأ إليها الخايفون ــ ولا قوّة إلاّ بالله!

لقد كان لذلك في نفسي من الأسف والأسَى ما لا أقدر أن أعبّـرُ عنه؛ ولكن، الحمد لله، خيّب الله آمالهم، وأذلّهم وأرجعهم منكوبين.

وها أنا الآن عازمٌ على تنفيذ أحكام الله في أولائك أهل الفتنة ــ منهم من سيُضْرَب عُنُقه عملاً بكتاب الله وشريعة رسول الله**، ومنهم من ستُقَطّع أَيْدِيهِمْ وَأَرْجُلُهُمْ من خِلافٍ ــ شريعة الله ــ شريعة محمد بن عبد الله ــ شريعة النبـي الذي جآء بهذا الدين والاسلام!

وأُحذّر الحاضرين ــ والحاضر يَعْلِم [كذا] الغائب ــ أنّني أُقسِم بالله قَسَماً لا هَوَادَةَ فيه أنّه لا يُرْفَع إلَـيَّ بحقّ عن أيّ شخص، كان من أبيض[124] [كذا] أو أسود* يسْعَى في الإخلال بالأمن، وإخافة الضُعَفا، ومخالفة الأوامر، والتنكّب عن شريعة الله* ــ لا يَبْلُغني ذلك عن أيّ فرد، عن أيّ شخصٍ كائنًا من كان، إلاّ جَزَزْتُ راسه بالسيف*؛ وأقول مكرّرًا مُـحَدّرًا[125] ــ ومن كذّب فليجرّبْ ــ وهذا الفَرَسُ وهذا الميدان!*

أما علمتم أنّ النصارى وأذنابهم وخَدَمَة الكافرين يسعَوْن بكل جدّهم وبكل جهدهم، بلا كَلَلٍ ولا مَلَل، يقصدون تفريق الكلمة؛ وتشتيت الجماعة، وقطع السبيل، ومخالفة الإمام، ومخالفة شريعة الله؟*** وإنّ الواقعة التي كانت في تعزّ، والتي كانت في صنعآء لم تكن بنت ساعتها،

124. Note the Imām's faulty grammar! In places he lapses into colloquial forms.
125. Unclear, translated as if *muḥadhdhir-an* is read.

ولكنها مدبَّرة من الخارج. والدليل على هذا أنّه قد وُجد بعض الذهب مع بعض المخذولين المغرورين... حجّة واضحة لا شكّ فيها ولا مِرْيَه. فهل يُرْضيكم مثل هذا*؟ هل ترضَوْن بالسفهآء والأشرار أن يتحمّلون [كذا] المستعمرين على ظهورهم إلى وطننا العزيز يُريدون إذلالَه وإذلال الشعب اليمني الباسل؟

فقد كانت تلك آية من الله سبحانه وتعالى أظهر فيها ما هو الشعب اليمني وما هورجاله، ثابتون على الدين، ثابتون على الموالاة، ثابتون على أمر الإمام وطاعته، لم يغترّوا بالذهب، ولم يغترّوا بالكلام المعسول الذي أوّله حَلاوة وآخره نارٌ وظلم.

إخواني وأولادي ـ أستودعكم الله وآخْلُدوا إلى السكينة والاطمئنان*؛ ولا تخافوا، ولا تقلقوا ـ فإنّي حريص على أمانكم وراحتكم ولو أضحّي بنفسي!

والسلام عليكم ورحمة الله وبركاته.

Supplementary note

A valuable source not drawn upon for this paper is *Ḥawliyyāt Yamāniyyah min sanat 1224 ilā sanat 1316; aw al-Yaman fi-ʾl-qarn al-tāsiᶜ ᶜashar al-mīlādī*, ed. ᶜAbdullāh Muḥammad al-Ḥabshī, Ṣanᶜāʾ, n.d., but author's preface dated Adhār 1980, Wizārat al-iᶜlām publications. The interplay of the rivals for the imāmate, the citizens of Ṣanᶜāʾ and the northern tribes is richly illustrated in this chronicle year by year. The text is in need however of full annotation to cover the senses of Yemeni words and expressions not explained by the editor.

Appendix II

Imām Aḥmad's Speech at Hodeidah, 1959

My brothers and sons, God deliver you.

I greet you a warm greeting that springs from the bottom of my heart, from esteem for you and in recognition of what you have accomplished in the way of steadfast loyalty and affection *(mawadda),* and in not harkening to and believing the evil men - those who would (create) dissension, who want to upset (public) security, make the road(s) and women *(al-shawfa)* unsafe, to (create) trouble *(fitna)* and injustice, and to carry on without shame before God or heed of Him.

It was foreknown to God in His wisdom[126] that your Imām would go abroad for (medical) treatment and hospitalization. And now I have returned to you in excellent health (CHEERS) and full of strength! I praise God and thank him for his bountiful favours! I greet my Yemeni people *(sha^cb),* steadfast in (their) religion, loyalty, affection, calm and tranquility, their avoidance of the Christians and their aides. I greet my noble people whose telegrams reached me where I was, enquiring after my health and strength. This is an impressive indication of (their) true love and affection *(al-maḥabba wa-'l-mawadda)* - Praise God, Lord of the Worlds!

There took place what there did on the part of some foolish irresponsibles and deluded abandoned evil-doers - they upset (public) security in Ta^cizz and murdered a sacred human life - they plundered property, made roads unsafe and rendered unsafe the territory of Islām to which those in fear take refuge - There is no power but in God![127]

On account of this there is in my heart such grief that I cannot bear to express, but, God be praised, God has frustrated their hopes, humbled them and sent them back in distress.

And here am I now - resolved to put into execution the laws of God upon those trouble-makers! Some of them will have their heads struck off in accordance with the Book of God and the law *(sharī^ca)* of the Apostle of God (LOUD CHEERS). And some of them «will have their hands and legs cut off from alter-

126. He means it was written *fi 'l-Lawḥ al-Maḥfūẓ,* in the Preserved Tablet.

127. The Imām in using this phrase is putting himself in a strong challenging position against his opponents.

nate sides» (Qur'ān, V,33)[128] - the *sharīʿa* of God, the *sharīʿa* of Muḥammad b. ʿAbdullāh, the *sharīʿa* of the Prophet who brought this religion and Islām!

I warn those present here - and let him who is present tell him who is absent,[129] that I swear by God an oath without remission that no case *(ḥaqq)* will be submitted to me concerning any person, be he of white or black (CHEERS), attempting to breach (public) security, to upset the security of[130] those who do not bear arms *(ḍuʿafā')*, to disobey orders and deviate from the *sharīʿa* of God (CHEERS) - I shall not hear this of any individual or any person, be who it may, but I shall strike off his head with the sword (CHEERS). (This) I say repeating and warning[131]. Whosoever says (this is) a lie - let him try! This is the horse and here the battlefield! (CHEERS)[132]

Don't you know that the Christians,[133] their tails and the servants of the infidels, are striving might and main, neither flagging nor faltering, seeking to divide the unity (of the Yemen) and break up the body (politic), to cut the road(s), [to foster] disobedience to the Imām and to the *Sharīʿa* of God (CONTINUOUS CHEERS)...[134] The incident in Taʿizz and that in Ṣanʿā' did not take place on the spur of the moment but was hatched from outside. The pointer to this is that some gold was found with certain abandoned deluded persons... a clear proof with no doubt or argument about it. Does such a thing as this win your approval? (CRIES of «No» and BOOING) Will you consent that irresponsible fools and evil men should bear the colonialists on their backs to our beloved homeland, wishing to humiliate it and bring the courageous Yemeni populace into subjection?

This has been a sign from God, Praised and Exalted, whereby he made manifest what the Yemeni populace *(shaʿb)* is and what its men are - steadfast in the faith, steadfast in loyalty, steadfast in (obedience) to the Imām's commands and in obeying him, not deluded by gold, not deluded by honied words the first of which are sweetness and the last of them Hell and oppression! (CHEERS)

My brothers and my sons, I consign you to God - so abide forever in (God's) peace and tranquillity. Fear not nor be troubled, for I am intent on your security and well-being, though I were to sacrifice myself (to achieve it)!

Peace upon you and God's mercy and blessings.

128. The quotation says this is to be the penalty of those who fight God and his Apostle and work up dissension *(fasād)* in the land.

129. A traditional formula at public announcements which remounts to pre-Islamic times.

130. *Ikhāfa,* causing fear, but used in sense of insecurity.

131. Recording unclear, see f.n. 125.

132. Al-ʿIzzī Ṣāliḥ al-Sinaydār, *Amthāl Yamaniya wa-fukāhāt Ṣanʿāniyya,* Aden (?), 18/vi/61, ii, 9, cites a proverb, *Farasak wa-'l-maydān.*

133. The Imām means the British, and by «tails» probably the Aden Protectorate sultans, but as al-Shāmī said, they had nothing to do with this situation.

134. Continuous cheering makes the Imām, if speaking, inaudible.

IV

THE ᶜAWDHILLAH CONFEDERATION WITH SOME REFERENCE TO AL-HAMDĀNĪ

My interest in the ᶜAwdhalī tribes dates from 1940 when I first went to Aden, sent by London University to study south Arabian dialect, but in the emergency following the fall of France I joined the Aden Protectorate Government Guards and it was in December that year that I obtained permission to accompany the political officer to Zārah, the ᶜAwdhalī Sultan's village. The political officer had come to settle a dispute between the Sultanic house and the tribes of al-Ḥaḍn. In the course of discussions the Sultan produced a most interesting document called the '**sharᶜ**' of the ᶜAwdhillah, a translation of which I published in the **Admiralty Handbook of Arabia** in 1946 but I have since studied it and its curious language in far greater depth. I have re-visited the Sultanate on several occasions since, notably in 1954 and consulted Sultan Ṣāliḥ on various aspects of customary law, most recently in Jeddah, but one enquiry has led to another and I have never found enough time to publish my research on the ᶜAwdhalīs from which this present paper is drawn.

That the ᶜAwdhillah are an ancient confederation that, at my first visit, had changed little over a thousand years or more was at once evident. It cannot be mere coincidence that a pre-Islamic inscription mentions ᵒŪd/ᶜAwd and Dathīnah close together in the same context. Landberg has suggested that after Islam the Awd tribe called itself Awd Allāh, later becoming Awdh Allāh — this would be analogous to the either Quraysh Allāh, indicating that the tribe owed allegiance to a particular god, and in fact probably constituted a tribal theocracy. He thinks that a change in name would indicate a change of politico-religious allegiance. I see however no particular reason why they should not have been so called before Islam.

The **Tāj al-ᶜArūs** has a long passage on the ᶜĀʾidh or ᶜAyyidh Allah (with ᶜ**ayn**) who are probably to be connected with the ᶜAwdhillah —whom incidentally I have also heard called ᶜAyādhillah. Al-Zabīdī links them with Saᶜd al-ᶜAshīrah b. Madhḥij, a genealogy which is given in fact by Ibn al-Kalbī. Some writers trace back the poet Afwah al-Awdī to Saᶜd al-ᶜAshīrah and al-Hamdānī says he came from Wādī Naᶜwah near the modern town al-Bayḍā. **Al-Aghānī** calls Afwah one of the great poets of the ancients (**al-qudamāʾ**) of the Jāhiliyyah, a leader in their wars, one of their judges (**hukamāʾ**) whose judgement (**kalām**) was highly valued. In the published **Dīwān** of Afwah I have found nothing to confirm that he came from the tribe we know today as the ᶜAwdhillah, though he was of Madhḥij to which the ᶜAwdhillah seem to belong.

It appears that the Awd tribes extended rather further north than the present day habitat of the ᶜAwdhillah, into Sarw Madhḥij, to judge by what al-Hamdānī says, but he singles out for mention the Dahbalī, the Ashrāf of the Banū Awd and their Lords (Sādah) and this house still flourishes today — incontrovertibly the Awd are the forebears of the ᶜAwdhillah. The mediaeval **Ṭurfat al-Aṣḥāb confirms** that the Awd are of Madhḥij, as also are the Juᶜfīs, the Banū Dayyān and the Nakhaᶜ. The Dayyān and Nakhaᶜ at the present time are **ḥabīṭs** of the ᶜAwdhalīs. The **Ṭurfah** also makes Madhḥij a descendant of ᶜAryab — which today is the name of an ᶜAwdhalī village of al-Ẓāhir.

Sultan Ṣāliḥ al-ᶜAwdhalī made the significant statement to me that all the tribes except al-Manṣūrī are Ahl ᶜAwdhillah and the name ᶜAwdhillah is only applied to the tribes who follow the Dahbalī. Landberg commented in 1897 that the Dahbalīs were vastly more powerful than the Sultans of Zārah themselves. The well known journalist, the late Muḥammad ᶜAlī Luqmān, who visited the ᶜAwdhalīs in 1946, reported that the Sultanic family is descended from the famous Sultan ᶜĀmir b. ᶜAbd al-Wahhāb the Ṭāhirid who reached Dathīnah in 908/1502-03 and he printed a genealogy supplied to him there. I think we should need more precise evidence to confirm this and I have at least not heard of it from Sultan Ṣāliḥ.

My present working theory is that the Dahbalī of al-Hamdānī were the original Lords of the Awd/ᶜAwdhillah in the early Islamic centuries, whether as purely secular arbiters and repositories of customary law, or whether they had also some theocratic type of function — but of this last I find no evidence. The present Sultanic house is more recent. They may have been the leaders and arbiters of the Manṣūrī group which may have entered and settled in the territory at some date unknown, but of course after the time of al-Hamdānī. In the historical material available to me, in print or Ms. form, I have found virtually nothing about the ᶜAwdhillah, but one hopes that documents may turn up containing some data upon them.

A Geographical sketch of ᶜAwdhalī territory

ᶜAwdhalī country lies east and north of Aden, its chief market centre being Lawdar, some hundred miles distant from it as the crow flies — or should one say the **qaṭā**, sand-grouse? Its borders were defined by an Aden paper as the territory of the ᶜUlahiyyīn on the east, Yāfiᶜ and the Yemen on the west, on the south the Dathīnah borders, and the Yemeni border on the north. During the later years of the British Protectorate the ᶜAwdhalī borders were defined (in order to avoid disputes I suppose) by the action of the British Agent and demarcated by pillars.

A glance at the map shows that ᶜAwdhalī territory is split into two parts by the great mountain range, the Kawr, the crest of which is called al-Ṭaffah — Sultan Ṣāliḥ called it Rās am-Ṣabar. The district of al-Ṭaffah includes Dhirwah, Bilās and Arḍ al-Sulṭān. The highland plateau to the north beyond al-Ṭaffah is known as al-Ẓāhir. The slope of this range to the south with the plain below it is known al-Kawr or Kawr al-ᶜAwdhillah. Al-Bāṭin is the flat ground south of the range, a part of which is known as al-Ḥaḍn.

Leading north-east is the Wādī Ruqub to which al-Hamdānī refers, flanked on the north by the Kawr and on the south by a high mountain range which I suppose even now is not well known. Ruqub is an important route to the east but I recall that it was not very secure.

The seat of the Sultanate is at Zārah, one of the low but steep defensible hills, projecting from the plain at the south of ᶜAwdhalī territory. Opposite it lies Shirwān hill, the top of which still has the ruins of a **ḥuṣn,** and where Sultan Ṣāliḥ b. Ḥusayn built a new castle. In the plain to the east lies Lawdar market, occupying a central position where tracks cross from Dathīnah, Ruqub, via the traditional religious centre of am-Nijdah, the Aden-Shuqrah route, and the various passes up the Kawr, including the most important, the Wādī Thirah. Wādī Thirah runs from west of Zārah and Lawdar and passes through Lawdar itself. The top of the Thirah pass has pre-Islamic paving and there are traces of a paved causeway all the way down to the Dathīnah plain but the causeway itself has long been badly eroded. Customary law forbids fighting on the Thirah pass. During the latter years of the British Protectorate a new motor road was built up near the Thirah pass, but when I climbed it in late 1940 we could only go on foot though some people rode camels or donkeys. The land below Zārah is called am-Māzim.

The Bāṭin became a rich agricultural district as a result of the establishment of security in the early 1940s and cultivation was greatly extended so that it became able to supply the Aden market with fruit and vegetables. Here the houses are mostly of inferior architectural quality to those of al-Ẓāhir and there are fewer traces of the ancient pre-Islamic culture. Between my first, second and third visits in 1940, 1954 and 1964 there were great signs of prosperity because of the remittances sent from Aden and sale there of local produce.

The Ṭaffah-Kawr range which by its wildness and imposing, almost perpendicular heights, has captured the imagination of the people in their song and verse, is about 7,000 feet high, some 3,000

— 4,000 feet higher than al-Bāṭin. Al-Ẓāhir plateau behind it contains a number of small towns such as ᶜAryab, in stone architecture. These have ancient paved threshing floors and terracing, and the great but now entirely ruined city of am-ᶜĀdiyah which has cisterns, temples, walls and numerous inscriptions, the last hardly touched at my first visit. The climate of al-Ẓāhir is mild, and can be sharply cold; I noticed some perennial streams.

Al-Ṭayyib ... Bā Makhramah says of it, 'Al-Ẓāhirī is the **nisbah** to al-Ẓāhir ... a tract in the Yemen above Dathīnah from which wheat (**ḥinṭah**) etcetera, is imported to Aden and elsewhere'. Even in mediaeval times, then, it supplied Aden with comestibles and it was at the village of Mukayrās that the Aden Government set up its centre of agricultural experiment before World War II.

On the Yemenite side of the border from Mukayrās the important Yemeni market of al-Bayḍā has always had close connections with the ᶜAwdhalī tribes.

A further point of interest is the stone circle of pre-historic times which the local people call the bride and bridegroom with their retainers, near al-Ṣawmaᶜah.

While in Zārah in 1954 I attempted to identify the place-names in this territory with those cited in al-Hamdānī a copy of whose **Ṣifah,** edited last century by D.H. Müller, I had with me, and I was able on the basis of this work to make corrections to the map which the late Professor Hermann von Wissmann was compiling about that time. There are of course some errors in the D.H. Müller edition and Muḥammad al-Akwaᶜ has been able to correct some of these in his edition from informants though I would question some of his notes. Al-Hamdānī states that certain places belonged to the Awd who would obviously seem to be the ancestors of the ᶜAwdhillah and others to the Aṣābiḥ whom one is tempted to link with the Ṣubbayḥah west of Aden or the Ṣabāḥīs on the southern frontier of the YAR. Apparently however there are still Asābiḥ (with **sīn**) in al-Ẓāhir province according to Sultan Ṣāliḥ, and there is a Saint,

Waliyy, ᶜUmar b. Miṣbaḥī in al-Ẓāhir province. Al-Hamdānī also speaks of the Dahbalīs (who have survived to the present day) and of whom more will be said below. The von Wissmann sheets of the Aden Protectorate maps appeared in 1957, the placenames corrected by me as far as possible but it would require direct travel over the whole area as Dr Wilson did in the Ṣanᶜā' region to compare al-Hamdānī with what still is known of the toponomy of his day.

The tribes of the ᶜAwdhalī Confederation

Rarely or never do two lists of the tribes of any given confederation agree, yet the lists themselves may not be inaccurate necessarily. Most travellers, for instance, rely on a small number of informants who may be well acquainted with certain tribal groups, but know little of others. Some informants may omit smaller units or consider them part of an other larger group. Where lists of tribes compiled at considerable intervals of time are concerned, the virtual disappearance of certain **groups** and the rise of others can be the cause of the disparity when comparisons are made.

The first grouping which I give below, made in 1947, seems to be territorial rather than tribal: it has been supplemented with notes from other informants and sources.

Ahl al-Ẓāhir : Manṣūrī, Barkānī, Mukayrasī, Martaᶜī, Shihrī

Al-Ḥaḍn : Manṣūrī, Bijayrī, Ṭuhayfī, Qafaᶜī all live in al-Ḥaḍn and are known as the ᶜAwdhillah al-Kawr according to Landberg. His statement that the Bijayr al-Ḥaḍn and the Bijayr al-Raydah are the same tribe was confirmed to me. The Laqfāᶜ and Manṣūrīs have a common ancestor.

Ahl am-Shaᶜah : This tribe was formerly at war with the Sultan but is now (1947) under his rule. The sub-tribes of the group are ᶜUmayrī, Qufayshī, Dayrī, Dhiyaybī and ᶜUbahī, and they inhabit the Wādī Ruqub. The **bayt al-maᶜqalah** in which the headship lies, is Ahl al-Ghānim.

Ahl Damān : A people of the mountains (actually the eastern side of al-Ẓāhir) who refuse to obey the Sultan who can only enter their territory if invited. **Nahḍah** reported on May 18th, 1950, that the Damānī tribe had submitted to **al-aḥkām al-sharciyyah** and entered into obedience to the Sultan, a truce (**Ṣulḥ**) being concluded between them and the Dhiyaybī so that their differences could be explored. **Nahḍah** names al-Warkā as the residence of the **cāqil** of Damān. It seems that their country extends as far as Wādi 'l-Khaṭīb of the Upper cAwlaqīs.

A Damānī informant named to me the Damānī sub-tribes as: al-Qafacī (Laqfāc), al-Ḍamajī (also spelled as al-Ẓamajī), Siyyārī, Maḥrizī, cAnnānī, Shamrūkhī, Ḥaddād, Ahl Dāwūd (among whom the Ahl cAlī cUmar are the **ahl am-macqalah** or headman's house, with their present **cāqil** (1954) cUmar Sālim), the Bihiyyī, the Macwaḍī (Āl Macwaḍiyyah), and the Ahl cAlī b. Shaykh, from which latter personage springs the ancestor of this group. The caskar am-Damānī were also vaguely mentioned to me, perhaps in the same social category as the soldiers of the cAwdhalī Sultan. Landberg avers the tribe has thirteen sub-divisions.

Sayyid Muhammad cUmar al-Jifrī who should be in a good position to know, gives the following list of tribes which seems in no way to clash with the territorial list **supra.**

Al-Manṣūrī : The tribes al-Barkānī, al-Shihrī, al-Ṭuhayfī, and a section of al-Bijayrī come under (**tābicah**) the Manṣūrī and are included under the name Manṣūrī. It may well be, however, that as an cAwdhalī state official, al-Jifrī shows a certain bias in calling these tribes Manṣūrīs. According to Sultan Ṣāliḥ b. Ḥusayn, the five tribes (**qabā'il**) of al-Ẓāhir are Manṣūrīs and, in fact, the land is really Arḍ al-Manṣūrī. The other tribes such as the Bijayrīs, are said to have come in from elsewhere as individuals to defend the land, and to have stayed. They are, said the Sultan, somewhat opposed to the Sultan and the Manṣūrīs. The assertion that some at least of these tribes are not so native to the country as the Āl Manṣūr is probably correct, and certainly al-Hamdānī's **Ṣifah** seems to indicate a considerable movement in population in this part of the Yemen, even as between his day and the Jāhiliyyah. Apart from the Bijayrīs, the Bū Ṭuhayf are reported by Landberg to have come from Ḥarīb.

The ancestor of the Manṣūrī tribe is said to have been the **ra'īs** of the ᶜAwdhalī tribe. Another informant told me that the Āl Ḥaydarah b. Manṣūr in Abyan are descended also from the same Manṣūr. A Manṣūrī maintained that Manṣūrīs do not intermarry with other tribes, but only among themselves and with the Sultanic house. Formerly they paid no tithes and a Manṣūrī was never put in prison (**mā yaḥtabis**). A Sultan, on the contrary, denied that Sultans intermarried with Manṣūrīs, averring that they only marry each-other. I understand his statement to refer to Dawlah girls only, for I cannot think that the Dawlah would not take girls from the tribes if they wished.

Al-Bijayrī : I assume al-Jifrī means Bijayr al-Raydah.

Al-Ghānimī : This name was explained to me as equivalent to am-Shaᶜawī, for al-Ghānimī is, as stated, the **bayt am-maᶜqalah,** headman's family, and their ancestor is al-Ghānimī.

Al-Damānī : Cf. **supra.**

Al-Muḥammadī : This name is identical with the Āl ᶜAlī Muḥammad who have as their ᶜ**āqils** the family of al-Dahbalī known to al-Hamdānī. The Āl ᶜAlī Muḥammad are settled in Shurjān at am-Darb, Shawḥaṭ, al-Ruqub, and ᶜArābah etcetera. This group is known as Miḥimmadī, and includes among its sub-tribes am-Marzūqī, am-Juᶜaymalānī and Āl-Manṣūr bir (= bin) Aḥmad.

To the above an informant in 1954 added am-Yazīdī, a tribe given in the **Handbook of the Western Aden Protectorate** as part of the Ahl Wuḥaysh settled in the Martaᶜah region of al-Ẓāhir: they and the Bijayr al-Raydah do not seem to be large tribes.

In this connection it may be mentioned that the Ahl Dayyān and al-Nakhaᶜī of Ḍalaᶜah were described to me as the **ḥabīṭs** of the ᶜAwādhil, and in fact Dathīnah was also a **ḥabīṭ** to them. The term **mutaḥābiṭīn** is synonymous with **mutakhāwīn**, brothers of each-other, it is said. **Ḥabīṭ** is further stated to mean 'neighbour' in ᶜAwdhalī tribal law, equivalent to the classical Arabic **jār**, this last statement confirming Landberg's rendering of the word as **contigu, voisin**. This term however requires further enquiry for it obviously implies a fixed known relationship implying certain obligations. It is nevertheless clear that to be the **ḥabīṭ** of another implies no form of subjection and Dathīnah so far from being subject to the ᶜAwdhalīs, or vice-versa, was until fairly recent times to some degree tributary to the ᶜAwlaqīs.

Arbitration, the Sultan and the Dahbalīs

The Ahl ᶜAwdhillah are in al-Ẓāhir and al-Kawr, but al-Ẓāhir is divided into Arḍ ᶜAwdhillah and Arḍ al-Manṣūrī — which latter is Arḍ al-Sulṭān, the Sultan's territory. The Arḍ al-Ẓāhir has many headmen (ᶜ**uqqāl**), but the Dahbalī is the source of reference for tribal custom (**marjaᶜ al-ᶜawā'id al-qabīliyyah**) or, as Sultan Ṣāliḥ also expressed it, **'Al-Dahbalī maradd fī manṭiqat al-Ẓāhir, Arḍ ᶜAw-**

dhillah, The Dahbalī is the source to which reference is made in al-Ẓāhir district'.

Maradd, with its synonum **marja**ᶜ is an ancient term which I have discussed in my study of the so-called 'Constitution of Medina', in document F of which any incident or quarrel (**ḥadath wa-'shtijār**) the ill consequences of which are feared is to be referred back to Allāh... and to Muḥammad Rasūl Allāh (**maraddu-hu ilā Allāh...**). Colonel H.F. Jacob alludes to the 'titular "Marad(d)" or Chief' of the Ahl Quṭayb, but I imagine that their Maradd would be really a repository of law and custom, a kind of arbiter, rather than a chief. I have also come across the term in the former Wāḥidī sultanate.

It rather looks as if, from the purely legal point of view, the Dahbalī Ashrāf even in al-Hamdānī's time would have held a position not unlike that of the Prophet in Medina, in the sense that they were the sources of opinion on customary law. I do not know whether the Dahbalī Ashrāf go back to the pre-Islamic era. It would be interesting to find if they are mentioned in any of the inscriptions, but they are not mentioned by Ibn al-Kalbī in **Jamharat al-nasab** though he does give a genealogy of Awd.

Tribes used to go to the Dahbalī of their own free will so that he could settle their differences. He also had the **khuṭūṭ al-Dahbalī,** the Dahbalī documents which are said to have contained the record of his customary rights, but these were apparently carried off by Imām Yaḥyā's Zaydī troops. The said documents contained a record of such customary rights as the fee of a **thawb** — in practice two riyāls — which had to be paid to the Dahbalī in the case of a woman marrying outside her tribe. I think their **khuṭūṭ** may well have been somewhat similar in certain respects to the ᶜAwdhalī **shar**ᶜ a translation of which I published many years ago. The chief family of the Dahbalīs seems to be the Ahl Sufyān. Muḥammad al-Akwaᶜ says that the present day Dahbalīs live in Wādī Shurjān of al-Ẓāhir.

The ᶜAwdhalī Sultan at Zārah appears to have had no sovereignty over the large Damānī tribe who seem in fact to have been linked to him by only the most tenuous of threads. The Damānī ᶜ**āqil** is appointed by a ceremony similar to that of the ᶜAwdhalī Sultan. When one ᶜ**āqil** dies they crown his son with the turban (ᶜ**ammamū walad al-ᶜāqil**). Three of the ᶜ**ashshārīn,** collectors of the tithe (ᶜ**ashīr**) belonging to the ᶜ**āqil's** tribe come and each links a loop of the fuse of the Arab gun (**dhabīlat al-bunduq al-ᶜArabī**) round his head, three loops (**thalāth layyāt**), one after the other. In return for this he gives them a present. This custom will at once be recognised as pre-Islamic for ᶜAbdullāh b. Ubayy, the arch-**Munāfiq** was about to be crowned this way in Yathrib when the Prophet arrived and his ambitions were disappointed. Till about the 1950s the Damānīs seem to have been little known and to a great extent isolated in their mountains.

The Shaᶜawīs, Sultan Ṣāliḥ told me, are greater than either the Dahbalīs or Damānīs, and in order of precedence the Shaᶜawīs would be followed by the Dahbalīs and then by the Damānīs. The important point is that the Sultan of Zārah is the **maradd** or arbiter in any quarrel (**khilāf**) between these three large tribal groups, but in war the Manṣūrīs and the Sultan fight side by side as a single group, whereas the other tribes may fight separately and conclude separate peaces.

The Drum: sign of authority

'Le tambour', says Landberg 'est et l'a toujours été, la prérogative du pouvoir dans le Sud. Chaque petit Sultan a son **ṭabl** ou **marfa**ᶜ qui a même un nom particulier. Il y a également des ᶜ**āqil** qui, de souche ancienne, ont leur **ṭabl** qu'ils frappent lorsqu'ils veulent convoquer leur guerriers'. In Rasūlid histories there are constant allusions to the **ṭabl-khānah** and we have in fact discussed this in our forthcoming volume on Ṣanᶜāʾ; Governors seem to have been sent kettledrums and a banner by the Rasūlid Sultan, though this may be a custom derived from Syria and Egypt. The **Rawḥ al-rūḥ** alludes to drums being beaten in a house to summon tribal help, and I recall that for similar reasons when in Shahārah in 1964 I heard drums beaten there.

There are significant parallels to this on the western bank of the Red Sea. In the 'Empire of Zayla^{c}' the right to have drums beaten belonged to the king in the early Middle Ages. Its usage in Ethiopia is well established and I may refer to al-Ḥaymī's journey to the Emperor there. According to J. **Baeteman** provincial governors are preceded on their progress through the country by a drum carried on mules. The great royal drum which was beaten at ceremonials, e.g., the entry of Ṣarsa Dengel into Aksum in 1580 A.D. had the name Deb Anbasā, Hyena and Lion — it was a large **nagārit** (Ar. **naqqārah**) reserved for the king. When Menelik conquered Gurage in 1875 he divided it into five 'drum-districts' called **nagārit.** For the curfew the Zaydī Imām's troops used to beat the drum in the evening, and when in Bayḥān at Sūq ^{c}Abdullāh I remember the drum was beaten every night at 10 p.m. for the curfew, there known by the Turkish term, **yasaq.**

I must mention here the famous copper drum of Yāfi^{c} which is said to have **ṭalāsim siḥriyyah,** magic talismans on it — I have not seen it but it might be ancient, even pre-Islamic.

The drums of the ^{c}Awdhalī Sultan of Zārah have no names it seems. What is significant however is that he is not the only possessor of a drum in the ^{c}Awdhalī confederation. Landberg refers to the drum (**marfa^{c}**) of 'the independant territory of Damān which is a sign of ancient power. Myself I have heard that the Damānī chief has a drum and a thread (**lah marfa^{c} wa-khayṭ**). The thread is a sign of authority and is drawn from the Sultan's **mi^{c}waz** or kilt and sent out as a sign of his command to a tribesman to come to Zārah. The Manṣab of the saint ^{c}Umar b. Sa^{c}īd at am-Nigdah of Wādī ^{c}Aydarī also has a thread which he sends to a tribesman wishing to perform the **ziyārah** as a sign of the protection of the saint from whose **bayraq** it is drawn. Again this is a custom that goes right back to the Jāhiliyyah for al-Marzūqī alludes to a loop of hair or wool which a pilgrim would wear going on the **ḥajj**, for the same reason.

The drums of the Damānī ^{c}**āqil** are called al-Naṣṣar and al-Muṣabbiḥ — the latter is so named because it 'attacks the foes early in the morning (**yuṣabbiḥ al-khuṣūm ghabash**)'. The drummers (**shuḥ-ḥādh**) beat on these two drums and as the drums are beaten thus will the bullets fly. Landberg also states that the ᶜ**āqil** of the independant territory of al-Shaᶜah to the south of the Kawr and of Zughayrah, al-ᶜUmayrī has his **ṭabl** or **marfa**ᶜ called al-Ghassān. On the other hand I was informed that the Dahbalī, despite the fact that his family is so ancient, has no drum.

This and other evidence reinforce the conclusion that the Zārah Sultans had little if any suzerainty over either the Shaᶜawī or the Damānī. Yet when the ᶜAwdhalī Sultan has his drums beaten and announces that he has been attacked by any tribe, then all — Shaᶜa-wī, Damānī and Dahbalī come to his aid.

The tribes which respond to the Sultan's drum are called Ahl al-Marfaᶜ and the list of these given me in 1941 was al-Qafaᶜī, al-Ṭuhayfī, al-Bijayrī, and al-Manṣūrī, i.e., the Kawr tribes, but in 1954 the tribes Barkānī, Shihrī, Mukayrasī, Dhirwī and Muḥammadī were added to my list — all these latter are tribes of al-Ẓāhir, and this looks perfectly correct. Sultan Ṣāliḥ b. Ḥusayn expressly stated that al-Miḥimmidī, al-Shaᶜawī and al-Damānī are not Ahl al-Marfaᶜ.

The saint ᶜUmar b. Saᶜīd and his authority

At the same time and, presumably, side by side with the secular authority of the Sultan and ᶜUqqāl, there was what one might call a spiritual power or authority which extended beyond the territory of the ᶜAwdhalī confederation. The Āl ᶜUmar b. Saᶜīd are Manāṣib, Lords of the sacred enclave in which the domed tomb of ᶜUmar b. Saᶜīd lies. One of the **Khādims** of his shrine (**khādim** here being an honourable term and his office highly respected) told me that before the entry of the British into the country (he meant before the 1940s or so) the Āl ᶜUmar b. Saᶜīd were the judges of the country (**ḥuk-kām al-bilād**), sending out 'the thread' as a sign to cease warring. He added that the ᶜAwdhalī Sultan's power was restricted to Lawdar and its immediate district, al-Ḥaḍn, and al-Ẓāhir up to ᶜAryab.

The **Khādim** of the shrine brings the banner of the Saint and intervenes between the tribes (**yigīb al-bayraq ḥaqq al-Waliyy wa-yifra^c bayn al-qabā'il**) after the outbreak of war. This incidentally is also common procedure in Ḥaḍramawt, associated with Manṣabs of **ḥawṭahs**— The warring tribes in the field at once separate because they reverence the **bayraq (yistaḥramūn-ah)** and out of respect for the Saint (**istiḥrām li-'l-Waliyy).** When the **bayraq** goes out to a **qabīlī** and he is armed (**mustalib**) he must fire a salute (**ta^cshīrah**). When the **bayraq** goes to a house it is absolutely **de rigueur** that a head (a sheep) be slaughtered for it, or perhaps more accurately for the Saint it represents.

The Mashāyikh of ^cUmar Sa^cīd used to judge cases by tribal law. The **sharī^cah,** I think, was hardly known. I have attended both **^curfī** and **sharī^cah** courts in Zārah and Mūdiyah in 1954 and while the **^curfī** court was always thronged with vociferous litigants the **sharī^cah** court was often quite empty. When the **khuddām** of ^cUmar b. Sa^cīd intervened between two contending parties no fee was payable to the Saint. He had in any case certain fees as well as his **ziyārāt** or pilgrimages at which sheep and cattle (**^canam wa-qurūsh**) were brought to him.

The territories from which the Saint drew revenue are indicative of his influence, or rather that of the Lords of his shrine. They were am-Sha^cah ḥaqq am-Sha^cawī lā mājil al-Ḥaḍn, Mūdiyah, ^cUlah, am-Raydah ḥaqq al-Bijayr, Arḍ al-^cAwdhalī min ^cUrr (al-Bayḍā) lā Marwaḥah, Shurjān bilād al-Dahbalī, Arḍ am-Dhiyabī, etcetera. The Ahl Damān are also one of the tribes of ^cUmar b. Sa^cīd and even now (1954) the Saint receives the **^cushr** or tithe of sheep (**ghanam**) and grain (**ḥabb**) from Damān. The Saint used to have the **^cushūr** from the Ḥasanah. Mayāsir and Sa^cīdī of Dathīnah, but the British Government took these away from the Saint. This, I was told was to provide revenue for the local administration.

This country then was the property (**milk**) of ^cUmar Sa^cīd, over which he had judgement (**kalām**) and from which he received tithes. On every field (**jirbah**) a furrow (**tilm**) went to the Saint, and one in every hundred head of sheep and goats. According to another informant, ᶜUmar Saᶜīd had, on the country of the Sultans, merchants and soldiers (**bilād al-Dawlah wa-'l-tijār wa-'l-ᶜaskar**), one third of the tithe (**lah thilith**), and in each field he received a long furrow by the bund (**wa-lah fī 'l-widin tilmṭūl**). He had half of the tithe (**nāṣifah am-ᶜashīr**) of the tribes of al-Ḥaḍn, al-Ẓāhir and the Kawr. On tribal land (**bilād al-qabā'il**) he had one of the furrows in the field of those that run across the breadth (**sāliq fī 'm-widin min gayz al-sawāliq**) and half of the tithe (**nāṣifat am-ᶜashīr**). A correspondent wrote to me in 1957 that 'in the past the **khuddām** of ᶜUmar b. Saᶜīd collected a third of the tithes of grain from the whole area of al-Kawr and used it for their own'. Half of the ᶜ**ashīr** used to go to ᶜUmar Saᶜīd, but half was called ᶜ**ashīr Miryam** — my informant identified this Miryam with Miryam bint ᶜImrān, Mary mother of Jesus. This term ᶜ**ashīr Miryam** is used all over the area because she guaranteed the cultivator from the sun so that it would not harm him (**ḍammanat al-batūl min al-shams lā tashūf-uh** (= **lā taḍurr-uh**). When the grain arrived at the threshing floor (**waṣar**), simply a smooth circle of hard clay ground with a ring of small stones to define its limits, the portion of the poor would be measured out and they would come there to receive it.

In 1947 my Ḥaḍnī informants expressed the same thing in slightly different form. All the tribes of al-Ḥaḍn, they said, are raᶜiyyat ᶜUmar b. Saᶜīd, his subjects. They pay tithes to him, a portion of which goes to the Waliyy, i.e., the Manṣab, and a portion to the poor (**naṣīf li-'l-Waliyy wanaṣīf li-'llāh**). The **khuddām** of the Saint would come out to collect the ᶜ**ashīr** — now all this ᶜ**ashīr Miryam** and ᶜUmar Saᶜīd's portion is in the hands of the ᶜAwdhalī Sultan.

All the afore-going recalls statements made by Ibn Hishām as also by Ibn al-Kalbī. They speak of ᶜUmyānis (ᶜAmmanas) a pre-Islamic god of Khawlān. Between this god and Allāh they used to divide a portion of their cattle (**anᶜām**) and crops (**ḥurūth**). The Arabic for 'portion' is **ḥaqq — ḥaqq ᶜAmm Anis** and **ḥaqq Allāh.** The passage is not easy to interpret. Mary's tithe reminds one that Christianity was at one time widespread in the south, and of the passage in the Qur'ān, sūrah iii,37 (Āl ᶜImrān), 'Whenever he came into Mary in the **miḥrāb** he found provision with her. He said, "Whence do you have this"? She said, "It is from God, God makes provision for whomever he willeth without reckoning" '.

The daughter of ᶜUmar b. Saᶜīd, Saᶜīdah bint ᶜUmar, whose tomb (which I have visited) lies near the coast between Shuqrah and Aḥwar receives what Landberg designates as the **votive** furrow, and the Miṣbaḥī shrine at Midmanah receives the first furrow and one tenth of the corn after the harvest. Of this, half (**ḥaqq Allāh**) is distributed to the poor by the sanctuary, and half is the property of the Mashāyikh.

The origins of the ᶜAwdhalī Sultanic family

The origins of the Sultanic house at Zārah are not really known, but it is believed the family is of ancient and honourable descent. Sultan Ṣāliḥ quoted to me the following verses which ascribe Quraysh descent to his ancestors, but similar claims are made by other noble families in southern Arabia that do not seem to have much evidence to support them. Whether this particular claim is genuine or not it has at least the merit of being some four or five centuries old.

جِدِّي قُرَيْشي من الْقِبْلَة تَهَبْهَبْ وَهَبْ
لا ما سَكَن طَفَّة آلْكَوْر المَنيع العَجَبْ
ذِي رَتَّب آمذِيب مَمْرَط وآمْنِمِر وآمْخَنَبْ

Of Quraysh was my forebear from the Qiblah took he urgent way,
Till at the Kawr's mountain crest, wondrous steep, he came at last to stay.
He't was who, over lean-flanked wolf, leopard and ibex cow held sway.

For their rallying cry the ᶜAwdhalīs and their Sultan, the ᶜAwlaqīs (but the Maᶜnīs say **Anā dhīb Maᶜn**) and the Ahl am-Saᶜīdī use the call **'Anā dhīb al-Kawr,** I am the wolf of the Kawr'. It is not without significance that the leopard is the epithet of the warrior, and in other districts, but not here, the ibex is associated with the ritual hunt. One says, **'Fulān nimr,** So and so is a leopard'. If you say, '**Fulān dhīb**, So and so is a wolf', it means he is skilful and cunning (**ḥādhiq wa-shāṭir**).

Another origin is suggested by a certain Shaykh Aḥmad Bā Riḍwān a Ms. copy of whose work I saw for the first time in Bayḥān entitled **al-Qawl al-ḥasan fī maᶜrifat baᶜḍ sukkān Ḥaḍramawt wa-'l-Yaman** in 1954. I cannot say on what authority Bā Riḍwān speaks, but he does draw on such known mediaeval sources as Muḥammad b. Saᶜd Bā Shukayl and Aḥmad b. Ibrāhīm al-Ashᶜarī.

'This is the **nisbah** of the sons of ᶜIff b. Yazan al-Ṣayᶜarī al-Kindī — among his sons is numbered ᶜAzzān b. ᶜIff, and the posterity of Āl ᶜAzzān settled in al-Sarw and Qintār b. ᶜIff and the posterity of Āl Hashshām and some of the inhabitants of al-Ṭaffah (the crest of the Kawr) and Manṣūr b. ᶜIff. The posterity of the latter are three, Aḥmad am-Manṣūr, ancestor of Āl Aḥmad am-ᶜAwsajī and his male relations (ᶜ**aṣabah**) and Ḥasan (text Ḥisan) am-Manṣūr (89) and the posterity of Āl Ḥasan the inhabitants of the Kawr — i.e., the Ghudr and ᶜĀmir, and Aḥmad b. Hamīm from whom is descended (**fī-hi**) Shams bint Aḥmad — she being the wife of Manṣūr am-Farīd al-ᶜUrayfī (or ᶜArīfī), mother of Jamīl and his brothers, and from him (Aḥmad?) is descended her sister, wife of Ḥusayn b. Yaḥyā, (and the third is the wife of am-ᶜAwsajī'.

Landberg considers al-ᶜAwsajī to be the family name of the ᶜAwdhalī Sultans and he points to a family of ᶜAwāsij in what is nowadays ᶜAsīr mentioned by al-Hamdānī who were Ashrāf Ḥimyar, but there may be no connection between these ᶜAwāsij and the ᶜAwdhalīs.

The name al-ᶜAwsajī seems to be limited nowadays, to a branch of the house from which Sultan Ṣāliḥ is descended also, but which has seemingly lost all power, settled at Sākin am-Ṣawma^{c}ah in the district called am-Ṣurr. In company with the political officer I paid a brief call on Ḥusayn b. Muḥammad ibn im-^{c}Awsagī there in 1964 — it is not far from Zārah. The ^{c}Awsagī/^{c}Awsajī still has some judicial function. I should like to have spent some time there to consult him on the ^{c}Awdhalīs but the political officer was pressed for time and even a **rās ghanam** slaughtered in the courtyard for our entertainment could not detain him longer. So often circumstances such as this lose one the opportunity for enquiry into the ancient and still surviving culture of southern Arabia.

Short Bibliography

N.B. Since this paper is extracted from a much larger study fully foot-noted with references to sources but as yet unpublished, only a summary bibliography directly related to the text is cited here.

Admiralty, Naval Intelligence Division, **Western Arabia and the Red Sea,** Oxford, 1946.

Afwah al-Awdī, see ^{c}Abd al-^{c}Azīz al-Maymanī, **al-Ṭarā'if al-adabiyyah,** Cairo, 1937, 1-24.

Bæteman, J., in **Dictionnaire Amarigna-Français,** Dire-Daoua, 1929, co. 522.

Caskel, Werner, **Ǧamharat an-nasab: das genealogische Werk des Hišām ibn Muḥammad al-Kalbī,** Leiden, 1966.

Al-Hamdānī, **Ṣifat Jazīrat al-^{c}Arab,** ed. D.H. Müller, Leiden, 1884-91, and ed. Muḥammad ^{c}Alī al-Akwa^{c} al-Ḥiwālī, al-Riyāḍ, 1394/1974.

Jacob, H.F., **Perfumes of Araby,** London, 1915.

Landberg, Carlo de, **Études sur les dialectes de l'Arabie méridionale,** II, **Daṯînah,** Leiden, 1905-13. **Arabica IV,** Leiden, 1897. **Glossaire daṯînois,** Leiden, 1920-42.

Luqmān, Muḥammad ^{c}Alī, **Fī Arḍ al-Ẓāhir,** Aden, 1946.

Bā Makhramah, al-Ṭayyib b. ^{c}Abdullāh b. ^{c}Umar, extracts in R.B. Serjeant, 'Two sixteenth-century Arabian geographical works', **BSOAS,** London, 1958, XXI, ii, 270 seq.

Al-Malik al-Ashraf, ᶜUmar b. Yūsuf b. Rasūl, **Ṭurfat al-Aṣḥāb,** ed. K.W. Zettersteen, Damascus, 1949.

Al-Marzūqī, **Kitāb al-Azminah wa-'l-amkinah,** Ḥaydarābād, 1332 H., II, 166.

Al-Nahḍah, Aden newspaper editor and proprietor late ᶜAbd al-Raḥmān Girgirah.

Rhodokanakis, N., **Altsabäische Texte,** Wien-Leipzig, 1927, I, 25

Serjeant, R.B., **Studies in Arabian history and civilisation,** London, 1981 (collected papers from 1954-78).

Addendum

P.101/13 In the 4th century A.D. the Arabian monarch Imru' al-Qays was evidently crowned in this way as he was *dhū aṣr al-tāj*. See Irfan Shahid, "Philological observations on the Namâra inscription", *Jl. Semitic Studies*, Manchester, XXIV, 34 in *Byzantium and the Semitic Orient before the rise of Islam*, London, 1988. A like form of crowning was also the practice in Swat till quite recently. See F. Barth, *The last Wali of Swat*, Oslo, 1985, 40. The tribal elders "tied the turban around my head. It was a very simple affair: the head qazi tied the first loop of the turban, and next the Darmei Khan did it." Then every Khan followed.

V

Dawlah, Tribal Shaykhs, the Manṣab of the Waliyyah Saʿīdah, *qasāmah*, in the Faḍlī Sultanate, South Arabian Federation

About April-May 1964 Stephen Day, then in the Aden Political Service, invited me to spend several weeks with him at Abyan, during which time we visited various places in the Faḍlī Sultanate and briefly passed through ʿAwdhalī country. I am more than happy to express my thanks to him for a pleasurable and profitable time during which he enabled me to make contacts with a wide variety of people. My main concern was the corpus of tribal law manuscripts I have long been engaged in editing and which I discussed with tribal informants, notably Muḥammad ʿAlī Bāqis, a Murqushī (of the qabīlat al-ʿāqil Muḥammad ʿAlī b.Lahmān) living in Murqushī country at that time. I was also permitted access to records of cases kept in the Faḍlī administrative office for which I am grateful to Sultan Faḍl b. Miḥsin. Of these I took preliminary notes intending to return to the area to develop my enquiries, but my attention became taken up with many other interests and after 1967 it was no longer possible to visit the former sultanate.

The Faḍlī Sultans

The Government handbook, *An Account of the Arab tribes in the vicinity of Aden,*[1] recounts the tale that about three hundred years ago from 1909, a Sayyid brought from Constantinople an Arab woman with child by a sultan of Turkey. She landed at Shuqrah and proceeded to al-Surraihah (? al-Sarriyyah) where her child was born, named Osman. He was selected by the Murqushī tribesmen as their sultan and begot a child named Faḍl from whom the Faḍlī derive their name – a descendant some generations later became Sultan in 1789. The Faḍlī, says the handbook, do not appear to have ever been subject to the Imāms of Ṣanʿāʾ. Landberg's[2] rejection of the ʿUthmānī origin of the sultans is confirmed by the author of *Ḥawliyyāt Yamaniyyah*[3] writing in 1257/1811-12 who states that ʿAl-Mahdī ʿAbbās (1161-89/1748-75) had made ʿAbd al-Raḥmān al-Faḍlī, whose origin (*aṣl*) was from Bilād Ānis of Mikhlāf Banī Faḍl, governor over Shuqrah, adding that the Banu 'l-Faḍlī at the date of writing are their posterity. If any credence is to be given to the legend of Turkish descent it can only be suggested that the family may have been Yemenized Turks whose ancestors came to the Yemen in the first Ottoman occupation.

When the British bombarded ʿAṣalah in 1865, the Sultan abandoned Dhawbah and al-

1 Government Central Press, Bombay, 1909, 34.

2 *Arabica V*, Leiden, 1898, 149.

3 Ed. ʿAbdullāh Muhammad al-Ḥabshī/Hibshī, publ. Wizārat al- Iʿlām wa-'l-Thaqāfah, Ṣanʿāʾ, date of preface 1400/1980, 100.

Sarriyyah in which he resided alternately and settled at Shuqrah.[4] We visited al-Sarriyyah in the foothills of Jabal ʿArīs[5] on April 30th, 1964 and saw the houses of the Faḍlī sultans.[6]

In more recent times an official publication[7] states that, to elect Faḍlī sultans, the chief members of the ruling family, called Bayt al-Amr,[8] after asking counsel of the tribal heads (*ru'asā' al-qabā'il*) – who are themselves elected – give their opinion to the Majlis al-Dawlah[9] which is composed of thirteen members considered to represent all the classes (*ṭabaqāt*) of the community. Each tribe is represented by its important headmen (*kibār ʿuqqāli-hā*), while the fishermen,[10] the cultivators, and those engaged in business, also have their representatives.[11] These thirteen members confirm the election of one of the members of the ruling house.[12] Part of the ceremony of inauguration of the new sultan/dawlah consists in the deputy head of the Majlis al-Dawlah, the Amīr Faḍl Muḥsin, the senior member of the Faḍlī House winding the *dhabīlah*[13] round the Sultan's head. Later there is a *mawkib al-qabā'il*, a ceremonial procession of the tribesmen. In those I have seen they marched in pairs and concluded by firing on a mark. These ceremonies are similar to others I have witnessed or recorded in several other places, but there were some modern adjuncts to this one, notably a fly-past by the RAF.

However, on referring to al-Jarmūzī's *al-Sīrat al-Muwakkiliyyah*, it is clear that a Faḍlī Sultan existed in the day of this Imām (1054-87/1644-76) who took action against him. At one time the Imām was holding the sultans of the Mashriq in Ṣanʿā', but was induced to set them free. Some of the sultans stood surety for others. The ʿAwlaqī sent his son as hostage (*rahhan*) and stood surety (*ḍamman ʿalā*) for the Faḍlī, writing a document (called *mashrūḥ*) on this, and the Imām set them free giving them generous presents. The Faḍlī however set to cutting the roads once more and seizing any unarmed persons (*ḍuʿafā'*) he could. So the Zaydīs took action against the Faḍlī and he became a fugitive but had eventually to give himself up and was imprisoned up to the time when, as Jarmūzī says, he was penning his account of these events. Jarmūzī records the name of the Faḍlī sultan who sought *amān* in 1072/1661-2 as Ḥaydarah b. Faḍl b. Aḥmad b. Ḥaydarah. This information does not tally with that of *Ḥawliyyāt Yamaniyyah*, but it demonstrates that the Faḍlī was, if only for a brief space of time, an unwilling subject of the Imām.

4 C. de Landberg, *Études sur les dialectes de l'Arabie Méridionale*, II, *Daṯinah*, Leiden, 1905, 1486.

5 Jabal ʿArīs and al-Sarriyyah are both marked on the map of H. von Wissmann, Royal Geographical Society, Aden Protectorate, sheet 1, London, 1957.

6 The houses were built of large stones with smaller stones inserted in the interstices and arches were used; the masonry seemed ancient and the stones were bonded, a bond being called *rabṭ*, pl. *rubūṭ*; sherds of blue and white Chinese ware were scattered over the site.

7 *Inaugural ceremony Sultan Ahmed Bin Abdullah Al Fadhli Zingibar* Aden, 20th January, 1963 (Arabic title *Iḥtifāl al-Tansīb* . . .).

8 *Amr* is also used by the ʿAwdhalīs in this sense, meaning *sultan/dawlah*.

9 An institution probably introduced on British advice.

10 The fisher headman (*ʿāqil al-sayyādīn*) at Shuqrah was Hasan Aḥmad ʿAmr.

11 It is not stated whether these representatives were, for instance, the fisher *ʿāqil*, or some other person.

12 Compare the 'Appointment of a Mansab. . .' in my 'Two tribal law cases (documents), *JRAS*, London, 1951, II, 166 seq., where this is made by election by all classes of the community.

13 The *dhabīlah* is the cord of the matchlock. The ʿAwdhalī Sultan has described to me how this ceremony was performed for him in his country. Cf. the intended 'crowning' of ʿAbdullāh b. Ubayy at Yathrib, etc.

The Faḍlī tribes

The 1909 Government handbook[14] gives a list of the Faḍlī tribes of that time, but many of these are not really to be accounted as such. Those with which this paper is concerned are the Murqushīs, the Ahl Ḥanash and the Nakhaʿīs. The last-named are famous in the early Islamic period for the chief Ashtar al-Nakhaʿī, the supporter of ʿAlī b. Abī Ṭālib, but nowadays they are obviously less important than the Marāqishah. The relative size of these three tribes may be judged by the number of fighting men they can muster. In 1909, both the Marāqishah and Ḥanashīs were credited as able to field six hundred apiece, but the Nakhaʿ only one hundred. The original home of the Nakhaʿiyyīn is said to be in the district called Baṣāmah in Wādī al-Shiʿb where at a junction of wādīs is a ruined castle (*ḥuṣn*) known as am-Kharibah on a hill close to Sākin am-Shuʿbah. In am-Shuʿbah village I saw a *bakrah* pillar[15] for the Sayyid saint al-Ḥāmid, a family of Ḥaḍramī origin, but this branch of it lives mostly at am-Ṣurrah now (1964). There are many graffiti on the rocks at Sākin am-Shuʿbah and stones covered with both Ḥimyar and archaic Arabic writing. I also saw rocks covered with incised outline drawings of camels in a wādī near Baṣāmah – it is significant that in this wādī they make interdicted pastures (*yiḥajjirūn, maḥjar*) which have known boundaries but are not defined by landmarks.

Of the Marāqishah it was said to me – *hum quwwat al-Dawlah* – they are the strength of the Sultan. There are two groups of them, Marāqishah al-Ḥayd and Marāqishah al-Sāḥil, the Mountain and coastal Murqushīs. The sections of the tribe are listed in the 1909 handbook as Ahl Sālim, Ahl Sanad, Ahl ʿAbbād, Ahl am-Bishaʿ, Bi-'l-ʿĪdī/ʿAydī, Ḥawṭalī[16], Maḥmarī, and some of these sections figure among the records of cases *infra*.

The Murqushīs and Nakhaʿīs are Ḥimyar, but the Murqushīs are not mentioned in the Rasūlid *Ṭurfat al-aṣḥāb*, while Nakhaʿ is accounted of Madhḥij.

Under protection of the Sultan and tribes (*taḥt ḥimāyat al-Sulṭān wa-'l-qabāyil*) were the Ḥigrīs, believed to hail originally from Wādī Ḥagar,[17] of dark complexion and ethnically distinct from the Arabs. The Sultan protected some groups and the tribes others. Families of Ḥigrīs settled in Abyan were Bā Ḥarb, Bā Rādhim, Bā Nāṣir, Bā Jāmzah, Bā Thawr, but there are many subsections (*fakhāyidh wājidah*) of Ḥigrīs in various places. It is significant that their blood-wit is the full *diyah*, i.e. 700 1/3rd *riyāls* like every other man. In reply to my question it was agreed they practised some magic (*siḥr*) and the *miʿfī* of the Ḥigrīs is one who can afflict you with the evil eye. They are mostly labourers and cultivators.

Other groups are the fishermen and there are *dallāls* in Abyan, brokers,[18] and probably elsewhere. The latter are *nās ḍiʿāf*, i.e. not men of arms; my notes say they bring a stipulated amount to the headmen (*shī muqarrar li-'l-ʿuqqāl*) of Marāqishah al-Sāḥil, taxes (*ḍarā'ib*) and gifts to

14 Op. cit., 43. Later Aden Government publications and of course the Government archives, now being calendared by the Commonwealth Relations Library where they are deposited, could most likely provide more detailed lists and a deal of other information on the Faḍlīs and Kāẓimīs.

15 The *bakrah* is described in my 'The "White Dune" at Abyan: an ancient place of pilgrimage in southern Arabia', *Journal of Semitic Studies*, Manchester, 1972, XVI, 80, with drawings. It is often set up for a *waliyy* and contains a niche in which to place a lighted lamp.

16 The handbook, 43, writes Hautari which may represent the known l/r variation in the country. A poet, ʿAlī b. Sālim al-Hawṭalī, recited a *qaṣīdah* to us. The handbook spellings have been adjusted.

17 Landberg, *Glossaire daṯînois*, Leiden, 1920-42, 362 seq., describes the Hagrī as *nāqiṣ al-aṣl, dūn*, of low degree, and gives a very full account of the Hugūr who are here to originate from Wādī Hajr, the upper part of Wādī Mayfaʿ which is extremely malarious and, for medical reasons, probably unsuitable for Arab settlement. Cf. *Arabica V*, Leiden, 1898, 181-82.

18 The *dallāl* is an intermediary in market transactions, in Hadramawt acting between the tribesman come to market and local merchants, buying and selling on his behalf.

friends. Both these groups and the shopmen and craftsmen must, I am not in doubt, also have come under the protection of the Sultan or tribes.

In the old days when passing by the houses of the Dawlah in Shuqrah one would dismount from one's camel or donkey and walk on foot by them out of respect. If a tribesman arrived at the Sultan's place, for any reason, he fired off a round as a salute, and the soldiers relieved him of his *bunduq* and food (*ṭaʿām* (grain), *ruzz* etc.) was brought him, but seemingly they would not slaughter an animal for casual entertainment, except if it were an *ʿāqil* arriving.

The Lower ʿAwlaqīs

The famous warlike ʿAwlaqī (ʿAwāliqah) tribes are first mentioned (so far as is known to me) by the author of the *Ghāyat al-amānī*[19] under the annals for 524/1130. But this was only to describe a route and so it is no evidence that this tribal name was known so early. However, in 1065/1654-5, Imām al-Mutawakkil Ismāʿīl when preparing to invade Ḥaḍramawt wrote to the ʿAwlaqīs who must have been well established by that time. Of the Bā Kāzim of the Lower ʿAwlaqīs with whom the Faḍlīs were so often embroiled, my 1954 notes say: The following tribes, all Bā Kāzim, set out, about a century ago (from 1954), to take Aḥwar[20] from the Zaydīs – Āl al-Ḥaṭalah (or Laḥṭalah), brothers of the Āl Saʿd, Ahl Wabar, ʿUmaysī, Yislamī, ʿUfawī (in Aḥwar) – they and the Āl Sālim, ʿAmbūrī, Busaymī and ʿAlawī of Ahl Bū Luqaysh, etcetera. The attacking tribes took shrouds (*akfān*) with them to scare off the Manṣūrīs who left them at Lūdiyah which flows into Wādī Ḍayqah, for fear of defeat – so they did not share in the land (*ṭīn*) of Aḥwar, but all those tribes which took part in the conquest of Aḥwar from the Zaydīs have shares in it. In those days these tribes lived in the mountain passes (*shiʿāb*) and had no villages (or fixed camps ? *maṭāriḥ*), but since then they have made *maṭāriḥ*. The tribes, in order to keep the peace between themselves, brought in a *dawlah* (sultan) from Yashbum in Upper ʿAwlaqī territory, the brother of the Sultan of Anṣāb of those days. He was put in office there (Aḥwar) as a *nāyib*, to eliminate *fitnah* (dissension) between the tribes and to distribute the tithes (*muʿashsharāt*) among them. But if the septs (*fukhudh*) of the Dawlah dispute among themselves the Āl Saʿd descend (from the areas about the head of Wādī Ḍayqah). Āl Saʿd are the important element in the country and, wherever the Saʿdī goes, the Dawlah follows him for security (*ḥayth mā mashā al-Saʿdī yitbaʿ-ah al-dawlah li-'l-amānah*). My notes show that the Saʿdī includes the Shamʿī and Jāraḍī sub-tribes[21] and the 1909 handbook[22] says the Shamʿī take the lead, presumably precedence, in processions or in a *majlis*.

I was told that previously (to 1954 at least) the Lower ʿAwlaqī Sultan paid dues to Ahl Saʿd of

19 Yaḥyā b. Ḥusayn b. al-Qāsım, ed. S. A. F. Ashur, Cairo, 1388/1968, I, 293.

20 Al-Jarmūzī, *al-Sīrat al-Mutawakkiliyyah*, Mukallā Ms., 235, says of it about 1069/1658:

احور بندر على ساحل البحر ومحاده لبلاد العوالق وما اليها من قوم
يسمون آل ذُيَيْب وآل باكازم وهو سوق مجمَع لتلك القبائل من
أجناس مختلفة .

21 There are twelve of the Bā Kāzım tribes listed ın the Government handbook, op. cıt., 36. The Jāradī seem to be the tribe marked as Qarala on von Wissmann's map (I was unable at the tıme to check thıs name), *jīm* and *qāf* both beıng pronounced as *gāf*, and *ḍād* "as a palatalized l" – see *Gloss. daṯ.*, 2164.

22 My 1954 notes state that at *haffahs*, processıons, the Shamʿah used to be next to the Dawlah, then came the Jāralī/Jāradī, then the ʿUmaysī, then the rest of the tribes.

al-Manqaʿah. This is understandable, the Sultan being originally put there by the tribes for the purpose of distributing the tribute they had imposed on Aḥwar. I was told that the ʿAmbūrīs were banned in all the Lower ʿAwlaqī sūqs and Robin Bidwell who served in the area informs me that this took place about 1952 or 1953 because they had murdered the Lower ʿAwlaqī Sultan, ʿAydarūs b. ʿAlī! The ban was lifted some years later.

In relation to the Faḍlī office records on raids and counter raids, it is interesting to look back at the Government handbook[23] and its statement: "The ʿAulakī (Lower) has constantly evinced a disposition to attack the Fadhlī, or make a raid into Fadhlī territory"!

Taxation

In former times no *muʿashshar*, tithe, was paid to the Dawlah, i.e. the Sultan, by such Faḍlī tribes as the Murqushīs, the Nakhaʿīs. However, the Qabīlat al-Jabal, the Jabal al-Dawlah, being inhabited by the ʿAṭawī and Dahwalī tribes, did pay tax to the Sultan (the word *ʿushūr* was used), but only on sheep-and-goats, one per cent, *fi 'l-sanah rās*, a head per annum.

At that time however the *raʿiyyah* in the Nakhaʿī district did pay *ʿushūr*, which Dawfān managed to collect for the Faḍlī at am-Ṣurrah. Dawfān was a man of slave origin who was made *ḥākim* of the Dawlah and collector of taxes on the *raʿiyyah*, i.e. the farmers, subjects as Landberg[24] puts it, of the sultans and the ʿuqqāl, headmen of the tribes, and Dawfān would be responsible for paying these *ʿushūr* to the Dawlah. He would inform the Dawlah how much grain he had received, paying the Dawlah cash for it, taking the grain himself and selling it by permission/licence (*rukhṣah*) from the Dawlah.

Though the Sultan did not then receive tithes from the tribes certain other dues were paid him. At al-ʿAlam, the boundary post between Aden Colony and Faḍlī territory, four annas was charged on each camel load (*bawlah ʿala 'l-baʿīr*) entering Faḍlī country. Each load (*ḥamūl*) of the ʿAwlaqī, Yāfiʿī, ʿAwdhalī and Dathīnah people passing through Faḍlī territory paid six annas on the *farāsilah*.[25] The Manāṣib (i.e. the Mashāyikh Lords of sanctuaries[26] and the Marāqishah were exempt (*jibār*, sing. *jabr*) and paid nothing. I have no positive information on the other Faḍlī tribes, but as the Ḥasanīs (of Dathīnah), are also *jabr*[27] in Shuqrah, because they became allies of the Faḍlī Dawlah, it is hardly likely they paid these duties. A Ḥasanī, for example, if passing through Shuqrah with twenty ʿAwlaqīs would go free while they would have to pay.

Shopmen (*madākinah*) in the sūqs paid *ʿushūr*. When a marriage in the Bayt al-Salṭanah took place, the Sultan received a *jalabah*, sheep-or-goat, either the beast itself or cash, as a *rifd/rafad*, a marriage present – this custom obtained elsewhere among the large tribes of the southwestern area.

Nowadays (1964) all, even the tribes, great and small, pay *ʿushūr*, tithes, to the *Bayt al-Māl*. The amount chargeable is assessed by *taḍmīd* = *takhmīn* ,[28] and a calculation made of how much

23 Op. cit., 60.

24 *Gloss. daṯ.*, 1325.

25 Usually 20 *raṭls*, but it varies.

26 See my *Studies in Arabian history and civilisation*, London, 1981, especially '*Ḥaram* and *ḥawṭah* .' and the article on social structure in south Arabia.

27 عندما يكون يوم (= مِسْراح / فتنه) على القبايل (الدوله)
يطلب مَعونَه من الحَسَنَه .

28 *Taḍmīd*, probably linked to *ḍamd*, acre.

grain is payable, but actually a cash payment is usually made, this after the harvest (*baʿd al-thamarah*). In some cases landowners pay *ʿushr* on the crops on their land to the Saint (*Waliyy*) – this was stated to be the case also in the ʿAwdhalī sultanate. So in effect these persons had now arrived at a position where they paid double the tithe they formerly paid, one tithe still to the spiritual power, the other to the secular. In the previous era no *ʿushūr* were paid on the cotton crop, but by 1964 so much cotton was being grown, especially in Abyan, that the *ʿushūr* on grain, etc., produced a greatly diminished revenue for Saʿīdah. I did not enquire whether cotton was taxed by the *Bayt al-Māl*.

This radical change in the incidence of taxation must, I assume, have come about through advice and pressure from the Western Aden Protectorate Office seeking for revenues to support the local administration. From antiquity the tribal supporters of a ruling house enjoyed such privileges as exemption from taxation – the change cannot have been popular with them or with the Mashāyikh of Saʿīdah, be this a salutary measure or otherwise. As elsewhere in the Protectorates the central secular authority, the Dawlah/Sultan and his house, was strengthened at the expense of the spiritual authority, the Manṣab, and the tribal supporters of the Sultanic house.

The importance of the theocratic element in the power structure of the Faḍlī state is closely paralleled in the Lower ʿAwlaqī sultanate. The late E. R. (Johnny) Johnstone, a well known and experienced political officer, records in a paper dated 1957[29] that the Bā Kāẓim of Maḥfid pay tithes to the Bā ʿAzab, Bā Ḥājj or Shaqqāʿ shaykhs, *but not to their sultans*. Some if not all of these Mashāyikh houses have shrines of the usual kind.

In former times the Faḍlī Sultan maintained a regular establishment of soldiers in permanent service with him, about twenty *qabīlīs* and a number of *ʿabīd*. The soldiers were paid 5 *riyāls* per mensem (as in Imāmic Yemen) and subsistence (*maṣārīf*) in kind, i.e. grain (*ṭaʿām*, probably *dhurah*), *bunn*, coffee, and oil (*dihn*). Five *riyāls* was good pay in those days. The Manṣab, Zayn b. Nāṣir ʿAmūrah, was a soldier at that time so this employment must have been honourable. In the event of war the Dawlah, i.e. the Sultan, assembled all the tribes (*lamma 'l-qabāyil kulla-hā*) by sending out a soldier to each tribe to avert them (*yinabbī-hum*) and raise them. First he sent to the Marāqishah, then to the Nakhaʿīn, then to the Āl Bi-'l-ʿAyd, this being their order of precedence. In those days hardly anyone could write, even the Sultans, and when the Sultan sent out a message he drew a thread out of his *fūṭah* for a soldier to take to the tribe – this was also the practice with the ʿAwdhalīs and probably other tribal confederations. As the Mashāyikh are arms-bearing, they also come out and fight alongside the tribes. Should war break out, for example with Yāfiʿ, the Sultan will request the Manṣabs of Saʿīdah to come to the headquarters (*murkuz*), bringing with them the crescent standard (*bayraq*/*bāriq*) of the saint Saʿīdah which remains with the Sultan at the *murkuz* until the war ends, or they may leave it in the Sultan's house till the time of the *ziyārah* on Rajab 15th. The *bayraq* is brought to the Sultan accompanied by songs with dancing, known as *maḥāgil* (sing. *maḥgal*). This is a *karāmah* (honour, bounty ?) from Saʿīdah.

If there is any trouble between the Faḍlī tribes themselves the Manṣab of Saʿīdah comes with the *bayraq* which he interposes between them to stop it; this again is general in the south. There is a Murqushī verse quoted by Landberg:[30]

بارِقْ سَعِيدَهْ لايَقَعْ عاذِرْ لكُمْ ، وَٱللهْ بِنَهْ بِهَا يِسُقُطْ وقام

Saʿīdah's standard will be no exempter for you.

29 *A Day at Mish'al with the Nakhai*, copy in Middle East Centre, Cambridge.

30 *Arabica V*, op. cit., 151. The metre of the final two words seems incorrect; should *yisaqqit* be read?

By God one must go on (fighting), falling (in war) and rising.

The verse shows the strength of feeling of the poet in that even veneration or fear of offending Saʿīdah is not to hold back the person addressed from fighting.

The Manṣab makes a truce between the two parties, called *ṣulḥ Saʿīdah*. He then arranges a dialogue/parley between them (*yisawwī bayna-hum murājaʿah = yukhāṭib bayna-hum*). The truce he makes is not a judgement (*ḥukm*) but a peace by mutual consent. At the end of the term of the *ṣulḥ* there is a *bara'*. quittance, absolvement, from the truce, and a state of war re-ensues. Then after a time the Manṣab makes another *ṣulḥ*. This, they said, was how things operated until the *Ḥukūmah* (the Aden Government) pacified the country. At the *ziyārah* of Saʿīdah on Rajab 15th any trouble between the Faḍlī tribes is brought to the Sultan and he settles it.

Of the Mashāyikh of Saʿīdah in whose house the Manṣabate is hereditary,[31] my Murqushī informant, Muḥammad ʿAlī Bāqis, said: *Khasārat-hum wa-fāyidat-hum min al-Marāqishah* which, though I did not ask him to explain exactly what he meant, is to be understood as "Their expenses/outgoings and what they gain comes from the Marāqishah". He added that *amr Saʿīdah yimshī fī bilàd al-Faḍlī, wa-'l-bilād al-thānī fī kull bilād fī-hā waliyy*, "the command of Saʿīdah is operative (throughout) Faḍlī territory, but in other territory there is a saint in each district of it." The Manṣab of Ḥimyar brings the tribes together as noted above, an interesting title, for the Marāqishah and Nàkhaʿīn are both accounted Ḥimyar, and probably the lesser tribes as well.

The functions of the Manṣab and the Sultan and their relation of one to the other follow a pattern which I think may be discerned in at least some of the other former sultanates. Also the situation is perhaps quite similar to the roles of the house of ʿAbd Manāf and the powerful chiefs of Quraysh at Mecca. The Manṣab of Saʿīd is not, on the basis of the evidence set down here, an arbiter or judge. It is true he might settle minor (lit. 'light') cases – e.g. he might arrange a *conciliation* over a theft (*yisidd fī nahb*) – but serious cases such as murder (*qatl*) were settled by the Sultan. Yet the judgement of the Sultan or his representatives involved taking the oath – which a Faḍlī tribesman would perform at Saʿīdah. The Sultan greatly *yisharrif*, holds in honour, the Shaykh (Manṣab) of Saʿīdah. If the Manṣab were to suffer any aggression he would go to the Faḍlī Sultan and the latter would take active steps to put it right. So before the changes in the post-World War II era the Manṣab seems to have been the most powerful person in the country enjoying the prestige of spiritual authority, an assured revenue from the land, and great political influence. However, in his position superior to that of the Sultan, he was above taking sides with any Faḍlī tribe in disputes. He would, as seen however, fight alongside them against an enemy from outside. Had circumstances permitted further enquiry I should have asked about the origin of this house of Mashāyikh, but if they are descendants of the saint of am-Nigdah,[32] ʿUmar b. Saʿīd, they would not belong to any of the Faḍlī tribes, and would therefore have no built-in local commitments. The chiefs of the large tribes not only judged or arbitrated in disputes among their own tribesmen, but, in conclave, actually made law when this was required. The Sultan obviously had quite limited powers and probably limited income, but could summon the tribe to war and seems to have acted as an arbiter.

31 But elective within the family.

32 A shrine near Lawdar in ʿAwdhalī territory. For ʿUmar b. Saʿīd's descendants see *Daṯīnah*, op. cit., 454.

Tribal customary law and judges

With al-Shaykh ʿAbdullāh Sālim bir al-Dhayb al-Murqushī, I had some discussion on the customary law of the Faḍlī tribes. His is the family of the chief tribal judges in Murqushī country, and the Bir al/am-Dhayb are appeal judges (*manqad*)[33] in the sultanate – they are tribesfolk, i.e. secular judges, not Mashāyikh. My notes indicate that ʿAbdullāh Sālim of the Bir al-Dhayb belongs to the Āl am-Bishʿah tribe of the Marāqishah, the *nisbah* being Bishaʿī. I did not follow up the question, but the name must arise from their exercising the function of *mubashshiʿ*, trial by ordeal. The *Arab tribes in the vicinity of Aden*[34] states that *bishʿah* 'is still in use in this and neighbouring tribes, but not much resorted to, except for serious crimes. There are numerous methods, but the usual one is the application of a heated knife to the tongue'. Elsewhere I have quoted a Quʿayṭī government official on the effectiveness of this ordeal among tribesmen.[35] Murqushīs said of Bir am-Dhayb that he is *Sabṭ al-Faḍlī*, explaining the word *sabṭ* as *silqat-nā*, our court.[36] Questioning them on the term *manqad*, they said it means *ḥukm*, adding that one says: *Al-manqad ʿind Bir al-Dhayb* – he judges between the qabāyil al-Faḍlī. Sometimes the *ʿurfī* court (probably established only in the post-war period) sends a case to him if it cannot decide it itself.

ʿAbdullāh Sālim has all the Faḍlī *sawābil*, precedents, these being known as *sawābil mashrūʿ*, and one also speaks of *shurūʿ al-qabāyil al-sābiqah*. This *sharʿ* has nothing to do with the Islamic *sharīʿah* but is employed for the customary laws of the Faḍlīs, ʿAwdhalīs and all the tribes of the region. I also heard it employed in the same sense at Ṣaʿdah of northern Zaydī Yemen. It is also found in the *Sabaic Dictionary* of which the late Professor Mahmoud Ghul was one of the editors, and when one looks at the inscription to which the passage refers it has basically the same sense there.[37]

Where no precedents already exist according to which a case is to be settled, the headmen (*ʿuqqāl*) of all the Marāqishah would meet, four or five of them, and they would set up a new precedent[38] by *qiyās* or *ʿaql* (perhaps the latter is the word more native to the region) and they would *yuwassisū-hu bi-'l-riḍā*, set up a new basis[39] for it by consent. Nowadays (1964) these precedents would be written down, but in days not so long ago when few Faḍlīs could write, they were not written down but remembered.[40] When I asked the Shaykh about a case where there were neither precedents nor analogy, Bir am-Dhayb said: *Bā asuwwī fikr qiyās mashrūʿ* which I suppose means "I shall think about making an analogy that would be according to customary *sharʿ*". He would seek the opinion (*ra'y*) of the *ʿuqqāl* until their *ra'y* became one, but any such new precedent would have to be established by consent and agreement of all the *ʿuqqāl*.[41] In all

33 At one time I thought *manqad* houses were few, but have since come across quite a number in various parts of the south.

34 Op. cit., 54. The *mubashshiʿ* at Ḥālimayn in Upper Yāfiʿ was mentioned. A man cleared of guilt is *ṣāfī*, innocent.

35 In my draft preface to Dr Oweidi's study – see fn. 40 infra. For a reference to pre-Islamic *bishʿah*, see my chapter in M. Loewe & C. Blacker, *Divination and oracles*, London, 1981, 219. Cf. my discussion on this subject in *Cambridge History of Arabic Literature*, 1983, 125 seq.

36 *Silqah* is a mat woven of palm-frond.

37 Publication of the University of Sanaa, Louvain-Beyrouth, 1982, 133, ed. Beeston, Ghul, Müller, Ryckmans.

38 Cf. 'Two tribal law cases (documents)', *JRAS*, London, 1951, I, 38.

39 Cf. ibid., 34, *sās*, ordering of procedure.

40 The way in which precedents are established and preserved among the Jordan tribes is described by Ahmad Oweidi ʿAbbadi in his Cambridge thesis (Ph. D., 1982).

41 My impression from this conversation was that the distinction made in Islamic law between *ra'y* and *qiyās* really did not come into the consciousness of these people.

circumstances of decision-making there is in southern Arabia no such thing as a minority dissenting view!

When I asked them about the (Islamic) *sharīʿah*[42] they maintained that resort to tribal law (*shurūʿ al-qabāyil al-sābiqah*) was much better than to *sharīʿah* because of the interminable delays in the latter and the appeals, etcetera, which drag out a case. Their own procedure was preferable because it was plea and counter-plea in one day, judgement in one day and payment/settlement in one day (*daʿwā wa-jawāb fī yawm wāḥid wa-ḥukm fī yawm wāḥid wa-kharj*)![43] If the *ḥukm* were just, they said, the tribes would rise against the offender in the case in point, should he not make proper amends – i.e. they constituted the executive element in a decision (*ḥukm*) to see it enforced, should this be necessary. The tribes in fact, they said, protect the country and the Sultans. The Sultans judged by precedents (*sābilah*, pl., *sawābil*) some of which were written down (*maktūbah*), and some with the elders (*shuyūbah*). If the Sultans went out in person to deal with a case they were entertained but they received no fee. Were they to send out a soldier for any reason he might be given something *ʿalā qadar al-ḥāl* in accordance with the circumstances, but there was no law about this.[44]

Procedure when a crime or hostile act has been committed

When a state of truce (*ṣulḥ*) exists and if, for instance, a Kāzimī were to kill a Murqushī, this is an *ʿayb*, a shaming act – the Kāzimī has *kasar al-ṣulḥ*, violated the truce. The procedure now is that the Kāzimī who has assumed responsibility for maintaining the truce that his fellow-tribesman has broken, or on whose face (*fī wigh-uh*) it is, as they say, the duty to maintain it, sends a prisoner – it would be his own son – to the Murqushī on whose face it is, correspondingly, to maintain the truce.

The two tribes then meet, twenty on each side, at al-Rawḍah of Jaʿdanī country to the north because the Jaʿdanī is *amīn*, trusted by them. The Jaʿdanī makes an entertainment for them and they talk. There will be two guarantors each undertaking to maintain the peace on his face (*fī wigh-uh*), known technically as *ṣalīḥ*, one from each side. They will judge the blame-money for breaking the peace (*al-lawm fi 'l-ṣulḥ*) to be 420 (shillings, I think, in 1964, but it might be *riyāls*). A murdered man cannot be compensated for by a cash payment, so the Murqushīs must then kill the offender or a member of his tribe after the expiry of the immediate truce under which they were able to meet. I noted in Arabic that *amman-ah al-Manṣab*, the Manṣab (of Saʿīdah) makes/sets up security and *yaḍummu-hum Manṣab Ḥimyar*, the Manṣab of Ḥimyar brings them together. This probably refers to the Manṣab making the truce, as he often does, for instance in Ḥaḍramawt, but after twenty years I cannot be quite sure! When a member of the offender tribe has been slain in retaliation, the Kāzimī will kill another Murqushī in return – and so the thing goes on!

Besides murder and robbery, other crimes include *ḥasf al-zirāʿah*, slashing down a standing crop with swords, or sometimes it would be burned. Sometimes tribesmen will cut out the tongues of cattle which die as they are no longer able to eat. Not only Faḍlīs take such actions but

42 In this frank statement they were quite uninhibited by any religious consideration of respect for the *sharīʿah*. Indeed it was when the Aden Government set to developing a more modern style of government in the tribal districts that in many places *sharīʿah* courts seem to have been set up.

43 This view is also held in certain other parts of Arabia.

44 The ʿAwdhalī Sultan also sends out a soldier as a messenger, and of course so did the Zaydī Imāms, but their soldiers had various perquisites, some legal, some not.

also Yāfiʿīs and other tribes. I have noted similar cases in Mayfaʿah.[45] Rape is considered *akbar jarīmah*, the major crime, and the tribe would take up arms against the perpetrator.

Saʿīdah bint ʿUmar: a waliyyah, female saint

The sanctuary of Saʿīdah lies on the coast road between Shuqrah and Aḥwar, in the sector of the sultanate east of it, but inside Faḍlī territory. Stephen and I visited it in 1964. Saʿīdah's father, ʿUmar b. Saʿīd, is buried at am-Nigdah in ʿAwdhalī territory which I have also visited and studied. Landberg[46] remarks of the shrines found in every district: "Souvent ces sanctuaires ne sont que la perpétuation du culte sabéo-himyarite". So although Saʿīdah is accorded a respectable ancestry in a family of Islamic saints,[47] incidentally unknown to al-Sharjī or other biographical works consulted, and about whom I obtained no information locally, the existence of a pre-Islamic deity Saʿīdah cannot be ignored. According to Ibn Ḥabīb[48] her cult was spread widely. 'Saʿd Hudhaym and all Quḍāʿah except Banū Wabarah used to worship Saʿīdah and Manāt. Azd also used to worship Saʿīdah and her temple-guardians (*sadanah*) were of Bayt ʿAjlān,[49] her place being at Uḥud.[50] A '*talbiyah* of a *nask/nusuk* pertaining to Saʿīdah' is quoted by Ibn Ḥabīb. A *nask* would be a pilgrimage bringing an animal to slaughter at a shrine;[51] *nusuk* means 'obedience and worship (*al-ṭāʿah wa-'l-ʿibādah*). The *talbiyah* of the deity al-Nasr and his *talbiyah* is discussed elsewhere,[52] i.e. verses in *rajaz* type metre sung or declaimed, probably to a sort of dancing step, by tribesmen approaching a sanctuary. In the *talbiyah* of Saʿīdah *infra*, words to be eliminated as surplus to the metre are bracketed – this justified by the quotation in the *Tāj al-ʿarūs*[53] of a *talbiyah* of the people of the Jāhiliyyah, citing two verses: *Ji'nā-ki li-'l-naṣāḥah. Lam na'ti li-'l-raqāḥah*, (the verses in that order).[54]
Of the three latter stanzas the rendering is proposed:

We come [to you] not to seek a favour,
Nor do we seek to trade.
We have come to you for advice/sincere worship.[55]

The *Tāj* defines *miyāḥah* (v.3) as conferment of a favour, but it might also be possible to understand it as 'intercession'; and *raqāḥah* (v.4) it calls *al-kasb wa-'l-tijārah*. This last recalls the

45 'Two tribal law cases. . . ,'I, 42.
46 *Datīnah*, op. cit., 457.
47 Ibid., 455.
48 *Al-Muḥabbar*, Haydarābād, 1942, 316. To Professor M. J. Kister I am indebted for a copy of *Jerusalem studies*, 1980, containing his 'On a monotheistic aspect of a Jāhiliyya practice' (II, 33-57) which includes a text of Muqātil b. Sulaymān (ob. 150 H.) on *talbiyahs*, but he suggests that some are inserted from other early sources by the transmitter of the *Tafsīr*. Saʿīdah and these verses, also used in some *talbiyahs* to other deities, are mentioned, as also the tribes Saʿd Hudhaym, Azd and Quḍāʿah who used to worship her.
49 ʿAjlān b. ʿAbdullāh of Rabīʿah (Ibn Durayd, *Ishtiqāq*, Cairo, 1378/1958, 296).
50 This is not a location for Saʿīdah cited by other sources consulted. Ibn Durayd, *Jamharah*, Beirut reprint, n. d. II, 272, col. i, refers to Saʿīdah as a temple to which Rabīʿah used to make the *ḥajj* in the Jāhiliyyah – he thinks this is near Kufah. Yāqūt cites him as locating it in Iraq, and Ibn al-Kalbī as on the bank of the Euphrates.
51 See my *South Arabian hunt*, London, 1966, 51.
52 Ibid., 9.
53 Kuwait, 1385/1965 -, VI, 398.
54 A third *labbayk* would bring line 2 to the same length as line 1.
55 The second sense from Lane, Lexicon.

لَبَّيْكَ أَللّٰهُمَّ لَبَّيْك	‖ – | – ᴗ – – | – ᴗ – –
لَبَّيْكَ لَبَّيْك (54)	| – | – ᴗ – –
لَمْ نَأْتِلْكَ) لِلسِّيَاحَه	| – – ᴗ | – ᴗ – –
وَلَاطَلَبْنَا لِلرَّقَاحَهْ	‖ – | – ᴗ – – | – ᴗ – ᴗ
(وَلَكِنْ) جِئْنَاكَ لِلنَّصَاحَهْ	‖ – – ᴗ | – ᴗ – –

Islamic phrase *ḥajj wa-ḥājah* and the Ḥaḍramī *ḥajj wa-bayʿ masābiḥ*, pilgrimage and selling rosaries,[56] and Qāḍī Ismāʿīl al-Akwaʿ quotes *ḥijj wa-bayʿ masābiḥ/wa-laqqāṭ masābiḥ*..

Though these citations do not allude to worship of Saʿīdah in southern Arabia, the sanctuary at Uḥud (if the reading be correct) is, in relative terms, not remote from Shuqrah, and if the name Saʿīdah for a pre-Islamic goddess and an Islamic saint is merest coincidence, the pilgrimage ceremonies at the sanctuary in Faḍlī country today are certainly somewhat Jāhilī in character.

Landberg[57] states that Saʿīdah's sanctuary is looked after by a *khādim* who receives the votive offerings (*nudhūr*) and *ʿushūr*. This is an honourable office, and in other places a saint's tomb will be attended by a family not of the Mashāyikh house connected with the saint, usually his descendants. There are three *bayts* of the Mashāyikh family which provides the Manṣab of Saʿīdah. These are:

Al-Ḥasan b. Ḥaydarah, al-ʿĀṭif. He bears (*yishill*) the *bayraq/bāriq*, the insignia of saints, a pole with a crescent and other ornaments.

Zayn b. Nāṣir b ʿAmūrah, Hal ʿAlī. He was Manṣab according to Bāqis, but when I am not certain.

Ḥaydarah bir Ṣāliḥ bir Wālid, Hal Sumur.

Bāqis said: *Dāʿī-hum wāḥid* – which would mean that they all respond to one summons (to war etc.),[58] in other words they form a single political entity.

The Sanctuary of Saʿīdah bint ʿUmar

The shrine lies in a kind of cleft in the wādī. A clay bank diverts the *sayl*-flood water from the cemeteries close to it.[59] The old *karīf*, a basin or tank for holding water, which they also called *mājil*, had been renewed. The water here was sweet. The place was certainly imposing as such sanctuaries can be, as is Qabr Hūd in Ḥaḍramawt. A round wall roughly north-east of the shrine had vertical lines in relief plastered white at which shots were fired as a salute to the saint.[60] There were some huts of brushwood with matting and palm frond roofing.

The shrine has three tombs, Saʿīdah's in carved and polished wood, probably a *tābūt* though I have not recorded this; a second tomb was somewhat broken down with stones inside it and no

56 Sayf b. Husayn al-Quʿayṭī, *al-Amthāl wa-'l-aqwāl al- Hadramıyyah*, Ms. in Haydarābād, proverb no. 148.

57 *Daṯīnah*, 455.

58 For a definition of *dāʿī*, see *Gloss. daṯ.*, 797.

59 Fairly recently there had been large and destructive floods here but there is little arable land upon which to use the water.

60 It seems rather strange to have salutes fired so close to, or actually in, the sanctuary.

wooden cover while a third tomb in clay and plaster was heavily oiled[61] but it was not known who was buried there. An old round lamp (*miṣbāḥ*) of steatite with several compartments for wicks radiating out from the centre, hung by a chain; *sesame* (*gilgil*) oil is burned in these lamps and they had here a black wick (*dhabalah sawdā*). Inside the building was decorative plasterwork of some interest, and what may possibly have been ibex (*wiʿl*) horns.[62] The tomb also contained the *bayraq*, the pole with a crescent that is the banner of saints in this part of Arabia.

The Mashāyikh are buried near Saʿīdah's tomb but outside the building. Tribesfolk are buried in separate parts of the cemetery related to the direction from which they come, bodies being brought from some distance on a (fishing?) net stretched over poles and borne on men's shoulders. The Murqushīs and ahl al-Jabal and Shiʿb al-Dawlah from above ʿUqmah (lit. a bank in the wadi to divert water onto the fields but seemingly a place-name here). The Nakhaʿīs and people of the upper plain are not buried here – the Nakhaʿīs come to Saʿīdah by way of am-Ṣurrah (Ṣurrat al-Nakhaʿīn or Ṣurrat al-Misḥāl), where it seems they stop the night on their way to Shuqrah. Other groups stop at Ṣanīf[63]. The Bā Kāzim of the Lower ʿAwlaqī sultanate also visit Saʿīdah.

I noted arches in the tombs made of clay (perhaps for lamps (RBS, 1984)) and on two of the tombs there was a sign which, without doubt, must be a drawing in outline of the *bayraq* of Saʿīdah – I did not enquire why this should be done, but obviously it would in some way put the grave under her patronage or protection. Ships, i.e. country craft, are always being wrecked on the coast at Saʿīdah and some of the tombs appear to be constructed from old ships' timbers. Inside a wall is the tomb of Sinān/Sanān al-Ṭayyār and at his grave within the wall are buried the old Sultans of al-Sarriyyah of the Faḍlī house. Sinān[64] is an ancestor of the Faḍlī Sultans at some period before the earliest known Sultan (apart from the governor said to have been appointed by Imām al-Mahdī ʿAbbās), ʿAbdullāh b. Aḥmad (1789-1805).[65] The son of the last-named, Aḥmad al-Mukassir (d. 1819), is buried in Saʿīdah – Mukassir might be a title referring to his activities against the tribes.

Every saint has an annual pilgrimage (*ziyārah*) and these have been described many times;[66] the annual *ziyārah* to Saʿīdah takes place on Rajab 15th. The ceremony includes a *mawkab*, procession, to the saint with sung verses. At this ceremonial and of course on other appropriate occasions, is declaimed the *ʿazwah*, slogan[67] of the Dawlah, the Sultanic house, the ʿAṭawī, Dahwarī and Jahhaynī, tribes of al-Jabal, *Anā dhayb Sanān*, I am the wolf of Sanān! This would be in reference to the Faḍlī ancestor already mentioned. The full cry at Saʿīdah was quoted to me and the form is rather like that of the ancient *talbiyah*:

Layk wa-bayn adayk (=*aydayk*/*yadayk*),

61 The oil is probably a gift to the denizen of the tomb. I recall vaguely however having seen a *bakrah* upon which oil was poured and burned.

62 For ibex-horns in sanctuaries see *South Arabian hunt*, passim.

63 My 1964 notes, the interpretation of which here I am not absolutely certain, seem to describe the boundaries of the *ḥawṭah*, sacred enclave, of Saʿīdah, within which I presume tribal law and custom would not rule. The *maradd*, boundary on the east is at Wādī Ṣanīf, at a place called Zayt, in the wādī, with water. The southern boundary of the *ḥawṭah* is the shore; on the west it is at al-Kawd al-Kathīb on the wādī called al-Maḥjal. On the north it is at al-Mithār near a place called al-Sharj, and *al-midʿā*, a little pillar with a recess to hold a lamp (for a description and illustration of which see 'The "White Dune" at Abyan . . .', loc. cit.) is at the top of al-Sharj (*al-midʿā fī rās al-Sharj*). These pillars are often used to define the limits of a sacred enclave – as may well be the case here.

64 Bāqis said that people in Dirjāj/Dirgāg and Fulays still call their sons Sinān/Sanān – it is a name handed down there but he did not know of it elsewhere.

65 For this and subsequent Fadlī sultans see the Government handbook, 34.

66 E.g. my 'Heiligenverehrung in Südwestarabien', *Bustan*, Vienna, 1964, II, 16-23.

67 *Gloss daṭ.*, 2290, *rapport d'origine, filiation; cri de ralliement.*

Wa-iḥnā tawakkalnā ʿalayk,
W-anā dhayb Sinān!

The Kashmīmī however would use the *ʿazwah*, *Anā dhayb al-Kawr*, because they claim that their ancestor hailed from the Kawr escarpment to the north.[68] A Murqushī, if fired upon, would exclaim: *Dhayb Ḥimyar!* This, they said, is because the wolf is brave. *Dhayb/dhīb* is widely used by the tribes in this way and I have ʿAwdhalī slogans of the same pattern.

There is a minor visitation by heads of families, about mid-year – when they bring a young animal (*ṭaliyy*) and they light a lamp for the saint (*yisarrigūn al-waliyy*). At our casual visit an historical *qaṣīdah* of the poet Dawʿan whose verses are much quoted by Landberg was recited by the Manṣab. When a child (*ʿāqibah*) has come to be born one makes a visitation with a *riyāl* and a sheep-or-goat and they deposit it with him (the Manṣab), *Lammā yigī wāḥid makhlūq yisawwī ziyārah ʿalā riyāl wa-jalabah wa-yiwaddū-hā ʿind-ah*. I. e. in the case of a baby (*nīnū*) they take it to the saint on the fortieth day after it is born, showing it to the saint and presenting the animal.

Dues paid to Saʿīdah

The tribes that make payment to Saʿīdah are the Marāqishah, Nakhaʿī, Mathūthī, Kashmīmī, Dahwalī, ʿAṭawī, Mughawwarī, Miṣḥarī. A man not a Murqushī or other tribes of the above group whose *waliyy* Saʿīdah is, if he marries, for instance, a Murqushī woman then he too must make some contribution to the saint – he would pay once a year a sheep only, but no tithes etc. This would be the case were the husband, for example, a Ḥanashī. The Manṣab collects for the *ziyārahs*, which are an expensive affair, going round the tribes a month before the *ziyārah* to collect gifts (*nudhūr*). If a man should not happen to meet the Manṣab at the time the latter is going his rounds then at the time of the *mūlid* (= *ziyārah*) he must bring his animal. A poor man brings one or two *riyāls* instead.

My notes do not make it clear whether *nudhūr* are distinct from the tithes paid to Saʿīdah, but I think they are. In the case of livestock the minimum on which one contributes is one in ten *ghanam* (sheep-and-goats) owned. With large animals (*bawsh*) a *faḥl* bull is contributed, if there are over ten animals, and with camels (*bil*) a *qaʿūd*, young camel, when one owns twenty. A few *riyāls* only are payable if one does not possess the requisite minimum number. A mark (*ʿalam*) is put on the animal contributed.

In the case of grain, cultivators all over the country used to leave the tenth furrow (*tilm*) when they harvested and the Manṣab of Saʿīdah's representative would come and cut it, or the cultivator might cut it himself for him. Even the Faḍlī Dawlah used to pay over the tenth furrow. The Mashāyikh of Saʿīdah receive these *ʿushūr* or tenth furrows, and Āl ʿĀṭif makes division of them following their custom (*ʿalā ʿādat-hum*) into three parts one of which goes to each Mashāyikh house. Landberg[69] says that not only the Mashāyikh subsist on this income but also the saint's '*desservants*' presumably the *khādim* who looks after a shrine, and his family. One could hardly be wrong in saying that this system of taxation in what is in effect a theocracy goes back long before Islam.

Furthermore, over and above the tenth *tilm* the saint used to receive the first measure (*awwal mikyāl*) measured out, also termed *awwal ḍarbah*, for Saʿīdah's luck, *yikūn tabarruk li-Saʿīdah*. At the threshing floor (*waṣar*) itself the tribes used to give ten per cent to the poor, known as

68 See the von Wissmann map.
69 *Daṯînah*, 457.

Ḥaqq Allāh[70] on grain and sesame (*gilgil*). Both of these gifts were customarily made by the Murqushīs, Nakhaʿīs and some of the Bil-ʿAyd. Landberg[71] reports slightly differently of a Mashāyikh family of al-Ẓāhir: 'On met aussi à part pour eux la dixième partie du blé, amoncelé après la récolte, en la mesurant. De çela, une moitié est distribuée aux pauvres par le sanctuaire, *Ḥaqq Allāh*, et l'autre moitié devient la propriété des Mashāyikh'.

Al-Qasāmah, the multiple oath[72]

The evidence goes to show that the collective oath (*qasāmah*) was a well established practice in both southern and northern Arabia well before Islam. Our late friend Professor al-Ghūl understood *ʿahd b-mqs'm* in inscription C 548/2[73] as "to take the collective oath" while Ibn Ḥabīb[74] states that "one of the things that Quraysh made a *sunnah* is *al-qasāmah* (*Mimmā sannat Quraysh al-qasāmah*)". He quotes a well known narrative in this connection which, if it has a slightly

70 This looks like a practice remounting to the pre-Islamic age.

71 *Daṯînah*, 457.

72 Dr ʿAbdullāh Maqṭarī has written on *qasāmah* in a thesis at the London SOAS, *The Qasāma mode of proof in Islamic criminal law* (1961?), according to the four Sunnī Schools. In the final stages of preparing this paper I received from Professor Kister, *Jerusalem studies in Arabia and Islam*, 1984, IV, with P. Crone, 'Jāhilī and Jewish law: the *qasāma*', 153-201, a very well documented study with much interesting detail. However its main purpose appears to be to demonstrate that a passage of Deuteronomy, an account of the law in the case of a man found murdered between two villages, has been taken by early Muslim lawyers as 'an account of their own compurgation which it reshaped to fit the Pentateuchal mould'. Unfortunately the argument has numerous flaws and shows an imperfect understanding of Arabian society. The argument mainly concerns the discovery of a corpse of a murdered man between two villages. Especially at this late stage, my paper cannot deal with these flaws, apart from the following. 'Since the institution (*qasāmah*) presupposes some sort of authority, a bedouin origin is ruled out'. Yet in point of fact, as the law concerns villages and therefore settled tribesmen, there is no difficulty about the existence of a settled authority, be it only the *shaykh al-ḍamān* of a confederation, in the Jāhiliyyah. In the thousands of Yemeni villages it is inconceivable that a murdered man was never found between two of them with relative frequency, and that resort to calculating the distance between them and the corpse did not form part of the procedure before Islam. The *qasāmah ḥadīths* al-Wāqidī quotes on the *qasāmah* at Khaybar (probably in fact an ancient *sunnah*) affirm that the Prophet's ruling and Jewish procedure were in accord and it may not be arbitrarily assumed that *qasāmah* was 'a Jāhilī institution being reshaped to fit a Biblical blueprint'. Indeed the Arabian Jews, to judge by the *Maghāzī*, fitted into the Arabian system of society in a way indistinguishable from the Arabs – which is not surprising because, as Professor M. Gil shows in the same issue, numbers were Arabian converts anyway. It is notable that one of the authorities in a Ḥanafī *isnād* is Ibrāhīm al-Nakhaʿī and elsewhere traditions on *qasāmah* are given a Yemeni setting. Yet the testimony of the Nakhaʿī is arbitrarily rejected.
The following passage from ʿAlī b. Saʿīd al-Miʿzābī (pointing uncertain) in his *Talqīh al-ḥukkām*, from the tribal law corpus I am editing, perhaps medieval but undated, lays down the procedure in the Yemen in customary law:

> 'As for the slain man for whom neither of two groups of houses (*ḥillah*) or villages seeks aid and support (*najdah*) the *ḥākim* will look to which of the two *ḥillahs* or villages he is closer and (?that to which) he is closer is the guarantor (*ḍāmin*) of the blood- money (*diyah*) on account of the duty of protection and inviolability (*li-ḥaqq sitr al-waṭan wa-ḥurmati-hi*) of the country.'

Ḥurmat al-waṭan he defines as being an obligation:

يجب على الناس أن يحموا اوطانهم {حتيا / حتى} لايحظى فيها أحد
بحق ولا غيره .

73 *Sabaic dictionary*, 108.

74 *Al-Muḥabbar*, op. cit., 335; cf. *al-Munammaq*, Ḥaydarābād, 1384/1964, 140.

legendary air about it, authenticates the fact of its existence and the procedure followed. Khidāsh, accused of a murder of a man of the ʿAbd Manāf house (he himself was of ʿĀmir b. Lu'ayy) is made to swear at the head of fifty of his fellow tribesmen that he is *barī' min dam ʿAmr b. ʿAbd Manāf*. All but one took the oath at the Corner of the Kaʿbah (*ḥalafū ʿind al-Rukn*), perjuring themselves, and none of those who swore saw a year pass, i.e., they perished.

According to al-Wāqidī;[75] *Kānat al-qasāmah fi 'l-Jāhiliyyah, thumma aqarra-hā Rasūl Allāh*. He illustrates his statement with the well known account (in more than one version) of the murdered man discovered in a well at Khaybar. The Prophet says that the Khaybar Jews in whose territory the body was found should produce fifty men to swear fifty oaths by Allah of their innocence, but it is objected that they are *qawm kuffār* so the Prophet imposes a *diyah* upon them because he was killed in their *ḥaḍrah*.[76] This is alleged to be the first *qasāmah* (in Islam).

In certain *Ḥadīth* narratives, as for example quoted by al-Bukhārī, there was clearly some reluctance to accept *qasāmah* as justification for imposing a sentence, though the hypothetical circumstances suggested by its opponent are not those under which sentence of death would ever be even likely to be imposed in Arabia. It cannot however be supposed that, during the first century and more, of Islam, the tribes in the conquered lands ceased to settle their disputes by the procedure of *qasāmah* just as they had done before and as they do to this day in southern Arabia, and when they were living in cantonment cities in Iraq. I incline to the view that, though effective in tribal society, *qasāmah* may have lent itself to abuse in urbanized centres from the second *hijrah* century onwards where the strict tribal ethic was giving way to the easier morals of the mixed population. Be this so or not, *qasāmah*'s effectiveness must depend on the character of the witness(es) and of course on their real fear of the consequences of perjury, i.e. the punishment that would be meted out for it by Allah or, in other contexts, the *waliyy*, saint.

The *Kitāb al-Ādāb wa-'l-lawāzim fi 'l-manʿah* (ca. 8th/14th century)[77] is categorical about witnesses. *Al-shāhid fi 'l-manʿ man yaqūm bi-'l-manʿah wa-yuʿraf bi-hā – wa-'l-tājir wa-'l-qammāṭ lā shahādah la-hu*. This means that those bearing arms are acceptable as witnesses, but not the merchant or the cattle-dealer.[78] I do not think the testimony of the *dallāl*, broker or commission-agent, would be accepted in tribal society and it is interesting that the Shāfiʿī faqīh, Ibrāhīm b. Muḥammad Jaʿmān (ob. 1034/1624-5), had the question of the testimony of the *dallāl* put to him[79] and, perhaps both as a *faqīh* and non-tribal, he says his *shahādah* is to be accepted providing it is not on a matter of which he has been put in charge, but he rejects the testimony of a *dīwānī*, an official, during the first Ottoman occupation of the Yemen.[80] Ibn Jaʿmān[81] issued two *fatwās* on individuals slain in what looks like tribal affrays, under the heading *daʿwa 'l-dam wa-'l-qasāmah*.

The taking of the oath

In the disputes between the Faḍlīs and the Kāẓimīs, each tribe would take the oath at tombs of its own saints, i.e., the Murqushīs would either do so at Saʿīdah, where in fact it is mostly the

75 *Al-Maghāzī*, ed. Marsden Jones, London, 1966, II, 715.
76 *Ḥaḍrat al-rajul qurbu-hu* (Ibn al-Athīr, *Nihāyah*).
77 See 'Materials for south Arabian history, II', *BSOAS*, London, 1950, XIII, II, 589.
78 A *qammāṭ* was defined to me as *alladhī yajlib al-baqar bi- kathrah ila 'l-aswāq*.
79 *Fatāwā*, Ms. in my possession, 384b.
80 Ibid., 385b.
81 Ibid., 335b.

custom,[82] or at another saint called al-Shaykh Aḥmad on the coast *fī ḥadd al-Faḍlī fi 'l-Khabr* – I do not know if the other Faḍlī tribes have other saints or who those saints are if so. The Kāzimīs would take the oath at shrines in the ʿAwāliq al-Suflā territory – but each side, Faḍlīs and Kāzimīs, would accept oaths taken at shrines in the other's country. The oath can either be taken where one happens to be, or one can actually go to the Waliyy to swear, but there is a slightly different formula in the former instance.

The oath-takers proceed to whatever *waliyy* it is at whose shrine they intent to swear. Landberg[83] who published his *Notes sur quelques serments et pratiques chez les bédouins de l'Arabie* in 1898, says they form a circle around the *tābūt* (in my own experience usually a sort of wooden ark with corner posts) (*yḥajjirūn ʿala 'l-tābūt*) or simple tomb (*qabr*), but if the *misgid* or *qubbah* is small they line up (*yiṣṭaffūn*) outside the door. While swearing the oath the oath-taker puts his hand on the *tābūt or qafaṣ* of the *waliyy*. At Saʿīdah the oath is taken outside the tomb in front of the door in a *shukhṭ*, a circle, as described by Landberg,[84] and, as they stand outside the door of the shrine, first the accused (*al-mathūm*) swears, then the other oath-takers.

Landberg says that when several persons are called upon to take the oath they march round the sanctuary in pairs, one after another, singing *marāgīz*.[85] When they arrive they fire salutes (*taʿshīrāt*) which sometimes the *waliyy* accepts, but sometimes he does not. He adds that a Sayyid or Shaykh is always present at these ceremonies to prevent bloodshed as there is great excitement.

I was told that if one goes to the *waliyy* the form of the oath would be: *W-allāh al-ʿAẓīm wa-'l-Bārr*[86] *al-Raḥīm (wa-hādha 'l-Waliyy), mā ʿindī lak shay, lā gamal* . . .etc. By God the Almighty, the Creator, the Merciful, I have not got anything that belongs to you, no camel. . . etc. If you do not go to the Waliyy you omit the reference to him. A statement which might follow the above oath could be: I am innocent of the matter of which such and such a man accuses me.

إني بريِ من القضيـة الذي يدّعي بها عليَّ فلان آدمي

The others taking part in the multiple oath would swear in support of him: By God the Almighty the oath of such and such a man is true[87]

واسه العظيم يايمين فلان آدمي انه حق

The following formula was given to me in such crude writing that one phrase could not be read by any of us:

بدع اليمين يقول واسه العظيم والبار الرحيم ياهذا الشخص لاهو أعرفه
ولامن سلبي ولامن أصحابي ... نحن نقول ياماحلف به صاحبنا أنهو
حق فلاعرفنا شي

82 *Ḥadd al-Fadlī mā bayn al-ʿAwāliq al-Suflā Bā Kāzım ṭarīq al- Maʿjalah.*

83 *Arabıca V*, 124 seq.

84 Ibid., 131 seq.; *Ḥaḍramoût* (Études . . ., I) Leıden, 1901, 618.

85 Ibid., 141. Thıs may be compared wıth the pilgrims ın ancient Arabıa arrıvıng at the shrıne with the *talbıyah*.

86 *Arabıca V*, 277, defines *al-Bār* = *al-Bārr* as Dieu et lune, parce que *Bārr ʿala 'l-dunyā, domıne tout l'unıvers*, but (136) he translates al-Bārr as Creator.

87 *Yā* perhaps corresponds to classical Arabıc *ıyyā*.

He commences the oath by saying: "By God the Almighty, the Creator, the Merciful, concerning (?). This person I do not know him, nor is he of my family[88] nor of my fellows. . . [and the others?] We say concerning (?) what our fellow has sworn to, it is truth, and we know nothing". Landberg[89] quotes one example employing the above form of oath, denying a crime and all knowledge of it (*lā ʿallayt wa-lā ʿalimt*). This formula is ancient and al-Wāqidī[90] for instance quotes the Jews in the *qasāmah* case as denying knowledge of the murder with the words: *Mā la-nā bi-hi ʿilm*. Indeed in Wāḥidī country in 1947 meeting a tribesman by chance his first words were *ʿIlm-ak*, What news? To this, I made the conventional reply: *Mā shī ʿilm*,No news. But in this context *ʿilm* means news of such incidents as murders, raids, robbery, etc.

At the Mūdiyah customary law court in Dathīnah which I used to attend in the summer of 1954 the oath was taken by a witness holding his right hand in that of *al-ḥākim al ʿurfī*, but these were not serious cases like murder and raiding, indeed they were mostly about land and water rights. I noted the following:

والله العظيم البار الرحيم أعطيت فلان آدمي كذا كذا

By Allah, the Creator, the Merciful, I have given such and such a man such and such a thing.

بالله والنار الحامي هذا برِّي كما محمد بريّ من النار

By Allah and the Hot Fire (Hell) this (man) is innocent as Muḥammad is innocent/free of Hell.

احلف بالله العظيم العالم بالغيب والشهادة قاطعة الصِيب والنصيب
يَقطع حَبْلك من السما والارض

I swear by Allah, the Mighty, the Aware of what is hidden, and by the testimony which cuts off posterity[91] and portion and cutting off your link/rope[92] from Heaven and Earth.

In the court I heard an oath uttered in the ordinary way of the proceedings, *wa-'lladhī ʿajan-ak* (=*ansha'-ak*), lit. by Him who kneaded you!

If the accused takes the oath he is acquitted (*in ḥalaf kharag*[93]).

The way in which a case opens in Wāḥidī country I have already described[94] and the procedure in Faḍlī and Bā Kāzim territories was probably basically the same. The plea (*daʿwā*) is met with a counter-plea or defence (*taqwā*), the latter most interesting term is Wāḥidī, but I do not know if it is employed elsewhere. In discussion with a number of persons from several tribes at Abyan, an ʿAwdhalī said the plea might be: Before God and you o Judge, so and so came on me with red eye and black heart [threatening] that he would kill me.

The Faḍlī tribesmen present said they would use this form of plea, and the *mujawwib*, defendant,

88 *Sulb* is probably to be understood as *ṣulb*; cf. *ṣadr/sidr* the prow of a ship.

89 Op. cit., 136.

90 *al-Maghāzī*, II, 714; cf. Balādhurī, *Ansāb al-Ashrāf*, ed. Ḥamīdullāh, Cairo, 1959, 19, *lā ʿilm lī*, a denial of a crime, though there is no mention of *qasāmah*.

91 Cf. a similar form of oath in 'Two tribal law cases . . .' II, 159. Perhaps my informant should have said *taqṭaʿ*.

92 *Gloss. daṯ*, quotes a verse of Farazdaq, *Naqā'iḍ*, 101, in a panegyric on the Caliph Hishām, *Wa-hablu 'llāh hablu-ka*, *ḥabl*, having the sense of protection. *Gloss. daṯ.*, 342, also notes *ḥabl-ah/uh maqṭūb*, he cannot do any more, he has no consideration, no power. Cf. Qur'ān, III, 101, *Wa- 'taṣimū bi-ḥabli 'llāhi*.

93 Cf. *Khārag bayna-nā*, He settled things between us.

94 See 'Two tribal law cases. . .', I, 34.

فلان جا فوقي بعين حمرا وقلب أسود انّه با يقتلني

would reply to the plaintiff (*mindaʿī*): God forbid! I did not come on him, either with red eye or black heart, but this man has lied against me.

حَيْش اَلله ماجِيت فوقه لابعين حمرا ولا بقلب أسود إلّا كذب عليَّ
هذا الرَجّال

The ʿAwdhalī confirmed that this would be used in his country.

With regard to the number of men required to take the oath there is a sort of tariff in accordance with the seriousness of the offence. It was stated that in a murder (*qatl*) case forty are required to take the oath at a *Waliyy*, any *waliyy*; this differs from Islamic *qasāmah* which requires fifty men.[95] For theft of a camel or cattle, five are required to swear, and for a sheep-or-goat one. These figures do not exactly tally with the lists below – perhaps there may have been circumstances that modified the decisions of arbiters.

Cases pertaining to marriage, marital relations, etc., belong to a category, *zawjiyyah* – in a Wāḥidī case[96] of this sort five *ḥallāfah ḥattāmah* were to be produced to swear an oath by the saint Bā Lahmān. *Ḥattāmah* qualifies the oath-taking and means that five different persons must each swear a single oath, not one person five oaths. Rape is considered the greatest crime (*akbar jarīmah*) and the tribe of the assaulted woman would fight the man who committed it.

> "If a man is accused of having got a girl with child and denies it, he must produce not less than five persons, in the case of an important woman ten persons, to swear to his innocence. The father of the pregnant girl chooses the oath-takers".[97]

Faḍlī-Kāzimī disputes and *qasāmah* decisions

At the Faḍlī Sultanate office at Abyan in 1964, by courtesy of Sultan Faḍl Muḥsin, I was permitted to copy entries recording incidents of aggression and counter-aggression, occurring during a period of over two years, between Faḍlī tribesmen and their eastern neighbours, the Bā Kāzim. These were probably dealt with by the conciliators or peace-makers (*ṣalīḥ*) in the manner already described. Each party to the case chose the men of the opposite side whom it wished to take the oath. It was stated that in the disputes listed infra the Faḍlīs were ready to swear by Saʿīdah, but the Bā Kāzim were unwilling to do so. When one sees that certain members of the Manṣab house connected with Saʿīdah were involved in the incidents this strikes one as not unnatural. However it seems that both sides were willing to swear by ʿUmar b. Saʿīd, already mentioned, in ʿAwdhalī territory.

The language of these court records must be that of a clerk but it reports, more or less verbatim, the words of the arbiters and tribesmen. Pronunciation would differ as between a tribes-

95 Cf. *Arabica V*, 137-8. This number of oath-takers in the case of a murdered man is also confirmed by documents in my corpus of tribal law writings.

96 'Two tribal law cases. . .', II, 159 seq., 165.

97 'The "White Dune" ', op. cit., 82. Evidently *qasāmah* could be resorted to in paternity cases in the earliest period of Islam (and doubtless before) to judge by a threat made in Muʿāwiyah's time:

همت أن آتي بقسامة من قريش يحلفون أن أبا سفيان لم ير
سُمَيَّة قط .

Balādhurī, *Ansāb al-Ashrāf*, IVa, ed. M. Schloessinger & M.J. Kister, Jerusalem, 1971, 194.

man and a clerk, especially if an Adenese, to say nothing of diction. There is no consistent use of *am* or *al*[98] even in tribesmen's names which in themselves are interesting.[99] Colloquial language or grammatical usages occurring in the records are quoted in transliteration as they too are interesting. The definite article is transliterated as *al* even before *ḥurūf shamsiyyah* as is conventional.

Cases of The Faḍlīs brought against Bā Kāzim

1. Plea: on 31 iv 60:
   Laʿwag b. Yislam b. Sarīʿ ʿAnbūrī Kāzimī and his five brothers of the Lower ʿAwlaqī (al-ʿAwāliq al-Suflā) tribes committed an unlawful/hostile act (*iʿtadā*); they committed an unlawful act and looted the Marāqishah camels (*bil*), four camels.
   Counter-plea:
   The accused replied with denial (*inkār*) [of the charge].
   Judgement: The judgement (*ḥukm*) on the accused is twenty oath-takers (*ḥallāfah*).
2. Plea: on 28 xii 60:
   Ahl Bā Kāzim committed a hostile act on the borders[100] of the Jaʿādinah and cut some timbers, firewood and palm-frond (*ʿazaf*) while it was still green, in interdicted land.[101]
   Decision:
   Investigation (*baḥth*) between Ahl al-Faḍlī and Ahl Bā Kāzim [led to the affirmation] that whatever side [it be] should not commit an unlawful/hostile act against the other by cutting *sarḥ*, *ṣarḥah*, the *ḍubyānah* and the *ʿilb* trees[102] of the two sides unless they are not in disagreement about it through mutual consent in accordance with the tribal customs observed between them (*illā mā taʿājaw*[103] *ʿalay-h bi- tarāḍā*[104] *bi-mūjib al-ʿawā'id al-qabaliyyah al-muttabaʿah bayna-hum*), henceforth and from now onwards.
3. Plea: on 1 ii 61:
   Mahdī b.al-ʿĀqil al-Yaḥawī (son of the Yaḥawī *ʿāqil*, headman) and Sāḥim al-Ḥaydarī of Ahl Bā Kāzim committed a hostile act[105] and prevented the *makīnah* (mechanical plough?; *makīnah* is usually a pump) of Saʿīd b. Ṣāliḥ b. Yaʿqūb nicknamed al-Ṭirs (the Tooth), and his brother from ploughing the land. The aggressors (*al-muʿtadūn*) are Ahl Yaḥāwiyah.
   Counter-plea:
   Bin Yaʿqūb came over the question of a field (*jirbah*) called Jawbah[106] and both (*kull[in] min*) Bū Bakr b. Aḥmad and Nāṣir b. ʿAbdullāh had already inspected this place and they stopped everything in this place.
   Judgement: We decided that a committee consisting of the Nā'ib Aḥmad b. ʿAbdullāh and

98 For the dialectical use of *am* which he calls *tahmīr*, see al- Hamdānī, *Ṣifah*, ed. D. H. Müller, Leiden, 1884-91, 134.
99 Note also Laʿwag = al-Aʿwaj, Maḥmarī = am-Aḥmarī, Maḥwal= am-Aḥwal.
100 *Ḥudūd* also means 'territory'.
101 *Khaḍrā' maḥjūrah*. Presumably cutting it while green injures the palm. The *arḍ maḥjūrah*, interdicted land, is al-Rawḍah (not on von Wissmann's map), between Bā Kāzim and Jaʿādinah country. They do not permit Badu to camp there, make fields (*yijarrib al-tīn*), cut trees, or the pasturing (*raʿī*) of cattle there. For the *maḥjar* in the Yemen, cf. Serjeant & Ronald Lewcock, *Sanʿā': an Arabian Islamic city*, London, 1983, index 584b.
102 *Sarḥ/ṣarḥ*, arbre sans épines (*Gloss. daṯ.*). The *ḍubyānah* tree was said to be like the *sumur* (acacia) and bees to 'eat' of it, the honey being of good quality. *ʿIlb* is Zizyphus spina Christi.
103 *Mā taʿājaw*, paraphrased as *mā saddaw shī*, they did not agree at all. Cf. *Gloss. daṯ., taʿājā, être en difficulté, en désaccord*.
104 *Bi-'l-tarāḍā* may be intended, but as written this is a common orthographic error.
105 I. e. he stopped all agricultural activities. Cf. 'Two tribal law cases. . .', I, 39.
106 *Jawbah, Gloss. daṯ.*, bowl, basin. It was described as a *widin*, field.

the Nā'ib Bū Bakr b. Aḥmad[107] should go out to look into this question and resolve it in a just fashion.[108]

4. Plea: on 21 ii 61:
Complaint of looting by Abū Sitt[109] al-ʿAlawī of Ahl ʿAlī[110] Bā Kāẓim. He looted the young riding camel (*qaʿūd*)[111] of ʿAlī b. Muḥammad b. ʿAbdullāh Abū Bakr al-Maḥmarī, and the camel was a purchase from the Bā Kāẓim camels (*bil*), which the Marāqishah took – and Bā Kāẓim received payment for that (*fulūs muqābil dhālik*) by hand of the Regent (al-Waṣiyy).[112]
Counter-Plea:
The accused replied with denial [of the charge].
Judgement: The judgement on the accused is five oath-takers.
5. Plea: on 8 xi 61:
Ahl Bā Kāẓim laid an ambush (*kamin*) for some of the Marāqishah, they being Munaṣṣar b. ʿĪdah b. al-Khamsī ʿAnbūrī, Ḥasan Munaṣṣar b. al-Ṣindaʿī[113] ʿAmbūrī[114], ʿAlī b. Bābā and his brothers, Yislamī and ʿAlī b. ʿAbdullāh b. Hādī Busaymī – this was in Wādī Haram[115] – their objective being to kill Zaʿlān al-Murqushī[116] or someone else.
Counter-plea:
The accused replied with denial.
Judgement: The accused must [produce] ten oath-takers that they did not lay an ambush for Zaʿlān or anyone else.
6. Ahl Ḥaydarah Bā Kāẓim, Aḥmad Ṣāliḥ b. al-Ṭaḥar[117] and his brother Saḥm and Maṣar b. Nāṣir Ḥaydarī[118] committed an unlawful act and cut four bunds in the land (*jabbū arbaʿat aswām fī ṭīn*) of ʿIyāl Ḥasan b. Maḥwal when they were dry (*jidib*[119]) and ʿAwaḍ b. Ḥusayn (sic) Maḥwal entered Aḥwar to make a report (*yaʿmal rabūṭ*), but the answer was prison! He stayed (lit. sat) in prison for a spell and during this time seven *bil* were taken from Ahl Maḥwal. Two of them they found in the Shārīʿ[120] of Ahl al-ʿUmaysī and they took them back and those that remain are five *bil*.
Counter-plea:
The accused replied with denial.
Judgement: The accused must [produce] twenty oath-takers.

107 The Faḍlī and Kāẓimī, respectively. Bū Bakr is Regent (Waṣiyy) and now, since the Federation (Ittiḥād), in 1964 Nā'ib.

108 My notes state that Ṣāliḥ b. Ḥusayn, the ʿAwdhalī Sultan, in his capacity as a Minister in al-Ittiḥād, gave this decision.

109 Abū Sitt, with six fingers. The extra finger comes after the little finger. Here it is accounted as *barakah*, an extra blessing from God. The Faḍlī sultans are known to have this as an hereditary feature. Cf. A. M. Honeyman, 'Some south Arabian instances of polydactyly', *Man*, London, 1961, LXI, 161-2.

110 Āl ʿAlī Bā Kāẓim live in al-Miʿlā (the upper part) of Wādī Aḥwar and receive (flood)-water before Aḥwar.

111 This is the lexical sense of *qaʿūd*; it might have a more specific sense in the area.

112 I. e. Bū Bakr b. Aḥmad of fn. 107.

113 Ṣindaʿī was an ʿAmbūrī ʿāqil, but the Marāqishah eventually killed him.

114 ʿAm̱būrī/ʿAṉbūrī, written interchangeably.

115 A wādī said to flow into Wādī Aḥwar.

116 Zaʿlān was an *ʿāqil*. The bloodwit of men of rank in the south is in general more than that of an ordinary tribesman, but I have no information on this point for the Faḍlīs and Bā Kāẓim.

117 *Ṭaḥar, Gloss. daṯ.*, class. rejeter, but the local sense is unknown to me.

118 *Maṣar(r)* is a scarf tied under the chin (*Ṣanʿā'*, op. cit., 231b (n)) or *mouchoir, fichu (Gloss. daṯ.*, 2123).

119 *Arḍ mamṭūrah* and *arḍ jadb* are contrasted; *jidib* is an unwatered field, fallow; *mijiddibīn*, those who do not water their fields. The bunds are cut at flood-time, though under certain conditions, but there was no water at this time, therefore no cause to cut the bund.

120 *Shārīʿ* = *sākin*, settlement, tents. *Sākin* is in common use.

7. Furthermore six *bil* were taken from ʿAlī b. Fāṭimah, the bastard (*zanū*[121]) of Ahl ʿAbbādī, the person who seized (*al- akhkhādh*) [them] being Ṣāliḥ b. Laʿdhan.
Counter-plea:
The accused replied with denial.
Judgement: The accused must [produce] twenty oath-takers.
8. Plea: on 5 v 62:
Ahl Bā Kāzim took six head of cattle (*sittah ru'ūs baqar*) from the Marāqishah, Ahl ʿAmr b. ʿAlī, and two head of cattle from ʿAlī b. Muḥammad b. ʿAbdullāh Maḥmarī. They took the cattle from Wādī Taṣabah, and they took a heifer (*ʿijlah*) belonging to Aḥmad al-ʿAwnī ʿAbbādī, and they took from Ṣāliḥ son of the Manṣab Muḥammad b. al-Kubaysh[122] two small bulls (*ithnayn tibʿān*[123]).
Counter-plea:
The accused replied with denial.
Judgement: The accused must [produce] ten oath-takers.
9. Plea: probably in 1962.
After ʿĪd al-Aḍḥā al-mubārak, Ahl Bā Kāzim looted from ʿAlī Barṭam Qaynāshī a she-camel for riding (*rāḥilah*[124]), and from Ṣāliḥ ʿAbdullāh Maḥmarī a *qaʿūd* and a *rāḥilah*, and from ʿAlī Ḥaydar b. Sālim Maḥmarī, a *qaʿūd* – they took them from Wādī Taṣabah – the takers (*al-akhkhādhah*) were Ahl al- ʿUmaysī. Counter-plea:
The accused replied with denial.
Judgement: Ṣāliḥ b. Rāgiḥ and his nephew (*ibn akhū-h*) Bin ʿArṣūṣ must [produce] twenty oath-takers.
10. Plea: undated[125] (June 1962?):
Ahl Faḍl pleads that in month six[126] Ahl Bā Kāzim took from Sūbān b. Aḥmad two camels (*ithnayn bil*), the looter (*ṭammāʿ*) being Bin al-Ḍirsī.[127]
Judgement: He will attend at the time of the appointment for the putting of judgements (*aḥkām*) into execution, and if he denies [the charge] he must [produce] ten oath-takers.
11. Furthermore Ahl al-ʿUmaysī looted two camels (*bil*) from ʿIyāl Muḥammad Ḥaydarah – the takers were Bin Laḥmar and Bin Lādhin.
They replied with denial.
The judgement is ten oath-takers.
12. Plea: on 14 iv 62:
They took from ʿAlī b. Muḥammad Maḥmarī a camel (*baʿīr*) and from ʿAlī am-Ṣawbī a *baʿīr* and from Barṭam al-Qaynāshī fifty head of sheep-and-goats (*khamsīn rās ghanam*) – the looters (*al-nahhābah*) were Muḥammad ʿAwaḍ al-Ṭawīl al-ʿUmaysī and al-Nāshirī of Ahl

121 For *zanū*, see 'The "White Dune"', op. cit., 80 seq.; *Daṯînah*, 433, 944. The Government handbook, op. cit., 32, remarks: 'Among the eastern sub-divisions [of Faḍlī country], and especially the Markashí, a curious practice obtains, of holding a "Zanw", or base-born son, in higher estimation than the legitimate issue, and such a sobriquet is held to be no mark of dishonour, but rather the reverse. The men of this class are fond of calling themselves after their mothers, as "Bin Fatima," etc., their fathers being ignored.' This seems a little exaggerated though broadly true.

122 The Manṣab is of the Bil-ʿĪdī, but I have no information about the shrine with which he was connected.

123 Sing. *tabʿ*, *baqar dhukrān*.

124 *Gloss. daṯ.*, *rāḥilah* = *chamelle qui a déjà mis bas et pouvant porter une charge*.

125 Omitted by the records or by me.

126 This usage of numbering the months of the Christian year was quite common in 1964, but I do not recall it in 1954.

127 Written Zirsī with *zāʾ* for *ḍād*, perhaps the same as al-Ṭirs in case 3.

Laʿgam and ʿAwaḍ al-Kārūf[128] and Yislam b. Ṣādiq nicknamed al-Bard[129] of Ahl Ilḥāq.
Counter-plea:
The accused replied with denial.
Judgement: The accused must [produce] forty oath-takers.

13. Plea: on 20 ii 62:
A *rāḥilah* was taken from Saʿīd Ḥaydarah Aḥmad Bil-ʿAydī.
The accused was Ṣāliḥ b. Lādhin.
The accused is [to produce] five oath-takers.
14. Plea: on 25 ii 62:
Two *bil* were taken from Sālim Masʿūd Banī ʿAlī from Wādī Taṣabah.
The accused are Ṣāliḥ b. Saʿīd ʿUmaysī and Bin Ṭubayq al- Laʿgamī.
They have to produce five oath-takers that they had not looted them nor withheld[130] them (*mā salabū-hā wa-lā iʿtaqalū-hā*).
15. Plea: on 11 iii 62:
A *rāḥilah* was taken from Aḥmad am-Wārid Faḍlī (a Qaynāshī) by Laʿwag b. Sarīʿ al-ʿAnbūrī. The judgement was that the accused should produce five oath-takers.
16. Plea: on 14 iii 62:
A *qaʿūd* was taken from Ḥaydarah am-Ṭayūzī Qaynāshī Faḍlī. The accused was Laʿwag b. Sarīʿ who was required to produce five oath-takers.
17. Plea: on 14 iii 62:
A *baʿīr* was taken from Ṣāliḥ ʿAbdullāh Qaynāshī. The accused, Nāṣir ʿAwaḍ b. Aḥmad al-ʿĀqil (the Headman), denied the charge and was required to produce five oath-takers.
18. Plea: on 15 iii 62:
A *gamal* (probably merely a beast of burden) was taken from Ṣāliḥ Muḥammad Maḥmarī. The accused Sālim b. al-ʿĀmah[131] al-Bishaʿī is to attend and, if he admits the theft, to return the animal. If he denies the charge he must produce five oath-takers.
19. Plea: on 21 iii 62:
Sixteen *rās ghanam* were taken from Aḥmad ʿAlī b. Muṭʿim.[132] The accused are Laʿwag b. Sarīʿ and his brothers. If they deny the charge they must produce five oath-takers.
20. Plea: on 10 iv 62:
A *rāḥilah* and her foal (*ibn-hā*) were taken from ʿAlī Barṭam. The accused Aḥmad Ṣāliḥ and (name unclear) . . . ʿĀdī al- Sūd/Al-Aswad/al-Sawd(?), if they deny the charge are to produce ten oath-takers.
21. Plea: on 21 iv 62:
A *qaʿūd* was taken from ʿAlī Saʿīd am-Wārid between Wādī al- Misayl (in Murqushī territory). The accused, Ṣāliḥ b. Nāṣir b. Lādhin, if he denies the charge must produce five oath-takers.
22. Plea: on 21 iv 62:
A *gamal* was taken from Ḥaydarah b. Sālim Maḥmarī by Ṣāliḥ Ṭubayq and Nāṣir b. Yislam. They are to present themselves at a time fixed and if they deny the charge, to produce five oath-takers.

128 Al-Kārūf, an Ilhāqī, from *karā*, *yikruf*, to smack, *Gloss. daṯ.*, *donner une claque*.
129 So called because cold (*bard*) goes everywhere – he used to scare (perhaps – make insecure) people (*yikhawwif al-nās*), and hence the nickname.
130 *Iʿtaqala* could also mean to tie an animal's leg with the *ʿiqāl*.
131 This name looks doubtful.
132 *Muṭʿim* in the classical sense.

23. Plea: on 22 iv 62:
Fifteen *rās ghanam* were taken from Muḥammad Ḥasan Qaynāshī by Ruways b. ʿAwlah (a Busaymī) and two others.
If the accused deny the charge they must produce five oath-takers.
24. Plea: on 22 iv 62:
Fifteen *rās ghanam* were taken from Ṣāliḥ ʿAbdullāh Qaynāshī.
No names of the takers are given, but if they deny the charge they must produce five oath-takers.[133]
25. Plea: on 22 iv 62:
Thirty *rās ghanam* were taken from ʿAlī ʿAbdullāh Maḥmarī.
If the takers, un-named, deny the charge they must produce ten oath-takers.
26. Plea: on 4 v 62:
Twenty-five *rās ghanam* were taken from Saʿīd am-Marbaʿī Qaynāshī.
The accused, Bin Ṣāliḥ b. Bāḥī (? – this and a following name unclearly written) and Bin Laʿwar, if they deny the charge are to produce ten oath-takers.
27. Plea: on 4 v 62:
Two camels (*thintayn bil*) were taken from am-Ṣāfī Qaynāshī by Bin Ruways and Bin ʿAwlah Busaymī.
If they deny the charge they must produce ten oath-takers.
28. Plea: on 4 v 62:
Three camels (*thalāth bil*) were taken from Aḥmad Ṣāliḥ b. Muthannā Qaynāshī by ʿAwaḍ al-Zayn and Bin Laḥmar D r ʿ ḥ/g (unclearly written). If they deny the charge they must produce fifteen oath-takers.
29. Plea: on 3 vi 62:
Four camels (*arbaʿ bil*) were taken from Muḥammad Ḥaydarah Qaynāshī from Wādī am-Mukaylah [in Qaynāshī territory] by Aḥmad al-Dādah and ʿAlī . . . (?).
If the accused deny the charge they must produce twenty oath-takers.
30. Plea: on 3 vi 62:
Thirteen *rās ghanam* were taken from Aḥmad Ḥaydarah am-Ṣawbī by ʿAlī b. ʿAwaḍ b. Ghabrah.[134]
If he denies the charge he must produce five oath-takers.
31. Plea: on 3 vi 62:
Seventeen *rās ghanam* were taken from Muḥammad Ḥaydarah am- Ṣawbī[135] Qaynāshī.
The accused, un-named, if they deny the charge must produce five oath-takers.
32. Plea: on 5 vi 62:
Seven camels (*sabʿ bil*) were taken from al-Khiḍr b. Muṭʿim from Wādī al-Ṭuyū by ʿAwaḍ al-Dīk ʿAmbūrī.
If he denies the charge he must produce twenty oath-takers.
33. Plea: on 5 vi 62:
A bull was taken from ʿAlī Barṭam Qaynāshī from Wādī al-Ṭuyū by Muqbil b. ʿAlī ʿAlawī.
If he denies the charge he must produce five oath-takers.

133 Perhaps the plaintiff did not know the names in this and the next case, or the clerk tired of writing them down.
134 Vocalisation uncertain.
135 My transcript has am-Sarbī which seems incorrect.

The cases (*qaḍāyā*) in which Ahl Bā Kāzim make accusation against Ahl Faḍl and the counter-pleas (*ajwibah*) of Ahl Faḍl and the judgement (*ḥukm*) in them

1. Ahl Bā Kāzim allege that, on the day 12 v 61, Zaʿlān and Bin Saʿīd b. ʿUmayr of the tribes of the Faḍlī committed a hostile act, firing at ʿAwaḍ al-Kārūf of the tribes of Bā Kāzim and hitting him with fragments of cartridge (*ṣābū-h bi-quṭuf*[136]).
   Counter-plea:
   The Faḍlī replied with denial [of the charge]. There is no proof (*ithbāt*).
   Judgement: Ahl Faḍl must [produce] ten oath-takers (*ḥallāfah*).
2. Ahl Bā Kāzim alleges that, on the day 17 xii 61, Bin am- Muḥannah al-Murqushī and Bin Nāṣir b. Saʿīd Maḥwal committed an unlawful act and seized two camels (*ithnatayn bil*) belonging to Nāṣir b. ʿAlī al-ʿAmbūrī of the Bā Kāzim tribes
   Counter-plea:
   Nāṣir b. ʿAlī states: They took from him two *bil* which can be seen (*bānū*[137] with the Jaʿādinah at [the place of] ʿIyāl al-Maẓlūmī, a she-camel for riding (*rāḥilah*) and her foal, and another with her foal (*wāḥid w-ibn-hā*) at [the place of] ʿAlī Muhallab [Jaʿdanī]. Sālim Masʿūd admits to the *rāḥilah* which is with ʿAlī Muhallab, but he states that it was seized before the truce (*ṣulḥ*).
   Judgement: The decision was taken to select five oath- takers (*riqāb*)[138] from the Marāqishah to swear (*yaḥlifūn*) that these camels (*ibil*) were seized before the truce – and, if not, they will give up (*yiksirūn*[139]) [the camels] and they have five oath-takers (*riqāb*) from Bā Kāzim. With regard to the two camels (*min sha'n al-ithnayn al-ibil*) which are with ʿIyāl al-Maẓlūmī they will invite them to admit and prove whence they bought them (*yadʿūna-hum an*[140] *iʿtarafū wa-sannadū-hin min ayn ishtaraw-hin*), and if they state that they are part of their property they must [produce] five oath-takers (*ḥallāfah*) to [confirm] that these camels (*hādha 'l-ibil*) are part of their property.
3. Ahl Bā Kāzim allege that, on 24 xii 61, ʿAlī Barṭam and ʿIyāl am-Ṣawbī of the tribes of the Faḍlī committed an unlawful act and looted three head of cattle (*thalāth ru'ūs baqar*) belonging to Saʿīd Umbārak ʿUmaysī of the tribes of Bā Kāzim.
   Counter-plea:
   The Faḍlī replied to that (*ajāb ʿalā dhālik*) with denial. Judgement: It was judged upon the accused (*al-mathūmīn*) Muḥammad am-Ṣawbī and Muḥammad Ḥaydarah ibn/bir[141] am-Qaydah and Saʿīd am-Ṭuyūzī (that they should produce) five oath-takers (*khamsah ḥallāfah*) (to swear) that they did not seize the afore-mentioned cattle (*al-baqar al-madhkūrāt*), and upon Nāṣir Saʿīd b. ʿAmbar b. ʿAbbādī and Daymaḥ (a Rabīzī[142]) and Ḥaydarah b. Sālim their oaths (*riqāb-hum*) (or oath- takers) that they do not know, have no news of, and did not see them with their fellow [tribesmen] (*lā yiʿallūn wa-lā yaʿlamūn wa-lā shāfū-hin maʿa aṣḥāb-hum*).[143]

136 *Qaṭf*, pl. *quṭūf*, small fragments of bullet, explained as *fadhakh* or *qaṭan*, neither of which seems to be classical.
137 I. e. *tabayyan*.
138 Sing., *raqabah*. One says: *Ashill fī raqabatī*, I undertake on my neck (to do). Hence the word comes to mean takers of oaths. *Cf. Gloss. daṯ., Amānat-ak fī raqabat-ak, Ton honnêteté est à ton cou.*
139 *Yiksirūn* explained as 'will give them the camels'. *Kasara*, to give up, I have heard in coastal Hadramawt.
140 *An* might here be read *in*. *Sannadū-hin* was explained as *athbatū ʿalay-hin*. I am not altogether sure of the sense of this passage.
141 Written *bin* but informants said *bir*.
142 The Rabīzīs are of the Mahājir confederation of the Upper ʿAwlaqīs. There was much *fitnah* between them and Aden in 1954 when we visited the area. Perhaps this Rabīzī had somehow joined Bā Kāzim.
143 *ʿAllā* = *yaʿrif*; cf. supra.

4. Ahl Bā Kāzim allege that, on the day of 16 ii 62, Saʿīd b. Sālim Dawkam and Saʿīd am-Ṭuyūzī[144] of the tribes of the Faḍlī committed an unlawful act and seized six head of cattle belonging to Laḥmar b. Farīd al-ʿUmaysī of the tribes of Bā Kāzim.
   Counter-plea:
   The Faḍlī replied with denial.
   The judgement is an oath [to be taken] by the accused (*yamīn ʿala 'l-muttahamīn*) aforementioned [i.e.] ten oath-takers that they did not seize these cattle; and Bin/Bir Maḥwal and Sālim Masʿūd must [take] an oath (*raqabah*)[145] – as for these cattle they did not raid after them (*yā hādha 'l-baqar lā ghārū qafā-hum*[146]), [neither] they nor ʿIyāl al-ʿUmaysī, and they have no news of them (*wa-lā yaʿlamū bi-hin*[147]) being with the group (*jamāʿah*).[148]
5. Ahl Bā Kāzim alleged that, on the day of 25 iii 62, Muḥammad Ḥaydarah and ʿAbdullāh am-Ṭayūzī and Bin ʿAbdullāh b. Saʿīd of the tribes of the Faḍlī committed an unlawful act and looted thirty *rās ghanam* belonging to Muḥammad b. ʿAwaḍ Laʿgam of Ahl Bā Kāzim.
   Counter-plea:
   The accused replied with denial.
   The judgement on the accused is [that they produce] ten oath-takers [to swear] that they did not loot these cattle.
6. Ahl Bā Kāzim allege that on 17 iv 62 Bin Ṣāliḥ am-Zanū[149] of the tribes of the Faḍlī committed an unlawful act and seized one young female camel not yet put to the male[150] (*bakrah*) belonging to Aḥmad b. Nāṣir b. ʿAwaḍ Yislamī of the tribes of Bā Kāzim.
   Counter-plea:
   The accused replied with denial.
   The judgement on the accused is [to produce] five oath-takers.
7. Ahl Bā Kāzim allege that on month five, 1962, they received a telegram from the Assistant Adviser (*musāʿid al-mustashār al-thānī*)[151], Aḥwar, and he informs [them] that he has received a report from the ʿUmaysī ʿĀqil that Barṭam and Muḥammad and ʿAlī, ʿIyāl am-Ṣawbī, and Bin am-Ṭuyūzī and Dawkam and Bin am-Qaḍā', Ahl Saʿīd and Ahl Bā Qaynāsh, and ʿAydarūs b. Muḥammad b. ʿAbdullāh Maḥmarī and his brothers, and Ṣāliḥ b. am-Shaybah and the son of the Manṣab and Nāṣir b. Saʿīd Maḥmarī of the tribes of the Faḍlī have committed an unlawful act and looted nineteen head of cattle belonging to the ʿUmaysī ʿĀqil and his brothers, of the tribe of Bā Kāzim.
   Counter-plea:
   The accused replied with denial.
   The judgement on the accused is [to produce] twenty oath-takers.

In the series of raids and counter-raids, mainly to steal livestock, members of Manṣab houses (Faḍlī case no. 8; Kāzimī case no. 6) and of those of headmen (*ʿāqils*) were involved – I find it a little surprising that the former should have taken part in these actions. To deny an accusation seems to have been the convention, possibly so that all past and present circumstances could be

144 Al-Ṭayūzī supra.
145 *Raqabah* seems to mean an oath here, not oath-taker.
146 For *yā* cf. fn. 87; here it seems to mean 'as for'.
147 Cf. fn. 90.
148 Presumably of raiders.
149 Cf. fn. 121.
150 *Gloss. daṯ.*, *bakrah*, 'camel which has not yet borne off-spring.'
151 Robin Bidwell tells me the Junior Assistant Adviser (JAA) would be an Arab, most likely a former officer in one of the Arab units.

discussed. The changes that the federating of the protected sultanates had begun to introduce are evident as in Faḍlī case 3 where the Faḍlī Nā'ib Aḥmad ʿAbdullāh (later Sultan) and the Lower ʿAwlaqī Regent Bū Bakr b. Aḥmad are appointed by the Federal Minister Sultan Ḥusayn al-ʿAwdhalī to settle a dispute between their tribes. Later in these records a junior assistant adviser, a government not a local man comes into the picture. In Kāzimī case 2 "the truce" is mentioned but I do not know whether this was part of the general security established in the Federation or simply a local truce.

Apart from the stealing of animals the records contain the case of infringement of a common interdicted pasture (*maḥjar*) and the banning of cultivation. Though forty oath-takers are required in the case of a murdered man (*qatīl*) only ten are required in the case of ambush with intent to kill, and for firing at and slightly wounding. This is to be compared with the twenty required in the case of cutting a bund and stealing five camels. The following table may give some indication of the 'tariff'.

Animal	*Number*	*Oath-takers*
Rās ghanam	13-15	5
	17-30	10
	50 + 2	
	baʿīr	40
baqar	1-3	5
	6	10
	19	20
	6 + heifer	
	& 2 small bulls	10
Camels	1-2	5
	2	10
	3	15
	4,6-7	20
	Rāḥilah &	
	qaʿūd	20
	Rāḥilah	5
	Rāḥilah &	
	foal	10

But obviously one should not attach too much importance to such tables.

Of *qasāmah* in *Encyclopaedia of Islam* (2) avers: "It does not appear that this institution functioned much, even in the past". The persistence of *qasāmah* as an important legal procedure in tribal south Arabia up to the present day is evidence to the contrary. It is much more likely that it was normal procedure for Arab tribes, outside the cities of Iraq and Syria at least, for centuries. Has it in point of fact ever really disappeared among them in practice?

Transliteration

For classical Arabic the system of *Arabian Studies* is followed. For colloquial Arabic this system has been to some extent adapted to reflect local pronunciation; this is not always consistent and so slightly different spellings occur.

Supplementary Notes

P.111, fn.3 — Further historical data on the Faḍlī sultans are to be found in *al-Sīrat al- Mutawakkiliyyah*, Mukallā Ms., 260-64 and ʿAbdullāh b. ʿAlī al-Wazīr, *Ṭabaq al-halwā*, Chester Beatty Ms. 28a, 41a, printed Sanʿā', 1405/1985, index.

p.112, fn.13. — In the pre-Islamic period the Bishop of Najrān was also crowned in this way.

P.113, line 10. — *Ṣurr*, I was informed means *kharaz* trees, probably, like *silim*, acacias, which a *surr* also means, but *tin surr* means *ṭin ṣulb*, hard soil.

Pp.130, line7; 131, line 32, passim.

Abū Makhramah, *Arabische Texte zu ... Aden im Mittelalter*, ed. O. Löfgren, Leiden, 1936-50, 242, refers to a qāḍī of Aden called al-ʿĪdī (ʿAydī ?) al-Abyanī (661-735 H.), and (p.253) to the Aʿyūd (plur.) of Abyan, presumably of this same house.

Addenda

P.135/fn.8 Wyman Bury, Shukra to Bêhân via Makatein (Ms.) "It will be observed that 'Amir' is a Turkish title, and is not known among the Bedouin tribes to the eastward who use the synonym 'Amr'."

P.139/38 In the Prophet's time the noble lady Umm Qirfah, whose family was the Bayt Ghaṭafān, when there was a dispute among the Ghaṭafān tribes, would send her headcloth (*khimār*) raised up on a spear to interpose between them and they would make a truce (*yaṣṭaliḥūn*). Was she linked to Ghaṭafān's goddess al-ʿUzzā? Ibn al-Ḥabīb, *Muḥabbar*, 119 & 461; Ṭabarī, *Tārīkh*, I, III, 1557–58; Ibn Durayd, *Ishtiqāq*, Cairo, 1378/1958, 284.

P.140 The Aden paper *al-Ayyām* (7/iv/63), reports the Faḍlī Sultan Aḥ. b. ʿAbdullah as displaying a volume printed in 1957 which contained the *nuẓum* and *qawānīn* acted upon in the Sultanate but without indication of their nature.

P.147/6 Cf. *Bāb al-Qasāmah* of the Zaydī, Aḥ. b. Yaḥyā b. al-Murtaḍā, *al-Baḥr al-zakhkhār*, Cairo, 1368/1949, V, 295–303.

VI

Yāfiᶜ, Zaydīs, Āl Bū Bakr b. Sālim and others: Tribes and Sayyids

This is my modest tribute to Professor Oscar Löfgren who, with another Swedish scholar, Count Carlo de Landberg, has laid an enduring foundation for the study of south western Arabia of the Islamic era. I am happy to have the occasion to acknowledge my personal debt to Professor Löfgren's scholarship.

Yāfiᶜ is an ancient and important congerie of tribes – agriculturists and warriors – established in lofty steeply rising mountains lying north of Aden and bordering on the present day Yemen Arab Republic. The name Yāfiᶜ already occurs in the pre-Islamic inscriptions and places to which reference is made here already figure as Yāfiᶜī territory in Hamdānī's geography[1]. So inaccessible is Yāfiᶜī country that it rarely comes under a centralizing power and then not for long. It does not for example seem to have paid taxes to the Rasūlids[2] though Yāfiᶜīs served them as mercenaries. In Ḥaḍramawt to which they also came as mercenaries in the 11-12th/17-18th centuries (on one occasion at least at the instance of the ᶜĪnāt Sayyid house of Bū Bakr b. Sālim[3]), they became the dominant power. Many were employed as mercenaries in India, notably Ḥaydarābād. Towards the end of the 19th century and onwards the (British) Indian Government entered into a series of treaties with various Yāfiᶜī groups, the *naqībs* of al-Mawsaṭah, the Muflaḥīs, the Ḥaḍramī tribe, and the Ibn Harharah shaykh[4], aiming to keep other powers out of these areas – the chiefs received tiny stipends in return. In 1909[5] it was stated that »the Aden Residency has little communication with the Upper Yafai tribes«. It was really only after World War II and the Aden Government's penetration policy that any serious attempt was made to develop relations with Yāfiᶜ. Aden's troubles with Muḥammad son of Sultan ᶜAydarūs of Lower Yāfiᶜ are rather sketchily discussed by Sir Kennedy Trevaskis[6] and a Yāfiᶜī element was part of the small communist NLF to which the 1967 Labour Government resolved to hand over Aden and its dependencies. The iron curtain descended and news of the tribes filters out rarely with refugees. It

[1] *Ṣifat Jazīrat al-ᶜArab*, ed. D.H. Müller, Leiden 1884-91, p. 89; ed. Muḥammad . . . al-Akwaᶜ, al-Riyāḍ, 1394/1974, p. 176, with some modern notes. Al-ᶜUrr, Dhū Nākhib, Taym, the Banū Qāsid and Yahar, as well as other places are mentioned.

[2] The *Mulakhkhaṣ al-fiṭan* (1411-12) does not list revenue from Yāfiᶜ.

[3] Cf. p. 103.

[4] Printed in *An Account of the Arab Tribes in the vicinity of Aden*, Government Central Press, Bombay 1909. W.H. Ingrams, *Report on . . . Hadhramaut*, Colonial 123, London 1937, lists the tribes of Lower and Upper Yāfiᶜ but the spelling and possibly part of the information is unreliable.

[5] *Account . . . op. cit.*, 63.

[6] *Shades of Amber*, London 1968, *passim*.

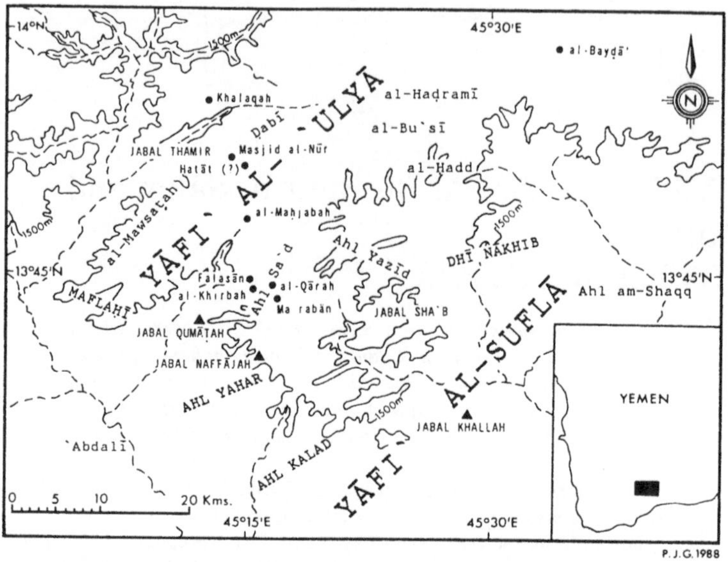

Map of Upper Yāfiᶜ and part of Lower Yāfiᶜ. *(Courtesy of Peter J. Grove)*

is not, however, to be expected that the junta at present ruling in Aden has control of the mountains of Yāfiᶜ.

Yāfiᶜ divides into Upper (al-ᶜUlyā) and Lower (al-Suflā) Yāfiᶜ. The high mountain districts are not known to have been visited by Europeans; the maps are mainly based on aerial survey – I have myself flown over Yāfiᶜ. Lower Yāfiᶜ lies partly in the Abyan plain. In ancient times ᶜĀd (ibn Shaddād) and Thamūd were in Yāfiᶜ, they say, and point to the Shaddād tribe in the Faḍlī sultanate. Al-Qārah, chosen for its strategic position, was the old capital of the Sultans of Banū Qāsid, a tribe known to al-Hamdānī[7]. The Sultan had five tribes, Kaladī, Saᶜdī, Yazīdī, Yaharī and Nākhibī. The only visit paid by a British official to al-Qārah was that of Sir Tom Hickinbotham[8] in the fifties, an edgy affair, fraught with danger, political officers told me.

The Upper Yāfiᶜ capital is al-Maḥjabah of the Mashāyikh family Āl Harharah. His tribes are also five – from west to east, al-Mufliḥī, al-Mawsaṭī, al-Ẓabī/Ḍabī, al-Buᶜsī, al-Ḥaḍramī. According to the 1909 handbook[9] Sultan Sayf of Lower Yāfiᶜ had in his employ a clerk, Ibn Harharah, much loved by him, an able man to whom he granted by deed of gift, a district called al-Sufāl, from which originated Upper Yāfiᶜ. Perhaps this is not quite consistent with other versions of the Āl Harharah Sultan's antecedents. Aḥmad Faḍl al-ᶜAbdalī[10] (Ibn Harharah is related to the ᶜAbdalī Sultans of Lahej) maintains that Shaykh Abū Bakr b. Sālim of ᶜĪnāt, before his death in 992/1584, appointed (*naṣaba*) the very learned shaykh ᶜAlī Harharah as a conciliator (*muṣliḥ*) and religious guide

7 Al-Hamdānī, *loc. cit.*.
8 *Aden*, London 1958, p. 134, with pictures at al-Qārah.
9 *Account of the Arab tribes*, p. 63.
10 *Hadiyyat al-zaman fī akhbār mulūk Laḥj wa-ᶜAdan*, Cairo 1351 H., p. 108.

(*murshid*) in Upper Yāfiᶜ – his son Aḥmad succeeded him and the latter's son Ṣāliḥ followed him. Ibn Harharah, says Ibn Hāshim[11] was of the noblest houses of Yāfiᶜ (*min ashraf buyūtāt Yāfiᶜ*).

In their fratricidal struggles for power during the twelth/eighteenth century the rival Kathīrī Sultans of Ḥaḍramawt called in Yāfiᶜī tribesmen to support them. In 1116/1704–5 the Manṣab of ᶜĪnāt[12] summoned (*istaṣrakha*) Yāfiᶜ to his aid, while at the same time the Kathīrī Sultan Muḥammad al-Mardūf sent sacrificial animals (*ᶜaqāʾir*) to Jabal Yāfiᶜ to invoke aid against his rival, Sultan ᶜUmar b. Jaᶜfar al-Kathīrī, who had adopted the Zaydī school. Though at this point, the Manṣab seems to have made common cause with Sultan al-Mardūf, he had also been instrumental, it seems, in bringing Yāfiᶜīs to support Sultan ᶜUmar al-Kathīrī. ᶜUmar b. Ṣāliḥ b. Harharah arrived to support Sultan al-Mardūf with 6,000 Yāfiᶜīs and gained control over all Ḥaḍramawt. He returned home but left ᶜUmar b. ᶜAwaḍ al-Quᶜayṭī in command of the Yāfiᶜī tribesmen in Ḥaḍramawt – Yāfiᶜī dominance there does not however come into our story.

Yāfiᶜ is famous for its coffee, grown in sheltered places on its lofty mountain sides. Yāfiᶜīs are also fine masons. They are not unknown as scholars, notably ᶜAfīf al-Dīn ᶜAbdullāh b. Asᶜad al-Yāfiᶜī the biographer (ob. 768/1367).

The Sultans of Lower Yāfiᶜ and their Tribes

In the brief and limited discussion I had, mainly with Sultan ᶜAlawī b. Aḥmad al-ᶜAfīfī, relations between the tribes and Sultan were said to fall into two categories (*al-aḥkām ᶜalā nawᶜayn*) - *qayd* and *sumᶜah wa-tubᶜah.*

Qayd seems to mean something like bounden duty or it might mean treaty, but we did not develop this theme.

Sumᶜah wa-tubᶜah, literally, to hear and follow, means that the *qabāʾil* respond to the summons of the ᶜAfīfī Sultan and follow him to war - i.e., when the Sultan declares war they rally to his support, but there is no bond (*qayd*). It seems there are stipulations governing this relationship for the *ḥākim* (sultan?) says: »If I do you wrong then it is upon my neck (*ẓalamtu-ka - ᶜalā raqabatī*[13]). To this the *qabīlī* replies, giving his allegiance; »I undertake by the pact of Allah on the Qurʾān that I will listen to you and obey, and moreover I will pay the tithes (*Anā badayt bi-ᶜahd Allāh ᶜalā khitmah annī bā akūn sāmiᶜ lak ṭayiᶜ, wa-baᶜd bā usallim al-ᶜushūr*)«. The ᶜAfīfī, if they disobey him, would say to them: »If you do not listen to my words (decision?) Allah will bring a calamity upon you (*In mā samiᶜt al-kalām ḥaqqī Allāh bā yajᶜal lak muṣībah*).«

[11] Muḥammad b. Hāshim (of Āl Yaḥyā), *Tārīkh al-Dawlat al-Kathīriyyah*, Cairo 1367/1948, p. 90.

[12] *Ibid.*, p. 91.

[13] *I.e.*, I am responsible. *Cf.* C. de Landberg, *Glossaire daṯînois*, Leiden 1920–42, p. 1342. *Raqabah* is the side of the neck.

The Sultan and Wazīr of al-Qārah, capital of the sultanate of Lower Yāfiʿ in the early 1940s

Like other rulers the ʿAfīf Sultans have their *ʿaskar al-Sulṭān*, men who have left their tribes and become »sons of the Sultan, under the Sultan's protection (*ibn al-Dawlah, taḥt ḥimāyat al-Dawlah*).« Of such a soldier it is said: »There is no war/hostility from him or toward him (*Lā minnuh sharr wa-lā lah/luh sharr*[14])«. So the *ʿaskarī* can move freely among the tribes who do not molest him. The Sultan of Lower Yāfiʿ used to rule it from al-Qārah which is a *ḥawṭah* inhabited by only the Āl ʿAfīf and their hereditary *ʿaskar* who are divided into five houses each of which has the function of dealing with its own special *maktab* or tribal section, in collecting *ʿushūr*, etcetera. There appears also to be a small group (of *ʿaskar* ?) dealing with a small tribe or section outside the five *maktabs*, known as Mashʾalī[15] of whom it is said: »The (grain-)measure (*kās*[16]) goes to al-Qārah but the head belongs to Upper Yāfiʿ (*Al-kās li-ʾl-Qārah wa-ʾl-rās li-Yāfiʿ al-ʿUlyā*)«. That is they pay their tithes to the lower Yāfiʿī Sultan but in fact they are rijāl al-Miflaḥī, i.e. belonging to Upper Yāfiʿ. A parallel case is that of certain Faḍlī tribes who pay the *ʿushūr* to Lower Yāfiʿī but fight in war on the Faḍlī side.

Of grain crops the Dawlah receives the tenth measure (*al-kaylat al-ʿāshirah*[17]) or to be more precise, half of it. The other half goes a quarter to the poor (*miskīn*) and a quarter to the saints (*waliyy*) of the district for the Yāfiʿ tribes used to pay the *ʿushr al-ʿashar* and the tithe on coffee (*ʿāshir al-bunn*) to the Manṣab of ʿĪnāt who was one of the descendants (*aḥfād*) of Ḥusayn b. Abū Bakr b. Sālim. I do not know if the payments were made to ʿĪnāt up to the British withdrawal or if they ceased before that. The same division of the *ʿushūr* is made for the Ibn Harharah Shaykh and the local poor and saints. This is an act of benevolence (*ḥasanah*) on the part of the tribes, and not exacted by force on Ibn Harharah's part.

In every distict there are of course saints special to it. Lower Yāfiʿ has some *awliyāʾ* at ʿAzzān and Asʿad b. ʿAlī of Yahar seems to have close links with the ʿAfīfīs. Ribāṭ al-ʿAbbādī of the Mashāyikh Ahl al-ʿAbbādī was also mentioned. Ṣāliḥ ʿUmar Muḥammad Ghālib writes to me that Āl ʿAbbād are Umayyads[18] who fled after the collapse of the Umayyad dynasty and today are spread over all districts of Lower and Upper Yāfiʿ, coming second in rank after the Sayyids. Before the British withdrawal they used to teach the Qurʾān and deal with documents relating to marriage contracts and sales (*marāsīm ʿuqūd al-nikāḥ wa-ʾl-buyūʿ*). The Ribāṭ is in Yahar of Banī Qāsid of Lower Yāfiʿ. The Āl Bā ʿAbbād of Ḥaḍramawt are connected with the Tomb of Hūd[19]. About half a mile west and south of Khanfar rock and west of the road from Khanfar to Zingibar is the Qubbah of ʿAbdullāh b. ʿUmar b. Bū Bakr al-Saqqāf with old wood carving of some interest. The ʿAfīf are buried by the tomb of this Sayyid saint who however seems unknown to the hagiologies.

[14] *Gloss. daṯ.*, 2033. *Cf.* T. Nöldeke, *Delectus*. . ., Berlin 1890, p. 87.

[15] So pronounced, written al-Mashālī.

[16] The *kās* is, in some areas, a fixed cubic measure. In the ʿAwdhalī district of al-Ẓāhir three *kūs* (pl.) are equivalent to one *kaylah* in that of al-Bāṭin.

[17] Ṣāliḥ ʿUmar says the *kaylah* is a wooden grain measure of 4 *athmān*, approximately 12 kilograms, when the grain has been separated from the stalk and winnowed. They say also *kaylat ʿishr*.

[18] This tradition is quoted by Sayyid Muḥammad b. Ḥasan al-ʿAṭṭās, *Riśalah fī ansāb al-qabāʾil*, transcript in my possession, writing in 1331/1913. A variant tradition he cites is that they were *mawālī* of the Umayyads.

[19] Cf. my Hūd and other pre-Islamic Prophets of Ḥaḍramawt, *Le Muséon* LXVII, Louvain 1954, p. 130.

AL-QĀRAH. South at the head
Courtesy of the former Information Office, Aden
Al-Qārah showing its location in relation to the surrounding countryside. This photograph was probably taken about 1953

The Drum of Yāfiᶜ and their Wars with the Zaydīs

The drum plays an important role in tribal life both in the Yemen of the Zaydī Imāms and the former Aden Protectorates[20]. It is, says Landberg[21], the »prérogative du pouvoir dans le sud« and the Sultans are *ahl al-marāfiᶜ wa-ʾl-ṭuwas*, people of drums and kettledrums[22]. It is the signal of the chiefs and is beaten after the prayer. I heard it in al-Qārah (of north Yemen), headquarters of Imām al-Badr in 1964, beaten in one mountain after another to warn probably of the thrust of Nasserite troops to the north. The copper brass (*naḥās/ṣufr*[23]) drum (*ṭabl*) of Yāfiᶜ is particularly famous. It is said to have been found in the ruins at Ḥaṭāṭ (near al-Mawṣatah?). Informants thought the drum might have Ḥimyar writing on it and remount to the time of ᶜĀd. It is said to be square-ish in shape and have writings on it described as *ṭalāsim siḥriyyah*, magic talismans.

For the part played by the Drum in the wars with the Zaydīs that follows I am indebted to ᶜAlawī b. Aḥmad al-ᶜAfīfī of Jiᶜār, a Governmental official in 1964.

[20] See, in particular, of references in my writings, R. B. Serjeant & Ronald Lewcock, *Ṣanᶜāʾ: an Arabian Islamic city*, London 1983, indices.
[21] *Ḥadramoût*, Leiden 1901, p. 642-3.
[22] *Gloss. daṯ.*, 1337.
[23] In the Yemen *naḥās* can mean »brass«. See *Ṣanᶜā*, *op. cit.*, p. 226a.

AL-QĀRAH. South at the head
Courtesy of the former Western Aden Protectorate Office
Al-Qārah is a mesa nearly inaccessible and well fortified. The main gateway or Siddah (right front) is in shadow, with roads leading to it. When tribes enter the Siddah they become like brothers (*ikhwān*), hostilities being suspended. The cluster of domed buildings will be tombs of saints. The four domed building is probably the Jīlānī Mosque and an earlier photograph shows a minaret on its northern side. A cistern shows at the middle top, collecting the run-off from the rising ground to the left of it. Terracing for cultivation has been constructed wherever possible

»We heard from the old people (*qadīmīn*) that it [the Drum] was in Jabal Jār hill about three miles from the north side (*al-shiqq al-qiblī*) of al-Qārah. When the Yemenis occupied bilād Yāfiᶜ their headquarters (*al-maḥaṭṭah al-rayīsiyy* (sic)) was Masjid al-Nūr. Than the Copper Drum (*ṭabl al-naḥās*) moved (*itḥarrak*), with it being the Amīrah Nūr bint al-ᶜAfīf[24] and the entire Qāsidī branch [of Yāfiᶜ], the Copper Drum beating of its own accord in front of the tribes like a band (*al-muzīkah*), without anyone seeing it, but hearing it. When the Yemeni tribes (*qawm al-Yaman*) heard it and the [Yāfiᶜī] tribes they fled from Yāfiᶜ. Yāfiᶜ al-ᶜUlyā and Yāfiᶜ banī Qāsid joined together[25] against the Yemeni tribes. The last post (*maḥaṭṭah*) with the Yemenis was in al-ᶜUrr[26] in which they settled for many years. Then Yāfiᶜ contrived and burrowed in the ground under the mountain until they reached the fort in which the Yemeni tribes were living, using hammers, mallets (*maḍārib*) and chisels (? *f r ṣah*[27]). They spent fifteen years in burrowing before they came under the fort. As soon as the Yemeni tribes heard the burrowing underneath them they fled beyond Yāfiᶜī territory (*ḥudūd*) and have stayed in al-Bayḍā᾽ up until this time. Then the Copper Drum returned to Jabal Jār. In olden time Jabal Jār was inhabited but now (1964) it is devoid of inhabitants. This is what we/I know«. Masjid al-Nūr is in al-Mawsaṭah and the tomb of Nūr bint ᶜAfīf is there. Women were formerly fighters and she was killed while fighting for the ᶜAfīfīs. I was told that the Drum is with Haddār b. Muḥammad, a Sultan of Āl ᶜAfīf, but I have no further information about this person.

The afore-going narrative displays a recollection of events some two centuries and a half earlier; perhaps this is oral tradition, but perhaps not entirely so for the Ahl Bin ᶜUbādī living in the village of al-Najd of Maᶜrabān of Yahar who were Quḍāt al-Dawlah, Sultanic Qāḍīs, were said to have history (*tārīkh*). Traces of the Zaydī occupation in the form of ruins survive, they say, especially at Qumāṭah, Jāz, al-Ḥadīdah, Wādī Ḥaṭāṭ, Jabal Wādī Ḥummā, Jabal Ṣanam/Sanam[28] and a *qaryah* above al-ᶜIrqah. I recall also in Faḍlī territory Qaryat am-Qaḥāb, Harlots' Village, said to be so called after the Zaydī soldiers who frequented it!

[24] In Yāfiᶜ as also among the ᶜAwdhalīs, the Sultan was called *Amr* and his amīrs were known as Sultan, but there seems to have been a change in nomenclature over latter years.

[25] The Arabic is a little ambiguous – it might be that the Amīrah united the tribes, but this is unlikely.

[26] Ḥusayn Hādī ᶜAwad says al-ᶜUrr is near al-Ḥadd and in it is a large building, Ḥuṣn Ibn Kirbāl with writing on pillars.

[27] Cf. *Ṣanᶜā᾽*, *furaṣ*, etc., pl. *furāṣāt*.

[28] I wrote *ṣanam*, but Sāliḥ ᶜUmar says *sinam* is correct.

Al-Qārah – its Special Status

ᶜAlawī b. Aḥmad al.ᶜAfīfī told me that al-Qārah is a *ḥawṭah.* He also distinguished two types of *ḥawṭah*, a saint's *ḥawṭah* (*ḥawṭat al-waliyy*) and the rulers' *ḥawṭah* (*ḥawṭat al-ḥukkām*), the latter being an entirely new concept to me – other persons indeed have denied that such a category exists. In the Zabīd district of the Yemeni Tihāmah I found *ḥawṭah* to be used in the sense of a cemetery; as a cemetery generally has at least one saint's tomb, the term may have come to apply to the sacred enclave in general that surrounds a saint's tomb. In al-Qārah itself the main mosque is called Masjid al-Jīlānī after the famous Ṣūfī saint and there are said to be many mosques in Yāfiᶜ bearing his name, but this can hardly be the reason for calling it a *ḥawṭah.* However, be what may, up to approximately one mile out of al-Qārah in all directions is holy (*muqaddas*) territory. Tribes in a state of hostility with other (Yāfiᶜī) tribes if they go straight into al-Qārah through their own territory would not clash with them, but if they happen to meet with oneanother on their joint boundaries they might do so, but there is of course no fighting once they are in al-Qārah. Perhaps it is more like the Yemeni *hijrah*[29] than a *ḥawṭah*, perhaps its »holy« nature is even pre-Islamic.

Like the other tribes Yāfiᶜīs have their own tribal slogans[30] – Yaḥarīs shout »I am the wolf of Ḥimyar, *Anā dhīb Ḥimyar*«, while the others cry »*Anā dhīb Kalad*«, etcetera. Yāfiᶜ's proud boast is:

> Into ten parts tribal honour is split.
> Yāfiᶜ has nine parts – the rest – the tenth bit.

> اَلْقَبوَلَهْ عَشَرَهْ قسُومْ يِتْقَسَّمْ[31]
> تِسعَهْ لِيَافِعْ وآلبَقِيّه العَاشِرْ

To this Āl ᶜUmar Bā ᶜUmar (of al-ᶜAwābithah) made the riposte:

> Bū Sitt[32], prithee, who 's he when honour 's split?
> With us is he, or you in the tenth bit?

> بآنشِدْك مَنْ بوْ سِتّ لَمَّا تَقَسَّمَتْ
> هْو عِنْدَنا أو عِنْدَكمْ فيِ العاشِر؟

The allusion is to the fact that Yāfiᶜ has no port or direct access to the sea and used to pay to the Faḍlī Sultan, Bū Sitt, when passing through his territory *ᶜushūr*, a capitation tax on each person – which was considered

29 See for *hijrah*, *Ṣanᶜāʾ*, p. 39–43, *passim.*

30 Cf. my 'Dawlah, tribal shaykhs, the manṣab of the Waliyyah Saᶜīdah, qasāmah, in the Faḍlī sultanate, South Arabian Federation', *Maḥmūd al-Ghūl Commemoration Volume* (forthcoming), p. 122.

31 *Rajaz* metre. In the second line *wa-ʾl-baqiyyah al-ᶜāshir* is pronounced *wal-baqīyil-ᶜāshir* which fits the metre, the final *hāʾ* of *baqiyyah* being eliminated through it is felt to be there. I have noticed a similar phenomenon in Iraqi printed colloquial verse. The verses were quoted to me by Muḥammad ᶜAbd al-Qādir Bā Maṭraf.

32 The nickname of the house of the Faḍlī Sultans. See article cited in fn. 30, p. 129.

the greatest humiliation (*hiyānah*). This was distinct from any tax that might be paid on goods.

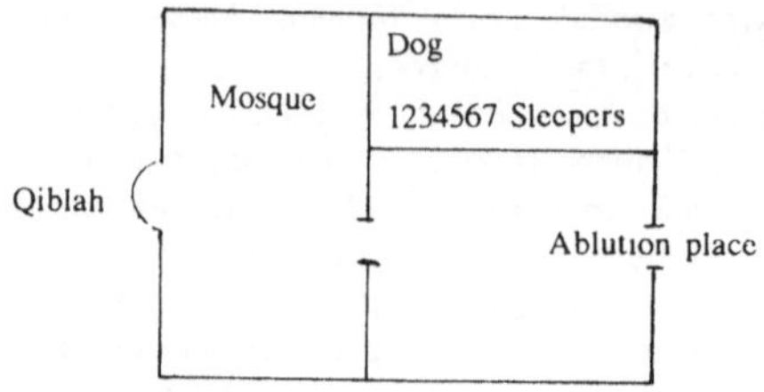

Rough sketch of the tombs of the Seven Sleepers in the Saʿdī tribal district

Some Places to which Legends are Attached

In Saʿdī territory the Seven Sleepers (Ahl al-Kahf) have a mosque (*masjid*) and grave/cemetery (*maqbarah*) with special domes (*qubab*) and also a cave in a mountain which I recorded as Jabal Ṣanam[33] but Ṣāliḥ ʿUmar writes to say it should be corrected to Sinam, which overlooks Falasān village. The cave is near a village called al-Maṣnaʿah. The mountain is said to have the shape of a person prostrating himself in the direction of Mecca, and the cave is situated in relation to the sun exactly as described in Sūrah XVIII,16 – »And you would see the sun when it rose inclining from their cave towards the right and when it set passing them by on the left, while they were in an open part of it. The old town nearby to which the Seven Sleepers, called here al-Sabʿ al-Sujūd, the Seven Prostrators, went when they woke up, is called nowadays al-Khirbah (map al-Kharibah), the Ruin. It was the place of the family al-Baṭāṭī, known to me in Ḥaḍramawt. Ibn al-Mujāwir[34] says the Seven Sleepers' cave is one of the caves of Jabal Ṣabir of Taʿizz: and I was told in the Yemen that it is still known, east of the mountain under the peak and there is a *masjid* there. If you enter the cave carrying a light it goes out. The Ahl Saʿd and the Sultan often meet together at al-Khirbah.

At Rahwat Jār[35] said to be a »white mountain« there is a stone which is a sort of *mashhad* (perhaps best rendered with Lane as »a place of religious visitation«) that belongs to Miryam. Any person passing by it for the first time places some offering there, e.g., sweet basil (*shuqr*[36]), eggs or stone (*ḥajar*). Where the name Miryam occurs in this and other places in the Yemens I suspect that it is a vestige of Christianity easy to assimilate into Islam.

[33] My informant must have understood the names as *ṣanam*, an idol, because he remarked that if a person indulges in frivolous talk (*kalām khafīf*), it might be said to him: *Ant rūḥ taʿbud al-ṣanam*, You go and worship the idol/Ṣanam mountain!
[34] O. Löfgren, *Descriptio Arabiae Meridionalis*, Leiden 1951-54, p. 158.
[35] Nigel Groom, *Dictionary of Arabic topography and placenames*, Beirut-London 1983, p. 237, gives as the best sense for *rahwah*, »hillocks on elevated ground«.
[36] For *shuqr*, sweet basil, associated with Shaqr the pre-Islamic Moon God, see Walter Dostal, Some remarks on the ritual significance of the bull in pre-Islamic South Arabia, *Arabian and Islamic Studies: articles presented to R. B. Serjeant*, ed. Robin Bidwell & G. Rex Smith, London 1983, p. 197, reading *mashqūr* for *mashkūr*.

Judgement, Trial by Ordeal (bish^cah)

The law, customary law in the main we may be sure, and the hearing of pleas, probably follows procedures similar to those I have reported from the Faḍlī Sultanate[37]; some practices, I noted, were also current in the ʿAwdhalī Sultanate. With Sultan ʿAlawī al-ʿAfīfī, unfortunately, I only had the opportunity to discuss *bishʿah*[38] – conveniently translated as trial by ordeal. I have found an allusion to it in pre-Islamic Yemen[39] and it may still not have entirely disappeared in northern Arabia[40] though there and in the south it comes under heavy attack from Islamic reformists and the 'enlightened' *shabāb*. It used to be practised by the Yaharī, Kaladī and Yazīdī/Ahl Yazīd tribes, but with appeal to al-Qārah. Mutual consent of the two parties to a suit to proceed to *bishʿah* is necessary. There are three types, *bishʿat al-nār, bishʿat al-khayṭ* and *bishʿat al-qirbah.* For each there is a different formula which is inscribed onto the instrument with which the *bishʿah* is performed. The first and third types were stated, in 1964, to be still current.

Bishʿat al-nār is the well known ordeal with the red hot iron. If the tongue, after being flicked with the iron, remains red the accused is innocent (*bariyy*). The *bishʿat al-qirbah,* ordeal of the water-skin has a special *sijill* (formula ?) of *ṭalāsim* and *asmāʾ*, names (probably of Allah) and they write: »So and so, if he be innocent exonerate him and if he be guilty declare him guilty (*Fulān b. fulān idhā hū bariyy ibrī-h wa-in hū āthim āthmī-h*)«. The water-skin is then slowly inflated, the two (plaintiff and defendant) standing in front of it. As it expands so does the stomach of the accused *al-mathūm* if he is guilty!

No data on *bishʿat al-khayṭ*, the thread ordeal, were forthcoming but Ṣāliḥ ʿUmar writes of *al-ḥilyah/ḥulyah* or *bishʿat al-khayṭ* that it is a precious stone (*min al-aḥjār al-karīmah*) about the size of a large olive, tied by a thread to the ring (*khātam*) of the person undertaking this process. The two suspects come and seat themselves before the *mubashshiʿ* who has in front of him a glass or enamelled iron bowl which he fills half-full of water. On one side of the bowl he writes the name of one of the litigants (*al-mutakhāṣimayn*) and the name of his mother and, on the other, the name of the second man and that of his mother also. »Then the *mubashshiʿ* ups, as if speaking confidentially (*yunājī*) to someone, and goes on stirring the ornament (*ḥilyah*) around in the bowl«. When the stirring stops and the stone comes to rest on one side or the other the process ends and the name of the guilty party is disclosed. Perhaps the names of the parties' mothers, not their fathers, are written because of the existence of the custom of *tawrīd* or provision of a concubine for the guest[41]. Ṣāliḥ comments that »all these processes are a sort of sleight of hand (*shahʿwadhah*) which Islam does not ratify – sometimes they hit and often they miss«.

The occasion did not permit of a systematic enquiry into tribal codes,

[37] See article cited in fn. 30, p. 118.

[38] Heinrich Freiherr von Maltzan, *Reise nach Südarabien*, Braunschweig 1873, p. 294 *seq.* reports that 'the ʿAfīfī is the most famous »Gottesrichter« and »Feuerrichter« (*mubashshiʿ?*) in this part of south Arabia'.

[39] Cf. *Cambridge history of Arabic literature*, 1983, I, p. 125 *seq.*

[40] *Bishʿah* was, up till fairly recently at least, practised in Jordan.

[41] I have not actually heard that *tawrīd* is known in Yāfiʿ but it was very widely practised in south Arabia as we know from Ibn al-Mujāwir. See p. 94-5 *infra*.

written or unwritten, of offences and penalties, but it was said in the course of conversation that, in the case of a hen or a cock entering standing crops, different fines are imposed – the cock is always looking about him but the hen concentrates on feeding, thus causing greater loss of grain! Likewise with cattle a tail-less animal causes less damage to standing crops than a beast vigorously swishing its tail from side to side! It would be interesting to follow up other aspects of agricultural customary law.

Al-Jarmūzī on the Zaydī Conquest of al-Raṣṣās and Yāfiᶜ (11th/17th Century)

Let me now turn from these brief notes on Yāfiᶜ made almost in passing which might nonetheless form the basis of further fieldwork, to be correlated also with the Aden archival material housed in the Commonwealth Relations Office Library. In 1964, through the courtesy of the Mukallā Residency I was able to xerox the copy of al-Jarmūzī's *al-Sīrat al-Mutawakkiliyyah* in the Sultanic Library, which covers the reign of Imām al-Mutawakkil (1054–1087/1644–1676). It gives a vivid account of the resounding victory at Najd al-Salaf in 1065/1654–55 over the Mashriq tribes and the conquest of al-Raṣṣāṣ and Yāfiᶜ, followed, in a short space of years by that of Ḥaḍramawt as far as Ẓafār[42]. The Zaydī leaders seem to have used mainly Zaydī tribal contingents. This was the peak of their expansion but the Imāms' power gradually declined and the tribes broke free of central government. The Yāfiᶜī version supra of these event compares with al-Jarmūzī's contemporary report of them; it seems a little blurred into legend but the two accounts are not inconsistent.

Before dealing with the campaign – *al-Makhraj al-manṣūr ilā jihāt al-Mashriq wa-nawāḥī Ḥaḍramawt*[43], al-Jarmūzī gives a revealing description of the Manṣab of ᶜĪnāt in Wādī Ḥadramawt and of his relations with the tribes of Yāfiᶜ.

> 'Now Yāfiᶜī country (*bilād Yāfiᶜ*) and what adjoins it exercise authority (*yataḥakkamūn*)[44] for a man of Āl Abī Bakr b. Sālim of the Ashrāf, the Āl Bā ᶜAlawī, it being said that they are of the offspring of al-Ḥusayn b. ᶜAlī (peace upon him[45]) and of the posterity of Mūsā b. Jaᶜfar (peace on them both), as al-Ahdal[46] has mentioned in his history called *ᶜUmdat al-ṭālib fī ansāb Āl Abī Ṭālib,* and they are devoted to speaking of him, alleging that he has supernatural phenomena (*al-khawāriq*) which exert an influence on the world. They hate people of learning (*ᶜilm*), on which [subject] they [talk] at length, and they especially detest the Zay-

[42] The Zaydīs and Ibāḍīs of Oman clashed here. See my 'Omani naval activities off the southern Arabian coast in the 11th/17th century from Yemeni chronicles', *Journal of Oman Studies*, VI, I, p. 81 *seq.*
[43] Mukallā Ms. p. 129 *seq.*
[44] I have translated *yataḥakkamūn* in accordance with the senses in the lexicons, but I wonder if it means that they take their cases for judgement to ...
[45] The Zaydī abbreviation علیلم is always used.
[46] This is the title of a well known work by Ibn ᶜInabah (C. Brockelmann, *GAL.*, *Sup.*, II, p. 271). There is a Zaydī author, al-Husayn b. ᶜAbd al-Rahmān al-Ahdal, who wrote *Tuḥfat al-zaman bi-dhikr Sādāt al-Yaman* about the early 9th/15th century. So al-Jarmūzī may have confused the two. One must remember his *Sīrah* was not completed and there appear to be errors and mis-spelling of names in a number of places.

diyyah and other people of learning, though they perform the prayer, fast and go on pilgrimage; music (*ṭarab*) they deem lawful and all musical instruments (*al-malāhī*), considering them obedience (to Allah[47]). The inhabitants of Ḥadramawt, its badw and settled folk (*ḥaḍar*) alike, go along with what has already been remarked.'

'My learned cousin (? *al-ṣinw al-fāḍil*), Ghawth al-Dīn b. Muḥammad, God rest him, told me that in the year 1038/1628 or 1039/1629–30 he came across a man from the western districts (*maghārib*) of Dhamār wearing the dress of the inhabitants of Ḥadramawt and the patched garment (*khirqah*) of Sufism, with a humility and responsiveness (*iqbāl*) about him. (He continued) 'So I asked him where he had been and he said: »With the Ḥabīb[48] Ḥusayn«, the account of whom and some of his characteristics comes (later), he having been with his father Abū Bakr b. Sālim before him. (He added) that he entered into their *ṭarīqah* with them until the strong desire overcame him to put abominations (*istiḥsān al-qabā'iḥ*) to rights. Then he told them many things about them[49].'

'One of these was that he met with a man, an inhabitant of a town (*balad*) (which he named – I think it was the town of the Sultan – who was there[50] with a woman of high standing among them, as had the man also, and (he continued) »whosoever came she had intercourse with them«[51]. [So he said], disapproving of them: »Are you not committing evil actions and doing what is forbidden?« and he made much outcry against them. So the two said together: »This is no action of ours; that is the ruling of the decree and determination (*ḥukm al-qaḍā' wa-l-qadar*) [of Allah] only«[52]. Then their case was disclosed to a person with pretensions to learning (*ʿilm*) and there was a great quoting of authorities (? *ʿaẓuma l-riwāyah*) and mighty volume of highminded talk (*fakhuma 'l-ḥikāyah*) and [finally] he said: »Praise to Allah who inspired us with the doctrine of the decree and determination (of Allah)«. Then he commanded that everyone should proceed at a trotting pace (*yazuff/yaziff*[53]) to his house, honoured and respected. (He con-

47 A case in point is at the Saqqāf Mosque in Tarīm with its musicians, the Servants of the Saqqāf who sing Sufi songs to pipe and drum. See my *Prose and Poetry from Ḥadramawt*, London 1951, p. 40 *seq.* I have attended a *ḥaḍrah* in the Ḥuraydah Mosque where Sufi *nashīds* were accompanied by music.

48 Ḥaḍramī Sayyids are addressed by the title Ḥabīb.

49 There is confusion here over the application of the pronominal suffixes.

50 Reading *wujida*.

51 This appears to be an allusion to the custom of *tawrīd*. It is a little surprising to find this tribal custom in Saywūn in the 11th/17th century. In 1964 I noted that the Ḥumūm tribes have a custom (*silfah*) with wife or daughter, that she is lent to a guest. This is a loan in the real sense since the guest will provide the same in return when he is visited by the tribesman who had provided him with this entertainment. The Ḥumūmī says: '*Ḍayfī*, my guest!' and the woman sleeps with him. A Ḥumūmī woman may say of a child of hers: '*Kasabtah*', literally 'I earned him', perhaps adding: 'This is the child of a Sayyid', or 'an *ʿaskarī*', etc. All this is said quite openly, the child having been conceived while the woman's husband was away. The narrator is a little prudish for similar customs were current in the Yemen of the time of Ibn al-Mujāwir and even today I was told the story of a tribeswoman who asked which of her three daughters would like 'to keep the guest warm'. By implication a *Ḥadīth* indicates that it was recognized that the wife whose husband was away might take a lover in the Prophet's time, but I hope to develop this theme further. What perhaps is most surprising about this case is that a Ḥaḍramī *ʿālim* seems to have found an argument for tolerating the custom.

52 The argument appears to be that since their actions are pre-destined they are not responsible for them, hardly a belief likely to appeal to the Muʿtazilī Zaydīs.

53 *Zaffa*, trottiner à petits pas (*Gloss. daṯ.*), conduct a bride to her husband's house. 'Honoured and respected' is plural.

tinued): »And when I saw this come from them I realised my mistake in entering with them [into the *ṭarīqah*] and myself fled to this country, repentant, withdrawing from staying among them«. As for the badw of them they are the same as the others of them, the description of whom will come [below] if Allah wills.'

Al-Jarmūzī now turns to the despatch by the Imām al-Mu'ayyad of a shaykh, al-Asadī, a bedouin (*bādī*)[54], a truthful and religious minded man, to the Sultan of Ḥaḍramawt, ʿAbdullāh b. ʿUmar b. Badr b. Jaʿfar al-Kathīrī[55] in 1040/1630–31 or 1041/1631–32, with a letter the content of which consisted of imāmic invocations and exhortations. Al-Asadī's account follows verbatim.

'When the Sultan acquainted himself with it (the letter), he being at the time in his place (*maḥall*) known as Saywūn, he said to me after (my) staying with him for about a week[56]: »The reply to the Imām will be only after making (it) known to the Ḥabīb[57] and receiving his honourable advice and you will be with us until his reply comes back«. He, meaning the Sultan, gave orders to his secretary to go to the afore-mentioned Ḥabīb to his place known as ʿĪnāt, sending with him the letter of the Imām (peace upon him). So I said to the Sultan: »And I should like to visit (*ziyārah*) the Ḥabīb«, my purpose being to get to know about his circumstances so as to inform the Imām (peace upon him) of them. So they had me ride with them and we arrived at his place with part of the night still remaining and they left me in a resthouse and the Sultan's man in another, each of us being next to the Domed (Tomb) of his father the shaykh Abū Bakr b. Sālim in which the lamps[58] were lit but there were no carpets in it and the tomb also was bare while in and around it were about four hundred persons, the majority of them of Yāfiʿ, declaiming *lā ilāha illa 'llāh* and shouting at the top of their voices: »Yā Ḥabīb, yā Ḥabīb!« meaning the afore-mentioned Ḥabīb, the while beating drums and tambourines (*ṭārāt*) and playing (*yarfaʿūn*) pipes (*shabbābāt*[59]). (He continued): So I questioned the man who had been put in charge of entertaining us about them, and he said: »There are some who stay a month, some who stay for two months, and less and more, without seeing the Ḥabīb, and sometimes he closets himself with one of them and discloses to him (? *yaẓhur ʿalayhi*) and informs him about himself and the name of his wife[60], his own name and the name of his village (*balad*)«.

The afore-mentioned Shaykh said in his account:

So I realised that he leaves them like that until he become apprised of much information about them and links news of their notables/

[54] Al-Asadī is described as *min ḥudhdhāq al-ʿawāmm*, (probably) a headman of the ordinary folk. It looks as if he were a village tribal elder.

[55] Muḥammad b. Hāshim, *op. cit.*, p. 67 *seq.*

[56] *Thamāniyah ayyām.*

[57] *I.e.* Ḥusayn.

[58] *Qanādīl*, perhaps 'candelabra', but in *Ṣanʿā'*, p. 230a, *qanādīl* are evidently pottery lamps.

[59] A Ḥaḍramī *shabbābah* is illustrated in W. H. Ingrams, *Arabia and the Isles*, London 1942, frontispiece. *Yarfaʿūn* lit., 'raising'.

[60] Yemenis would probably consider it *ʿayb* that the name of the wife be disclosed.

familiars in their country with him[61]. So they spread about in the land[62] and testify that he has knowledge of hidden things. (He continued): And we/I likewise were/was not permitted [to enter his presence]. As for the Sultan's man he was given permission.

When the second or third day arrived I was permitted (to enter) so I entered his presence and found him in a large room filled with[63] his entourage (*ḥadafah*[64]) while various kinds of musical instruments were being played beside him, one after another (*wa-ālāt al-malāhī ʿalā ʾanwāʿi-hā tuttakhadh ʿinda-hu shayʾan fa-shayʾan*)[65]. I perceived him to be a stout man with a lot of hair, his head not shaven[66], his moustache unclipped, his nails untrimmed. By him stood two women teasing out his hair with combs, wearing fine clothes and jewellery. I asked about them and they said: »[They belong] to the dancers (*min al-laʿʿābīn*) whom they call beggar minstrels (*shuḥḥadh*[67]) whose profession is music (*ʿādat-hum al-ṭarab*) and whose women dance at the [places] of the immoral«. They were to be found among the people of the Yemen all over, before the Imāms (peace upon them) took possession of the Yemen. They (i.e. the two women) have devoted themselves (*waqafā anfusa-humā*) solely to the service of the Shaykh (al-Ḥusayn). (He continued): We were thus (engaged) when, from another door at the lower end of the reception room (*al-īwān*[68]), a youth appeared [who looked] as if the hair had (just) begun to sprout on his face. For him was placed a chair upon which he sat, two women being with him, likewise combing his hair for him. So I inquired about him and was told: »This is al-Ḥusayn's son called Aḥmad Jaḥḥāf«[69]. Then (al-Ḥusayn) began to question me about the Imām, the gist of what he said, though it was more *verbatim,* being: »Where al-Sayyid Muḥammad (Imām al-Muʾayyad) is concerned there is good (*barakah*) in him, but as for the such-and-such (in terms not per-

61 Imām Aḥmad of the Yemen is said to have found out details about the relatives of tribesmen and others visiting him and surprised and overawed them by asking them about their fathers, uncles of brothers, sometimes displaying a knowledge of certain intimate details about them.

62 Though not actually Qurʾān this phrase reflects Qurʾānic passages.

63 Text, incorrectly, *mamlū-an*.

64 *Ḥafadah* can of course mean 'grandchildren' and a Sayyid *majlis* in Ḥaḍramawt could well have many family members.

65 I recall having heard either *maʾkhadh* or *mawkhadh* somewhere in south Arabia as meaning a certain type of ditty but I have been unable to discover this in my field notes or elsewhere.

66 The *ḥaḍar* in general and certainly the ulema, in my experience, have their heads shaven and for al-Ḥusayn and not to shave his moustache would be an affectation of bedouinism/tribalism. Yāfiʿī soldiery have moustaches.

67 See *Gloss. daṯ.* 2623 *seq.* These dancing girls undoubtedly are of the same class of south Arabian society as the group I encountered in Dathīnah in 1954. See my 'The Maʿn »Gypsies« of the West Aden Protectorate', *Anthropos*, Posieux (Fribourg), LXVI, 1961, p. 737-49. As the so-called Maʿn girls are supposed to come from the Yemen they might even be descendants of, or related to the *shuḥḥadh* described by al-Asadī. The Maʿn would move via Mukayras, am-Ṣawmaʿah to the top of Wādī Bayhān to purvey their wares. There are indications that similar groups existed in the time of the first Zaydī Imām al-Hādī ila ʾl-Ḥaqq. *Cf.* ʿAlī b. Muḥammad al-ʿAbbāsī al-ʿAlawī, *Sīrat al-Hādī ila ʾl-Ḥaqq*, ed. Suhayl Zakkār, Beirut 1392/1972, p. 94.

68 *Īwān* is probably equivalent here to *dīwān*, Rossi's sala per ricevere.

69 *Cf. infra* p. 104. The biographers do not mention the name Jahhāf.

> missible to repeat) al-Ḥasan and al-Ḥusayn[70] they did this and that with Ḥaydar Pasha, and with ʿĀbidīn Pasha, this and that«[71].'

Since the Ḥabīb and those present believe that nobody may contradict him, al-Asadī replies tactfully and rises to kiss his feet. While this was going on –

> 'The muezzin gave the call to mid-day prayer and those there said: »The Ḥabīb has left, the Ḥabīb has left«. (He continued): And there he was, still, not moving, as if he were dead, they, the while, saying to one another (*yatalākatūna*[72]) that he had gone to Mecca. (He continued): So they waited a long time for him – then lo and behold, he stirred and spoke, and they got up to greet him.'

Al-Jarmūzī says that he had heard from others that up until now no private or public reception (*majlis*) is without musical instruments. He was told of a dome in Ḥaḍramawt 'over one of their ignorant (*jahalah*) persons', doubtless a saint, with a mosque around it where he attended a *majlis al-qirāʾah* where he heard 'lying tales and frivolous irreligious stories with music (*fi ʾl-ṭarab*). In a book there on the virtues (*manāqib*) of the Shaykhs it was said of Shaykh Fulān that the Almighty Lord manifested Himself to him, and of Shaykh Fulān that prophethood was offered him on several occasions but that he refused it out of veneration for the Apostle of Allah, and suchlike outlandish things. In the country of the Raṣṣāṣ and adjoining Musʿabayn and Murād tribes not one in a thousand can be found who prays[73] or is acquainted with the obligations of the divine law or reason (*al-taklīf al-sharʿī aw al-ʿaqlī*), the badw of them especially who take pride only in hospitality (*ḍiyāfāt*) and security of the roads. An eye-witness told al-Jarmūzī's son that when Sultan Aḥmad b. ʿAlī al-Raṣṣāṣ died his corpse 'was borne from his house on poles accompanied by women on both sides weaving their hair (*nāshirāt*) [their heads] uncovered[74] to a cemetery of theirs. As for the women playing lutes (*ʿawwādāt*), those with musical instruments and the dancers to whom the Mashriq[75] has become a home and for whom the properties of the inhabitants of it has become a place to eat, they go along by his corpse and shave some of their hair and hock (*yaʿqirna*) their camels, their menfolk doing likewise till, at each pace or paces, there are many *ʿaqīrahs*[76], while their voices are loud in wailing and lamentation'.

Of the Raṣṣāṣ, al-Jarmūzī remarks that the kings of the Yemen neglected

[70] Imām al-Muʾayyad's brothers, active in the campaigns leading to the expulsion of the Ottoman Turks.

[71] Ḥaydar Pasha was the last effective Ottoman governor of the Yemen. A. S. Tritton, *Rise of the Imams of Sanaa*, Madras 1925, mentions as following him, Aidin, for which ʿĀbidīn seems a better reading.

[72] Enquiries have been unable to elicit the sense of this word so the rendering is conjectural. This episode examplified what is known colloquially as *khaṭwah* or *daḥqah*, lit., 'step'; it occurs in the hagiologies. The Sufi moves in spirit to some other place, temporarily leaving his body in situ.

[73] This is not exaggeration – for tribal ignorance or disregard for the Fast and Prayer see *Ṣanʿāʾ*, p. 310.

[74] For weaving the hair *cf.* my *South Arabian Hunt*, London 1976, p. 66, 109.

[75] Al-Mashriq is the eastern side of the Yemen.

[76] Landberg, *Ḥadramoût*, p. 459, says an *ʿaqīrah* is always 'en vertu d'un vœu', adding that 'le Sâdah n'en veulent pas savoir et le considèrent comme *makrūh*'.

them and none paid them any attention except Sinān[77] Pasha who conquered their country and that of Yāfiᶜ and the adjoining territories in about four years, but when the Imām rose the Turks removed from them, and they returned to their former state. The Raṣṣāṣī Sultan, he says, has no creed (*iᶜtiqādāt*) but hate of the Āl Muḥammad (i.e. the Zaydī Imāms)[78] and has no regard for the Zaydiyyah but orders the non-arms-bearing classes (*ahl al-ḥaḍar*[79]) in his country to make the *khuṭbah* in the name of the Ottoman Sultan (*Sulṭān al-Rūm*) as also the blessing on him (*al-duᶜā lahu*) in imitation of the afore-said Shaykh al-Ḥabīb (Ḥusayn b. Abī Bakr b. Sālim).

In their triumphant progress of conquest of the Yemen following on their expulsion of the Ottoman Turks, the Zaydīs determined to bring the Raṣṣāṣīs and other tribes under their domination.

The Zaydī Conquest of al-Raṣṣāṣ and Yāfiᶜ

The Zaydīs opened their campaign by moving to al-Zahrā[80] where they established a camp from which to invade the territory of the Sultan al-Raṣṣāṣ. He in turn assembled over 30,000 men from the ᶜAwāliq, Yāfiᶜ and other Mashriq sultanates. They prepared to engage the Zaydīs at Najd al-Salaf[81] 'it being the gate to their country and the only road to it', and they imposed a daily levy of dirhams, sheep and grain on al-Bayḍāʾ.

Al-Ḥabīb Sālim b. Aḥmad wrote to al-Raṣṣāṣ, saying that 'the Zaydiyyah will be a morsel (*ṭuᶜmah*[82]) for you', declaring he had delivered them over to him and sending him a rosary which would take the place of great armies. On a further occasion he despatched one of their ill-favoured banners (*rāyāt-hum al-mankūsah*[83]) with a slave to bear it. The Sultan placed entire confidence in what the Ḥabīb had promised him while the Ḥabīb's messenger accompanying 'the banner of error' declared that the words of his Shaykh were true and that bullets would not hit him[84] but if

[77] Aḥmad b. Muḥammad b. Ṣalāḥ al-Sharafī, seemingly the author of the text used by Tritton (perhaps the *'akhbār'* noted by al-Shawkānī, *al-Badr al-ṭāliᶜ*, Cairo 1348 H.; Ms. f. 32a), states that, in 1004/1595–6, Sinān conquered Yāfiᶜ and built a fort at Khalaqah later beseiged by Yāfiᶜ. 'The Amīr Sinān used to respect the people of Yāfiᶜ because of what he had come to know of their great courage at the time of his entering their country and their fighting him in it'. For this reason doubtless the Faḍlī Sultans and certain of their tribes have the slogan (*ᶜazwah*), *'Anā dhayb Sanān/Sinān* I am the wolf of Sinān'. See *Mahmūd al-Ghūl Commemoration Volume*, p. 122.

[78] Al-Jarmūzī was told that the Sultan 'may, each Friday, pray two *rakᶜahs*, not in the proper way of prayer (*ᶜalā ghayr ṣifat al-ṣalāh*) after washing his hair with *sidr* (Zizyphus spina Christi) leaf. He has two women who tease out his hair with the comb. All the people of the afore-said district go in for very long hair'.

[79] The villagers?

[80] Ṣāliḥ ᶜUmar says this should read Zāhir.

[81] Najd al-Salaf/al-Aslāf or Najd al-Ḥājj is south of Yarīm (*Ṣanᶜāʾ*, p. 80b). Yāfiᶜ had inflicted a heavy defeat on the Turks there about sixty years earlier.

[82] *Ṭuᶜmah* is 'an assigned means of subsistence' etc. (Lane) but Ḥabīb Sālim has probably in mind the Hadīth: *Wa-qitāl-un ᶜalā hādhihi l-ṭuᶜmah* where *ṭuᶜmah* is said by Ibn al-Athīr, *al-Nihāyah*, III, p. 38, to mean *fayʾ*, booty.

[83] *Mankūsah*, lit., upside down. I have rendered it in the sense given by Dozy, *Supplément*, défavourable, but Ṣāliḥ ᶜUmar says that this is a custom – to send a banner reversed – to incite the tribes to one's aid. The Manṣab used to have a green and white *bayraq* with him to indicate his arrival or to protect himself at tribal battles and 'loosen the interlocking of those fighting oneanother'.

[84] He would be what the Yemenis term *'muṣarraf'*. The late Imām Aḥmad of the Yemen was popularly believed to have immunity from bullets or sword cuts.

they did it would only be to wound him. So the Zaydī musketeers poured lead into him, very few bullets missing, his skull scattered into splinters and he fell down into Hell-fire! His head was cut off and his banner became a plaything for those in the Imāmic sūq.

The Zaydīs advanced to Qāʿ al-Rumāh, north-west of Najd al-Salaf around which the Sultan al-Raṣṣāṣ had built a wall to act as a sangar (*matras*) and his tribesmen with those of Banu ʾl-Arḍ, Murād, Yāfiʿ, the ʿAwāliq and others drew up on a front over two miles long. But the tribesmen were defeated, the Sultan al-Raṣṣāṣ was slain and his head cut off, the ʿAwlaqī horse routed, though some of al-Raṣṣāṣ's women escaped on the ʿAwlaqī horses. After the battle the Zaydī leaders collected the women together in a single tent and put them in charge of persons of repute. Later the women and children were sent to Sultan Ṣāliḥ al-Raṣṣāṣ, brother to the slain Sultan who had fled to a place ʿUbarah[85] in the mountains near Bayḥān as he could find none to give him refuge. Eventually he sought safeconduct (*amān*) which the Imām granted him with a firm pact (*ʿaqd muʾakkad*) to that effect. Sultan al-Raṣṣāṣ's head was sent to the Imām and hung up at al-Ḥuṣayn[86] so that all might see he had been slain. Following his death *Allāh fataḥa ʾl-amṭār*, opened up the rains[87].

The Conquest of Bilād Yāfiʿ

In the year 1065/1655 when peace had been made in the Mashriq by direct contact or through correspondence Zaydī forces took up position in al-Khalaqah[88] and Yāfiʿ fortified themselves in their high mountains one of which was the inaccessible mountain called al-ʿUrr[89], constructing on it high walls (*dawāʾir*[90]) and curved sangars (? *matāris mulawwiyah*) that they garrisoned with many men and muskets.

The Zaydīs now invited Sultan Ṣāliḥ al-Raṣṣāṣ to al-Bayḍāʾ where they had established themselves. He was met by the Zaydī leader, obviously bent on a policy of conciliation, who invested him with a spendid robe (*kiswah*) while still on his way there. An eye-witness reports that he nearly refused to accept it 'because they are unaccustomed to the *kiswah*, their costume being, like the other Mashāyikh of the Mashriq, a waist-wrapper (*mīzār*) and shoulder-cloth (*liḥfah*) of the select top quality of al-Shiḥr cloth (*bazz*)[91], and his weapons a musket like others. He is at pains to decorate it and the powderhorn (*yubāligh fī ḥilyati-hā wa-ḥilyat al-ʿiddah*) [with silver mounts[92]], the chiefs of his fellow (tribesmen) having mostly the same weapons'. The Sultan does not ride horses but goes along with his fellow tribesmen like one of them. 'They wear their hair long and comb it out, so that Sultan Ḥusayn al-Raṣṣāṣ's hair, as one who actually

[85] Unidentified.
[86] Unknown to me, perhaps in the Ḍawrān region where al-Mutawakkil had taken up residence.
[87] This is a sign of *barakah*, perhaps Divine approval of the Zaydī conquest?
[88] See p. 102 *infra*.
[89] See fn. 26.
[90] Sing. *dāʾir* (*Ṣanʿāʾ*, p. 576a).
[91] For Ḥaḍramī cloth in Ṣanʿāʾ Sūq see *Ṣanʿāʾ*, p. 182.
[92] The lawfulness of ornamenting the *bunduq* with silver is discussed by Ḥusayn b. Muḥammad b. al-Ḥusayn Ibrīq al-Ḥaḍramī al-Ḥabbān, in his *Taḥrīḍ al-ikhwān al-kirām wa-badhl al-naṣīḥah fi ʾl-taḥarruz min Yām al-liyām wa-afʿāli-him al-qabīḥah* composed about 1800 (my photocopy).

saw it told me, was nearly two *dhirā*ᶜ (a metre) long and he had servants to comb it out. They do not dwell in settled places (*lā yaskunūn al-ḥaḍar*)' [93].

Al-Jarmūzī concludes that, following Sultan al-Raṣṣāṣ's submission, came that of the ᶜAwlaqī Sultan, Manṣūr b. Ṣāliḥ, whose place is a little town called Yashbum – he and the people of his country are *ahl al-ḥaḍar* with many sūqs in their country, and they ride horses. He sought *amān* for his country which was duly granted. The Faḍlī sultan's son also came in, and the Zaydī leader wrote to all districts, receiving responses from the Wāḥidī, ᶜAmūdī[94] and others.

The Zaydīs now heard that the Ḥabīb Sālim had left Ḥaḍramawt and was making for Yāfiᶜ who had written him many letters. He took the route through the country of Ibn ᶜAbd al-Māniᶜ[95] and Aḥwar territory[96]. The Zaydīs therefore despatched a contingent of cavalry and infantry to intercept him before he could reach Yāfiᶜ. The infantry were at 'the town of Dathīnah' (probably al-Ḥāfah[97]). When close to Aḥwar the cavalry learned his son the Ḥabīb[98] with a body of Yāfiᶜ had already passed through and realized that he had given them the slip but they hung about till they confirmed that Sālim al-Ḥabīb (sic) had returned to his home in Ḥaḍramawt. These cavalry when at a place called al-Madārah[99] were recalled to the Zaydī army and proceeded to it by way of the Thirah pass (*ᶜaqabah*)[100] which they found steep and difficult to climb. They went on to a village of the Banu ᵓl-Arḍ and there they learned that the Zaydī troops, called by al-Jarmūzī '*junūd al-ḥaqq*' [101], had fought and dispersed Yāfiᶜ tribesmen who were driven back to al-ᶜUrr which the Zaydīs apparently took[102] then capturing Marfad[103], to take houses there belonging to the Shaykh Ibn Harharah. So the cavalry contingent moved to al-ᶜUrr where they prayed and going to a place above Marfad they fired off many rounds. This action further dispirited the Yāfiᶜīs whose chiefs came to the Zaydī camp to ask for safe-conduct (*amān*). They were welcomed by the Zaydī general al-Ṣafiyy and granted *amān* and an investiture; he took them to his brothers who did the same.

> 'As for the Shaykh ᶜAbdullāh b. Harharah who is in charge of the collection (*qabḍ*) of the *awqāf* belonging to the afore-said Ḥabīb Sālim, his votive gifts (*nudhūr*) and taxes (*zakawāt*[104]) and to whom ultimately come the commodities in Yāfiᶜ which are forwarded to the Ḥabīb in Ḥaḍramawt, our Lords[105], Allah preserve them, commanded that such grain (*ḥubūb*) belonging to the afore-said Ḥabīb as was found in his house, consisting of money, grain, horses, the three flocks

93 Sense uncertain.
94 Famous Mashāyikh family of Wādī Dawᶜan.
95 Mashāyikh family of Jōl ᶜAbd al-Māniᶜ.
96 Lower ᶜAwlaqī country.
97 A ruined mediaeval town I visited in 1954.
98 Presumably al-Jarmūzī means the son of al-Ḥabīb Sālim, but I can find no reference to him in Sayyid genealogies.
99 Al-Madārah is a Mayāsir village between Mūdiyah and al-Shāfiᶜiyyah.
100 In ᶜAwdhalī territory, the famous pass up the Kawr.
101 'The troops of righteousness/right/justice/truth' !
102 See fn. 26.
103 Marfad is in the Qabīlat al-Ḥaḍramī territory.
104 *I.e.* the *ᶜushūr*.
105 The Zaydī leaders.

(*al-an*ᶜ*ām al-thalāth*[106]) and the coffee plantations (*ṣawāfī bunn*[107]) should be seized'.

The Dhū Nākhib people had declined to come in to the Zaydī leaders because of the steepness of their mountains which were garrisoned by brave Yāfiᶜī tribes but after the safe-conduct (*amān*) accorded Shaykh ᶜAbdullāh b. Harharah they also petitioned for *amān*. Al-Ṣafiyy sent them to the Imām. They, knowing that repentance would be accepted (*al-tawbah maqbūlah*), made a show of repentance. The Imām presented their chiefs with clothing, money, weapons and horses to those of them who were accustomed to [ride] them.

Governors were appointed over Yāfiᶜ, Raṣṣāṣ and Dathīnah and Zaydī troops moved to al-Khalaqah, rebuilding the fort there which commands the *sūq*. News arrived of the submission of the Sultan of Ḥaḍramawt. The Mashāyikh of Yāfiᶜ, Ibn Harharah and those of the Mashāyikh who had come in were informed by the Imām of their *wājibāt*, i.e. the taxes they must pay – he wrote them a pact and took an oath from them.

The situation was still unsettled with under 100 Zaydī soldiers remaining in Yāfiᶜ, and when the harvest (*al-thamarah*) was ready and assessors were sent out Ibn al-ᶜAfīf prevented them from making their rounds. The Zaydī governor who had married locally had engaged about 400 Yāfiᶜī troops and they agreed to follow him against Ibn ᶜAfīf who went to Jabal al-Naffāj between al-Mawsaṭah and Banī Qāsiṭ (sic). All Yāfiᶜ then rose except al-Muflaḥī, but the Sultan al-Raṣṣāṣ dissociated himself (*aẓhara ʾl-barāʾah*) from the rising. Zaydī forces went to al-Khalaqah, Marfad and al-Mawsaṭah. The Yāfiᶜī allies of the Zaydīs used to 'show obedience by day and raid the (Zaydī) soldiers to their places at night', like the Yemenis did with Nasser's forces in the sixties! The Zaydīs however moved from al-Khalaqah to Masjid al-Nūr in al-Mawsaṭah and mounted an attack on the ᶜAfīfīs and Nākhibīs on al-Naffāj who were defeated with the loss of 300 tribesmen.

After some days the shaykh Maᶜūḍah and his son asked for *amān*. Some Zaydī troops meanwhile had found in a pass 'a woman with slave-girls (*jawārin*) of hers with instruments (*ālāt*) so they took her and those with her and she was the wife of Ibn ᶜAfīf'. Perhaps the 'instruments' were arms. The Zaydī general ordered her to be taken with trusty persons to Radāᶜ fort, making her a hostage (*rahīnah*). The news of her capture was brought to Ibn ᶜAfīf who was much grieved as he thought she had escaped. Perhaps this is the lady called Nūr bint ᶜAfīf (p. 90) who was said to have fought the Zaydīs. The Zaydī general ordered all the weapons of bilād b. ᶜAfīf to be collected, guns (*banādiq*), clubs, (leather) shields (*daraq*), or no *amān* would be given. Musical instruments and drums (*ṭāsāt*) were confiscated also. After this there seems to have been general submission to the Zaydīs, all this in year 1066/1655–56. The Imām ordered the musical instruments to be broken, but he appears to have tried to win over Ibn ᶜAfīf, Ibn Harharah, and al-Nākhibī to whom he assigned maintenance while detaining them with him, and to whom he made gifts.

[106] I.e. *al-ibl wa-ʾl-baqar wa-ʾl-ghanam*, camels, cattle, sheep and goats, upon which *zakāt* has to be paid.

[107] I translate *ṣawāfī* as plural of *ṣāfiyah*, a category of landholding, but *bunn ṣāfī* is the pure coffee-berry.

The Zaydīs lose Yāfi'

About a quarter century later Yāfi' expelled the Imām's governor and repulsed expeditions sent against them so that the Zaydīs were compelled to retire on Radā'. Again in 1101/1689–90, a Zaydī expedition reached al-'Urr but was defeated. After defeating the Zaydīs in Yāfi' in 1120/1708–09, 'Umar b. Ṣāliḥ Harharah and the Mashriq tribes even ravaged the town of Ibb. While in 1144/1731–32 in the time of Sultan Sayf b. Qaḥṭān b. Ma'ūḍah al-'Afīf the Yāfi'īs drove the Zaydīs out of Lahej and Aden. The Zaydī empire was now well on the way to disintegration and the Yemen on the return to tribal anarchy.

The Āl al-Shaykh Bū Bakr b. Sālim, Manṣabs of 'Ināt

Though the informants marshalled by al-Jarmūzī are hostile to the Āl Bū Bakr b. Sālim house, taking a cynical view of the way in which it exercises its functions, they do present a fair and authentic picture. The Āl Bū Bakr b. Sālim is probably the largest Ḥaḍramī Sayyid house and in the era of migration it had many branches settling in Indonesia, East Africa and elsewhere. I have found no actual account of how its founder Bū Bakr established his ascendancy but this was probably gained through strength of personality, political acumen and playing to the full on his 'spiritual power' [108] inherited from the Prophet. The family, says the editor of *Shams al-ẓahīrah*[109], 'has a *dāllah*[110] over the arms-bearing tribes like Yāfi', Kindah, the Manāhīl and Mahrah. Because of the prestige/influence (*wajāhah*) that their *manṣabs* have, they employ it to reconcile contending parties and to extinguish the fire of dissension (*fitnah*) when it intensifies. They had hands in appeasing dissensions and arranging truces between people in an age when anarchy prevailed'.

Al-Shillī (ob. 1093/1682) assigns a lengthy biography to Bū Bakr b. Sālim (919–992/1513–4–1584) known as Ṣāḥib 'Ināt. He was born in Tarīm where he studied with its ulema, subsequently moving to 'Ināt[111]. Both *al-ḥāḍir wa-l-bād*, the settled and bedouin, profited through him and his virtues (*manāqib*). His place (*janāb*) became a refuge for any person in danger (*khā'if*) and after his death whosoever came to seek protection at his tomb (*istajāra bi-qabri-hi*) became protected (*maḥrūs*). All his property deriving from his estates and what was brought to him (*manqūl*) and animals was 'in the name of' (i.e. spent upon) the needy the *ḍu'afā' wa-ḍīfān* (unarmed classes[112] and guests). The revenues in kind from Yāfi' would come under the heading of *manqūl*. Al-Shillī lists his writings on the usual religious

[108] *Al-sulṭat al-rūḥiyyah*. I imagine the term is of comparatively recent usage in Ḥaḍramawt.

[109] Muḥammad Ḍiyā' Shihāb ed. 'Abd al-Raḥmān b. Muḥammad al-Mashhūr *Shams al-ẓahīrah*, Jeddah, 1404/1984, I, p. 276. There is an earlier lithographed edition.

[110] Lane's rendering of *dāllah* perfectly describes the manners of a great Manṣab – a placid, grave manner of deportment with pleasingness of mien, a kind of boldness towards a person in whose estimation one holds a high place. Bū Bakr b. Sālim used to cajole the rude bedouin (*ajlāf*) and they did not upset him (*lā yuz'iju-hu*).

[111] Muḥammad b. Abī Bakr, *al-Mashra' al-rawiyy*, Cairo, 1319 H., II, p. 26. The Āl Kathīr Sultans laid out (*ikhtaṭṭa*) 'Ināt al-Qadīmah in 629/1232, but the area in which he built his house became known as al-Jadīdah.

[112] *Da'īf* in Ḥaḍramawt – workers in clay, builders, potters, field workers, but probably here of more general application.

topics including *taṣawwuf* but avers that he used to hold aloof from the manifesting of miracles (*iẓhār al-karāmāt*) and supernatural phenomena (*khawāriq al-ʿādāt*) though al-Jarmūzī quotes al-Ahdal to the contrary with regard at least to the Āl Bū Bakr b. Sālim in general. Nevertheless, like other holy men, he revealed (*kāshafa*) to a group of his companions what was in their hearts. The following story recalls the cynical remarks of the Zaydī al-Asadī supra.

Certain merchants sailing from India to bandar Mokha were delayed by an adverse wind, it being the end of the monsoon (*mawsim*). One of the ship's company saw in a dream Bū Bakr b. Sālim who instructed him to make votive gifts and to be of good cheer. This he promised to do and a favourable wind took them to Mokha. This man arriving in ʿĪnāt, had this tale recounted to him by Bū Bakr before he could open his mouth, with the demand: '*Hāt al-nidhr*, Hand over the gift'! 'Not until you tell me what it is', said the man, and Bū Bakr told him in exact detail.

It vas Abū Bakr's son, al-Ḥusayn (ob. 1044/1634–35), who was visited by al-Asadī in 1041/1630–31. Al-Shillī[113] declared him to be unequivocally 'the imām of his time', widely famed, following the *sunnah*, perfectly exercising his office (*manṣab*[114]), entertaining the *fuqarāʾ* and *masākīn*[115], strangers and orphans. The tribesmen (*ʿurbān*) used to come to him from all quarters of the land. He disliked tyrants (*jabābirah*) - by these he probably means haughty tribal chiefs - and would only look at them askance. 'When the Imām of the Zaydiyyah wrote to the people of al-Diyār al-Ḥaḍramiyyah summoning them to enter into obedience to him, and everyone to whom a letter came from him gave a (positive) reply' except al-Ḥabīb al-Ḥusayn, 'he neither replied to him (assenting) nor did he sent him a letter'. It is to be inferred from the text, though unvoiced by it, that the Ḥaḍramīs considered the Zaydī Imām to be one of the Jabābirah!

When al-Ḥusayn died it was agreed by consensus that his son Aḥmad had the best claim to the office of *manṣab*. He, like his group (*jamāʿah*) followed Bedouin ways[116], their bodies were bedouin and their hair bedouin (*abdānu-hum wa-shuʿūru-hum bādiyah*). In 1948 the branch of the Āl al-Shaykh Bū Bakr lower down the Wādī Ḥaḍramawt at Khōn were still bedouin in their dress and arms-bearing though not the Manṣab house at ʿĪnāt which seems to have abandoned bedouin ways and conformed to Sayyid dress[117] Aḥmad died in 1061/1651.

The Sālim who figures in the narrative of al-Jarmūzī would be Sālim b. Aḥmad b. al-Ḥusayn. He is not included by al-Shillī in *al-Mashraʿ* but he is recorded in *Shams al-ẓahīrah*[118] with the title Sālim al-Muhājir, the latter epithet to be interpreted as the emigrant seeking protection. He died in al-Ghayẓah/Ghayḍah in 1087/1676–77. Sālim may have been manṣab after his father's death, but it rather looks as if he was obliged to take refuge from the Zaydīs in the coastal Mishqāṣ district east of al-Shiḥr.

The link between the ʿĪnāt Sayyids and Yāfiʿ still persisted till our own

[113] *Op. cit.* II, p. 92. Al-Ḥusayn was opposed to tobacco and had a proclamation prohibiting the use of it made in the *sūq*.
[114] The title 'Manṣab' seems to derive from the office.
[115] The *fuqarāʾ* in Ḥaḍramawt may mean Sufis and *masākīn* petty traders, but perhaps here the terms are used in the general sense of 'poor'.
[116] *Al-Mashraʿ*, II, p. 53; *Shams al-ẓahīrah*, I, p. 301.
[117] See my *Saiyids of Ḥadramawt*, London 1957.
[118] *Shams al-ẓahīrah*, II, p. 302.

time and a notice in the *Tārīkh al-shuʿarāʾ al-Ḥaḍramiyyīn*[119] mentions that a noted Ṣūfī scholar ʿAlī b. Sālim, eleventh in the line of descent from Shaykh Bū Bakr b. Sālim, travelled probably round about 1850 to Jabal Yāfiʿ 'for worldly purposes, trading (*fī sabīl al-ḥayāt al-dunyawiyyah, mutājir-an*) among a multitude of traders, but his spirit was not at ease with this wordly life and he quickly withdrew to Ḥaḍramawt'.

It is the writer's pleasure to acknowledge his indebtedness to Ḥusayn Hādī ʿAwaḍ of the Madhḥij of Maʿn formerly of Wādī Yashbum and Ṣāliḥ ʿUmar Muḥammad Ghālib of al-Ḥaḍramī tribe of Yāfiʿ al-ʿUlyā, originally from near al-ʿUrr, for information gratefully received and to thank them and Dr Robert T. O. Wilson and Mr Peter J. Grove for their valuable advice on the cartography of Yāfiʿī country and Mr Grove for his expertly drawn sketch map of this little known region.

Addenda

P.86 The person on the right is the Lower Yāfiʿī Sultan, ʿAydarūs b. Muḥsin. His son Muḥammad attended the Coronation but turned dissident; he was eventually given safe conduct by the NLF after the British withdrawal but murdered by them.

P.88 Ṣāliḥ ʿUmar says it was an ordinary copper drum with a leather cover on both ends. NLF officials impounded it to prove to the Yāfiʿīs that the rulers used to deceive them by pretending it was a sacred drum, and they lodged it in Aden Museum!

P.89 Ḥusayn Hādī ʿAwaḍ writes that the only two mosques in al-Qārah are those of ʿAbd al-Qādir al-Jīlānī and Shaykh Saʿīd b. ʿĪsā, ancestor of the Dawʿan ʿAmūdīs. Other domes are the tombs of the ʿAfīfī chiefs.

P.105 ʿAbdullah b. Aḥ. al-Wazīr, *Ṭabaq al-ḥalwā*, Ṣanʿāʾ, 1405/1985, 137–43, provides a secondary account of the Yemeni conquest of Yāfiʿ drawing on al-Jarmūzī. Sultan Ghālib al-Quʿayṭī has given me a new book by ʿAbdullah b. Aḥ. al-Nākhibī, *Riḥlah ilā Yāfiʿ aw Yāfiʿ fī adwār al-tārīkh*, Jeddah, 1410/1990.

[119] ʿAbdullāh b. Muḥammad al-Saqqāf, Cairo ca. 1359 H., IV, p. 72.

VII

The Ma'n "Gypsies" of the West Aden Protectorate

Every night during my stay at Mūdiyah, the principal village of Dathīnah, the scene some fifty years ago of the love affair of Sham'ah that stirred up a tribal feud still well remembered [1], I heard the singing and drums of the Ma'n gypsies. That is until Ramaḍān, for then, through the representations of the Qāḍī and certain prominent men of the village, they were restrained from giving their performance. About half a dozen of the high square black goat-hair tents of the Ma'n, known as *karbah* (pl. *karābī*) [2], were pitched round the tribal guard fort in which I had taken up brief residence. The Ma'n seemed to be very prosperous, for they possessed excellent camels and other beasts.

The Ma'n are variously said to have appeared first from the north-west (*al-qiblah*), from Khawlān of the Yemen, and perhaps from other places. When mischievous people wish to tease the proud and warlike 'Awlaqī tribes of the Ma'nī Shaikhdom they make play with the possibility of a common ancestry of the gypsies and tribesmen – which of course, is an *'aib*, an insult. In the Yemen, to say, "*Wallāh innak dawshān*, By God, you are a minstrel", would be insulting indeed. On questioning the well-known MUBĀRAK 'ABDULLĀH AL-ṬAWṢALĪ [3] some years later, he said that the gypsy tribe was probably called Ma'n simply because they accompanied the Ma'n group of Upper 'Awlaqī tribes down to Dathīnah, but that they had no proper tribal name known to him (his knowledge of tribal matters is encyclopaedic), and are called *shaḥath*

[1] C. DE LANDBERG, Dialectes de l'Arabie Méridionale, Daṯînah. Leiden 1909-1913. I, p. 5 s. and p. 179 s. I read out passages from this volume to friends at Mūdiyah who were amazed to find the story in print, pointing out to me from time to time the descendants of the principal actors. Al-Qufl, the *ḥuṣn* which figures in the story, still stands to the east of Mūdiyah village.

[2] There is a Ḥadīth that the Ka'bah was a tent, and I have wondered if these tents of cube-like shape were not indeed the prototype of the Ka'bahs of Mecca and Najrān. The black cloth covering of the Meccan Ka'bah would bring it very near to these tents. The Ka'bah is the Bait, which is after all the Arabic for tent, as opposed to *dār*. Karbah and Ka'bah differ only in one radical. "Gloss. Daṯ." suggests the word is Persian in origin. C. DE LANDBERG, Glossaire Daṯînois (Leiden 1920-1942).

[3] His picture, with a sensational, not entirely correct caption, appears in WENDELL PHILLIPS, Qataban and Sheba (London 1955), p. 33.

or *shaḥadh*, that is to say, beggar minstrels [4]. The 'Awlaqīs do indeed claim certain rights or dues in Dathīnah as a result of this incursion, to this day [5].

Some Ma'n are settled in the 'Awdhalī village of am-Nigdah famous for its shrine, living in houses there. They are said to have nothing of the lewd gypsy ways of the other branches of the tribe – the Ahl al-Muzaiyad whose tents were pitched at Mūdiyah, and the Ahl al-Nawwāḥ with whom they were at variance, the latter being then encamped at one of the many villages clustering round Mūdiyah. Village scandal had it that the local officer of the tribal guards who has turned dissident since that time but was recently received back, had formed an attachment to one of the Muzaiyad girls, and so favoured the Ahl al-Muzaiyad by permitting them to stay close by Mūdiyah where most money could be made. To the other branch, the Ahl al-Nawwāḥ of whom I saw little, belonged a lovely girl, they told me, called Bū Sā'ah because she usually wears a wrist watch. When, later on, I had moved over to Zārah, the seat of the 'Awdhalī Sultans, an old beggar Ma'nī woman found her way into the house, by name Qamrah, at one time a dancer, belonging to the Āl al-Muzaiyad of am-Nigdah. Though her youth was long past, the bold look in her eye told the story of the days when she was young and beautiful like the Ma'nī girls of Mūdiyah, and her speech had the ingratiating wheedling way of beggars – a rain of blessings for fifty cents – *Allāh ḥaffaẓ-ak min al-qawm wa-'l-lawm, wa-'l-'āfiyah faidat (khairah) māl, Allāh yi'allī daragat-kum, man'ūm bi-'l-'āfiyah, Allāh yiḥyīk* [6].

On the occasion of the arrival of an Aden Protectorate Levies convoy the assistant political officer granted special permission for the Ma'n to hold a *samrah*, an evening's dancing. The headlights of the trucks were turned onto the crowd of village people and soldiers, my pressure lamp and all the lanterns from the fort were brought out, a circle was formed with the Ma'nī drummers sitting on the ground at one end of it, and the Ma'nī girls danced, or rather ran up and down in a sort of gliding trot, the weight of *riyāls* and silver ornaments with which they were covered jingling and tinkling all the time. Their heady perfumes and the thick dust lying heavy in the warm air, raised by the dancing and crowding of the villagers breathed a sharp catching

---

[4] Gloss. Daṯ., pp. 2023, 2704 s., *shāḥidh*, pl. *shuḥḥādh*. Datînah, pp. 165, 747 with illustration of drum, 1789.

[5] Aḥmad Faḍl al-'Abdalī, Hadīyat al-Zaman (Cairo 1351 H.), p. 142 records a raid of the 'Awlaqī Sultan 'Abdullāh b. Farīd on Lahej in 1234 H. (1818-1819 A. D.), and the "Account of the Arab Tribes in the Vicinity of Aden" (Bombay 1909), p. 56 notes that the 'Awlaqī threatened to build a fort at Qarn Murshid in 1882 which indicates that he must have had some effective sovereignty in Dathīnah at that time.

[6] *Qawm* "tribes", perhaps "tribal attack" ; *lawm* "disgrace" but it has also a technical sense ; *faidah*, probably *fā'idah*. Probably the phrase means, "Health is the best of goods. May God give you honour". *Man'ūm*, etc., is a common Dathīnah reply to the greeting *Kīf ḥālak*. This may be compared with a blessing I heard of a beggar of the Āl al-Shaikh Bū Bakr at Saiwūn, a Saiyid, *Allāh yaḥfaẓ-kum wa-yuṭawwil a'mār-kum, al-ḥabā'ib yad'ūn lakum min Āl al-Shaikh Bū Bakr, wa-sa'ad al-ḥabā'ib wa-yutammim kull maqṣūd-ak*, "God guard you and prolong your life, the Saiyids of the Āl al-Shaikh Bū Bakr pray for [or bless] you, the Saiyids give aid and he will realise all your aims."

excitement into the evening. No village women were there of course, although in Dathīnah like all tribal peasant communities, purdah in the strict sense hardly exists outside a few families of social distinction or wealth, but propriety dictates a woman's conduct; moreover it was murmured that the village women resented the presence of the Ma'n.

While as yet no one has ventured to dance, or at intervals between the dancing, two girls together at a time run or glide round the inside edge of the circle formed by the crowd. Sometimes the one holds the other's hand arched up in the air; this signifies the invitation – enter into the circle any one of you who desires us. Sooner or later some gallant will edge his way through the crowd into the circle and dance with them. The commonest dance naturally is a mime of courtship. The girl will run round the circle with her hand held to her ear, which means – you mustn't kiss me! She holds her skirt in her other hand. The man in turn will stretch forth his hands before him as to say – I am afire with thirst for you, let me but sip. This is ancient convention in Arabia; it is to be found too in such as the sophisticated but ardent Ḥaḍramī poet of the 19th century YAḤYĀ ʿUMAR who spent so many years in India, and in a mélange of Arabic and Hindustani, astonishingly like mediaeval Spanish verse with its Arabic *kharjah* he sings [7],

> You lovely thing,
> Your lover slake, donne un peu d'eau [8].
> Of pity's sake – tenderness show.
> See how wasted, how thin I grow.

Sometimes the dancer will grasp his belly in his hands, as if to say – for love of you I am a prisoner (*maqbūḍ*). He may touch his membrum virile even. The tribesman will strike his right hand on the hilt of his dagger to convey the boast – I am a tribesman, a *qabīlī*, a fine strong young fellow [9]. Another in earnest of his manliness made exaggerated strutting movements with his feet, while others jumped up and down [10]. At Khanfar I have already noted the dagger play at this type of dance. Sometimes the man creeps round on his toes with bent knees, but I did not discover the significance of this movement. A man would sometimes give a little quivering of his shoulder or some other part of his body, but I noticed that none of the Maʿnī women did this. In Southern Arabia this quivering is known as *lawq*, and is described by Europeans as belly-wriggling or belly-dancing, but it is certainly not confined to this part of the body alone. In the dance there is much of chasing and pursuit, frequent touchings and passionate gesture. Sometimes the girl will bring her elbow round to avoid a kiss – for the man makes a play of snatching a kiss from her, or perhaps indeed he seriously attempts it. In Ḥaḍramawt, for a man to kiss his wife in the presence of another, even a slave so menial

---

[7] Prose and Poetry from Ḥaḍramawt. London 1951, Ar. text, p. 91.

[8] These words are in Hindustani in the original.

[9] Cf. the picture in G. WYMAN BURY, Land of Uz (London 1911), p. 278 with a tribesman holding a dagger.

[10] Cf. Prose and Poetry, Pref. p. 22.

that a noble woman does not bother to veil before him, would be considered an act of indecency; I imagine the Dathīnah people too would find such conduct repugnant, but as the dancer makes his essay at a kiss, the *muṭabbin* or drummer shouts out, *"Ra'hā wāḍī!"* [11] This I first thought to render as, "See, she is ritually pure!" for I understood it to be conventional fiction that the Ma'nī girls are innocent or chaste, but I have since wondered if I was not mistaken, for *awḍā'* in the Ḥadīth can mean "prettier". So the drummer may have meant, "See how pretty she is!" Mubārak 'Abdullāh however writes that *Ra'-hā wāḍiyah*" is a joking expression. While dancing the girls exclaim, *"Sarā"*, which was explained to me as *"Nisrī"*, "we 're going to have a good time tonight". The men as they dance, pull out a five-shilling note and fling it with contemptuous abandon on the basket tray lying in front of the drummers. My own servant, an 'Āmirī of Tarīm, paid his *riyāl* and danced, but counted it dear, for in his native Ḥaḍramawt the villagers, men and women, dance together in a simplicity and Arcadian innocence quite different from these gypsy folk. Here in Dathīnah, people told me, when you have danced once it but serves to whet your appetite for more, and so you keep on returning to dance again and again, no matter what it cost you.

The dances, simple as they look, have, I am assured, a complicated footwork, and in every gesture lies some allusion to the arts of courtship and love. In their patterns of gesture they are closely linked with the conventional themes and idioms of Arabic love poetry in the spoken tongue. It may well be inferred that this is true of certain genres of ancient Arabic verse, but if so, it has been long forgotten. At a *tafrigah* or fantasia, an evening's entertainment, many dances, each distinguished by its own name, are performed – the *qar'ah* danced to flute (*mizmār*) and drum (*ṭabl*), the *sharḥ*-dance [12] which has already been described, the *'askarah* with a walking movement, which I take to mean "the soldier's dance", the *ṭannah* [13] where a man and woman facing one another, jump up and down. Each of these dances has its special traditional tune or tunes. I noted some verses of a Ma'nī song known as *miyāḥ* [14] sung to the *sharḥ*-dance [15],

Yā Aylamānī gadīdah   *Min dākhili 'ṣ-ṣundūq ḥinnī*
Lā dawn qalb-ak taghannā   *Minnak wa-lā ga 'l-'aib minnī* [15].

Sing out, o you Aylamānī rifle,
Drawn shining, brand-new, from within its case.
Your heart, did it perchance fall out of love,
'T were better than that I should lack in grace [16].

---

[11] Gloss Daṯ., *ra'ā* "regarder". Ibn al-Athīr, Nihāyah (Cairo 1311 H.), IV, p. 210, *awḍa'* means *aḥsan*. Cf. O. Rescher, Vocabulaire du recueil de Bokhârî (Stuttgart 1922), *awḍa'* "plus jolie, plus propre".

[12] Described in "Daṯînah", p. 1013; Prose and Poetry, pp. 22-23.

[13] Gloss. Daṯ., *ṭann*, "sauter, jaillir".

[14] Daṯînah, p. 1513, *māḥ* "danser une ronde, une farandole lorsqu'on se meut à gauche et à droite avec dignité. *Bā limīḥ* "nous allons danser une ronde (*sharḥ*)". *Miyāḥ*, "farandole".

[15] Metre : || – | – ⏑ – – | – ⏑ – – || – – ⏑ – | – ⏑ – –

[16] Gloss Daṯ., *ḥann* "résonner, whistle of a bullet", *lā* "if", *dawn* "peut-être". *Ḥann*

The Aylamānī rifle, i. e. the German "Mauser", is a complimentary epithet for the Maʿnī girl whose parure glistens with the heavy weight of silver metal.

With the al-Muzaiyad at Mūdiyah there were two drummers and one flute ; the girls stand near the drummers, issuing forth to join in the dance, and returning there when tired, to rest a little before joining the dance anew. Though the liveliness of the dancing demands no small exertion on their part, they can continue at it most of the night.

Throughout the evening I noticed an old woman making her round of the back of the crowd collecting money or accosting the spectators to visit the tents. Even in day-time if you pass by the Maʿnī tents an old woman will accost you and invite you to enter them, but many men seem to sit there simply to pass the time of day, though in such cases, they will in accordance with the established custom of Southern Arabia, bring coffee with them as a small present. On my last brief visit to the Aden Protectorate a soldier driver from the Upper ʿAwlaqī group recounted to us his experience with the Maʿn. Entering one of the Maʿnī tents, he sat down beside his N.C.O. who had visited the Maʿn before. A Maʿnī girl, he said, came and actually sat down between them, and from his acute embarrassment of actually sitting next to a woman in public he broke out into a sweat. Such embarrassment is very much a trait of the tribesman, and in like case the sophisticated Adenese would doubtless handle the situation very differently. The ʿAwlaqī soldier found he had paid 5/– each to the husband, the mother, and the sister of the girl, to say nothing of 15/– to the girl herself, so he felt he should receive the appropriate return for his money. Her husband turned over to sleep, covering his eyes (*yulabbis ʿuyūn-uh*).

As I was discussing the Maʿn some years before this with a friend in Mūdiyah, he too gave me an account of the conventions of approach to these girls which I found confirmed by an article in the Aden paper *al-Nahḍah* [17] attacking the Maʿn. According to the writer in the columns of this newspaper, when a man comes to the tent, the Maʿn say, "*Al-bait lak yā sīdī, wa-'l-khalā' lī dār,* The tent is yours, my lord, and the open country will be my house". If a man wishes to possess himself of a girl who has struck his fancy, he brings a sheep to the tent ; this the Maʿnī women cook for him, but give him only a small piece for himself, and they pass the evening in the tent singing. It was this singing that I used often to hear at night in the fort after the public dancing had ended, but it is in keeping with the times that I noticed a portable gramophone outside a Maʿnī tent. My Mūdiyah friend said that signs pass between the girl and the other occupants of the tent – including her husband, if she is married, and these persons depart on some pretext or another, perhaps for example to go to visit the *sūq*. If the girl is pretty, she is given two *riyāls* by the intent lover, and then, said my friend, he can have anything he wants, "*ḥatta 'l-ist*", if the suitor has a fancy to it !

---

was explained to me as *aqraḥī* "fire", but it means here "sing". *Taghannā* seems to accord with the explanations in E. J. W. Lane's Lexicon.

[17] Al-Nahḍah (June, 15th, 1950), I, xxx.

The Ma'n sometimes collected about 100/– of an evening between the hours of 9 p. m. and midnight when at Mūdiyah in the summer of 1954, but other persons variously put the figure between 80/- and 150/–. These are large sums for a Protectorate village, even a market-town like Mūdiyah. A young man from Aden, fat and a little foolish, who had come up to Mūdiyah on holiday, it being the village whence his family was sprung, and become enamoured of Bedouin, that is to say of tribal life, not unlike a certain type of young British officer, buying himself a rifle and a dagger heavily studded with imitation sequins in gold, was deeply attracted by the undoubted charms of the Ma'nī girls. Despite the expressed disapproval of his relatives, affronted by his conduct, he spent, as gossip had it, no less than 100/– a night on the Ma'n, and gossip even related that he paid as much as 300/- and a gold ring over and above, for the favour of spending a night with the girl known as Lubnān [18]. In quite recent years in one of the villages of Dathīnah they caused great disturbance as young boys were stealing sheep from their father's *ḥawsh* to take to the Ma'nī girls, and the influence of the *'āqil* or headmen was too far decayed for them to be able to restrain them.

Quite small schoolboys of the Mūdiyah government school were singing of their (no doubt theoretical) passion for Lubnān, to the great scandal of the respectable people of the place. Lubnān herself was a tall girl, young, with a face revealing no emotion, slim, and a lovely dancer ; she usually wore a frock of green silk velvet and, of course, the weighty silver ornaments – I watched her dancing many times. The village children would also sing, "*Ana amūt 'alā 'Ubbal*, I am dying [for love of] 'Ubbal". 'Ubbal was not the girl's real name of course, any more than Lubnān, for all the Ma'nī dancing girls have nice nicknames, and 'Ubbal was called after the German Opel car which is much sold in Aden. There were also, Umm al-Sā'ah, who may be the same as Bū Sā'ah mentioned earlier, Umm Ḥalā [19], and Abū Durg, but while I knew Lubnān and 'Ubbal by sight, I never identified the other girls.

In speaking of the Ma'n girls, the word *mu'arrasah* was used to describe them, though I did not sense that any deliberate insult was implied even as in the Egyptian, often semi-jocular "*yā mu'arris*". Amongst the Ma'n, contrary to all other Arabs, the girl is preferred, or nobler than the man – *al-bint afḍal 'ind al-Ma'n*, because she brings them in money. Throughout the countryside the Ma'n, because they allow and even encourage their women to prostitution, are regarded as of very low degree. It is interesting that in negotiations the chief woman comes with a man to deal with Government, and hers is by far the stronger personality.

A child born of a Ma'nī woman is attributed to her husband [20], but if

---

[18] I have no idea why she was called Lubnān, but the song, *Lubnān 'arūs al-kawn* "Lebanon is the bride of all creation", at once springs to my mind. Whether the Dathanīs would have heard this song on the radio and be punning on the name I do not know.

[19] *Ḥalā*, syn. *zain* "beautiful".

[20] Cf. the legal maxim, *al-walad li-'l-firāsh*. I am by no means convinced that this maxim derives from Roman law as I. Goldziher and J. Schacht have persuasively argued, for we find this principle here in customary law in a very un-Islamic setting in

a child is born out of wedlock, as happened recently here, it is her own. Unfortunately I have not recorded whether a child with no known father is named as the son of his mother, though this is likely to be so, or whether indeed all Ma'nī children are described in this way. Lubnān in fact, is said not to conceive, but other girls make use of a drug called *kawfar* to prevent conception ; one says of the women that they *yitkawfarīn* "make use of *kawfar*". One of my informants who, though he would never openly avow it, evidently knew all there was to know about the Ma'nī girls from direct experience, stated that a Ma'nī girl he knew practised "coitus interruptus" to avoid conception. In Dathīnah generally, a woman pregnant from a lover, it was said, will partake of a mixture of shark, dates, and honey, in an attempt to expel the foetus at its earliest stages, but there are women here who can expel the foetus by pressure on the body, perhaps massage, so that the woman aborts [21]. These devices, whatever efficacy they may have, I am sure must be known to the Ma'n.

When I questioned my informant on the matter of disease amongst the Ma'n, he maintained there was none since the country is clean and far from Aden. This may be true, or it may have been true, though I heard later that a Protectorate medical officer held different opinions on the subject of the Ma'n. Venereal disease has been known in Arabia since 807 H. (1404-5 A. D.), and a Yemenite medical Ms. in my possession calls it the Frankish, Persian, or Armenian disease [22] ; there are historical references to its appearance in the Yemen in the histories, but in the past Dathīnah was probably sufficiently isolated to avoid any great incidence of it.

Nowadays the Ma'n are said to visit Dathīnah, Baiḥān, and Raṣāṣī country in the Yemen. When they decide to leave any place they collect all the money they have earned and divide it in shares amongst men and women ; it does not seem, however, that they have any fixed times for moving from

---

a territory remote from the influence of Rome. SCHACHT's arguments (Origins of Muhammadan Jurisprudence [Oxford 1950], pp. 181-182) that this maxim was not acted upon as Islam developed, seems to postulate a society more Islamised and consistent than perhaps was actually the case.

[21] In the fragmentary treatises on Yemenite customary law made available to me for editing by the late ETTORE ROSSI, is the following interesting passage on tribal law relating to abortion :

> *Bāb idhā fa'alat al-imrāh bi-nafsi-hā fi'l-an mimmā yusqiṭ al-walad min baṭni-hā bi-shurb duwā aw ghairi-hā aw faḥs – lazima-hā li ahli-hi mā yalzam ghaira-hā fi 'l-jināyah, wa-lā budda min al-shahādah wa-illā lam yajib 'alai-hā qaṭ'ah, wa-'alā walīyi-hā, 'ala 'l-'ilm, 'ala 'l-niṣf min aymān al-rajul – farq mā bain al-rijāl wa-'l-nisā' fa-' 'lam dhālika.*

The gist of this passage is that a woman who induces abortion in herself through drinking some concotion, or massage, is liable to the child's tribe for damages. Provision is made for witnesses to her deed.

[22] Cf. H. P. J. RENAUD and G. S. COLIN, Documents Marocains pour servir à l'histoire du "Mal Franc". Institut des Hautes Etudes Marocaines. Paris 1935, p. XXVII. Syphilis in Socotra today is still known as *faranj* according to N. I. CORKHILL, Health Adviser's Notes on a Visit to Socotra in February and March 1956, PHS /193/5, and in Oman, AL-SĀLIMĪ, Jawhar al-Niẓām (Cairo 1345 H.), p. 186.

one district to another. About the time of the fair at Shaikh 'Uthmān [23] the Ma'n sometimes come down to Aden and perform their dances outside Dār Sa'd (*yil'abū fī Dār Sa'd*) [24], since they are not really permitted to enter the colony. Dancing does go on at the Shaikh 'Uthmān fair inside the colony, but on the one occasion I have attended it the performers looked to me like women of the pariah Khādim caste.

The curious thing is that the Ma'n were prohibited from coming to Mūdiyah before the British penetration into the country during the war years, though they were allowed to pass through Mūdiyah and spend the night there. It is said to have been an Aden political assistant, 'Abdullāh Ḥasan, who issued the order permitting them to stay there, whereas the Mashāyikh in Mūdiyah used never to allow this. In the old tribal days, however, it does seem that they were under general protection and were allowed to wander about freely. If, for example, one of the Ma'n were to be killed here in Mūdiyah, the headman (*'āqil*) would send to the killer's place and say, "You have killed a *rabī'* [i. e. a protected person] of mine, and I want restitution". The blood-price would be higher even than that for a *qabīlī*. This last remark I interpret to mean that, with all the additional fines payable for the circumstances of killing another man's protected person the blood-money would amount to more than that of a tribesman, for of course, the Ma'nī being a *shāḥith* of low social position, and *nāqiṣ*, i. e. of inferior status, it seems hardly possible that the basic blood-money would be identical in both cases. Even today, arriving near Miqbābah, they send to the village and two Ṣāliḥīs meet them and the Ma'n give them goats and receive their protection because the place where they camp lies below their *ḥuṣns* or castles. Still, as MUBĀRAK said of the Ma'nī, "*Al-silāḥ ḥaqq-uh lisān-uh*, His weapon is his tongue". It is an *'aib* or shame to speak back at the Ma'nī when he is insulting. Out of fear of his tongue the tribesman will slaughter an animal for the entertainment of the Ma'nī [25]. Reminiscing on the olden days, and he meant before the British penetration into the Protectorate, MUBĀRAK said that few people came to visit you, and there was far more entertainment and generosity of this sort than nowadays when so many people arrive at your door. In the eastern part of the Western Protectorate animals were slaughtered on the roofs, and the blood ran down the sides of the walls (he must have meant down the gutters onto the wall) ; this was a sign of nobility and of generosity.

---

[23] The name of this saint is al-Shaikh 'Uthmān b. Muḥammad al-Wuka'ī al-Zubairī al-Asadī, but I have not come across his biography in the usual sources. The *qafaṣ* over his tomb has a fine inscription with his name, and there is an old lamp in his mosque. The *manṣab* of Shaikh 'Uthmān in 1954 was 'Awaḍ Ḥamūd (Hal Hindī 'Umar), but the ancestor Hindī was an Arab by race, and the co-*manṣab*, his cousin, for there are always two *manṣabs* here, was Aḥmad b. Muḥammad 'Awaḍ 'Abd al-Raḥīm. The saint has *waqf* land in Lahej, Ḥuyūsh, etc., about which there is a dispute.

[24] It was to Dār Sa'd that during the short-lived ban on the import of *qāt* to Aden in 1957, that the *qāt*-eaters used to repair, and a shanty town sprang up where their needs were supplied. It had already fallen into ruin when I passed through it in 1958.

[25] Cf. infra, p. 748.

The Ma'n take their internal quarrels to the 'Awdhalī Sultan, Ṣāliḥ bin Ḥusain (now translated into Minister of Defence in the new Federation), for judgement, but the Sultan, with his strong reformist tendencies towards orthodox Islam, will not allow them to make money through the exercise of their profession. In former times I was told of the Ma'nī girls that *"mā kān yukassirhā illa 'l-Sulṭān,* Only a Sultan used to break her". "To break her" was paraphrased as *yiniḳ-hā*, and this custom is dealt with more fully in the passage translated below.

Again, I am told, if a noted headman (*'āqil*) dies, the Ma'nī will bring his drum to the grave, beat it, and stab it with his dagger. By this he implies, *"Ṭablī akbar 'aqīrah,* My drum is the greatest sacrifice I can offer". Or else he might say, *"Hādhā 'aqīratī 'alā hādha 'l-shaikh, mut'assif 'alaih,* This is my sacrifice for this *shaikh*, whose [demise] I regret". *'Aqīrah* is generally a sacrificial animal, but the Ma'nī presumably gives his drum at least a symbolic value greater than an animal's. This may be compared with the breaking of the spear-shaft in honour of the deceased, described by MUBĀRAK below. Not dissimilar is that when a Ma'nī is afraid of a *qabīlī* he will bring his drum and stab it at the *qabīlī's* house, there being many analogies with this in tribal customary procedure in that one kills an animal as a demonstration that one is seeking the assistance of a stronger party, but I shall deal with this at length elsewhere.

I am much indebted to MUBĀRAK 'ABDULLĀH for sending me an account of the Ma'n, not always consistent with the information supplied me by other informants in every detail, though the divergencies are small. It is written in near-classical Arabic and it has seemed to me worth while giving the original where the Arabic is in itself significant.

"As for from what stock they are descended, I do not know, nor do I think anyone does know. They are families (*'ā'ilāt*) with different names, and you find some of these families vying in pride (*tatfākhar*) with others, each of them saying, 'We are the original minstrels (*al-shaḥadh al-aṣlīyīn*) !' [26] Their dialect and customs (*taqālīd*) are like those of Banyar [27], and wherever they go, they return to al-Raṣāṣ country [28] ; when a dispute comes about between them their recourse is to the Raṣāṣ Sultan [29]. As for their true name, they are al-Shaḥadh or al-Shuḥḥādh (minstrels), and as for the word Ma'n it is only used in Dathīnah and in al-Kawr of the 'Awdhalī country. One section (*firqah*) of them maintains their origin is from the minstrels of the Upper 'Awlaqī Sultanate.

---

[26] *Aṣlī* means "pure, original, of good quality", etc.

[27] Banyar country is marked on HERMANN V. WISSMANN'S map as lying along the border of the Yemen and the Aden Protectorate north of al-Baiḍā' and south of Jabal al-Nisīyīn.

[28] The capital of Raṣāṣī country is al-Baiḍā' close to the 'Awdhalī border.

[29] Earlier I have reported that they refer to the 'Awdhalī Sultan. The Arabic, *"marja'-hum ilā Sulṭān al-Raṣāṣ"* is a most significant phrase in Islam. The meaning is that they will refer their disputes for arbitration to the Sultan in accordance with customary law upon which he is an authority.

As for their basic occupation (*qānūn shughl-hum*), it is of two sorts, dancing (*al-raqṣ*) and the evening entertainment (*samrah*, i. e. with dancing and music). In the case of the dancing they issue forth after sunset to an open place with the girls, the men beating the drums and [playing] the pipes. When the village people hear the drum and pipe they hurry out to them, some to watch, some eager to dance ; one of the dancers of the village comes out into the circle of the dance (*yibruz ilā ḥalqat al-raqṣ*) and one of the dancing girls comes out and dances with him. When the dance has gone on a long time another girl comes out, then a third, then a fourth, and thus the dance goes on. During the course of the dance, the dancer puts down some money, not less than a dollar a time, while some become exhilarated (*yantashī*) [30] and put down two or three times [as much] [31]. When he leaves [the circle] another dancer enters, and so on.

Once the dancing is ended they collect the money they have gained (*ghanamū*), the person they trust takes it, and there they divide it out according to their customs, i. e. [on the basis] that the woman gets the same as the man [32]. Then they leave the dancing-place, each going to his tent, and those persons desirous of them (*muwalla'īn bi-him* [33]) follow them inside their tents, entering where the pretty girls are, saying, 'we would like to have a party (*labā samrah*)'. So they spread out mats, rugs for them there inside the tents, but first of all the *sāmir* or *summār* (i. e. the person or persons who wish the party) bring a head or a couple of head of sheep. They slaughter these, and the old women or those with ugly faces cook them (*yingaḥin-hā al-'agāwiz aw qabīḥāt al-manḍar*), while as for the pretty ones, each sits beside one of their visitors and they spend the night in singing, their men-folk being at the door of the tent, and sometimes they play the pipes and the drums (*yiqra'ūn al-mazāmīr wa-'l-ṭubūl*). Any one beside her guest you will see making love to him while he makes love to her, this, in the eyes of the minstrels, not touching their honour (*fī naḍar al-shaḥadh lā yamuss karāmat-hum*). Most times they dance and sing (*yismarūn*) till morning, then the visitor or visitors (*summār*) make a collection of some money which they give to them, and then leave the tent. You will find the girl or girls in whose tent the party took place, boasting next morning over those girls who had no night visitors, because such meat and money as they have gained is the lot of the people of the tent in which the party was held.

Now if it be a Sultan or Amir or important chief (*shaikh kabīr*), the prettiest girl spends the night by his side and the expenses of the party come

---

[30] Gloss. Dat., to be in good humour, stolzieren.

[31] Here and elsewhere there are some interesting spellings in MUBĀRAK's letter. I do not think it merely an error in spelling that he should use *tanwīn* in *an* where a nominative is required by classical Arabic, an "error" which I have remarked many times in South Arabian Arabic. He has also some curious spellings with *tā' marbūṭah* for *tā'*, e. g., يموت الميتة، البناة، ثلاث مراة

[32] This is indeed surprising for Arabia. It will be recalled that actual blood-money for a woman is only half that payable for a man.

[33] *Muwalla'* is also a term used to describe a *qāt* addict.

from his private purse (*takālīf al-samrah takūn 'alā kīs-uh al-khāṣṣ*). Most times a party or parties are held at night (*tabāt samrah*) in all the tents, and the visitors vie as to which among them gives most animals to be slaughtered, and most money (*fa-yatzāyadūn al-summār man min-hum zaiyad fi 'l-dhabāyiḥ wa-a'ṭā al-nuqūd al-zāyidah*). This is the custom of the dance and the evening entertainment.

As for immoral acts (*al-af'āl al-danīnah*) [34], this is a difficult matter, except on rare occasions after one of the persons enamoured of them (*muwalla'*) spends his money and seduces them by presents (*yughrī-hin bi-'l-'aṭā*). Concerning the girls and the person who comes to them at their virginity (*man yaqa' bi-hin fī bukūrat-hin*) [35], it may be the lot (*naṣīb*) of the Sultans or the Amirs like al-Raṣāṣ. They say, when one of the girls becomes famous for outstanding beauty that he brings pressure to bear on her family until he takes her virginity (*yaḍghaṭ 'alā ahli-hā ḥattā yafukk bukūrat-hā*). This was in times past – the minstrels used to come to the country of the 'Awāliq, to Anṣāb, Markhah, and Khawrah up to the time of Sultan Ṣāliḥ [36]. Then they were prevented from coming to 'Awlaqī country because their safety became threatened, so since about forty years ago the land of the 'Awāliq has no longer known them, and the districts where they live are Dathīnaḥ, Bilād al-Raṣāṣ, Baiḥān, and Ḥarīb, they being prohibited from dancing in the land of the 'Awdhalī because the Sultan of the 'Awādhil believes that their actions corrupt morals.

There are minstrels throughout the whole of the Yemen, and in the Protectorates, but they differ from the wandering minstrels, for they do not display their women to people. Wherever the tribes come together in any place the minstrel comes forth (*yabruz*), a spear in hand, brandishing the spear in his right hand before the most prominent personage in that assembly, giving praise to him exceeding all bounds, and continuing to praise him until that personage gives him some money or piece of cloth [37]. The minstrel (*shāḥidh*) of each one of the Protectorate tribes is known and when a man dies (*yamūt al-maiyit*) the minstrel goes to near where the deceased is and proclaims the death of the departed (*yin'ā al-rāḥil*), praising him with praise most of which is extravagance. If he be a personage [of importance], he breaks the shaft (*ṣa'dah*) of his spear. Now the breaking of the [spear-]shaft is the greatest honour to the departed because it is [the subject] of a saying (*kilmah*) uttered when a man finds fault (*yadhumm*) with another man, saying, '*Fulān*

---

[34] The word *danīnah* is unknown to me, probably an error, but I am rendering it as equivalent to *danī'ah*, though this is subject to correction. From what I have reported from other sources I think MUBĀRAK with his tribal distaste for discussing anything he regards as improper or dishonourable, is making an understatement here. It seemed to me that the only difficulty confronting the would-be lover was the expensiveness of consorting with the Ma'nī girls, an ordinary soldier's pay certainly could not last long at the rate described by the driver.

[35] My rendering here is a little uncertain.

[36] Probably the Sultan Ṣāliḥ b. 'Abdullāh mentioned by C. DE LANDBERG.

[37] I have dealt with presents of cloth in my forthcoming study on the 'Awdhalī Sultanate.

mā yinkasir 'alaih al-rumḥ, The spear will not be broken for so and so!' i. e. When he dies the minstrel won't break the spear over him. So the family of the departed are generous (*yukrimūn*) to the minstrel, presenting him with sheep and money so that he will be placated. Then, of latter years however the minstrels have considered this profession despised (*mihnah ḥaqīrah*), so they have abandoned it and gone to honourable work, and only the name

Photograph by Flight-Lieutenant J. P. E. Williams

Gypsy dancing-girl, perhaps of the Ma'n, for her face is of a type common in Dathīnah. Her face is tattoed and may be smeared with yellow *hurud* (turmeric). Her necklace of Jewish workmanship will be set with red cornelians or red glass ; from it is suspended a charm of a known type, often set with a red stone. Some of the coins on the necklaces are Maria Theresa dollars, and she appears to be wearing a silver amulet case of pencil shape between the necklaces ; a silver waist-belt shows at the bottom of the photograph. The hair-style, if not that of Dathīnah, is almost identical with it, and she seems to be wearing silver ornaments on her hair. The costume of the Ma'n differs somewhat from that of the "nautch-girls" photographed by WYMAN BURY.

remains ; thus you find only an occasional one of them clinging to this profession. That, in my view, is because the minstrels were the servants of the ancient kings and used to gain a livelihood by praising kings, and entertaining[38] them with dancing and panegyrics, then they took this as a profession. I believe that the wandering minstrels will abandon this profession because some of them have now begun to buy land in Bilād al-Raṣāṣ and in Dathīnah, while a small number of them have abandoned this profession returning to buying and selling (i. e. trade). This is what I know of the minstrels in reply to your enquiry."

Where the Ma'n are concerned I fear Mubārak is right, that they will abandon the entertainment profession for other pursuits, for they are open to attack on all sides. I have recorded that a local school teacher attacked a *qabīlī* on the subject of the Ma'n whose dances he attended, asking why people should waste money on them, pointing to the wealth they had acquired in the numbers of camels and sheep they own – to which I mentally added the weight of bullion worn by the women about their persons. He also attacked the use of the *mizmār*-pipes which he said *ḥarām*, forbidden, in Muslim law. The tribesman only replied to such a learned assault on the Ma'n that they were harmless, and this, poor things, was their only form of livelihood. The Ma'n do indeed provide a great diversion for the villages lacking which they would be much the duller, and as one may gather from the tribesman's reply, there is much quite pagan tolerance for old-established customs however non-Islamic they be. Furthermore there is, underlying the orthodoxy of the country, a different and more ancient code of sexual behaviour, revealed in certain remarks of Ibn al-Mujāwir, and which may lie behind the accusations of sexual license levelled at the Carmathians who, it is worth remembering, found support in the tribe of Yāfi'. The Qāḍī of course, though a mild man, was in official opposition to the Ma'n by the nature of his calling, and it may be only a matter of time till the Islamic injunction that women must not mingle with men is applied here as it has been in the 'Awdhalī Sultanate and so many other places. So perhaps we shall lose the picturesque performance of the Ma'n, and public morality will be satisfied by driving what is at present open, underground to flourish in less romantic surroundings.

[38] Arabic, *y a r f hū 'alaihim*, my rendering being without confirmation.

ADDENDUM

P.743/9 Coitus interruptus, class. Ar. *'azl*. See al-Wāqidī, *al-Maghāzī*, ed. Marsden Jones, London–Oxford, 1966, III, 919, for a question put to the Prophet on this subject, and Cyril Elgood, Tibb al-Nabi or Medicine of the Prophet, *Osiris*, Bruges, 1962, 144–45.

VIII

A Judeo-Arab House-Deed from Ḥabbān
(With Notes on the former Jewish Communities of the Wāḥidī Sultanate)

THE Jewish community of Ḥabbān is no more. The Yemenite Jews have emigrated almost wholesale to Palestine, taking with them, indeed, a number of their books and documents, but they cannot now be studied in their homeland. For the further history of the Yemenite Jews Professor S. D. Goitein's article on the "Transplantation of the Yemenites" may be consulted, but my own brief and crowded six days in Ḥabbān during December, 1947, were probably one of the last visits paid by an orientalist to such a curious medieval community. In the melting-pot of the new state of Israel it is probable that the unique culture of the Yemenite Jews will not long survive the passing of the older generation.

It is generally accepted that the Yemenite Jewish communities known to us in the twentieth century were descendants of the pre-Islamic Jews and Jewish proselytes,[1] and I have already set down such reasons as there are for supposing that the Ḥabbān community may be descended from Ḥimyarī proselytes.[2] The writer Aḥmad Faḍl al-'Abdalī [3] holds that "the likelihood is that the Jews of the Yemen are Ḳaḥṭānīs, not Isrā'īlīs as they aver. On the contrary, they are survivors of the people of the Tubba' Yūsuf D͟hū Nuwās". Such an opinion is, of course, probably based upon a consideration of literary sources, but as far as I have been able to judge, the Arab does not consider the Yemenite Jew as *racially* different from himself. It may be that when the Jews were expelled from the Hejaz some took refuge with their co-religionists in South Arabia, for al-S͟hard͟jī [4] refers to the Ḳuraiẓis, "descended from the

[1] Cf. E. Brauer, *Jemenitische Juden* (bibliog.). Though there is an abundance of material from Jewish sources (cf. E. Brauer, "Bibliographie der Juden Jemens," *Kirjath Sefer* (Jerusalem, 1933–4), x, pp. 119 ff., and current material in subsequent numbers) much of it is not accessible to me. The Arabic material is less well known and it has been drawn upon for these notes. S. Jawneli (cf. Brauer, op. cit., p. xiv), writing in *Davar* on his visit to Ḥabbān, is not available to me.

[2] "Hūd and other South Arabian Prophets," *Le Muséon* (Louvain, 1953).

[3] *Hadīyat al-Zaman* (Cairo, 1351 H.), p. 297.

[4] *Ṭabaḳāt al-K͟hawāṣṣ* (Cairo, 1903), p. 99. Abū Mak͟hramah (ed. O. Löfgren, Uppsala, 1936–1950), ii, p. 135, names him as the k͟haṭīb of Aden in 754 H. (A.D. 1353), but says nothing of the Banū Ḳuraiẓah.

Banū Ḳuraiẓah, the well known tribe of the Banū Isrā'īl, in a place about a stage from the city of Aden." S͟hawkānī [1] cites a late seventeenth-century treatise on the tradition, "Expel the Jews from the Arabian Peninsula," in which it is argued that it was only required to expel them from the Hejaz, perhaps an endeavour to give legal justification for the existence of numbers of Jews in South Arabia.

The Status of Jewish Communities

Judging by Arabic sources, the Jews of South Arabia were not hardly treated by Muslim rulers, who in general seem to have dealt with them in fairly strict accordance with the provisions of the s͟harī'ah relating to the protected faiths. Nazīh al-Mu'aiyad,[2] for instance, states that they enjoyed in the Yemen certain rights which Muslims did not possess; they paid d͟jizyah, but were exempt from many other taxes which the Muslim ra'āyā must pay to the state. Mohamed Hassan [3] gives the poll-tax in Ṣan'ā' as 4 riyāls for each male in the Jewish Quarter, assessed by the 'Āmil Ṣan'ā' and the Āḳil (headman) of the Ḳā' al-Yahūd. My own impression is that from an economic point of view the Muslim peasant was often very much worse off than the Jewish craftsman in respect of tax-burdens.

Zaidī law no less than the orthodox mad͟hhabs protects the Jew from insult [4] and attack by a Muslim. If a Muslim insult a Jew he is fined, being forced to slaughter an animal which is distributed to the poor.[5] If he attack a Jew the latter will say, "Anā fī 'iṣmat al-Imām (or al-'Āmil), I am under the Imām's (or Governor's) protection." Both parties must then proceed to the Imām or 'Āmil and summary justice is dealt.[6] Hebrew documents were not, however, admitted by the courts [7] as evidence.

[1] *Al-Badr al-Ṭāli'* (Cairo, 1348), i, p. 230 seq. Perhaps this is the same as that cited in Brock., *Sup.*, ii, p. 74.

[2] Nazīh al-Mu'aiyad, *Riḥlah fī Bilād al-'Arabīyah al-Sa'īdah* (Cairo, 1937), i, p. 60. Anastase Marie de St. Elie, (edit.) *Bulūg͟h al-Marām* (Cairo, 1939) also contains some material on the Yemenite Jews. For material (as yet unpublished) in Arabic, see *Rivista d. Studi Orientali* (Roma, 1910), iii, 917.

[3] *Qalb al-Yaman* (Bag͟hdād, 1947), p. 166. In Ḥabbān the poll-tax was apparently 16 riyāls. Figures for the Ṣan'ā' poll-tax, as given by different authorities, do however vary.

[4] Cf. "An Early Zaidī Manual of Ḥisbah," *Rivista d. Studi Orientali* (Roma, 1953), p. 29.

[5] Nazīh al-Mu'aiyad, op. cit., i, p. 60.

[6] *Qalb al-Yaman*, op. cit., p. 167.

[7] Cf. "Divieto agli uffici statali yemeniti di accettare documenti in ebraico," *Oriente Moderno* (Roma, 1938), p. 41.

Outside the centralized Yemenite administration the Jew was protected by the Sultan, or even by the individual tribe or family; such was the case of the Ḥabbānīs (*infra*). The protectors would, of course, be of the arms-bearing classes or perhaps of the religious aristocracy. In South Arabia it is a shameful act for a tribesman to kill a Jew, as it would be to kill a woman. An excellent example of this form of protection in ancient times is to be found in a passage from the Fākhir of al-Mufaḍḍal b. Salamah.[1] A protected Jew of al-Ḥuṣain, the Saiyid of the Banū Sahm, was murdered by the Banū Ṣirmah, so the Sahm in turn slew a protected Jew of the Ṣirmah. Retaliation was then made on three Arab djīrān of the Sahm and the latter then slew three djīrān of the Ṣirmah. At this stage the Ṣirmah came to al-Ḥuṣain to discuss the matter. Al-Ḥuṣain replied, "You killed our Jew so we killed your Jew," adding that it would be a pity if two tribes closely related should actually engage each other in war.

The South Arabian Jew was subject to certain sumptuary laws [2] and to a number of religious restrictions. As I have found evidence that custom imposes certain sumptuary restrictions on the Muslim craftsman and cultivator, it seems to me likely that the arms-bearing tribes and religious aristocracy of South Arabia have laid restrictions of this kind on subjugated peoples and the menial classes from very ancient times. A case in point is the Ḥaḍramī tradition which ascribes the skirts shortened to the knee, worn by the women, and the tattooing of their faces, to an ordinance of the well-known 'Abbāsid governor Ma'n b. Zā'idah, who imposed these humiliating conditions on the country in punishment of a rebellion. Be this tradition historical or not, there is clearly a sense of the antiquity of such practices. Perhaps therefore it may be that these sumptuary laws were applied to the Jews as early as the period following the fall of Dhū Nuwās.

Individual Jews or communities were not, of course, always safe from occasional acts of fanaticism and, like the Muslim peasant, they must doubtless have been subject at times to unconstitutional exactions. Of the Imām al-Mahdī Aḥmad b. al-Ḥasan (ob. 1092 H. (A.D. 1681–2)) Shawkānī [3] says: "Among his noble actions and

[1] C. A. Storey, *The Fākhir of Mufaḍḍal ibn Salama* (Leiden, 1915), p. 103.

[2] For details see E. Brauer, op. cit., pp. 274 and 268.

[3] *Al-Badr al-Ṭāli'*, op. cit., i, p. 45. It is interesting to compare this with the Jewish account as related in S. D. Goitein, *From the Land of Sheba* (New York, 1947), p. 101.

qualities is the fact that he expelled the Jews whose houses were in Ṣan'ā', and they left it in flocks, selling such of their houses as were readily saleable. The Imām ordered the synagogue which they had in Ṣan'ā' to be nailed up, and that such books as it contained be taken out, and he poured away the wine which was in the miḥrāb. Then in the year 1091 H. he ordered the synagogue to be re-opened and destroyed, and he built in its place the mosque known as Masdjid al-Djalā."

On the other hand, the Jews did even play a part in the political life of South Arabia at times, and in fact they were not invariably held to the sumptuary laws.[1] There is, for example, the curious incident of the Jew of Baiḥān who set up as a semi-independent chief.[2] In Ḥabbān itself a Jewish tradition [3] mentions a certain Sulaimān al-Ḥākhām, who rendered assistance to the Muslim ruler when the town was besieged by Badr Bū Ṭuwairiḳ. Jewish sources would no doubt provide many other similar instances.

In folk tales from the Baiḍā' area the Jew figures as a cunning rogue, a poisoner, and a seducer of Muslim women ; but by contrast a number of writers record that Muslim and Jew lived not unkindly side by side. In Ḥabbān Arab guests seem to have attended Jewish wedding celebrations, and Arabs have described the head of the Ḥabbān community, Yūsuf b. Ibrāhīm, to me as a good fellow. In the Yemen it seems that the life of the two communities was more closely interwoven still.

In brief, while the Yemenite Jews did not enjoy the rights they hold in European society to-day, their position as Dhimmīs was generally upheld by the law, and the very existence of such large numbers after thirteen centuries of Muslim rule shows both that little pressure was put on them to alter their faith and that they were a useful asset to the tribes and rulers of South Arabia.

Emigration and Conversion in Ḥabbān

At the time of my visit one Jew had already accepted Islam and there was an interesting case before the Ḳāḍī of Ḥabbān regarding the custody of his children, as his wife had remained in her ancient

[1] Cf. al-Yāfi'ī, *Mir'āt al-Djanān* (Ḥaidarābād, 1337–9 H.), iv, p. 349, where mention is made of a Jew riding on horseback, *circa* 750 H. (A.D. 1349).

[2] " Materials for South Arabian History," *Bull. Sch. Or. and Afr. Studies* (London, 1950), xiii, p. 294. This has been dealt with at length from the Hebrew sources by S. D. Goitein in the Lit. Supplement to *Haaretz* of 17th November, 1950.

[3] Cf. T. Ashkenazi, *The Jews of Ḥaḍramawt* (bibliog.).

faith. According to the Ḳāḍī the decision regarding the custody of the children hinged upon whether the Ḥabbānīs were original Jews or Jews who had embraced Islam and then apostatized. I was shown a Jewish boy, son of the convert, who was being taught the recitation of the Koran, being maintained meanwhile by a Saiyid family. If this child were awarded to the father it was intended to send him to study at the Ribāṭ, in Tarīm. Even in the lawless and turbulent Wāḥidī Sultanate of that time there was quite clearly a certain regard for legal nicety where the D̲h̲immī was concerned, perhaps in part religious, in part due to the necessity of circumspection if the Arab Muslim protectors of the parties were not to be involved in feuds.

I am unable to deny or confirm the statement made to Touvia Ashkenazi that conditions had worsened since the war, and Sulṭān Ḥusain b. ʿAbdullāh (the regent) was pestering the Jews to accept Islam. The news from Palestine had, however, had a deep effect, even in remote Ḥabbān, and while I was there the news of the Aden riots arrived by radio and later through caravan or runner, much to the disquiet of the local Jewish community. Ultimately the community either accepted Islam or emigrated, the latter alternative being entirely voluntarily, I believe. The emigrants were mulcted of a portion of their silver bullion by the Sulṭān. Hard as this may seem, it is obvious that the departure of considerable quantities of silver from the country would be far from beneficial, and in the Ḳuʿaiṭī state there are actual restrictions on its export.

Jewish Settlements in Wāḥidī Territory

The field-notes below have now a certain historical interest, more especially as they were made on the occasion of the young Sulṭān's first state tour of the country.

ʿAzzān.

One family of Jews is found here, of small stature. The Jewish ḥāk̲h̲ām of the family is old and blind. A Jewish boy acts as domestic in the Sulṭān's house.

Al-Ḥawṭah.

Two families of Jewish silversmiths work here, three men in all. They have books which are kept on a wooden stretcher suspended from the ceiling by ropes, including Torahs and a Talmud printed in Jerusalem as well as MSS. bound in an unusual way. A Jewish boy reads to his father as he works. The MSS. are not on vellum but on paper. They speak in Hebrew but keep their accounts in Arabic in Hebrew character. They offer coffee, and are polite and submissive.

Al-Rawḍah.

Here the local Jews came into the assembly in the principal house to greet the Sulṭān, who had newly arrived; they drank coffee and then departed, saying practically nothing while they were there and not staying to eat. The exactions the Manṣab of al-Rawḍah imposes on the peasants he is also said to apply to the Jews. Here they say Allāh ya'izzak after mentioning the word "Jew" (as in the Yemen; the intention is to ask the listener's pardon for having mentioned something distasteful).

Ḥabbān.

The Jews were drawn up at the end of the long line of Ḥabbānīs (in order of precedence, Saiyids first) come to greet Sulṭān Nāṣir, who enters with firing of shots and a rattle from the Breda gun. They wear some indigo (nīl)—it is said that the Indian nīl gives a blacker dye, but the local ḥawīr is more lasting. These Jews have lighter complexions than the Arabs, but are certainly not tall [1] or distinguished in this way from them. None over the age of children wear the zunnār, but dress their hair in the Arab way. Many wear Jewish amulets known as taḥāfīẓ. Among themselves they speak Hebrew; the Arabs say there is no difference in the colloquial Arabic spoken by the Jews but they remark on a different intonation.[2] The Ḥākhām is Ibrāhīm b. Yūsuf, rather toothless. The Ḥabbān Jews kiss the hands of all.[3] They seem to be treated by the Arabs in quite a well-mannered way. The Jewish Quarter lies just below my window (in the Maṣna'ah). There are no ornaments on the battlements of the houses, but on some houses there are little patterns made with shells set in the mud wall. They burn dung [4]

[1] Contrary to Ashkenazi's informant (*supra*). Having notes on the article with me I particularly remarked on this fact.

[2] Those present when the Jewish boy converted to Islam recited the Koran made much of the fact that he spoke Arabic without a Jewish intonation.

[3] An important issue, for hand-kissing has of late years been the subject of much controversy in politico-religious circles in South Arabia.

[4] On this subject I should like to have been able to consult a work mentioned by Muḥ. b. 'Alī al-Shawkānī, author of "*al-Badr al-Ṭāli'*", op. cit., ii, p. 221, as composed by himself, *Ḥall al-Ashkāl fī Idjbār al-Yahūd 'alā 'ltiḳāṭ al-Azbāl*, but no copies of this work are at present known to Brockelmann.

and flat pats of it lie drying on the rocks at the foot of the Maṣna'ah, but it does not seem to be used by the Arabs here, as far as I can see. They are not agricultural but they keep fowls in a kind of coop made of mud with a wooden lid.

The Jewish cemetery lies south-west of the town; there are no old inscriptions because, they say, these have been destroyed by Arab children, but as the gravestones are of easily weathering sandstone this may not be true. The Jews, they say, held land once and some still keep the title-deeds, but the land was taken a long time ago by the Dawlah (Sulṭāns) and all they have now is their cemetery. The large mud karīf once owned by a Jew, and the sāḳiyah leading into it (Sāḳiyah Bā Ṭuwairiḳ), are filled from a bent tunnel hewn in the rock, the tool-marks showing on the side, but it only contains small pools just now.

I spent the afternoon of 8th December with the Jews and was shown various MSS., including two dīwāns. They use a book-rest formed of two crossed pieces of wood. Deeds in Arabic and Hebrew are produced. In the synagogues, of which there are two, are kept rolls of the law wrapped in cloth and with beautiful silver ends. Boys seem to be taught there in the evening. They make 'araḳ, but this was concealed when a soldier came in, but it is drunk secretly by some Muslims. At the Hanukka feast, which fell when I was in Ḥabbān, the Jewish girls wore all their silver ornaments and glass bracelets of the Am-Sailah type,[1] which were cheap at one time but are now dear as they are old.

There are five sections, called ḳaṣabāt, these are :—

(1) Shammākh. This is the first and oldest, and is said to be very ancient.

(2) Ma'ṭūf.

(3) Hilāl. For this section the Political Notebook has Sālim b. Manṣūr.

(4) Maifa'ī. This is presumably a nisbah from Maifa'ah.

(5) 'Adanī.

Most of the silversmiths of Ḥaḍramawt are said to be converted Jews, for no Jews can enter that country. The Jewish silversmiths are said to travel as far east as Rakhyah, Buḍah, and Bīr 'Alī, but not to enter Ḳu'aiṭī territory.[2] This may be true, as a family of silversmiths in Shibām is called Āl Bā Shammākh, and the names of

[1] Cf. *JRAS.*, 1938, p. 109.

[2] So the Political Notebook.

other families of Ḥaḍramī silversmiths, also said to be converted Jews, might possibly be Jewish by origin.

The Ḥabbānī House-deed.

The document *infra* was lent me by Ibrāhīm b. Yūsuf on my last afternoon in Ḥabbān. It illustrates very clearly the interplay of the D̲h̲immī and Muslim communities in a society which can have altered little since medieval times. The case obviously was quite a *cause célèbre* at the time. I quote from an informant :—

" Ṣāliḥ b. Yūsuf had a dispute with two sisters of his late father about a house in Bā Ba'air, the Jewish quarter of Ḥabbān. He sold the house to Mis'id b. Mḥummad (as they pronounce the names) who resold it on the same day to Ibrāhīm b. Yūsuf. The " siyāsah " of this procedure was to safeguard the buyer against any claims to be raised against him in the Jewish court of justice. He could then argue that he had acquired the house from a Gentile who was not under the jurisdiction of the Jewish Court. Indeed, the sisters proceeded against Ṣāliḥ for having sold to an ' Allom ', a term designing a lawless person, any transfer of property to whom would be void. Ṣāliḥ refused, however, to appear before the Jewish court. The case came before the Sulṭān Ḥusain b. 'Abdullāh, and it was decided after many vicissitudes that the sale was legal, but Ṣāliḥ had to pay Dumāyah (indemnities) and Mak̲h̲āsir (expenses)—which the husbands of the two aunts of Ṣāliḥ were prepared to accept instead of their share of the house, only after having been ' softened ' by various terms in jail. The affair nearly ended in a bloody feud between the Hil Mḳarmi', the d̲j̲ārs of the aunts,[1] and the Hil Yislam b. Manṣūr, the d̲j̲ārs of Ṣāliḥ."

[1] D̲j̲ār means both the protector and the person protected.

Arabic Text

صحيـح السّلطان علىّ بن محسن بن صالح الواحدىّ

(*Seals*)

الحمد للّه ربّ العالمين. وبعد، لمّا كان يوم الحَد[1] و٣ فى شهر محرّم عاشور
سنة ١٣٥١ الف وثلاثمـاية واحد وخمسين، فقد حضر لدَىّ وبين يدَىّ
صـالح بن يوسف بن هلال بن عَوَض اليهودىّ، وَقرّ[2] علا نفسـه اقراراً

[1] الاحد. [2] واقرّ.

صحيحاً شرعيًّا باءنّه[١] أباع إلّا مُسْعِد بِنْ محمّد بن احمد بن ناصر
البَابَكْرِىّ، وذالكَ البيت حَقُّه المعروف، بحافة اليهود، عُلْوَه وسُفَالَهْ،
وطين وعود، وحدّ وحدود، وابواب واخشاب، وحديد وجريد، وَحْجَار
وَمدَار[٢]، يحدّها بيت سَعيد بن سِحاق ذى تَصِلّا[٣] بيت بن دُوح، ويحدها
سّاس[٤] حقّها من قِدا صَرَحَت حسن لَكْسَرِ ومن قِدا الحافه على
ساسها ما لها مَخْرَج الّا حرَمها الشّرْعىّ بين اسْواسها أُلَرْبَعه، وجميع
مصالحها الدّاخله فيها والخارجه عنها، وما ينسَب اليها شرعًا وعاده. وذالك
بيعًا وشرا قَطْعًا قلاّطا بَتْرا مُنَجَّزًا، مستوفى الثّمن معلوم مقبوض بيد البايع.
وقَبَض البَيْع المشترِى القبض الشّرعىّ، يتصرّف ذِى الاملاك فى املاكهم،
وذى الحقوق فى حقوقهم. فلا عاد بقا للبيّاع حقّ من الحقوق، صار البيت
المذكور ملك من املاك المشترِى. واللّه الرّقيب. وكتب وشهد عبد الله
بن ابراهيم بن صالح بن ابراهيم بن عمر الشّبْلِىّ.

ושהיד עלא דליך חסן ן עוץ ן דוח
וצלם ן סחק ן דוח ואלה כאר לחצרין

צח מא רקמה
עבדלה : בריהים
אשבלי ואנא
צאלח : יוסף : הלאל

بتّاريخ[٧] اعلاه. فقد احال ما فى وجه المسطور إلّا ابراهيم بن يوسف بن
لَعرِيق اليهودىّ واخوانه، عوض، وسالم، وسعيد، حواله صحيحه شرعيّه، بقُنْع
مسعد بن محمّد ورضاه. واللّه الرّقيب. وكتب من تقدّم ذكره أعلا.
والدُّخَلا لَضوع يوسف بن لَعرِيق، السّلطان علىّ بن محسن الواحدىّ
واخوانه ومسعد بن لَحْمَد البَابَكْرىّ فيما نقط فى هذا الخطّ. والله كافى.

[١] بأنه. [٢] واحجار وامدار. [٣] تصل إلى. [٤] الساس. [٧] بالتاريخ.

Linguistic Notes

Spellings have been left as in the original text, but some of the tashkīl has been added for clarity or to indicate colloquial pronunciation.

TRANSLATION

Signature of the Sultan ʿAlī b. Muḥsin b. Ṣāliḥ al-Wāḥidī.

(*Seals*)

Praise to God, Lord of the Universe

Now when it was Sunday and the 3rd of the month of Muḥarram ʿĀs͟hūr (1), 1351 H. (A.D. 1932), Ṣāliḥ b. Yūsuf b. Hilāl b. ʿAwaḍ the Jew attended here before me, and made a valid legal (2) acknowledgment that he in fact sells to Musʿid (3) b. Muḥammad b. Aḥmad b. Nāṣir al-Bā-Bakrī (4), namely—the house in the Jewish Quarter (5) known to belong to him, its upper and lower parts (6), mud and wattle, borne and bounds, doors and timbers, iron and palm-branches, stone and clay; bounded by the house of Saʿīd b. Siḥāḳ (7) that extends to the house of B. Dūḥ, and bounded (also) by its own foundation-walls (8) on the side confronting the courtyard of Ḥasan Laksar (9), and by its own foundation-wall on the side facing the Jewish Quarter. It possesses no extra-mural area, but only the legal area belonging to it (10) comprised within its four foundation-walls, along with all its amenities within and without them (*or* it), and all pertaining to it in law and by usage (11). This is by (12) sale and purchase, executory, outright and unconditional (13), final and completed, and price being paid in full, known, and taken in the hand of the vendor. The purchaser has taken legal possession of the (property) sold, the owners of the properties having control of their properties, and those who hold rights (enjoying the exercise of) their rights. The vendor no longer retains any rights (therein), the afore-stated house having become a property of the purchaser. God is Overseer.

ʿAbdullāh b. Ibrāhīm b. Ṣāliḥ b. Ibrāhīm b. ʿUmar al-S͟hiblī (14) engrossed (this deed), and testifies to it.

(*Hebrew Script*)

Ḥasan b. ʿAwaḍ b. Dūḥ bears testimony to this, and (also) Sālim b. Siḥāḳ b. Dūḥ. God is the best of those present.

What ʿAbdullāh Brāhīm al-S͟hiblī wrote is true, and I am Ṣāliḥ b. Yūsuf b. Hilāl.

(*Reverse of the above, Arabic script*)

On the above date, that which is (contained) in the front page of the document was transferred to Ibrāhīm b. Yūsuf b. Laʿrīḳ the

Jew, and his brothers, 'Awaḍ, Sālim, and Sa'īd, a valid legal transfer, by consent and approval of Mus'id b. Muḥammad. God is Overseer.

The above-mentioned person engrossed (this deed).

The protectors of the dependents of Yūsuf b. La'rīḳ are the Sulṭān 'Alī b. Muḥsin al-Wāḥidī and his brothers, and Mus'id b. Laḥmad al-Bā-Bakrī, in accordance with what occurs in this document. God suffices (as witness).

Notes

(1) For the nomenclature of the Muslim months as used in the Wādī 'Amaḳīn see *Gl. Dat.*, p. 1449. 'Āshūr or Muḥarram in this district is reckoned the fourth month of the Muslim year.

(2) " Shar'ī " has been rendered throughout as " legal " but its full force in relation to the circumstances under which the contract was concluded would be " in conformity with sharī'ah law ".

(3) Pronounced Mis'id b. Mḥummad. So also Muḥsin is always pronounced Miḥsin. I have attempted no consistency in vocalization, employing both classical and colloquial vocalizations.

(4) Landberg, *Arabica V*, p. 226, mentions the Hal Bā Bakr, a sub-tribe of the Sa'd Ḥabbān, with their 'āḳil at Djuwairah.

(5) If my memory is correct the Jewish Quarter lies roughly on the south-west side of Ḥabbān and is overlooked by the neighbouring quarters. In this part of Arabia the aristocracy tend to build on the higher parts of the valley-side while the lower orders on the social scale build beneath them. In Ḥuraiḍah and perhaps other places in Ḥaḍramawt a Miskīn cannot even build a house as high as those of the Sādah. There seems to have been a similar distinction between the pre-Islamic Ḳuraish of the Ẓawāhir and Bawāṭin. *Arabica V*, p. 216, distinguishes four quarters in Ḥabbān. I was informed that the Miḥḍār Saiyids, the Āl Fad'aḳ Saiyids, the Ṣaban (indigo-workers), the carpenters, Jews, and the Āl Shiblī all had different quarters but that now they were mixed up to some extent.

(6) This legal term implies that the owner has the right to built on top of his house, should he so desire. I was informed that in Wādī 'Amd if you bought land in former times you could only build a single-storey house, but you had to pay a tax for each additional storey you added above that. House-deeds there are said to mention " al-bait hawwuh wa-djawwuh wa-'l-samā lī tawwuh, the house, its air (hawā-hu) and atmosphere and the sky adjoining it ". Though

this species of tax is known elsewhere it must have been established in South Arabia from antiquity. In Ṣan'ā' Jewish houses were usually of few storeys; according to Mohammed Hassan, *Heart of Yemen*, p. 168, the Jew's house must be of clay, or one storey of stone and the next of clay.

(7) Siḥāḳ, i.e. Isḥāḳ.

(8) For a description of the sās see *Building and Builders in Ḥaḍramawt*, pp. 276–7. It is the dry-stone foundation upon which an adobe house is built. The deed only mentions three sides; this is, I think, because the fourth side facing the famous Karīf of Ḥabbān attributed to Badr Bū Ṭuwairiḳ was on the edge of a steep cliff. The general plan of the houses is as follows :—

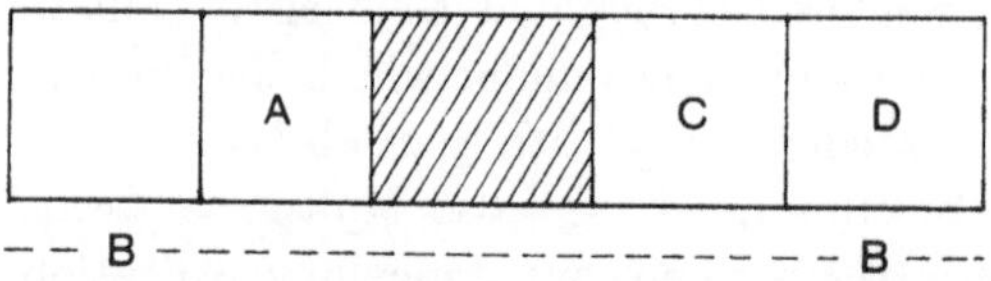

(A) The court of Ḥasan.
(B) Ḥāfat al-Yahūd.
(C) Dār Sa'īd b. Siḥāḳ.
(D) Bait Dūḥ.

This passage may be compared with Jean David-Weill, Un nouveau titre de Propriété daté, *Mélanges Gaudefroy Demombynes* (Cairo, 1935 45), pp. 141–6, and with a house-deed from the Faiyūm (British Museum, Or 4684, no. xvi) dated 405 H. (A.D. 1014–15), unfortunately so damaged that it cannot be reproduced here *in toto* :—

. . . بحده وحدوده ومدخله ومخرجه وكل حوله داخل فيه وخارج منه وما
اشتملت عليه حدود اربع حده الاول وهو القبلي . . .

The general substance and style of the document under discussion may be compared also with the prescriptions for the form of legal documents composed by Muḥ. b. 'Umar Baḥraḳ, al-Nubdhah al-Muḥarrirah, Princeton MS. Baḥraḳ was Ḳāḍī in Shiḥr in the late fifteenth century.

(9) The Hal Laksar are noted in *Arabica V*, p. 227, as one of the two main sections of Sa'd al-Shu'aib. In Landberg's day the *abū* of this section was Yislam b. Ṣāliḥ.

(10) My informants stated that the ḥaram means the outer sides of a house and a certain extent of ground in front, just a little beyond the walls. I assume that the owner of the house could not actually build on such outside ground. The makhradj or extra-mural area, on the contrary, might be an open space belonging to

the house, adjoining the street, or even a sort of adobe platform (in Aden, Ḥaḍramawt, " dakkah ") lying in front of the house, extending out from the sās. Mr. E. R. Johnson has drawn my attention to an interesting circumstance of recent occurrence in Saiwūn. An Adenese assaulted a Saiwūnī whom he found sitting upon his dakkah, on the grounds that he was making advances to his wife. It appeared subsequently that in Saiwūn a man can sit on another's dakkah without such impropriety, whereas in Aden it is taken as a sure sign of immoral intent! *Al-Fawā'id al-Sanīyah*, fol. 29b mentions a shop (ma<u>kh</u>zan) with a dakkah.

(11) Lit. " by custom ".

(12) Translated thus in accordance with the text as it stands, but in semi-colloquial documents such as this, an accusative is often written where classical grammar demands a nominative.

(13) It was stated that by " unconditional " (cf. *Gl. Dat.* " tout à fait ") the deed asserts that this transaction is a sale and not a mortgage.

(14) Al-<u>Sh</u>iblī is the Ḳāḍī of Ḥabbān of that time, a member of the well-known family of Ma<u>sh</u>ā'i<u>kh</u>.

(15) An endorsement on the back of a deed is a very common way of recording a transfer of property in South Arabia.

Note on the Wāḥidī Sulṭāns

The ruling Sulṭān of the Ḥabbān line in Landberg's day [1] was Nāṣir b. Ṣāliḥ who reigned, according to the Political Notebook, from 1314–31 H. (A.D. 1896–1912/13). It seems that his son Muḥsin b. Ṣāliḥ reigned between the years 1308–37 H. (A.D. 1890–1918/19), possibly concurrently with his father, as in ancient South Arabia.[2] 'Alī b. Muḥsin succeeded until 1365 H. (A.D. 1945–6), and it was during his reign that the above transaction took place. The present Sulṭān, Nāṣir b. 'Abdullāh, is the nephew of 'Alī b. Muḥsin. The ancestor of the dynasty is claimed by local tradition to be a certain 'Abd al-Wāḥid, who died in 991 H. (1583–4).

The Political Notebook remarks that the Jews generally settle their quarrels amongst themselves, but should that fail, *as it rarely does*, they appeal to the Wāḥidī Sulṭān (at that time Ḥusain b. 'Abdullāh).

[1] *Arabica V*, p. 180.

[2] Cf. Jacques Ryckmans, *L'Institution Monarchique* (Louvain, 1951).

Glossary

عاشور *Muḥarram.* Gl. Dat.

عُلْوَه وسُفَالَه *Top and bottom* (of a house). Sufālah is rendered by Gl. Dat., *le bas, la partie inférieure, le dessous.* Cf. ʻulw wa-sufl in A. A. Bevan, "Some Contributions to Arabic Lexicography," *Vol. of Oriental Studies presented to E. G. Browne* (Cambridge, 1922), p. 72.

ساس pl. أسواس Cf. Notes to Translation.

مَدَر pl. أمدار *Clay, adobe* (class). Cf. مَدْرَة *a brick,* مدّار *a potter.*

من قِدَا Gl. Dat. *du coté de.*

مَخْرَج Syn. دَكّة, *extra-mural space or area* belonging to a house.

حَرَم *Legal area of a house.* Cf. Notes to Translation.

قلاطًا Cf. Gl. Dat., قَلَطْ *tout à fait.* The Leiden Cod. Or. 7100 p. 128 (C. Snouck Hurgronje Bequest) containing Ḥaḍrami colloquial verse, also contains the phrase قطعاً قلاطاً

مُنَجَّز *Executory.* Gl. Dat., Vb. achever, finir, terminer. Cf. Muḥ. b. ʻUmar Baḥraḳ, *al-Nubdhah al-Muḥarrirah,* Princeton MS.

ذِى Said to be equivalent to ذوى , the latter presumably a colloquial form of ذوو.

قُنْع Commonly used in the formula ... بقنع, *by consent of . . .* Cf. al-Djāḥiẓ, Ḥayawān (Cairo, 1944), vi, p. 224,

قضى ... بين الجن ... بحكم وأقنعهم

دخيل pl. دخلاء *Guarantor, protector.* Gl. Dat., *associé.*

ضُوْح *Dependents.* Gl. Dat., *contribules; les gens de la famille et de la tribu.* One says, "كَيْف ضُوعَك and وِشْ هم ضُوعَك, How is your family?"

SHORT BIBLIOGRAPHY

Anon. "Jewish Nomads from the Hadramaut," *Crown Colonist* (London, September, 1947). (A copy of this article had actually reached Ḥabbān.)

Ashkenazi, Touvia. "The Jews of Ḥaḍramawt" (in Hebrew), *Edoth* (Palestine Institute of Folk-lore and Ethnology) (Jerusalem, 1946), pp. 58–71.

(I am indebted to my colleague Mr. I. Wartski, who drew my attention to, and translated this article for me.)

BRAUER, ERICH. *Ethnologie der Jemenitischen Juden* (Heidelberg, 1934).

Encyl. Islam. Art. " Ḥabbān ".

GOITEIN, S. D. " Transplantation of the Yemenites," *Commentary* (New York, July, 1951), pp. 24–33.

LANDBERG, C. DE. *Arabica V* (Leiden, 1898).

SERJEANT, R. B. " Building and Builders in Ḥaḍramawt," *Le Muséon* (Louvain, 1949), lxii, iii–iv, pp. 275–284.

Diagram of a silver plaque, a Hebrew amulet seen at Ḍāliʿ in 1940, probably to be read as above. The Ḥabbān Jews possessed various stones, supposed to have curative properties, which they offered me for sale at prices ranging up to 50 rupees. (Cf. Brauer, op. cit Index.)

ADDENDA

P.118 On the question of expulsion see Serjeant & Lewcock, *Ṣanʿāʾ; an Arabian Islamic city*, London, 1983, 399b seq. & Koningsveld, P.S., et alii, *Yemenite authorities and Jewish Messianism*, Leiden, 1990. *Ḥawliyyāt Yamāniyyah*, ed. ʿAbdullah al-Ḥabshī, covering years 1224/1809–1316/1899 has some references to Ṣanʿāʾ Jews as has *Ṣafaḥāt majhūlah*, Ṣanʿāʾ, 1978.

P.122/fn.4 The literature on compelling the Jews to collect dung is listed in our *Ṣanʿāʾ*, 394a (n) seq.

P.123/11 Of the Karīf the Aden paper *al-Nahḍah* (15/iii/51) reports that the Wāḥidī Nāʾib is preventing the Ḥabbānīs from drawing water from it though it is a *waqf sharʿī lā yubāʿ wa-lā yūrath ḥattā yarith Allah al-arḍ wa-man ʿalay-hā*. It is the *waqf* of Shaykh Muḥaymadān Dhiyaybān who bought it seven times from the Wāḥidī and ʿAwlaqī sultanates, arranged the excavation and repair of it, and made it a *waqf sharʿī* for those who dwell in this town (*bilād*). One can only guess at the vicissitudes of those depending on it in the wars between the Wāḥidī and ʿAwlaqī.

P.128/fn.8 Baḥraḳ's treatise is no. XI of this volume.

IX

FAMINE DEATH WITHOUT LOSS OF HONOUR IN ANCIENT ARABIA AND YEMENI ARḤAB

On 6 December 1966, with Muḥammad al-'Ubaydī, son of the *naqīb* of Shākir, as leader of my escort, I went to Sūdah in Arḥab, a black lava mountain, the place belonging to 'Iyāl al-Siḥaym. We had passed by Jabal al-Riyām and Ṣirwāḥ. The tomb of Ṣāliḥ [1] was on the north side, a domed building. This tomb had, or used to have, *'ushūr*, tithes paid to it. In the houses which were on the south side there was only one man, the rest of the villagers being women. The men were away at the war or perhaps employed in Ṣan'ā'. Water was short here and I believe (though this is not in my notes) brought from quite some distance. Sūdah had the look of a hungry place. Yet in the area there was much drawing on the rocks, some quite recent, including a Hebrew graffito which too had the appearance of being recently made, and it seems that Jews used at one time to live here.

In the open country we saw a number of *ma'fadas*, mass graves of people buried together according to Ṣāliḥ, one of the tribal escort. There was no visible sign of these graves though I recall some rocks in the ground—the place was memorable for me as my mule threw me in an unguarded moment on the hard, gritty ground! Ṣāliḥ gave me further particulars which I did not record in my field-book as I noted that 'there is no reason to believe this', but I was wrong. So I have to rely on my memory for what he told me. This was that in the time of famine, when there was no food left, or possibility of obtaining food, the tribesfolk, men and women, would collect together and sit down in a circle and wait for death—I think he said that they put on their finest clothes and jewellery. It was a matter of honour for the tribe that they should not beg for food.

When I showed the late Professor Maḥmūd al-Ghūl this word *ma'fada*, strange to me, he at once recognized its significance and referred me to the lexicons. There is also a quotation in the *Ghāyat al-amānī*: [2]

> Al-Hamdānī said: 'Most of the Āl Abi 'l-Jaysh perished in the drought (*ḥuṭma*[3]) of 290/903 after their monies (*amwāl*) were exhausted and their chiefs had given unstintingly because of the problem. So they sat in their houses and locked their doors until they died. Only one small infant girl of them survived whom some of the Banu 'l-Azhar b. 'Abd al-Raḥmān took and she married into them.'

A cursory examination of the extant published writings of al-Hamdānī has failed to bring to light any information on these families, so the author may be quoting from one of the missing volumes of the *Iklīl*.

Al-Ṣaghānī [4] makes the following entry:

'*Al-I'tifād* is that a man locks his door on himself and begs (*yas'alu*) of nobody until he starves to death.'

Abū 'Amr [5] cites:

[1] This prophet is buried in more than one place in south Arabia.

[2] Yaḥyā b. al-Ḥusayn, *Ghāyat al-amānī fī akhbār al-quṭr al-Yamānī*, ed. S. 'Āshūr and M. M. Ziyāda, Cairo, 1388/1968, I, 190.

[3] *Sanat al-ḥuṭma = sanat al-shidda wa-'l-jadb* (loc. cit.).

[4] *Al-Takmila*, vol. ed. Ibrāhīm al-Abyārī and Muḥammad Khalafullāh, Cairo, 1971, II, 291 ff.

[5] Abū 'Amr (b. al-'Alā' al-Baṣrī) died in 151 or 159 A.H. Shamir was contemporary with Muḥammad b. Ziyād b. al-A'rābī (died 231/846). So this information was being reported to a Basran philologist as early as the first half of the second century A.H.

I think of[6] a lady saying 'This is a time of *i'tifād*'.
Who is it that survives the *i'tifād*?

Shamir said: Muḥammad b. Ans said: 'It was (their custom) when they suffered severe famine and were afraid they would [starve to] death, to lock a door on themselves and erect an enclosure of bush into which they would enter so as to starve to death'. He continued: 'A man met a girl weeping and said to her "What is the matter with you?" "We are going to lock ourselves up and starve to death", she said.' He continued: 'Al-Naẓẓār b. Hāshim al-Asadī said:

Fate/a time called to them to starve to death,
Starving that rends the unity of peers.'[7]

Shamir said: 'I found it in the book of Ibn Buzurj: "*I'taqada 'l-rajul*, with [the letter] *qāf*, *wa-aṭama*,[8] i.e., he shuts a door on him[self] when in [dire] need so that he might die".'

Nashwān b. Sa'īd (died 573/1117)[9] notes that

Ḥimyar say '*'Affada 'alay-hi bāba-hu*, He '*affada*-ed his door on him(self)', when he has locked it—the *ifti'āl* (form). *Al-i'tifād*, in the dialect (*lugha*) of Ḥimyar, is a man's locking the door of his house (*dār*) without coming out of it, until he dies. They used to do that in the time when grain was cut off from the Yemen in the [famine] years of Joseph, on him be peace, out of haughty disdain (*takabbur-an*) of begging, until two women of them instituted the loan (*sanna 'l-salaf*).

I'tifād was the final resort of those proud tribal people, frustrated and despairing, but unflinching in their resolve to die rather than beg. It is unlikely that the people of Yemeni cities in desperate straits through famine or siege would turn to *i'tifād* and Yemeni histories record that they ate dogs and cats and even occasional cases of cannibalism occurred, as with other peoples in like situations.

Although Nashwān seems to imply that the custom of *i'tifād* was pre-Islamic and he makes a cryptic reference to the introduction of loans, if this is in the literature it has so far escaped me. However, *i'tifād* doubtless was a pre-Islamic practice, but when the Arḥabīs, our own contemporaries, showed me the *ma'fadas*, presumably the site of the death and burial of their forebears, I do not think they were recounting an antique legend but events within relatively recent folk memory.[10] A curious incident quite unconnected with the above, but *en route* to Sūda, took place a little before we arrived at al-Ḥayfa. We met on the track a party of three or four persons returning from a wedding. Muḥammad al-'Ubaydī built a little heap of stones in front of them, later explaining his action as: '*Anā qarda't*, I set up a stone pillar (*qirdā'*, plur., *qarādī'*)[11]'. This laid an obligation on the wedding party to give us some of the food, in fact *laḥūḥ* (pancakes of fermented *dhura*), which they were bringing back from the wedding.

[6] cf. Wright, *Grammar*, II, 217, for this rendering of *wāw rubba*.

[7] *Tāj al-'arūs*, Kuwait, 1390/1970, VIII, 393 seq., reads *zamān mu'tafad-un* for *zaman-un mu'tafid-un* of the *Takmila*, the former to be rendered 'A time in which starving to death had to take place', or something of this sense. The reading of the *Tāj* is the easier of the two.

[8] *Tāj*, loc. cit., *āṭam* for *aṭam*. It looks as if the reading with *qāf* is simply a textual error.

[9] *Shams al-'ulūm*, GMS, XXIV, Leiden-London, 1916, 73. Nashwān was a Ḥimyarī of Jabal Ṣabir behind Ta'izz and it could well be that, in his time, *i'tifād* was only a memory there but survived in remoter districts of the Yemen.

[10] See also J. H. Mordtmann's notes on Glaser's 'Skizze der Geschichte Arabiens', *ZDMG*, Leipzig, 1890, XLIV, 192, 200.

[11] I noted this word as a term for stone pillars of vine trellises in Banī Bahlūl country near Ṣan'ā', with a variant *qirdāl* (1966).

Note

Professor Peter Holt has drawn my attention to R.C. Slatin, *Fire and sword in the Sudan*, London, 1896, 455: "I think the Jaalin [Jaʿaliyyīn], who are the most independent, as well as the proudest tribe in the Sudan, suffered more severely than the rest [in the great famine during the Mahdiyyah 1306/1888–89]: several fathers of families, seeing that escape from death was impossible, bricked up the doors of their houses, and, united with their children, patiently awaited death. I have no hesitation in saying that in this way entire villages died out."

X

THE "WHITE DUNE" AT ABYAN: AN ANCIENT PLACE OF PILGRIMAGE IN SOUTHERN ARABIA

In the Faḍlī state of the former Aden Federation, a few miles to the north-east of Dirjāj/Dirgāg, is to be found al-Kat͟hīb al-Abyaḍ or the White Dune, an enormous ridge of sand running in a more or less north-easterly direction, and facing Mount Ḥiryān/Ḥaryān, this last being a grey stone mountain forming with al-Kat͟hīb al-Abyaḍ opposite to it a sort of ravine or *wādī*. This is the Wādī Salā, the mouth of which is approached from the west; the *wādī* winds somewhat, the sand ridge getting higher the farther one goes up it. The White Dune has long been a place of pilgrimage. It may be recalled that the pre-Islāmic Prophet Hūd is stated to be buried in al-Kat͟hīb al-Aḥmar, the Red Dune, in Wādī Ḥaḍramawt,[1] so perhaps dunes occasionally had some notion of sanctity attaching to them, for one reason or another, as long ago as the Jāhilīyah.

HISTORICO-LITERARY NOTICES ON THE "WHITE DUNE"

A fairly cursory survey of the literature reveals that al-Kat͟hīb al-Abyaḍ is known from early times to South Arabian writers. Al-Hamdānī quotes a tradition, already ancient in his day, that there were four sacred places (*biqā' muqaddasah/marḥūmah*) in the Yemen, one of these being "Mirrā' Ma'īn, which is perhaps in Abyan, and contains the White Dune (al-Kat͟hīb al-Abyaḍ),[2] it being a *ribāṭ* (religious college or *zāwiyah*?)[3] to which people go out, even up to this present time of ours". Elsewhere al-Hamdānī alludes to Kat͟hīb Yarāmis (text, incorrectly, Barāmis) which is a *ribāṭ*.[4]

[1] Cf. my "Hūd and other pre-Islamic prophets of Ḥaḍramawt", *Le Muséon*, LXVII (Louvain, 1954), 127, *passim*.

[2] Al-Hamdānī, *al-Juz' al-t͟hāmin min al-Iklīl*, ed. Anastase-Marie al-Kirmilī (Baghdad, n.d. [1934]), p. 137. The term *ḥiqf* is also used.

[3] O. Löfgren, *Arabische Texte zur Kenntnis der Stadt Aden im Mittelalter* (Uppsala, 1936–50), glossary, p. 35, "Mönchshospiz, befestigtes Kloster".

[4] Al-Hamdānī, *Ṣifat Jazīrat al-'Arab*, ed. D. H. Müller (Leiden, 1884–91), p. 52. A place al-Kat͟hīb is also mentioned on the route between al-Suḥaib and Lahej, *op. cit.* p. 189, but if it should be al-Kat͟hīb al-Abyaḍ the traveller would be making a considerable detour.

The driver of the Aden Department of Antiquities, Sa'īd, a Ḥasanī tribesman, told me that his father used to go to visit Kat͟hīb Yarāmis, so this name has also persisted to the present day, Yarāmis being the well-known *wādī* into which the Wādī Salā debouches.

Among the *faqīhs* and *qāḍīs* of Abyan, Ibn Samurah mentions a certain 'Umar b. Muḥammad al-Kat͟hībī, not a very well-known person.[1] Again, al-S͟harjī quotes 'Abd al-Raḥmān son of al-S͟haik͟h al-Kabīr 'Abdullāh b. As'ad al-Yāfi'ī as saying, "I met on one occasion with a certain man of God on al-Kat͟hīb al-Abyaḍ, and he revealed (*kās͟haf*) to me many things and spoke of somewhat of my secret. I asked him about the man of the age, and he said, 'He is the s͟haik͟h Ismā'īl al-Jabartī'." (Al-Jabartī (d. 875/1470–1) was a Zabīdī.)[2] The father, 'Abdullāh b. As'ad, the celebrated author of *Mir'āt al-janān*, is buried, the Yāfi'īs claim, at Ma'rabān, and is a *walī bain ḥadd al-Sa'dī wa-'l-Yaharī*, a saint on the Sa'dī-Yaharī border, these latter being two large tribes of the Lower Yāfi'ī confederation. He has the respect (*iḥtirām*) of the tribes and he, i.e. his shrine, receives a quarter of the tithes (*'us͟hūr*) of the district in which it lies. Abū Mak͟hramah[3] and other authors however state explicitly that he died and was buried in Mecca, so if I am correct in assuming that the saint of Ma'rabān is the same person as the author, Yāfi'ī local tradition would seem to be without foundation.

As late a source as the *Tāj al-'arūs*, though apparently copying the *Takmilah*, describes al-Kat͟hīb as on the coast of the Yemen Sea "containing a mosque from which *barakah* is acquired". This brief description could fit the case, but if al-Kat͟hīb al-Abyaḍ was at one time a resort or even a permanent centre of residence for Ṣūfīs and scholars nothing of that appears to be left now. The Ḥaḍramī writer 'Aidarūs b. 'Umar b. 'Aidarūs al-Ḥabs͟hī (d. 1314/1895) repeats that al-Kat͟hīb al-Abyaḍ is at al-Ribāṭ near Abyan, and that the first mosque to be built after Islam is said to be near this dune: "al-Kat͟hīb al-Abyaḍ is the blessed (*mubārak*) dune in the district of Abyan, a resort for the pious servants of God. It is said there are graves there and also a company of the pious. It has great fame in that district, and each year, in the month of Rajab a great concourse of the people of the district assembles there in order to obtain blessing (*tabarruk*)."[4]

[1] *Ṭabaqāt fuqahā' al-Yaman*, ed. Fu'ād Saiyid (Cairo, 1957), p. 224, with useful notes. [2] *Ṭabaqāt al-k͟hawāṣṣ* (Cairo, 1903), p. 37. Cf. pp. 21, 54.

[3] Ed. Löfgren, pp. 109–13.

[4] *'Iqd al-yawāqīt al-jawharīyah...* (Cairo, 1317), p. 125.

THE "WHITE DUNE" AT ABYAN

The visitation to al-Kat͟hīb al-Abyaḍ falls on 15 S͟ha'bān, that is Niṣf S͟ha'bān; it may only be a coincidence that this nowadays is also the date of the pilgrimage to Hūd, he being buried in al-Kat͟hīb al-Aḥmar. Some people maintain that the visitation dates only from the time of the Prophet Muḥammad and that this is why it is respected. Another visitation seems to take place at the Mi'rāj on 27 Rajab, as stated by al-Ḥabs͟hī. The people eat their '*as͟hā*' there, and they make a *mawlid al-nabī*. When I first went to Aden in 1940 the recital and singing of *mawlids* was a popular diversion and it still remains so. One of the ceremonies is to fire from the top of the White Dune at marks on the other side of the *wādī*, i.e. on Mount Ḥiryān, which is usual also at many other *ziyārahs* in South Arabia. If you can run seven times up the White Dune from the *wādī* bottom you will have performed the equivalent of the *ḥajj* to Mecca, but I imagine few people can do this, and one scramble to the top plunging through the loose sand was enough for me and for our Faḍlī tribal guard driver! Yāfi' take dust (*turāb*) away from the dune for *barakah*, just as people take dust from the tombs of the saints, for there are said to be seventy-seven prophets (*nabī*) buried in the White Dune. If a camel goes up to the top of Al-Kat͟hīb al-Abyaḍ and dies there no worms will eat it, nor will *al-ḥaras͟h*, a word explained to mean wild animals and birds, devour it. In one or two other places I noticed holes under the rocks polished by human contact, just like the stones under Ḥajar al-Zinwān, the Bastards' Rock.

THE BASTARDS' ROCK

In the valley-bottom of Salā are trees and booths, the latter unoccupied of course, except during the *ziyārah*, the remains of fires, and other traces of the festival. People also camp on the mountain-side, and there were even some sticks which had formed the booths of a recent visitation on the top of the sand-ridge itself. A little way up, on the side of the mountain is the Ḥajar al-Zinwān,[1] the Bastards' Rock, a large square-shaped boulder, standing free, but poised on other rocks. It is just possible to crawl underneath it, and the entrance is picked out

[1] Sing. *zanū*. 'Alawī b. Ṭāhir al-Ḥaddād, *al-S͟hāmil fī tārīk͟h Ḥaḍramawt wa-mak͟hālīfi-hā* (Singapore, 1940), unpublished copy in my possession, p. 193, mentions Ḥuṣn ibn al-Zanū in the Ḥālikah country of western Ḥaḍramawt. In Anṣāb of the Upper 'Awlaqīs a bastard is *ḥalḥūl* (plur. *ḥalāḥīl*), syn. *zinwān* (plur.).

with plaster (*nūrah*). No person born out of wedlock can pass under the rock, but he will stick there, and any person failing to get through from one side to the other could only be released from the position in which he is stuck, by another person firing off a rifle. In actual fact it appears that there is some kind of trick in the way that one places the body in attempting to crawl through underneath the rock. This curious institution seems to give rise to a great deal of levity at the time of the *ziyārah*, with challenges and counter-challenges to prove the legitimacy of one's birth, and I was told of the case of a woman who burst into a fury of rage at her son because he stuck under the Bastards' Rock, and thereby unjustly impugned her honour!

Sa'īd al-Ḥasanī told me a story which illustrates the rather more serious purpose to which the Ḥajar al-Zinwān may be put. His grandfather (*jadd*) was doubtful as to whether a son of his wife's was his own child or that of another man, so the tribe put down as a pledge fifteen Arab guns (i.e. muskets) and a hundred camels (*ṭaraḥū min khamsta'shar bunduq 'arabīyah wa-miyat rāḥilah*). This was of course in earnest of their willingness to proceed to judgement. The two contending parties in the case were the Āl al-Sha'aif, Ḥasanīs, and the Āl Bā Ja'am/Ga'am (*wa-'l-mutashājirīn hum qabīlat Āl al-Sha'aif al-Ḥasanī wa-qabīlat Āl Bā Ja'am*). The boy they then took to al-Kathīb, and they made the trial as to whether he could pass under the Bastards' Rock – which in fact he was able to do, so the fault lay with the Āl al-Sha'aif, and they paid over the damages (blame-money), such and such a sum (*wa-ṣār al-ghalṭah 'ind Āl al-Sha'aif wa-dafa'ū al-lawm, al-mablagh kadhā*). It is to be remarked that the tribe, not the individual plaintiff, paid over the fine. The *lawm*-money[1] was to clear the face (*ṣafā al-wijh*) (i.e. the honour) of the Āl Bā Ja'am from dishonour. For this reason, that it can exonerate and exculpate, the Bastards' Rock is also known as Ḥajarat al-Barā'ah, the Stone of Rendering Innocent. The Murqushī tribe of the Faḍlīs do not follow the procedure I have just described. This form of trial was described to me as being a kind of *bish'ah*, trial by ordeal which is practised by hereditary shaikhs of the *bish'ah* in Upper Yāfi', Raidat Āl 'Abd al-Wadūd, and other places in South Arabia; it is also practised in Socotra. I now have detailed information on how *bish'ah* is conducted given me by the Āl 'Abd al-Wadūd shaikh, but the similarity seems to me only superficial.

[1] C. de Landberg, *Glossaire daṯînois* (Leiden, 1920–42), p. 2658, "outrage, dommages-intérêts".

X

THE "WHITE DUNE" AT ABYAN

How near the custom associated with the Bastards' Rock is to pre-Islāmic usages and even what survived in medieval Islām is demonstrable from the literature. Describing the divination arrows at Mecca, Ibn Hishām states that Quraish, if they suspected a man's descent (*nasab*), would take him with a hundred *dirhams* and a camel to be slaughtered to the God Hubal at the Ka'bah. The gifts they presented to the man in charge of casting the divining arrows, and then they would say, "O our God, this is so-and-so...produce the truth (*akhrij al-ḥaqq*) about him!" Then they would order the diviner to cast the arrows. If it turned out to be the arrow which had *min-kum* marked upon it, the man was a *wasīṭ*, i.e. of good quality in respect of the tribe; if it was marked *min ghairi-kum* then he belonged to another tribe and was an ally (*ḥalīf*), but if it turned out to have *mulṣaq* (syn. *dā'ī*) marked upon it he was, with regard to them, in a position without relationship by blood (*nasab*) or alliance (*ḥilf*).[1] Needless to say it is often necessary in tribal society to be sure of such relationships.

The celebrated knight and author Usāmah b. Munqidh, visiting Petra in the middle of the twelfth century A.D. which he knew as al-Raqīm, the Hebrew Reqem,[2] tells us, "I entered the mosque and prayed in it; but the cleft (*al-maḍīq*) in it I did not go through. One of the Turkish amīrs, however, who were in my company, named Barshak, came with the intention of entering through that narrow cleft (*shiqq*). I said to him, 'What art thou doing there? Pray outside of it.' 'There is no god but Allāh', he replied. 'I must then be a bastard (*bi-iḥrām rāḥatī in lam...*) if I cannot enter through that narrow cleft!' 'What is this that thou art saying?' I asked. 'This is a place', he replied, 'through which no son of adultery (*walad zinā'*) can enter. He cannot possibly enter therein.' This statement made me rise and enter in that place. I prayed in it and came out without, as Allāh knows, believing what he had said. Most of the troops thereupon came, went in and recited their prayers. But one of my officers, Barāq al-Zubaydī, had a black slave, devout and assiduous in prayer. The same, though one of the leanest and tallest of men, came in turn to that place, exerted every effort to get in, but could not do it. The poor fellow came back crying,

[1] *Sīrah*, ed. F. Wüstenfeld (Göttingen, 1858–60), pp. 97 ff.

[2] M. A. Murray, *Petra* (Glasgow, 1939), pp. 78–9, quoting the Old Testament and Josephus. There is supposed also to be a cave of the Seven Sleepers in the Yemen.

moaning and sighing for having failed to get in through the cleft."[1]

So much then, for the Bastards' Rock, in front of which, lower down the hill, lies what looks like a small cistern, about one foot deep and perhaps two or three feet in diameter, all picked out with *nūrah*. In front of this again, slightly lower down the slope of the hill, and picked out in *nūrah* also, are the footprint of the Prophet's horse (*khail*) and the hole made in the rock by the butt of his spear. There is also a whitened stone near the much larger Bastards' Rock, and up the hill yet another whitened stone; but nobody present was able to inform me what purpose these served. All about the Bastards' Rock are little heaps of stones built up on individual rocks; these our driver called *mad'ā* (pl. *madā'ī*).

The *madā'ī* have been described by Landberg as defining the limits of a type of sacred enclave,[2] but this is perhaps not always so. At Khanfar of Abyan in 1947 I saw various types of *mad'ā ḥaqq al-walī*, stone or mud pillars with a hole in the top for a lamp. The following account of the *mad'ā* was related to me:

لَمّا يكون واحد مريض يروح الى عند المدعا (الولىّ) ويشلّ معْهْ شَىْ من المأكول وياكلوا عند الولىّ (عند المدعا) . بعد ما ياكلوا يِدْعُوا عند الولىّ إنَّك تَدْعِى لنا عند رَبَّكْ يِعافِينا من المرض الذى جِينا من شانهُ ثم يَقْرَءُون الفاتحه ويروحوا .

إقْراءة الفاتحه — يقول الفاتحه الى روح ولى الفلانى إنّ الله يَنْفَعَنا بَأَسرارَه وِأَنوارَه وِيكون منا دَرْب وحِجاب من جميع لِأَسْباب . وبَعْدَيْن فى الآخَر يقولها لا روح النبى .

"When a man is ill he goes to the *mad'ā*, i.e. the saint, and brings some food with him, and they eat at the saint, i.e. at the *mad'ā*.[3] After that they pray to the saint, 'Pray for us to your Lord to cure us of the illness on account of which we have come.' Then they recite the *Fātiḥah* and go.[4]

[1] H. Derenbourg, *Texte arabe de l'autobiographie d'Ousāma* (Paris, 1886), p. 11; P. K. Hitti, *Memoirs of an Arab-Syrian Gentleman* (Columbia, 1927, reprinted Beirut, 1964), pp. 39–41.

[2] *Études sur les dialectes de l'Arabie méridionale*, II, *Daṯînah* (Leiden, 1905–13), p. 1786; and *Arabica*, v (Leiden, 1896), 145–6.

[3] Alternatively, coffee alone may be brought.

[4] The Fātiḥah (Koran, *sūrah* I) is said on behalf of some person upon whom God will in consequence send his light – so said my informant.

THE "WHITE DUNE" AT ABYAN

"Recital of the *Fātiḥah* – they say the *Fātiḥah* for the soul of saint So-and-so, may God avail us through his secrets and lights,[1] and may he be a wall around us and a screen from all causes (of harm).[2] Then, at the end, he says it for the soul of the Prophet."

These pillars with a hole at the top for a lamp are common enough in many districts of Aden Federation. At Wādī 'l-Gharīb, east of Shuqrā, a pillar containing a hole for a lamp was called a *bakrah min shān al-walī*.[3] The Faḍlīs told me that a *mad'ā* may be set up for any person, but a *bakrah* was set up for a *walī* exclusively, i.e. for a saint. In this case the saint was said to be a Ḥāmid Saiyid from Ḥaḍramawt. At Sa'īd of the Upper 'Awlaqīs, said to have been badly destroyed in the fighting between the 'Awlaqīs and NLF in 1968, I saw a *mad'ā* of a saiyid called 'Abd al-Raḥmān Daḥūm somewhere inside the town. Possibly the *mad'ā* and *bakrah* may be survivals of, or related to, the granite *naos* containing the alabaster bust of a man published by Ahmed Fakhry in his Ma'rib material.[4]

TRIBAL CUSTOMARY PROCEDURE WITH UNMARRIED MOTHERS AND BASTARDS

It may seem strange that bastards should be found in tribal society in south Arabia, though in the Ḥaḍramī tribes this is not without advantages for the tribe when a situation arises in which it must execute one of its own members. In such case a bastard may be put to death, since he has no near male relative to avenge him, and a new blood feud will not be set up thereby between his executioners and his family – or so I am told. In the tribal country of parts of the Federation, *tawrīd* or providing a woman for the guest is said to be widely prevalent, and the sexual code is really more pagan than Islāmic.

The procedure among the tribes eastwards from Shuqrā for dealing with the case of an unmarried girl who becomes pregnant is of very considerable interest. The girl is first asked who the

[1] I have given this a literal translation, but of course the word *asrār* has a great range of senses in religious parlance. The reference to lights may possibly be to the miraculous lights that appear over the tombs of saints in South Arabia.

[2] A *darb* is a wall, here a circular wall. Cf. *mudarrab* surrounded by a wall, rendered as *muḥaṣṣan* fortified, and *Gloss. daṯ.* pp. 742–3.

[3] Cf. *Gloss. daṯ.* p. 192, *bikār* "colonne", on the authority of Glaser. I am inclined to think that *bikār* should be a plural of *bakrah* rather than a singular.

[4] *An Archaeological Journey to Yemen* (Cairo, 1951–2), III, pl. xl.

PLATE I

A *mad'ā* (?) at Ṣa'īd in Upper 'Awlaqī Wādī Yas͟hbum

Mad'ā column with an aperture in the top for an oil lamp.

Mas͟hhad Bā Ṭawq at Ruḍūm of the Wāḥidī sultanate, with a *mad'ā* (left) and a *bakrah* (right).

(*Facing p.* 80)

man is. The man is then asked to marry her but if he *ya'giz bi-'l-ḥurmah*, i.e. *mā yishtī-hā*, "does not want her", yet "has made her pregnant (*ḥabbal-hā*)", then he must *yiksir-hā*, i.e. "give her the *kasīrah* which is 30 *rās*, *jalabah*, sheep", the word *kasīrah* being said to mean *lawm* or damages.[1] To these sheep given to the woman her father usually adds ten more, and says to her, *Barra' min baitī* "Get out of my house!" The girl in this case is considered as a *kalb*. The bastard is not called by his mother's name, but is known as, for example, Ṣāliḥ am-Zanū, Ṣāliḥ the Bastard. He is described as being *ḥalal bain ḥarāmain*, a lawful (person) between two unlawful (persons, things). He is therefore not ill considered, and his grandfather may and often does love him better than the rest of his, legitimate, grandsons. He belongs to his mother's tribe, and would, in the event of war with his father's tribe, fight against the latter, and might even kill his father. There is a sub-tribe of the Ja'danīs known as Ahl am-Zanū. If the girl's lover marries her the child remains with the mother at first, but later her family take it and, according to another informant, if the mother marries the *zanū* stays with his maternal grandfather. The child is called *ibn al-salqah*, i.c. *al-firāsh*, the *salqah* being a mat made of palm-leaf, and the phrase was explained as *ibn ahl al-ḥurmah*, the son of the woman's family.

If in a normal case of a child born in wedlock a boy's father dies, he is brought up by his mother and is called after her, as for example in the case of the ancestor of the Hal Miryam of the Nakha'īyīn tribe of the Faḍlī Sultanate, to which latter tribe 'Alī's famous adviser al-Ashtar al-Nakha'ī belonged.[2] This could well be one reason why a woman's name occurs in Arab genealogical series of the pre-Islāmic period, as for example the Madhḥij tribe of 'Ubaidah (? 'Abīdah), a Taghlibī woman who married into Janb, her children being named after her.[3] Theories that the occurrences of women's names in genealogical series indicate traces of a preceding matriarchal system have, in the Arabian context, always seemed to me highly improbable.

Another significant practice is that in order to maintain the

[1] C. de Landberg, *Gloss. daṯ*. p. 2574, "outrage, dommages-intérêts".

[2] 'Umar b. Yūsuf b. Rasūl, *Ṭurfat al-aṣḥāb fī ma'rifat al-ansāb*, ed. K. W. Zettersteen (Damascus, 1949), p. 35.

[3] *Ibid.* Al-Mubarrad, *al-Kāmil*, ed. Aḥmad Muḥ. Shākir (Cairo, 1937–56), III, 996, cites a case where a man is named as son of his mother's second (?) husband though his father's name is also given. The text does not show whether he was born out of wedlock or not. The literature could doubtless show many cases where a man is named as son of his mother.

sharaf of the two families party to a marriage, when a man marries a girl already pregnant without his being aware of this, he will keep her for a year and then divorce her so as not to bring disgrace upon her father. If however the girl pleases him he may keep her and the child is his. When it comes to inheritance his brothers may say to him that he is a bastard, and therefore not entitled to inherit. To this he will reply, *Ummī gābat-nī fī silqat abū-y wa-abū-kum, ishtī qism zaiy mā wāḥid min-kum* "My mother brought me forth on the mat (bed) of my father and your father, I want my share like one of you." They then go to the *shaikh al-qabīlah*, and if it be proven that the man was born on his father's mat, then he receives a share in the inheritance, but if born on the mat of another he does not.

Those people who live in houses in Abyan do not follow the custom of the tribes to the east of Shuqrā, but give an abortifacient *duwā* to an unmarried girl who has become pregnant, and the matter is kept concealed. They try to marry her to the man responsible, or to another man, before the pregnancy shows. The people to the west of Shuqrā all seem to take this course of action and so do the 'Awdhalīs to the north-east, but my informant said tribes like the Rabīz and Kāzimīs take the same action as the Faḍlī tribes. The existence of this customary law by which a child is considered to belong to the *salqah/silqah* of his father, among tribes so removed from external influences as these, can safely be assumed to remount to the pre-Islāmic period. If this indeed be so it would further weaken the Goldziher theory that the principle embodied in *al-walad li-'l-firāsh* was taken over from, or influenced by Roman law,[1] a maxim attributed indeed to the Prophet himself as pronounced at the farewell pilgrimage at 'Arafah.[2]

It might be remarked that if a man is accused of having got a girl with child and denies it, he must produce not less than

[1] Cited in J. Schacht, *The Origins of Muhammadan Jurisprudence* (Oxford, 1950), p. 182. Another indication that the principle, *al-walad li-'l-firāsh*, is a pre-Islāmic practice can be seen from al-Hamdānī, *al-Iklīl, erstes Buch*, ed. O. Löfgren (Uppsala, 1965), II, 67. Quḍā'ah is claimed as belonging both to Ḥimyar and to Ma'add. Now Mālik b. Ḥimyar parted from the mother of Quḍā'ah when she was already pregnant by him, and "Ma'add succeeded to her and she delivered her child conceived from Mālik on his bed (*firāsh*)". Nevertheless, strangely enough, the Prophet maintained that Quḍā'ah is the son of Mālik b. Ḥimyar, i.e. contrary to the dictum ascribed to him, that *al-walad li-'l-firāsh*.

[2] Ibn Hishām, *op. cit.* p. 970.

five persons, in the case of an important woman ten persons, to swear to his innocence. The father of the pregnant girl chooses the oath-takers. This process is reminiscent of the *qasāmah* – which also exists in Faḍlī country and in fact is common practice over much of South Arabia, though the number of persons required to take the oath varies according to whether the offence is a simple sheep stealing, or the serious crime of murder.[1]

[1] For oath-taking in customary law cases, see my "Two tribal law cases (II)", *Journal of the Royal Asiatic Society* (London, 1951), pp. 164–5.

ADDENDA

P.74/fn.2 Cf. *Iklīl II*, ed. Akwaʿ, Cairo, 1386/1967, 146: *Kathīb Yarāmis min nāḥiyat ʿAdan.*

P.74/fn.4 Al-Rāzī, *Tārīkh Ṣanʿāʾ*, Damascus, 1974, 240.

P.82/fn.1 Muslim lawyers are in some doubt about the tradition *al-walad li-ʾl-firāsh wa-li-ʾl-ʿāhir al-ḥajar.* Ibn Durayd, *K. al-Mujtanā*, Cairo, 1386/1927, says: "He means . . . that the lot of the fornicator is *ḥajar* (stoning/deprivation), i.e., he has nothing of the child. This dictum has two senses – either he meant that his lot (*ḥazz*) is harshness (*ghalẓah*) and rough treatment (*khushūnah*) through the infliction of the *ḥadd*-punishment by stoning or beating – or that, by *ḥajar*, he meant that by which he does not benefit and in which he has no advantage (*maḥṣūl*), meaning there-by frustration (*khaybah*). The milder interpretation would seem more in line with tribal practice. Al-Amīr al-Ṣanʿānī, *Subul al-salām*, 2nd ed., Cairo, 1369/1960, III, 210, a Zaydī ʿālim, says of *al-walad li-ʾl-firāsh*: "the *ḥadīth* is an indication of the establishment of the descent (*nasab*) of the child from the father". He cites variant views on the *firāsh*, bed, some say it means the woman, some the husband. It is discussed whether the tradition applies to a free woman or an *amah*, slave-woman – the case which gave rise to the ruling was that involving an *amah*.

XI

FORMS OF PLEA, A ŠĀFI'Ī MANUAL FROM AL-ŠIḤR

For a microfilm of the only copy of the MS. treatise of al-Nubḏah al-Muḥarrirah [1] li-'l-Da'wā al-Muḥarrarah known to western scholars I am indebted to the courtesy of Mr. Alexander Clark, Curator of MSS. of the Garrett Collection, housed in Princeton University [2], by whose kind permission the text (*infra*) is reproduced.

The author's full name is Muḥ. b. 'Umar b. Mubārak b. 'Abdullāh b. 'Alī al-Ḥimyarī al-Ḥaḍramī al-Šāfi'ī known as Baḥraq [3]. Born in Ḥaḍramawt in 869 H. (1465 A. D.), he studied in Aden and Zabīd. He was a pupil of al-Muzağğad [4] an extract from whose Fatāwī is quoted at the beginning of the treatise. He performed the pilgrimage in 894 H. (1489 A. D.) and subsquently became Qāḍī in al-Šiḥr. Later he went to Aden where his patron was the Amīr Marğān b. 'Abdullāh al-Ẓāfirī [5] (ob. 927 H. [1520-1 A. D.]). Amīr Marğān was already in power by 917 H. (1511-2 A. D.). It is quite clear from the internal evidence of the text with its various Ḥaḍrami terms and allusions, that the treatise was composed during Baḥraq's Šiḥr period, i. e. between the years 894-920 H. approximately. It is not possible, at present, to give the treatise a narrower dating. After Amīr Marğān's death Baḥraq went to Aḥmadābād to which many eminent Ḥaḍrami scholars had emigrated, there he died in 930 H. (1524 A. D.). He belonged to the period of great literary activity of that time in Ḥaḍramawt, with its strong Ṣūfistic and legalistic bias.

The Nubḏah does not figure in the list of Baḥraq's works in *al-Nūr al-Sāfir*. It may, of course, have formed part of another work, for he wrote on a variety of subjects [6] and was moreover, a poet as well as an authority on law.

---

[1] Or al-Muḥabbirah. See footnotes to text no. 1.

[2] P. K. HITTI etc., *Descriptive Catalog of the Garret Collection* (Princeton 1938), p. 541. No. 1818, 897 H.

[3] BROCK., *Sup.*, II, 554, to whose sources I might add Bal-Faqīh al-Šiḥrī, Mukallā MS., p. 162.

[4] BROCK., *loc. cit.*, wrongly Muzağğid.

[5] Ibn al-'Aidarūs, *al-Nūr al-Sāfir* (Baghdād 1934), p. 133, 106, etc.

[6] *al-Nūr al-Sāfir*, *op. cit.*, p. 144.

After comparing the content of the MS. with the *Principes du Droit Musulman* (Abū Ḥanīfah and al-Šāfi'ī) of L. W. C. Van den Berg (Alger, 1896) I see nothing which deviates from general Šāfi'ī practice [1], so, from a legal view-point the MS. is hardly novel. On the other hand from a sociological angle there is much of interest, and even much that is useful in present-day practice. The forms of plea set down here are evidently drawn from Baḥraq's day to day experience as Qāḍī of al-Šiḥr, and may therefore be held to represent the cases which commonly came to him for consideration.

In the notes to the text I have attempted to clear up obscurities and comment upon whatever seems to me significant. It is for instance useful to discover that at this period African slaves were imported from Damot (textual note 8), and to read of the duties of what today would be called ḫaddām al-naḫl, such as the care of irrigation channels, digging out the trench round the palm, fecundation, and other duties. Unfortunately Baḥraq does not go into great detail on the many aspects of date-farming.

My main object however in producing an edition of this treatise is the desire to compare its prescriptions with the actual form of document current amongst the tribes of South Arabia today, such as my *Two Tribal Law Cases* [2] where the law in question is 'ādah or 'urf. Baḥraq is by way of a touch-stone, being himself so orthodoxly Šāfi'ī, and his Arabic so classical. That Baḥraq knew 'ādah documents and had them referred to him, goes without saying, and his object in composing the Nubḏah may well have been the desire not so much to regularise pleas set forth in an unscientific manner–as he states, but to extend the šarī'ah into territory where 'ādah had prevailed.

Description of MS.

The text is in a good nasḫ hand, requiring very little correction, vowelled here and there, and carefully copied by the transcriber from several other MSS. There seem to be occasional small omissions of words, and Yemenite spellings, such as da'wā with alif and šāyi'an for šā'i'an, known also to other Arab countries.

---

[1] A view in which I am confirmed by Prof. N. Anderson who was kind enough to read through the text with Šaiḫ 'Alī 'Abd al-Qādir, and make some suggestions incorporated in this article.

[2] *Jl. Roy. As. Soc., loc. cit., infra.*

Summary of Contents.

1. Quotation from Fatāwī al-Muzaǧǧad.
2. Author's preface.
   Discussion on the Plea (*daʿwā*).
   Classification of the subject of the Plea into five categories [1]
   - i) *Plea concerning a specific object.*
     - *a*) Wrongful possession;
     - *b*) Loan;
     - *c*) Deposit.

3. ii) *Plea of Debt.*
   - *a*) Now due;
   - *b*) Prompt payment.

4. iii) *Plea of Contract.*
   - *a*) Sale;
   - *b*) Purchase;

5. *c*) Agency;
6. *d*) Partnership;
7. *e*) Letting & hiring;
   f) Bequest;
8. *g*) Marriage.
   iv) *Plea of Annulment.*
   - *a*) Sale;
   - *b*) Letting & hiring;

9. *c*) Marriage.
   v) *Plea of Proprietary Rights.*
   - *a*) Right of way;

10. *b*) Pledge;
    c) Pre-emption.

(*Appendix*) Plea of Present on Divorce, and Imposition of Maintenance.

Conclusion.

---

[1] The text does not follow exactly the arrangement into subsections of the five categories, as set out in the preamble.

Since the completion of this edition I have found a second copy of the Nubḏah in Tarīm, but unfortunately too late to collate with the Princeton text.

النُّبْذَةُ المُحَرِّرَة [1] للدَّعْوَى المُحَرَّرَة

تأليف الشّيخ الإمام العلّامة جمال الدّين
محمّد بن عمر بَحْرَق رحمه الله تعالى آمين ،
وصلّى الله على سيّدنا محمّد وآله وصحبه وسلّم
تسليمًا كثيرًا إلى يوم الدّين

الحمد للّه

فى «فتاوى» المُزَجَّد [2] رحمه الله تعالى: إذا حصل العلم بالمدّعى به من أحد الأفراد فقد حصل شرط صحّة الدّعوى وإنّما يقدح فى صحّة الدّعوى جهالة تمنع استيفآء المحكوم به ، وتوجيه المطالبة نحوه. وذلك حيث يكون المدّعى به مجهولًا ، متردّدًا بأن يكون هذا أو ذاك. وأمّا إذا سلم المدّعى به من هذا ، وكان محصورًا يحاط بضبطه فلا يقدح. كما نقله الغَزّىّ فى «أدب القضا» عن ابن الصّلاح [3] (انتهى).

بسم الله الرّحمن الرّحيم وبه نستعين ، وعلى الله نتّكل ، الحمد للّه ربّ العالمين ، وصلّى الله على سيّدنا محمّد خاتم النّبيّين ، وعلى آله الطّيّبين الطّاهرين ، وصحبه الهادين المهتدين ، التّابعين لهم بإحسان إلى يوم الدّين.

أمّا بعد فقد سألنى بعض الإخوان أن أحرّر له صورًا من الدّعوى التّامّة ، المحتاج إليها فى المعاملات العامّة ، فأجبته إلى سؤاله ، راجيًا بركة دعائه ، وحسبنا الله ونعم الوكيل.

---

[1] Pointed according to the marginal note. The copyist mentions a variant found in some MSS. « al-Muḥabbirah », and considers the latter preferable.

[2] See BROCK., *Sup.*, II, 964, to be corrected by *al-Nūr al-Sāfir*, *op. cit.*, p. 137. He is Aḥmad b. ʿUmar b. Muḥ. al-Madḥiğī (*sic*, as indeed always in Yemenite MSS.) al-Saifī al-Murādī al-Zabīdī (847 H. [1443–4 A. D.] – 930 H. [1523–4 A. D.]). Al-Muzağğad's *Fatāwā* were collected by his son Ḥusain, and later by a certain Ibn al-Naqīb.

[3] The Princeton Catalogue (p. 541) notes a text immediately preceding the Nubḏah, entitled 'Imād al-Riḍā fī Ādāb al-Qaḍā', of Abū Yaḥyā Zakarīyā' al-Anṣārī (BROCK., *Sup.*, II, 118) which is a commentary on a work by Šaraf al-Dīn ʿĪsā al-Ġazzī (ob. 799 H. [1397 A. D.]).

فصل

اعلم أنّ ضابِطَ الدّعوى الصّحيحة التّامّة هى الّتى يترتّب عليها فصل [1] الخصومة ، ولا يفتقر الحاكم معها إلى شىء آخر . ثمّ تارة تصحّ مع جهالة المدّعى به ؛ وذلك حيث كان مطلوب المدّعى متوقّفًا على تقدير القاضى ، كفَرْض النّفقة ، والمُتعة ، ونحو ذلك ، ممّا لا يمنع الجهالة فيه استيفاء الحقّ ؛ وسيأتى التّنبيه على صور من ذلك. وما لم يكن كذلك فلا بدّ أن تكون الدّعوى فيه معلومة مُلزِمة ، أى بأن يكون المدّعى بـه [2] فيها معلومًا لازمًا للمدّعَى عليه فى صورة الدّعوى ، (وأن لا تنافيها دعوة أخرى) [3].

فصل

ثمّ المدّعى به إمّا أن يكون عَيْنًا أو دَيْنًا ، أو عقدًا أو حلًّا ، أو حقًّا من حقوق الملك . فهذه خمسة أقسام ، وسأذكر من كلّ قسم منها صورًا من الدّعوى ليقاس بها غيرها ، فإنّ تفاصيل ذلك ممّا يتعذّر استحضاره ، ولا يمكن استقصاؤه . فأقول ، وبالله التّوفيق :

١) القسم الأوّل دعوى العَيْن ، وهى إمّا سالمة يطلب ردّها ، أو تالفة يطلب بدلها ، وكلّ منهما إمّا مثليّة أو متقوّمة . وذلك فى باب الغصب ، أو العارية ، أو الوديعة ، أو نحو ذلك . فإن كانت مثليّة مطلقًا أو متقوّمة سالمة فلا بدّ أن يصفها بصفات السَّلَم الآتية ; فتقول مثلًا : أدّعى بأنّ فلانًا هذا ، (أو الغائب ، غصب منّى ، (أو) أتلف علىّ ⟨(أو)⟩ وقعت يده لى على كذا وكذ⟨ا⟩ مكيالًا ، بمكيال [4] بلد

---

[1] For the use of the term faṣl in ʿādah law, see Two Tribal Law Cases (2), *Journ. Roy. As. Soc.* (London 1951), p. 158.

[2] Al-Muṭarrizī, *al-Muġrib* (Ḥaidarābād 1328 H.), says, المال المدّعى والمدّعى به لغو .

[3] Bracketed words inserted from margin; perhaps daʿwah should be read daʿwā.

[4] Before the Quʿaiṭī *Weights and Measures Decree* of January 26th, 1943 (14th Muḥarram, 1362 H.) which fixed the Mikyāl at 4 Muṣrās, the Muṣrā, I am informed, used to be called Mikyāl, but Tāribah used the Mikyāl Bandarī, while both Saiwūn and Šibām had cubic measures of their own. Cf. L. W. C. Van den Berg, *Le*

كذا ، مــن الذّرة البلديّــة الحمرآء ، (أو) الدّخــن البلدىّ الأحمر ، إلى آخر صفات السّلم ؛ (أو) غصــب منّى ، عبدًا حبشيًّا دَامُوتِيًّا[1] أسود ، صافى اللّون ، طوله نحو السّتّة الأشبار ، وسِنّه نحو العشر السّنيـن ؛ (أو) ثوبًا قطنًا ، وهو ملحــف ، طوله سبعة أذرع وعرضه أربعة أذرع[2] ، رفيع الغزل ، صفيق النّسج ، إلى غير ذلك من صفات السّلم. ويقول بعد ذلك : وأنا مطالب له بردّه ، (أو) ولى بيّنة بذلك. (إن كان غائبًا). وإن كانــت متقوّمــة بالغةً ذكر جنسها ونوعها وقيمتها ، كأَنْ يقول : أدّعــى على فلان هــذا ، (أو) الغائــب ، عبدًا حبشيًّا دَامُوتيًّا ، قيمتــه كذا وكذا أشرفيًّا[3] ، (أو) ثوبًا قطنًا مَلْحَفَة قشوريًّا[4] ، (أو) عمامــة بيضآء ، (أو) تفصيلــة[5]

Ḥadhramout et les Colonies Arabes (Batavia 1886), p. 77. A set of measures of çubic capacity can be seen in the Cambridge Museum of Archaeology and Ethnology; the Muṣrā holds exactly one pint.

[1] Abyssinian slaves from Damot (Dāmūt) are mentioned several times by Baḥraq so they must have been quite common in al-Šiḥr. About 1520 A. D. Damot was still largely pagan, but it was apparently under Christian domination as a rule (J. S. TRIMINGHAN, *Islam in Ethiopia* [Oxford 1952], p. 76). Perhaps these slaves were captives in the Muslim-Christian wars. Bal-Faqīh al-Šiḥrī (Mukallā MS., p. 215) mentions that Sulṭān Badr had ʻabīd-hu al-Nūbah in 942 H. (1535 A. D.). I was told that in relatively modern times, three categories of slave were distinguished: 1) al-Biḥārah, i. e. slaves from al-Sawāḥil; 2) Tulud (S. Talīd), slaves born and reared in Ḥaḍramawt; 3) Nūbah, Nubians. It will be noticed that further on a Damot slave-girl is described as yellow. M a q d i s ī, *Descriptio imperii Moslemici*, ed. De. Goeje (Leyden 1906), p. 97 mentions Abyssinians at Aden, in the context almost certainly slaves.

[2] The *malḥafah* is "grand châle long, teint d'indigo et à franges" (C. DE LANDBERG, *Ḥaḍramoût* [Leyden 1901], p. 709. Cf. Materials for a History of Islamic Textiles, *Ars Islamica* [Michigan 1951], XV-VI, pp. 31-2). The measurements given are interesting and an ʻAwlaqī informant tells me that they are precisely the same today in South Arabia. A typical measurement in my Tarīm notes gives 7 by 3 ḏirāʻ instead of 7 by 4. Weaving is carried on in oblong rooms in al-Šiḥr, and the length of the web must be determined by the length of the rooms which are no doubt of a standard size. To the best of my memory these rooms are longer than 7 ḏirāʻ and probably therefore a single web (šaraʻah) is divisible into lengths of 7 ḏirāʻ.

[3] Ašrafīs are commonly mentioned in Ḥaḍrami documents of this period such as Bal-Faqīh's history.

[4] This word is puzzling. STEINGASS, *Pers. Dict.*, gives *qišr* (pl. *qušūr*) garments, but qušūrīyāt are mentioned as an import in the earlier *Mulaḫḫaṣ al-Fiṭan* (Ambrosiana H. 130).

[5] For Tafṣīlah see Materials for a History of Islamic Textiles, *op. cit.*, *Ars Islamica* (Michigan 1948), XIII-XIV, p. 103.

سوداء محرّرة ، قيمتها كذا وكذا . ويقول بعد ذلك : وأنا مطالب له بقيمته . وإن كان غائبًا قال : ولى بيّنة بذلك أسألك سماعها .

٢) القسم الثّانى دعوى الدّين ، وهو إمّا حالّ أو مؤجّل . فإن كان مؤجّلًا 〈ف〉لم تسمع الدّعوى به إذ المدّعى 〈به〉[1] ليس بلازم ، ومن شرط الدّعوى أن تكون مُلزِمة كما سبق . نعم ، إذا كان بعض الدّين حالًّا وبعضه مؤجّلًا سمعت الدّعوى وثبت المؤجّل تبعًا ، كَأنْ يقول : أدّعى أنّى أستحقّ فى ذمّة فلان هذا ، (أو) الغائب ، مائة درهم فضّة من معاملة بلد كذا وكذا[2] ، خمسون منها حالّة ، وخمسون منها مؤجّلة إلى مستهلّ شهر كذا من سنة كذا وكذا . وأمّا الحالّ فلا بدّ أن يصفه بصفات السّلم أيضًا ، سوا أكان ثمن مبيع ، أو دين سلم ، أو قرضٍ ، أو حوالةٍ ، أو ضمانٍ ، أو صداقٍ ، أو عِوَض خُلْعٍ ، أو غير ذلك ؛ فيقول مثلًا : أدّعى بأنّى أستحقّ فى ذمّة فلان هذا ، كذا وكذا مثقالًا ذهبًا خالصًا مضروبًا مسكوكًا ، حالًّا فى ذمّته ، (أو) كذا وكذا أوقيّة فضّة خالصة . (ويقول) : وأنا مطالب له بذلك ، ولى بيّنة تشهد بذلك . إن كان غائبًا . وإن كان الدّين سلمًا قال مثلًا : أدّعى بأنّى أستحقّ فى ذمّة فلان هذا ، (أو) الغائب ، كذا وكذا مكيالًا ، بمكيال بلد كذا ، من الذّرة البلديّة الحمراء الصّفيّة الجديدة الحرثيّة ، (أو) العِرْقيّة[3] المسقيّة بماء العين ، (أو) بماء السّانِيَة ، (أو) من الدّخن الأحمر الشّتوىّ[4] الجديد (إلى آخره) ، (أو) من

---

[1] Al-Muṭarrizī, *al-Muġrib*, (Ḥaidarābād 1328 H.), says, المال المدّعى والمدّعى به لغو .

[2] It is probable that at this period Ḥaḍramawt was entirely dependent on foreign coinage. Such information as there is about local coinage may be consulted in Materials for South Arabian History, *Bull. School of Or. & African Studies.* (London 1950), XIII, II, p. 292, 294. In 913 H. (1507–8) the price of twist at al-Šiḥr rose to Šiḥrī ocques, and cotton to 10 ocques, as the result of a famine. This was probably during Baḥraq's tenure of office there. While the ocque-weight was local the actual coinage was probably foreign, but this remains to be proven.

[3] ʿIrq is land with much water and salt, giving growth to trees, especially tamarisk, according to classical usage. Perhaps the contrast is between flood and well-watered land. For Sāniyah cf. *Gl. Daṯ*.

[4] Šitawī is the crop planted at the star Baldah, and ripening in six months time. See Star Calendars and an Almanac from South Arabia, *Anthropos* (Freiburg 1954).

التّمر السُّقُطْرِىّ ، (أو) الشِّحْرِىّ [1] ، الجديد اليابس المنقّى الجليل الحبّ النَّثْر [2] ، (أو) من الحنطة الحمرآء الحبشيّة [3] ، (أو) البلديّة الجليلة الحبّ ، (أو) من العسل البلدىّ الخَرِيفىّ الأصفر الدَّوْعَنِىّ [4] ، (أو) الصَّيْفىّ الجبلىّ ، (أو نحو ذلك) . ثمّ يقول : وأنا مطالب له بذلك . وإن كان غائبًا قال : ولى بيّنة بذلك. وإن كان الدّين حوالة قال : أدّعى بأنّى أستحقّ فى ذمّة فلان هذا كذا وكذا ، أحالنى بها عليه فلانُ ابن فلان بدينى الّذى عليه ، المساوى له فى الصّفات . وقبلتُ الحوالة . وأنا مطالب له بها ، ولى بيّنة تشهد بذلك . وإن كان ضمانًا قال : أدّعى بأنّى أستحقّ فى ذمّة فلان ابن فلان ، (أو) الغائب ، كذا وكذا من جهة ضمانه لى بدينى الّذى لى على فلانْ ، وأنا مطالب له بتسليم ذلك ، (أو) ولى بيّنة تشهد بذلك. وإن كان صداقًا قال : أدّعى بأنّ فلانة مُوَكِّلتى تستحقّ فى ذمّة فلان هذا ، (أو) الغائب ، (أو) الميت ، مائة درهم فضّة ، معاملة بلد كذا وكذا ، وذلك صداق نكاحها الّذى عقد به عليها ، وأنا مطالب له به . وإن كان غائبًا قال : ولى بيّنة بذلك . وإن كان ميتًا قال أيضًا : وله تركة تفى بذلك . وإن كانت الدّعوى فى وجه [5] الوارث زاد أيضًا : ووارثه يعلم ذلك . كأن يقول : أدّعى بأنّى أستحقّ فى ذمّة فلان ، أخى فلان هذا ، كذا وكذا ، وهو يعلم ذلك ، وقد خلف تركةً فى يد أخيه هذا ، فيها وفآء دينى ، وأنا مطالب به . فمره بالخروج عن حقّى.

٣) القسم الثّالث دعوى العقد من بيع ، أو شرآء ، أو وكالة ، أو شركة ، أو إجارة ، أو وصيّة ، أو نكاح ، أو غير ذلك. فيقول فى الشّرآء مثلًا : أدّعى بأنّى

---

[1] The Socotran variety of palm is mentioned also in my *Prose and Poetry from Ḥaḍramawt* (London 1951), I, Ar. text, p. 129 as al-Suquṭrāwī. Šiḥrī is evidently another variety.

[2] Al-naṯr, dates still in their fruit form, whole and with the stone inside, separate and not pounded or crushed. Cf. *Prose and Poetry*, *op. cit.*, Ar. Text., p. 128, Verse 12.

[3] The import of Abyssinian wheat might imply that local supplies, even at this period, were insufficient. At one time wheat was little eaten outside the more affluent classes though this is not so today.

[4] I read al-Daw'anī for al-Dū'ī of the text. Al-Ḫarīfī is the Autumn crop, while al-Ṣaifī is that of the earlier summer. Cf. *Star-Calendars*, *op. cit.*, and W. H. Ingrams, Bee-Keeping in the Wadi Du'an, *Man* (London 1937), XXXVII, p. 32.

[5] Fī wağh, in the responsibility of. See *Gl. Dat.*

اشتريت من فلان هذه الدّار الفلانيّة. ويذكر حدودها[1] ، (أو) نصيبه فيها ، الصّائر إليه من فلان ، وهو النّصف ، (مثلًا) ، شائعًا فى الدّار المذكورة بجميع حقوقها ، (أو) الأرض الفلانيّة ، (أو) القطعة. ويذكر حدودها ونصيبه فيها ، بحقوقها وسواقيها[2] ومسافيها. فإن اشترى دارًا ، ما خلا بيتًا فيها ، قال: ما خلا البيت الشّرقىّ ، (أو) الغربىّ منها. ويحدّده. ثمّ يقول: وأنا مطالب له بتسليمه إلىّ. إن كان يستحقّ التّسليم ، إن كان الثّمن مؤجّلًا أو حالًّا وقد سلّمه ، ويذكر ذلك ؛ فيقول: بثمن مبلغه كذا ، قبضه منّى ، (أو) استوفاه ، (أو) مؤجّلًا إلى كذا. وإلّا قال: وقد أحضرتُ له الثّمن ، وأنا مطالب له بقبضه وإقباض المبيع المذكور. فإن كان المبيع فى يد غير البائع قال[3]: أدّعى بأنّى اشتريت أرضَ كذا ، (مثلاً). ويحدّدها . من فلان ابن فلان ، وهو يملكها يومئذ ، وهى باقية فى ملكى الآن ، وهى فى يده بغير حقّ ، وأنا مطالب له بردّها إلىّ. فإن كان المبيع نخلًا بمغارسها ، دون بَيَاض[4] الأرض ، ذكر ذلك ؛ ثمّ قال ما سبق. وإن كان المبيع ثمرة دون الشّجر قال: جميع ثمرة النّخل الفلانىّ ، وهو كذا وكذا نخلة من نوع كذا ، بعد أن بدا صلاحها ، بشرط التّبقية إلى الجِداد. وإن كان المبيع رقيقًا قال: جميع العبد ، (أو) الجارية ، (أو) الوصيف البالغة ، (أو) غير البالغة ، الحبشىّ الدّاموتىّ الّذى هو بيده ، المقرّ له بالمشرف ، المسمّى فلانًا. فإن كان الشّرا من ولىّ المحجور عليه قال: أدّعى بأنّى اشتريت حصّة الطّفل فلانًا ، (أو) السّفيه ، (أو) المجنون ، فى الدّار الفلانيّة ، وهى كذا ، (أو) جميع الدّار. ويحدّدها. من أبى الطّفل المذكور ، (أو) جدّه فلان ، (أو) وصيّه ، (أو) قيّمه المنصوب عليه ، وهو فلان ، لِمَا رأى له فى البيع من الغبطة ، (أو) المصلحة ، (أو) للحاجة إلى بيعها ، فيما يحتاج إليه من نفقة وغيرها ، ولا موجود له غيرها , واستوفى منّى الثّمن. أو يقول: أدّعى بأنّى اشتريت من فلان ، قيّم الحاكم فلان ، البائع بإذنه ، جميع الدّار الفلانيّة ، ملك فلان المحجور

---

[1] For an example of a house-deed see, A Judeo-Arab House-deed from Ḥabbān, *Jl. Roy. As. Soc.* (London 1953), p. 124.

[2] *Gl. Dat.*, rigole dans les champs.

[3] Reading ḳāl for fa-in of the text.

[4] Terrain arrosé et séche (*Gl. Daṯ.*). Ibn Sīdah calls it "barren land" which sense is doubtless intended here.

عليه بالصِّبَى ، (أو) السّفه ، (أو) الجنون ، لِما دعت إليه الحاجة من نفقة أو كسوةٍ وغيرهما ، بثمن مبلغه كذا ، بعد ثبوت كونه ثمن المثل لدى الحاكم المذكور. وقبض منّى القائم ، (أو) الحاكم المذكور الثّمن المذكور ، وأنا مطالب بتسليم الدّار المذكورة. وإن اشترى للطّفل السّفيه ، أو المحجور ⟨عليه⟩ ، عقارًا قال : أدّعى بأنّى اشتريت من فلان للطّفل فلان ولدى ، (أو) الّذى تحت نظرى ، بطريق الوصيّة لى عليه من أبيه فلان ، (أو) جدّه فلان ، (أو) بالولاية من الحاكم فلان ، الدّار الفلانيّة ، (أو) الأرض الفلانيّة ، (أو) النّخل. ويحدّدها. بثمن مبلغه كذا ، هو ثمن الدّار ، (أو) ذلك المبيع من غير حَيفٍ ولا زيادة ، وسلّمت عنه من ماله للبائع المذكور. وإن اشترت المرأة الدّار ، مثلًا ، من زوجها بصداقها ، أو دين آخر من تركة زوجها الميت ، قال وكيلها : أدّعى بأنّ موكّلتى فلانة اشترت الدّار الفلانيّة. ويحدّدها. من زوجها فلان ابن فلان المتوفّى عنها ، بمالها فى ذمّته ، من الصّداق ، (أو) الدّين ، بعد أن قامت بيّنة بموته ، (أو) أثبتت فى وجه الورثة بالدّين المذكور ، وحلفت أنّها تستحقّ ذلك القدر فى تركته. ويقول فى دعوى الوكالة : أدّعى بأنّ فلانًا وكّلنى فى المطالبة بحقوقه كلّها الّتى له على فلان ، (أو) ديونه ، حيث كانت وعلى من كانت ، والمحاكمة بسببها عند الحاكم ، (أو) فى الدّعوى على غرمآئه ، (أو) خصومه ، (أو) سماع الدّعوى عليه والجواب عنها ، (أو) فى بيع أملاكه واستيفآء أثمانها ، ولى بيّنة بذلك أسألك سماعها. ويقول فى دعوى الشّركة : ⟨أدّعى⟩ بأنّى عاقدت فلانًا على الشّركة بينى وبينه فيما جرّه الإرث إلينا من النّقد والمتاع الفلانىّ ، (أو) فيما اشتريناه شائعًا من نوع كذا ، (أو) فيما أخرجته من مالى ، وأخرجه من ماله ، من النّقد (أو) الطّعام ، (أو) الرّهن ، (أو) التّمر ، (ونحو ذلك من المثليّات). وخلطناه حتّى صار مالًا واحدًا لا يتميّز ، وأذن كلّ واحد منّا للآخر فى التّصرّف بأنواع التّجارات. ويقول فى دعوى القِراض : أدّعِى أنّى قارضت فلانًا ، (أو) قارضنى فلان (إن ادّعى العامل) ، على كذا وكذا من الذّهب ، (أو) الفضّة ، وقبضه منّى ، وصار عنده ، (أو) عندى (إن ادّعى العامل) ، على سبيل القراض ، على أنّ لى نصفَ الرّبح بعد إخراج المؤن ، وإذن لى أن أتجر فيما شئت وحيث شئت ، (أو) فى النّوع الفلانىّ ، (أو) فى البلد الفلانىّ ، على حسب ما جرت به المعاملة. ثمّ

يقول المالك: وأنا مطالب له بردّه. أو يقول العامل: وأنا مطالب له بحصّتى فى الرّبح ، (أو) وقد تلف ماله المذكور عندى بغير تقصير منّى. ويقول فى المساقاة[1]: أدّعى بأنّ فلانًا هذا ساقانى على غَيضته الفلانيّة ، بجميع ما فيها من النّخل ، على اختلاف أنواعها ، على أنّ علىّ سقيَها وتعهّدها ، وتسوية أنهارها ، وإصلاح حفرها وسواقيها ، وتلقيحها ، وحفظ ثمرها ، وجداده ، وغيره ممّا فيه صلاحها. ولى فى مقابلة عمل ذلك الثّلث ، (مثلًا) ، من الثّمرة الحاصلة منها ؛ وقد امتنع من ذلك ، (أو) هرب[2] ، (مثلًا) ، (أو) قصّر فى عمله ، وأنا مطالب له بالوفآء بما التزمه. ويقول المستأجر فى دعوى الإجارة: أدّعى أنّى استأجرت من فلان داره الفلانيّة ، (مثلًا) ، (أو) عبده ، (أو) دابّته. ويصفها. (أو) هذه الحاضرة ، للانتفاع بها فى كذا من سكنى ، (أو) خدمة ، (أو) ركوب ، (أو) حمل ، (أو) نحو ذلك ممّا استأجره له ، بكذا وكذا ، وأنا مطالب له بتسليم ذلك. ويقول المؤجر: أدّعى بأنّى أجرت فلأنا هذا دارى الفلانيّة بكذا ، مدّة كذا ، وأنا مطالب له بالأجرة المذكورة. أو يقول: أدّعى بأنّى استأجرت فلأنا هذا على خدمة كذا ، مدّة كذا ، وأنا مطالب له بتسليم نفسه. ويقول الأجير: أدّعى بأنّ فلأنا استأجرنى بكيت ، على عمل كذا ، (أو) مدّة كذا بكذا ، (أو) عن فلان الميّت بكذا ، على أن أحجّ وأعتمر عنه حجّة الإسلام وعمرته ، وزيارة قبر النّبىّ صلّى الله عليه وسلّم ؛ وقد فعلت ذلك ، وأنا مطالب له

---

[1] This is evidently a typical contract under which the agricultural labourer or miskīn agrees to work for the palm-grove owner or ṭabīn, the latter word being found in the pre-Islamic inscriptions. The remuneration of one third of the crop is cited also by VAN DEN BERG, *Principes du Droit Musulman*, as common in Šāfi'ī law.

Gl. Daṯ., p. 398 gives a case to the W. of Ḥaḍramawt where the ḥarrāṯ supplies animals, ploughs, etc., and obtains in return half, a third, or a quarter of the crop, as specified in the agreement. For Zaidī law and practice cf. Aḥmad b. Yaḥyā al-Murtaḍā, *al-Baḥr al-Zaḫḫār* (Cairo 1949), IV, 68 giving a draft of a Musāqāh document which may be compared with that of the Nubḏah.

[2] I suspect that something is missing in the text at this point for while what has preceded must be the da'wā of the cultivator against the ṭabīn what follows must clearly be that of the ṭabīn against the cultivator. For a rağaz on this matter see *Prose and Poetry from Ḥaḍramawt*, p. 39 (Engl. text.). Al-Nabhānī, *Ğāmi' Karāmāt al-Awliyā'* (Cairo 1329 H.), II, 118 mentions a zāri' (by which he probably means a share-cropper) who borrowed from a Saiyid in Tarīm till harvest-time but ran away. The Saiyid remarks that he will never reach his destination, and so it befalls.

بالأجرة. ويقول المستاجر: أدّعى بأنّى استأجرتُ فلانًا هذا الّذى أسقط عن نفسه فرض الحجّ والعمرة ، على أن يحجّ ويعتمر بنفسه عن الميت فلان ، بطريق الوصيّة إلىّ منه بذلك ، بأجرة مبلغها كذا. وقد حجّ واعتمر عنه ، وسلّمت إليه الأجرة المذكورة من تركة الميت المذكور ، ولى بيّنة بذلك ، (أو) وارثه هذا[1] يعلم ذلك. ويقول فى دعوى الإرث: أدّعى بأنّ فلانًا مات ، وأنا ابنه لصلبه ، (أو) أخوه لأبويه ، (أو) عمّه ، (أو) جدّه ، ويميّز الجهة ، الحائز لإرثه ، لا وارث له سواى ، (أو) المنحصر إرثه فىّ وفى فلان وفلان ، لا وارث له سوانا ، ولا مانع يحجبنا عن إرثه ، ولى بيّنة بذلك. ويقول فى دعوى الوصيّة: أدّعى الوصيّة ، أدّعى أنّ فلانًا أوصى لى بكذا ، وإنّى قبلت الوصيّة بعد موته ، وأنّها تخرج من ثلثه ، ووارثه يعلم ذلك ، وأنا مطالبٌ بتسليمه إلىّ. ويقول فى دعوى الإيصاء: أدّعى بأنّ فلانًا أوصى إلىّ فى أمر أولاده القاصرين ، أتصرّف عليهم ولهم ، على وجه النّظر والاحتياط إلى بلوغهم ، وإيناس رشدهم ، ولى بيّنة بذلك. ويقول فى دعوى النّكاح: أدّعى بأنّى نكحت فلانة هذه ، (أو) بنت فلان من أبيها ، (أو) جدّها ، (أو) أخيها فلان ، (أو) الحاكم ، (أو) منصوبه فلان ، بإذنها ، (إن اعتبر إذنها) ، وشاهدى عدل ، مع خلوّها من الموانع من زوج وعدّةٍ وغيرهما ، ولى بيّنة بذلك ، ويقول فى دعوى الدّم: أدّعى بأنّ فلانًا هذا قتل مورّثى وحده ، (أو) هو وفلان ، عمدًا ، (أو) خطآء ، وأنا مطالب له بالقصاص الواجب عليه ، (أو) بالدّية ، (أو) أنّه قطع يدى ، (أو) إصبعى عمدًا ، (أو) خطآء ، (أو) شجّنى هذه الشّجّة ، وأنا مطالب له بالقصاص ، (أو) الدّية ، (أو) الأرش على حسب الجناية. ويقول فى دعوى القِسْمة: ⟨أدّعى⟩ بأنّى قاسمت فلانًا فى الدّار ⟨(أ⟩و) الأرض (أو) النّخل الفلانىّ ، وجزّئناها[2] جزئين ، غربيًّا وشرقيًّا ، (مثلًا) ، وخرج لى بالقسمة الجزء الغربىّ ، ولى بيّنة بذلك. وإن كان فيها مناقلة زاد: ثمّ اشتريت منه نصيبه فى الجانب الغربىّ بنصيبى فى الجانب الشرقىّ ، وصار الجانب الغربىّ لى خالصًا بالمناقلة الشّرعيّة ، ولى بيّنة بذلك.

---

[1] Obscure, perhaps deleted.
[2] Original spelling retained.

٤) القسم الرّابع دعوى الفسوخ فى البيع ، والإجارة ، والنّكاح ، ونحوه . فيقول فى إثبات حقّ الفسخ بالعيب : أدّعى بأنّى اشتريت ، (أو) استأجرت من فلان الدّار الفلانيّة . ثمّ وجدتها واهية الجدران ، (أو) وسخة الحيطان ، (أو) مسوّسة الأخشاب ، (أو) مكسّرة الأبواب ، (أو) هذا العبد . فوجدته سارقًا ، (أو) آبقًا ، (أو) أصمّ ، (أو) أعور ، (أو) أحول ، (أو) أجهر ، (أو) خصيًّا ، (أو) مجنونًا ، (أو) هذه الجارية . فوجدتها كذلك ، (أو) مزوّجة ، (أو) حاملًا . (أو) : تزوّجت هذه المرأة . فوجدتها رتقاء ، (أو) قرناء [1] ، (أو) مجذومة [2] ، (أو) مجنونة ، (أو) برصاء [3] ، (أو) اشتريت هذه الدّابّة فوجدتها عضوضًا ، (أو) رموحًا ، (أو) جموحًا ، أو غير ذلك من العيوب . ثمّ يقول : وأنا لا أعلم بذلك ؛ وقد فسختها بالعيب المذكور . ويقول فى دعوى الطّلاق : أدّعى بأنّ فلانًا طلّق موكّلتى فلانة طلقة واحدة ، (أو) ثلثًا (أو) خالعها فى حال نفوذ ذلك منه ، ولى بيّنة بذلك . ويقول فى دعوى العدّة : أدّعى بأنّ فلانًا طلّق موكّلتى فلانة يوم كذا فى شهر كذا من سنة كذا ، وأنّها قد انقضت عدّتها بالأقرآء ، (حيث يكون ذلك ممكنًا) ، (أو) بالأشهر . ويقول فى دعوى فسخ النّكاح بالإعسار : أدّعى بأنّ موكّلتى فلانة ثابتة الزّوجيّة ، فى عِصْمة فلان هذا ، (أو) الغائب فوق مسافة القَصْر ، وأنّها باذلة الطّاعة ، ملازمة مسكنها ؛ وهى مطالبته بالواجب لها عليه شرعًا ، وهو مُعسِر الإعسار الشّرعىّ ؛ وإنّها مطالبته بفسخ نكاحها منه بذلك ، ولى بيّنة تشهد بذلك كلّه . ويقول فى دعوى العتق : أدّعى بأنّ فلانًا أعتق مملوكه فلانًا الحبشىّ الدّاموتىّ الصّغير ، (أو) البالغ ، (أو) مملوكه هذا ، عتقًا صريحًا منجزًا ، ولى بيّنة بذلك ، (أو) أعتق نصيبه وهو الثّلث ، (مثلًا) ، فى الجارية الحبشيّة الدّاموتيّة الصّفرآء اللّون البالغة ، (أو) مملوكته هذه ،

---

[1] "The qarn is like a swelling in women, found in human beings, sheep, and in cows. Of this is the Tradition of 'Alī: 'If one marries a woman and she has a qarn in her, if one wishes one may divorce.' It is like a tooth in the pudenda of a woman, preventing intercourse." (*Tāğ al-'Arūs*) In Ḥaḍramawt qirnah means the uterus – because of its two horns. Ğāḥiẓ, *Ḥayawān*, VI, 75 says that a woman's "womb (raḥm) has two qurnahs, i. e. the two corners of the womb."

[2] Text مجدومة .

[3] For the rejection of a slave-girl on account of 'aib at Aden, see Ibn al-Muğāwir, *Ta'rīḫ al-Mustabṣir*, ed. O. Löfgren (Leiden 1951), I, p. 146.

وإنّه موسر بقيمة باقيها ، (أو) بنصف باقيها ، (مثلًا). فسَرَى عليه العتق إليه ، ولى بيّنة بذلك. (أو): أدّعى بأنّ فلانًا علّق عتق عبده فلان ، (ويصفه) ، على كذا. فوجدت الصّفة المذكورة ، وعتق عليه. (أو) أنّه دبّر مملوكه هذا ، (أو) علّق عتقه بموته ، وقد مات ، وخرج كلّه ، (أو) نصفُه من الثّلث ، فعتق ، ولى بيّنة بذلك. (أو) أنّه كاتب مملوكه هذا ، على كذا وكذا درهمًا منجّمة عليه ثلاثة أنجم[1] ، (مثلًا). وقال له: متى أدّيت ذلك فأنت حرّ ؛ وأدّى ذلك الأجل المذكور ، وعتق بحكم الكتابة الصّحيحة. (أو) أنّه أقرّ أنّه وطئ مملوكته فلانة ، وعَلِقَتْ منه بولد فى حال ملكه لها ، وإنّه مات ، وعتقت بموته ، بحكم الاستيلاد الشّرعىّ.

٥) القسم الخامس دعوى حقوق الملك من حقّ ممرّ ، أو وثيقة رهن ، أو ثبوت شفعة ، أو نحو ذلك. فيقول فى دعوى حقّ الممرّ ، أو إجرآء المآء: أدّعى أنّى أستحقّ الممرّ ، (أو) إجرآء المآء إلى دارى ، (أو) أرضى هذه ، (أو) الفلانيّة فى أرض فلان هذا (أو) الفلانيّة ، من جميع جوانبها ، (أو) من جانبها الفلانىّ ، فى موضع كذا منه إلى موضع كذا. (أو): أدّعى بأنّى أستحقّ حقّ البنآء على ساحة فلان الفلانيّة ، من موضع كذا منها إلى موضع كذا ، طول كذا فى عرض كذا. فإن كان على سقف زاد[2]: وفى سَمْك كذا ، ولى بيّنة بذلك. ويقول فى دعوى الرّهن: أدّعى بأنّ فلانًا رهننى بدينى الّذى لى عليه ، وهو كذا وكذا ، جميع داره ، (أو) أرضه ، (أو) نخله الفلانىّ ، (أو) عبده ، (أو) جاريته ، ويسمّيها ويصفها ، وقبضتُه منه بإذنه ، على جهة الرّهن ، ⟨وإنّ⟩ المذكور قبض مثله. وأنا مطالب له بوفآء دينى. فإن ردّ الرّهن إلى الرّاهن لينتفع به زاد: وأنّه استردّه منّى لينتفع به مع بقآئه على حكم الرّهن. ويقول الرّاهن: أدّعى بأنّى رهنت فلانًا ملكى الفلانىّ فى دينه الّذى له علىّ ، وهو كذا وكذا ، وقبض[3] الرّهن منّى ، وقد أحضرت قدر دينه ، وأنا مطالب له بقبضه وتسليم الرّهن إلىّ. ويقول فى حقّ الشّفعة: أدّعى بأنّ فلانًا

---

[1] Paid by instalments.

[2] Perhaps an allusion to the right to add a storey to the roof of one's house which is not always permissible without fee, according to district and custom. See *Jl. Roy. As. Soc.* (London 1953), pp. 127–8.

[3] Text قبضه.

هذا اشترى من فلان حصّته فى الأرض ، (أو) الدّار الفلانيّة ، وهى الثّلث ، شائعًا بكذا ، وإنّى شريك لفلان البائع ، وقد أخذتُ المبيع المذكور بحقّ الشّفعة ، بقدر ما أخذها به . فمره بقبض ما يتوجّه علىّ ، وتسليم المبيع إلىّ .

فصل

وأمّا دعوى المتعة ، وفرض النّفقة ، ونحوهما ، ممّا تصحّ الدّعوى به مع جهالته ، فيقول : أدّعى بأنّ فلانًا طلقت موكّلتى فلانة ، بعد الدّخول بها ، وهى مطالبة له بالمتعة الواجبة لها عليه . أو : أدّعى بأنّ موكّلتى فلانة فى عصمة نكاح فلان ، باذلة له الطّاعة ، مطالبة له بفرض النّفقة لها الواجبة عليه . ويزيد فى الدّعوى : ولى بيّنة بذلك . كما سبق . فهذه صور يقاس عليها غيرها ، واللّه ولىّ التّوفيق ، ولا حول ولا قوّة إلّا باللّه العلىّ العظيم ، وصلّى اللّه على سيّدنا محمّد وآله وصحبه ، وسلّم تسليمًا مباركًا فيه ، إلى يوم الدّين ، والحمد للّه أوّلًا وآخرًا ، وظاهرًا وباطنًا وحسبنا اللّه ونعم الوكيل .

تمّت «النّبذة المحرّرة للدّعوى المحرّرة» للشّيخ العلّامة جمال الدّين محمّد بن عمر بَحْرَق الحضرمىّ ، رحمه اللّه تعالى ، بقلم الفقير إلى اللّه تعالى عبد الهادى بن ثابت النّهارىّ [1] عفا اللّه عنهما ، أمين .

[1] I been unable to discover a reference to the copyist in the usual sources.

Addenda

P.1 A more recent Ḥaḍramī writer, Sayyid Muḥsin b. Jaʿfar b. ʿAlawī b. Numayy, composed: *Taḥṣīl al-daʿāwī fī rafʿ al-shakāwī*, al-Mukallā, 1954, on similar lines. Baḥraḳ also abridged a work on music of which Leiden has a Ms.

P.11 Bā Makhramah, *Fatāwā*, 277a–b, has a crop-sharing *fatwā*.

P.13/fn.1 Cf. Ibn Ḥajar al-Haytamī, *al-Fatāwā al-kubrā*, Cairo, 1329, II, 252.

XII

Two Tribal Law Cases (Documents)
(Wāḥidī Sultanate, South-West Arabia)

DURING a year in Ḥaḍramawt I was able to collect a number of legal documents which contain valuable material for a study of the social structure of the country. Amongst these are two groups of deeds relating to the Ḥawṭahs of al-Ḥāwī and Thibī, typical examples of the sacred enclaves of this part of Arabia. Another set of documents defines the rights of the townsmen of the Sūḳ quarter of Tarīm, with some references to the ceremonies connected with hunting the ibex, and I have various other documents relating to tribal cases, a house-sale deed, etc.

The cases which concern us at present are written in a mixture of colloquial and classical Arabic, conventional in form and difficult to interpret. The law upon which they are based is not sharī'ah, but tribal custom ('ādah), and there are references to usages which must be pre-Islamic but flourish still to-day. Apart from the importance of such material for constructing a picture of contemporary Arabian society, documents such as these may assist in the interpretation of the language and content of pre-Islamic inscriptions. They are a sample of material abundant in tribal areas but, of course, they are typical of a more primitive form of civilization than that of the Yemen and Ḥaḍramawt.[1]

The Wāḥidī Tribes and their Country

For detailed information on the Wāḥidī Sultanate, with accurate lists and descriptions of tribes and excellent geographical information, mostly not so far utilized by cartographers, C. von Landberg's *Arabica V* (Leiden, 1898), pp. 177–234, Pays des Wâḥidi, is invaluable. The best map of the area is H. Von Wissmann's new draft map of the Aden Protectorate, at present in MS. at the Royal Geographical Society. Use has been made of the Political Notebook for the district, where more recent events are concerned, but tribal and geographical data therein must be checked by *Arabica V*.[2]

[1] For the Yemen, see E. Rossi, Il diritto consuetudinario delle tribù arabe del Yemen, *Rivista degli Studi Orientali* (Roma, 1948), xxiii, 36 pp.

[2] Several travellers have described Wāḥidī country. A small literature exists on the Vienna Expedition at the beginning of the century. C. von Landberg's Die Hunde von 'Azzān und ihre Bestrafung durch die Engländer, *Eine Errinerung an die Südarabische Expedition* (München, 1903), might be consulted. For photographs, Freya Stark's books are useful.

Landberg's analysis absolves me from describing at length the social structure of the territory. Class divisions, in more or less descending order, include saiyids (with no temporal power), sultans, mashā'ikh, two sanctuary-khādims—a very ancient class—and the tribesmen. Below the fully honourable status come soldiers of the Sultan (usually, if engaged in trading, but not if acting as soldiers), ra'īyah, ḥawīk (weavers), ṣubyān, slaves, and outside this Islamic society the ancient but alien element of the Jews. The ra'īyah are sub-divided into various types, tradesmen, artisans, labourers, and even some rich merchants and camel-owners.

At Aṣba'ūn, in the Wādī Maifa'ah, about an hour's journey on foot from the pre-Islamic city of Naḳab al-Hadjar, the Wāḥidī sultanate has an administrative centre, under the qaim, Muḥammad bin Sa'īd al-Wāḥidī, from whom these cases were obtained. With his aid, that of the assistant political officer, Muṣṭafā Rif'at, and any Bā 'Awḍah tribesmen present, they were explained.

We are here concerned with two different tribal confederations, firstly in the land case, the Bā Rashaid section of Bā Baḥar, of the Nu'mān confederation. The Bā Rashaid have their tribal centre at Raidat Āl Rashaid, a little to the north and east of Aṣba'ūn, and live in the villages of Al-Salāmah, Ḥuṣn al-'Uṭair, Raḥṭān, al-Ḳurain, and Thafar. The Bā Baḥar is an ancient tribe, mentioned in Hamdānī's *Djazīrat al-'Arab*, etc. The other tribe in the case of the run-away wife, is the Bā 'Awḍah, of the Āl Dhiyaib branch of Ḥimyar. I have talked with most of the individuals whose names occur in the texts. Few can write more than their names at best, yet the documents abound in formulæ and technical terms, some of which one occasionally sees in ancient Arabic poetry.

Procedure

Each case has its fixed conventional procedure. In the reports of the qaim of Maifa'ah, we find the sās or ordering of procedure, the da'wā, plaint or accusation, the taḳwā or defence and reply, and the ḥukm, judgment, all set forth, though in the first instance, the land case, the ḥukm is not given, as it was *sub judice* at my visit.[1]

According to my informants there are three types of ḥukm.

[1] The term sās (asās) seems to be used in Iraq, though its actual technical application may vary a little from that in Wāḥidī territory. See Farīḳ al-Muzhir, *Al-Ḳaḍā' al-'Ashā'irī*, edited with notes by Nūrī Shams al-Dīn (Baghdad, 1941), pp. 23 and 135.

There is that which is called riḍā, agreement or consent, ḳaḍā, the decision of a judge according to the merits of a case, and ṣalāḥ or iṣlāḥ, settling out of court, or without going to court. When a case comes before the tribal judges, a meeting usually takes place in the room of a dār, and the case is conducted, often amidst much heated argument. I have seen such cases in Wāḥidī territory, and also remember vividly one held at my camp at Am-Fadjarah, in Ṣubaiḥī country, in 1940, attended by representatives of both contending tribes, with the hostages they had given in earnest of their intention of proceeding to court, the latter in fetters.

The Land Dispute

Two sections each claim certain rights over land in the Wādī Maifa'ah. The matter is brought before the qaim of Maifa'ah, the procedure agreed and witnessed. The plaint is made and the defence is set out.

نَقْل من الدَّعَاوِى الّذى تَصْدُر فى مَحْكَمَةْ مَيْفَعَه من البادِيَه

الأكرام

(١) وِثْر حَقّ السّاس

حضر عندى فى محكمة ميفعه العاقل على بن حَمَدْ بن
لَعْجَمْ وقبيلته هل رَّشَيْد، وكذلك العاقل على بن سالم بن حمد
وقبيلته هَلْ على بن حَمَدْ هل رَّشَيْد، وقدّموا محبوسين من
الفريقَيْن بيد قايم ميفعه محمّد بن سَعيد الوَاحِدِى لبعضهم
البعض فى ما طالبوا فيه فى حقايق الأطيان وتجاديرها وغَلَلها وفى
حدود الطّين ونهب وعَثَرَهْ وتوقيف، كُلَّيْن هرْجَه له ولسانه له
وساسه له بُلْغَ الطُّرُق، مُخَلَّف الدّم وشَايِم ولَايِم. هذا براس

الحكومه تقدّمه أو تؤخره الى وقت ثانى صار بالقنع والرضا بين المذاكير، وكلن منهم حميل ورديم على قبيلته . وعلى القائم ان يختار لنا حكّام من روس عقّال القبايل فى قواعد البلاد وسوالفها وسوَاسها، وكلّ ركبه ينكرها الحكم هى معذوفه ما لها قبول من الجانبين، وكلّ من جاه فصل ولا تقبّله يتقبله العدالى، وهو يقطع الغريم ومن صابه صوب ولا بدّاه فهو المربوع فى رجل محبوسه ومن ما قابل على وعده، وخذ وانطا عند الحكّام كلّ ما ادّعوه ايّاه واضح وما هو له ماضح .

وذلك بحضرة الأشهاد، المنصب الشيخ عبد الله بن محمّد با قادر والعاقل حسين بن عمر با عوضه، والعاقل على ن عوض بن لكرش با عوضه، والعاقل على بن حمد بن عوض بن ذييب با عوضه .

(٢) دعوى

دعوى على بن احمد بن لعجم بن رشيد وقبيلته . ادّعا بالله وعندكم يا لحكام أنّ لى مال فى ساقية النّونجع والبزنعله بالعطف وأنّه سرح عليه وغلب عليه ومنع وكيلى وقفا على حقيقتى وله سنين عديده ويا من بعد ما قفا علا مالى إنّه جاب

لى عَشْرَهَ وحمّلنى اثنين قُتول . وَأُصِيبه وَأُلْزَمـه من عنـد الله
وعندكم يَاأَلحْكَام ببـوش مالى وغَلَلى . وعِنّى وَأُتْعِبنِى
بشُهُودى وَأُصِيبه بِـأَلحْمَـال الثّقيله والعبُرَ الجايِره من عند الله
وعندكم يا أَلحْكَام .

(٣) تَنْوَى

اِتّقَا عَلِى بن سالم بِن رَّشَيْد. عندُ الله وعندكم يا أُلحْكَام
أن سـاقِيَة النُّوَيْجِـع والبِزَيْعَلَه بين هَل رَّشَيْد، وكُلَّيْن سـارِح
يِتَعَصَّم من تحت يدّى حِصتّه بعوايد حَرْث مَيْفعه وأنّ على بن
أحمد بن لَعْجَمْ وقبيلته غَلَبَوْا يتعصّمون جيَزْ القُسوم وأنّهم يَبَوْن
يرسمون عَلَىّ عاده ثانِيَه، وأنّهم جوَنِى حَرَّابـه ضَرَّابـه إلى
مَطْرَحِى، ويا من عثر إن عَشْرَتَـه فى ظَهْرَه؛ ويحمانى الله، لا
غلبت عَـلَا عَـاصِمَة مثل هل رَّشَيْد، ولا يِلَزّمنِى حاكم بالجَوْر
والبُهْتان . وقدنى عند الله وعندكم يا أُلحْكَام.

Copy of the cases which appear at the court of Maifa'ah from the honourable tribes.

(1) *A Document of Procedure*

The headman ('āķil) 'Alī bin Ḥamad bin La'djam (1) and his tribe, the Ahl Rashaid (2), attended the court of Maifa'ah before me, and so also the headman 'Alī bin Sālim bin Ḥamad and his tribe the Ahl 'Alī bin Ḥamad Ahl Rashaid. They delivered over hostages from (each of) the two (contending) parties into the hands of the qaim (3) of Maifa'ah, Muḥammad bin Sa'īd al-Wāḥidī (4), as a guarantee of one (tribe) to the other in the matter of the claims they maintain regarding the rights to cultivated lands, the imposition of a ban (5) thereon, the crops therein, and concerning the boundaries of the cultivated land, theft, provocation of quarrels, and forcible stoppage of cultivation (6). Each (tribe) has its (right of raising) a plea, of pleading its (case), and of having its procedure detailed, from beginning to end; apart from matters involving blood (7), and that which touches a man's honour (8). The latter rests with the Government (9) to decide whether to bring forward the matter, or postpone it to a later occasion.

(The afore-going) was agreed to the satisfaction and consent of the afore-mentioned (contracting) parties, and each of them is a responsible guarantor on behalf of his tribe. It is the duty of the qaim to choose judges for us from amongst the principal headmen of the tribes, in accordance with the laws, precedents, and customary procedure of the land (10). Any unfounded claim (or petition) which the judge disallows is (thereby) rejected, and shall find no acceptance from either party (of the two tribes). (In the case of) any party who has a decision preferred against him, but will not accept it, the pledge-holder will, notwithstanding, accept it, and he will pay the (successful) party to the suit (11). Whosoever has a sentence passed against him, but does not make settlement of it, must pay the (fine) four-fold before his hostage can be released (12). Whosoever has not presented himself in accordance with his promise (or appointment), nor made his plea and defended himself before the judges, all that they (his opponents) have preferred against him is valid, and not null and void.

This (took place) in the presence of the witnesses, the Manṣab the Shaikh 'Abdullāh bin Muḥammad Bā Ḳādir (13), the headman Ḥusain bin 'Umar Bā 'Awḍah, the headman 'Alī bin 'Awaḍ bin Lakrash, and the headman 'Alī bin Ḥamad bin 'Awaḍ bin Dhiyaib Bā 'Awḍah (14).

(2)* *A Plaint*

The plaint of 'Alī bin Aḥmad bin La'djam bin Rashaid and his tribe.

He brings a plaint before (15) God, and you, oh judges, that I (16) have property in the water-channel of al-Nuwaidji' and al-Bizai'alah, in the Bend (17) (of the Wādī Maifa'ah), and that he (18) went out to work in it, and took it over, and would not allow my agent (access to it), but disregarded my right, and has been doing so for a number of years. Then, subsequent to his disregarding my property, he picked a quarrel with me, and made me responsible for committing two murders. I therefore attaint him, and lay on him the responsibility, before God, and before you, oh judges, of plundering my property and my crops. So help me (19) and trouble me (to produce) my witnesses. For I attaint him (with the responsibility for) heavy burdens, and grievous troubles, before God, and before you, oh judges.

(3) *A Defence*

ʿ Alī bin Sālim bin Ra<u>sh</u>aid (20) declares in his defence :—

Before God, and before you, oh judges, that the water-channel (21) of al-Nuwai<u>dj</u>iʿ and al-Bizaiʿalah is (common property) amongst the Āl Ra<u>sh</u>aid, and each is eligible to receive his share from my hand, his portion being in accordance with the customs of cultivation at Maifaʿah, and that ʿAlī bin Aḥmad bin Laʿ<u>dj</u>am and his tribe refused to take their shares like the (other) share-holders, but wished to prescribe another custom for me, and that they came to my place with hostile intent. Now, whosoever picks a quarrel, the (responsibility for) the trouble (resulting), falls on his own head, and, God protect me, I have not withheld his share (which is) the same as (that of) the Āl Ra<u>sh</u>aid. Nor will any judge hold me culpable of injustice or false accusations. I am before God, and before you, oh judges.

NOTES.

(1) Laʿ<u>dj</u>am, i.e. al-Aʿ<u>dj</u>am, a not uncommon name amongst the Aden Protectorate tribes.

(2) Pronounced Harra<u>sh</u>aid.

(3) The placing of hostages in the hands of a third party, in earnest of the sincerity of both contending parties' intention of submitting their case to arbitration, is ordinary procedure in Arabia.

(4) Muḥammad bin Saʿīd al-Wāḥidī is a member of the Wāḥidī family which provides the Sultan for that group of tribal elements known as the Wāḥidī confederation.

A sultan (dawlah) in Southern Arabia is never an absolute monarch, or even a king in the ordinary sense, but stands rather in the position of hereditary mediator between a group of tribes associated together in a sort of large confederation ; he acts too, as their leader in matters arising between the confederation and the outside world. I suspect that the sultanate is really a development from the offices of 'āḳil and ḥakam, which are themselves often hereditary. Sultans are probably of tribal stock, and those closely related to the ruling member of the family are respected, though not reverenced and feared like the Mashā'ikh. The poorer sultans, as a rule, enjoy but little consideration, and during our tour of Wāḥidī territory I met one sultan (of whom there are a great many as all their descendants are known by this title), a penniless beggar. This person arrived uninvited at every meal given by local men of influence in honour of Sultan Nāṣir, and would stuff pieces of meat left over into the leather bag he wore slung over his shoulder, taking them away to consume at leisure.

Some assert that the Wāḥidīs are of Turkish descent. Descent is also claimed from the Ḳuraish and from Ḥimyar, but whatever the case may be the Aden Protectorate sultans are physically indistinguishable from their tribesmen. I was told that the ancestor of the Wāḥidīs, by name 'Abd al-Wāḥid, was an Ottoman Turk, a qaim of the Ottomans probably, about the time of the famous Ḥaḍramī sultan, Badr Bū Ṭuwairiḳ b. 'Abdullāh b. Dja'far al-Kathīrī. The Faḍlī, I was told at 'Azzān, is also Ottoman, and so is Sultan 'Aidarūs bin 'Afīf al-Yāfi'ī; elsewhere I have heard it said that the 'Awdhalī Sultan is of Turkish descent. A passage from the history of Bal-Faḳīh al-Shiḥrī described in " Materials for South Arabian History I ", *Bulletin of the School of Oriental and African Studies* (1949), gives some credibility to the assertion that the ancestor of the Wāḥidīs flourished about this time. In the year 955 H. (1548 A.D.) the Sultan Badr went from Shiḥr to Ḥaḍramawt. After spending the 'Īd al-Fiṭr in Saiwūn, he " set out for Shabwah ", then, says the author :—

" There came to him Ibn 'Abd al-Wāḥid, the Lord of Ḥabbān, to Shabwah, and asked him to go with him against certain enemies of his (i.e. Ibn 'Abd al-Wāḥid's enemies) there, such as Bā Ḳab, the Lord of Yashbum, and Ibn Siddah. So the sultan (Badr) set out with him at the head of his troops, and he (Ibn 'Abd al-Wāḥid) brought him up to the citadel (of Ḥabbān). Now, when Bā Ḳab heard, he fled to the mountains, but Ibn Siddah sent the faḳīh 'Abdullāh Bā Makhramah (to him) with horses and breast-plates, and he (Badr) accepted (them) from him, and left him as he was in his land. Bā Ḳab made peace with the sultan (Badr) in return for a (present of) breast-plates and money, but later did not pay what he had promised in full. So the sultan sent his soldiers to Yas͟hbum, and they plundered and burnt it. Then the sultan returned to S͟habwah."

وصله ابن عبد الواحد صاحب حَبَّان إلى شَبْوَه وطلبه
المسير معه إلى خصوم له هناك مثل با قَب صاحب يَشْبُم وابن
سِدّه فعزم معه السّلطان بجنده وطلعه المصْنَعَه فلمّا علم بَا قَب
شرد إلى الجبال وأمّا ابن سِدّه فأرسل الفقيه عبد الله با مَخْرَمَه
بخَيْل ودروع فقبل منه وتركه على حاله فى بلده وبا قب اصطلح
هو والسّلطان على دروع ومال ثمّ لم يفِى (sic) بما ضمنه فجهّز
السّلطان عسكره إلى يَشْبُم فنهبوها وأحرقوها ثمّ رجع
السّلطان إلى شبوه .

From this it seems the son of the founder of the dynasty was alive in 955 H. According to the political notebook he was named ʻAbdullāh bin ʻAbd al-Wāḥid and died in 998 H. (1589–1590 A.D.). We have evidence then that the dynasty was established in the first half of the tenth century H. I noticed on several occasions that members of the Wāḥidī family were addressed by others as Yā ʻAbd al-Wāḥid, notwithstanding that their names were known to the speakers.

(5) For the process of imposition and removal of a ban, see C. Snouck Hurgronje, " L'Interdit Séculier (Rifgèh) en H'adhramôt," *Revue Africaine* (Alger, 1905), no. 256. Al-Fawā'id al-Sanīyah, f. 28*b* seq., notes a Sultan of Tarīm as interdicting a man from irrigating his fields till nearly ruined at the time the corn was in the ear. The man's prayer, however, brought a flood which saved the crop.

(6) Forcible stoppage of cultivation may be occasioned by a shot in the air, or at persons on their way to cultivate their fields accompanied by their animals, etc., or by firing at a man's servants or cultivators, or by taking his animals while he is looking.

I recall an incident in the Maifa'ah area when a tribesman stabbed someone's cows in the stomach, killing them. This strange act might perhaps be another method of forcible stoppage of cultivation.

(7) By blood, murder is meant, and perhaps also wounding, the latter being mentioned as a matter for the sultan's judgment in the 'Awdhalī tribal code.

(8) This phrase is common in Ḥaḍrami documents. In Ḥaḍramawt it has come to be applied to the levy made on the date-crop by tribesmen for their forcible protection of the crop from others. Here, however, it would seem to apply simply to matters which touch a man's honour, "that which shames and blames," and is used thus in its original sense. Into this category would enter presumably any dispute relating to a woman, or an attack on a protected person, etc.

(9) By "Government", I presume the Wāḥidī Government is intended.

(10) It will be noticed that the qaim does not himself judge cases but makes the necessary arrangements for the normal processes of tribal law to come into operation.

(11) The pledge-holder ('adalī) may be a different individual from the judge (ḥakam), or they may sometimes be the same person. In this case, the qaim of Maifa'ah happened to be the pledge-holder. The sense seems to be that if one party, i.e. the losing party, rejects the decision of the judge, the pledge-holder will, at any rate, return the pledge of the successful party at the trial. The Aḥkām al-Man'ah (see following note), however, declares (fol. 66*b*) : "If two men are in dispute for some reason, and each of them delivers a pledge to an Amīr, or to a judge (ḥākim), or to the Ḳāḍī, and the two go to law (taḥākam), and judgement is given (wadjab al-ḥaḳḳ) against one of them, the pledge of him against whom judgement is given is withheld (lazima) until he acquits himself (takharradj) of what he owes, and if he (the pledge-holder must be intended) delivers it, the (damages awarded by the) judgement fall upon the man who delivers (the pledge), except if the person in whose favour judgement has been made (ṣāḥib al-ḥaḳḳ) permits him to deliver (it)."

(12) That is to say the hostages handed over before the opening

of the trial. In the Kitāb al-Ādāb wa-'l-Lawāzim fī Aḥkām al-Man'ah of Aḥmad b. Yaḥyā al-Faḍl (740 H.) which I found in Tarīm, and which is described in " Materials for South Arabian History II ", *Bulletin of the School of Oriental and African Studies* (1950), much space is given to the definition of penalties for each offence or crime. These fines can be halved, doubled, quadrupled, or even charged eight times, according to the gravity of the circumstance.

(13) Shaikh 'Abdullāh is the manṣab of Ṣa'īd, my host for three days, a man of honesty and sterling character. He is known as Mawlā Ṣa'īd. Shaikh 'Abdullāh had, in his youth, run convoys of supplies through the Turkish lines to the British in Aden, and his son is a dresser in the Aden Government Guards. For a note on the manṣabate, see the appendix to the second part of this article.

(14) 'Alī bin Ḥamad of 'Azzān, a poet of the Bā 'Awḍah, one of our companions *de route*. He would compose, smoking a rishbah, and I have a long poem of his, on the twenty-eight stars of the agricultural year, in basīṭ metre. A curious feature of this case is that all the witnesses whose names figure at the end of this sās belong to the Bā 'Awḍah, although it is evidently concerned with the Bā Rashaid only, belonging to a different confederation. The one exception is the manṣab, who belongs to neither, but is of a Mashā'ikh family, and whose name would figure on all kinds of documents.

(15) The preposition might be rendered either " at God ", or " by God ". The phrase is reminiscent of naḥnu bi-'llāh thumma bika, We put out trust in God, then in thee, quoted by W. Wright, *Arabic Grammar* (Cambridge, 1933), ii, p. 163. Cf. A. Musil, *Manners and Customs of the Rwala Bedouins* (New York, 1928), 490, " tarâna blawbak (billâh w-bak) 'an flân." Behold we ask Allah and thee to protect us from so and so.

(16) Note the change of pronoun from " he " to " I ", both of course referring to 'Alī bin Aḥmad.

(17) Al-'Aṭf, used as a proper name, lying south of 'Azzān, running from it to Naḳab al-Hadjar and thence south. The region has at one time been heavily cultivated, and the old naḳab or channel of pre-Islamic times is still used ; it is a cut through a ridge west of the ruined city known as Naḳab al-Hadjar (lit. the cutting of al-Hadjar, the town).

(18) The pronoun must refer to 'Alī bin Sālim bin Rashaid of document 3.

(19) Help me to obtain justice by asking me to produce my witnesses, who will show that I am in the right.

(20) Pronounced Birrashaid. Landberg gives Rishaid.

(21) I suspect that the word sāḳiyah (water-channel) is here employed like bīr (well) in Ḥaḍramawt, to indicate not the channel or well itself, but the lands irrigated by it.

Glossary to the Text

N.B.—Gl. Dath. is C. von Landberg, *Glossaire Datînois* (Leiden, 1920–1942).

وِزْر pl. وُزُور. I also heard a variant وَزِيرَة. Syn. وثيقة. Used also in Wādī Ḥaḍramawt. *A written deed or document.*

سَاس pl. أَسْوَاس, whence, no doubt, سَوَاس. *Legal procedure, the analysis and arrangement of various charges contained in a single plaint.* One says : طرحت لك ساس *I have set forth the procedure for trial before you* (which must be agreed to, if the two parties are going to stand trial). معى ساس عليه *I have a right, or custom, against him.*

عاقل *Headman.* Gl. Dath., etc.

تَجْدِير pl. تَجَادِير. Syn. of جَدَر in this sense, جَدْب. *The act of imposing a ban on fields, or preventing by some forcible means or threat of force, their cultivation in any way.* It seems derived from جدر in the sense of, *to wall, enclose with a wall.*

عَتْرَة *Dispute, quarrel.* Gl. Dath. 2266. Cf. Lane, لا تَبْدَأم بِالعَثْرَة which he renders, *Begin not ye with them by war.* It seems to be a technical term for "*an incident*", and I have recorded it in the 'Awdhalī tribal code also. In doc. 2, *a cause of trouble.*

تَوْقِيف *Interdiction, stopping by force.* The usage is explained in the notes to the translation.

هَرْج Gl. Dath. *Conversation, Gespräch, Rede.* Syns. given by Wāḥidīs دَعْوَة plaint, كلام. See Landberg, *Festgabe* (Leiden, 1909), p. 28 f., 'Ārif al-'Arīf, op. cit., Glossary, p. 41.

بَلْغ الطُرُق The sense of this phrase is obviously *to the limit of the roads*, but I cannot explain the form of بَلْغ unless it be a pl. of بالغ.

مَتْخَلَف *Except, with the exception of.*

شايم This word is always used in the common phrase here شايِم ولَايِم. Cf. the classical شَأَم على *to draw ill-luck, evil fortune on.* Ṭāhir

b. al-Ḥusain al-'Alawī in his Makāmah fī Ahl al-Shirāḥah, says, hādhihi 's-sanah al-Kharīf illā shawm *This year the date-crop is a very little only.* شزم is said to mean شتم *a disgrace, insult.*

لايم One says, لزم عليك *a shame on you,* to a person, for instance, who is mean with a guest, or in any way infringes the canons of honourable conduct. Cf. Gl. Dath. لوم for allied senses. The jingle شايم ولايم means *anything that touches a man's honour,* and probably from that, *anything which it is his duty to protect.* Thence, no doubt, the term is commonly applied to shirāḥah, the protection of date-palms against a fee, so that شايم ولايم comes to have the sense of one's *rights over palm-plantations,* a tangible asset which could be bought and sold, in the Wādī Ḥaḍramawt at least, up to the British protectorate.

زديم Syn. of حميل ورديم is ضامن, *guarantor,* though حميل can also mean *a supporter.* Gl. Dath. ردم *couvrir, boucher.*

حَكَم pl. احكام. Syn. حاكم pl. حُكّام *a tribal judge.*

سالف pl. سوالف. *Precedent, custom.*

زَكْبَة *Unfounded claim, baseless petition.* Cf. Gl. Dath. يزكب بجنانه *he pretends to be mad,* etc.

مدذوفه *Refused, rejected.*

عَدَلِي *One who holds hostages or pledges, deposited by parties in earnest of their intention to procede to arbitration.* The *pledge* is عَدَل pl. عُدُول. Lane says: "The saying originally relating to the bloodwit (al-diyah), one says, لم يقبلوا منهم صَرْفًا ولا عَدْلاً *They did not accept from them a bloodwit, nor did they slay one man for him, of their people who had been slain.*" Here عدل is said to mean *slaying a man for a man,* and صَرْف *the taking of a bloodwit.* See H. Klein, *Kapitel xxxiii der . . . Kašf al-Ġumma* (Hamburg, 1938), p. 25, where perhaps the word عدول should be understood in this sense.

قطع Gl. Dath. *décider le prix, payer.* My informants rendered the phrase, *acting on behalf of the man in whose favour the decision has been made.*

غريم pl. غُرْمَان. Here rendered as, *one of the two contending parties,* in this case the winning party. Lane says, *one upon whom lies the obligation of a bloodwit or the like, adversary in contention, litigant.* It also seems to mean *responsible*, perhaps from the sense of *to pay.*

صوّب Syn. حُكم. *judgment, decision.*

بَدَا *Pay, clear, settle,* Gl. Dath. *payer une dette.* One says, بَدِّى دَيْنَك *Pay your debt.*

مربوع *Fourfold.*

رجل This is a conventional phrase, used also in the 'Awdhalī tribal code. A hostage's legs are shackled.

قابل Syn. حضر.

انطا *To give.* Gl. Dath. The phrase (أ)خذ وانطا here means *made his plea and defended himself.* Cf. F. Krenkow, *The Grant of Land by Muḥammad to Tamīm al-Dārī*, Islamica (Leipzig, 1925), i, 530.

وَاضِح *Valid.*

مَاضِح *Null and void.* Cf. Lane مضح عِرْضَهُ *impute, accuse of a vice, or fault, disgrace, dishonour.*

لَكْرَش i.e. الأكرش *The one* **whose** كِرْش *(ventricule) stands out,* i.e. *a fat man.*

إِدَّعَا Gl. Dath. *prétendre, soutenir.* One says, إِدَّعَا فلان *So and so brought a plaint or accusation.* Cf. اتقى below. دَعْوَى *a plaint, accusation.*

سَاقِيَه *Water-channel.* Gl. Dath.

عطف *Wadi-bend,* here a proper name.

سرح *Go out to work in* (على). Gl. Dath.

غلب (على) Gl. Dath. *enlever, refuser.*

قفا (على) *Reject, disregard.* Gl. Dath. *injurier.* See *infra.*

يَا No one could explain this word exactly. Some said it was superfluous (zā'idah). It occurs again, also in the taḳwā and in the da'wā of the second set of documents. It may perhaps be a simple introductory particle. One says يا خمسه يا سته *either five or six.* It may have the sense of *as for, concerning,* and might be connected with the Class إِيَّا.

اصاب *To have a claim against, accuse, make responsible for.*

يوش باش One says, باش الله, i.e. نبه, cf. Gl. Dath.

يَعِين عان *To aid, assist.* This looks like a derivative from Stem IV of عون, with the disappearance of hamzah, as in case of اصاب, reported by Landberg, and *infra.*

بالحال i.e. بالاحمال *Burdens, responsibilities.*

عِبرَه *Trial, example.*

جَايِر *Heavy, great,* according to my informants, but perhaps *cruel,* in accordance with Gl. Dath., would be better. See also Lane.

اتقى One says فلان اتقا *so and so prepared to defend himself against an accusation.* تَقَوِى *A defence.*

سَارِح *Eligible, having the right, in a position to* . . . So my informants ; but it may be used here in the sense simply of *being, becoming.*

تمصّم *To receive a share* (عاصة Syn. جبة, cf. text, *infra*).

حَرَث *Cultivation.* Gl. Dath., etc.

جَيْز *Like.* Gl. Dath., etc.

قِسم pl. قُسُوم *One who gets a dividend, share-holder.*

يَبَوَن from بِا , بِبَا Syn. بَنى.

عَثَر *To give a reason for offence.* Cf. Gl. Dath.

لزَّم *To make responsible.* Allied senses in Gl. Dath.

لَشرَف i.e. الاشرف.

(To be continued.)

Two Tribal Law Cases (Documents)
(Wāḥidī Sultanate, South-West Arabia)

(Continued)

2

The Dispute over the Runaway Wife

The general procedure in this case is very similar to that of the aforegoing, but here we have the decision of the tribal muḳaddam (pl. maḳādimah) or headman. Bin ʻAwzar's solution of the problem is, of course, very different from a legal decision in a European court to-day, but our methods would probably fail where decisions such as this are effective in obtaining justice. The two parties are constrained to produce other individuals to give evidence to clear or convict them, on an oath which, if false, they firmly believe will swiftly bring upon them the direst consequences.[1] Bin ʻAwzar, however, envisages a possibility that neither party will be able to produce suitable evidence, and should this happen, he has instructed them to refer back the case to him.

It is clear from this case that the plaintiff is not acting from a sense of outraged sentiment, but for economic reasons, for dowries are high in Wāḥidī territory. Amongst the raʻīyah, dowries of 1,300 Maria Theresa dollars have even been known, but perhaps their dowries are higher than those of tribal women. In Ḥaḍramawt the peasant-cultivator pays a dowry of 60 to 100 riyals for a virgin bride, because she is a useful economic asset, working in the fields and house, but the ma<u>sh</u>ā'i<u>kh</u> only pay about 35 riyals for a virgin <u>sh</u>ai<u>kh</u>ah, and even the ʻAlawī saiyids have a standard 40 riyals for a virgin bride, though by arrangement between the two families it

[1] Landberg has described how oaths are taken at the tomb of a saint : " On se range en cercle autour du coffin (tābūt), ou le simple tombeau (ḳabr), s'il n'y a pas de tābūt. Si le mis<u>dj</u>id (mosque) ou la ḳubbah (domed tomb) sont petits, on s'aligne devant la porte. Lorsqu' il y a plusieurs personnes appelées à prêter serment, on commence d'abord par une marche autour du sanctuaire, en se plaçant deux à deux, les uns après les autres. On chante des marā<u>dj</u>īz. Leur arrivée est signalée par des salves de fusil . . . Quelque saiyid ou <u>sh</u>ai<u>kh</u> est toujours présent à ces cérémonies pour empêcher que le sang coule, car l'excitation est toujours grande. Ce n'est pourtant qu' une partie remise ; hors du territoire du walī la vengeance cherche sa victime jusqu'à ce qu' elle la frappe. Cette pratique de se purger d'une accusation moyennant le serment est la ḳasāmah des anciens Arabes (*Arabica V*, op. cit., pp. 141–2).

may be more. The reason stated for the strange practice of the upper classes in paying less for their brides than peasants, is that their women do far less work than a peasant woman, or even none at all.

(٤)

حضروا عندى فى مَحْكَمَة مَيْفَعه سالِم بن حُسَيْن لَشْرَفْ با عَوْظَه وعلى بن سالم با تُرَاب دُمَيْدِم با عوظه . وقدّموا محبوسين بيد قايم ميفعه محمّد بن سعيد الواحدى لبعضهم البعض فى نَقَدْ وحَقّ عند القبيله هَلْ حَمَدْ بِنْ ذِيَيْب على ما فى سوالفهم وقواعدهم وذالك فى حُرْمة سالم بن حسين با عوظه لَشْرَفْ ، وغيره نهب الغنم والرّاحله ؛ وَاُجِيب لهم قائم ميفعه ، حُكّام الّذى اختارهم من اهل با عوظه .

(٥)

(نقل) دَعْوَى سالم بن حسين

بَاُللّه وعندك يا بن عَوْزَر إنّها سارت حُرْمَتى عند ابوها وإنّى تبعتها بيومها وطرحت عَدَلى فى ما تزتقر فيه حرمتى فى سَوَاس القبيله . وإنّه غلب با تُراب من عَدَلى ولا سَرّح حرمتى . وعِنّى وتَعِبْنى ؛ ويا ما نهبته على با تراب ، وهو مَقْفِى ، لا يَصيبُنى بقافِى على ما فى رَزِيَة هل با عوظه .

(٦)

(نقل) تَقْوَى على بن سالم با تُراب

تَقْوَاىْ يا بن عَـوْزَر إنّ عارِى جَاتنى بها هَدّه وتَقْصُور وإنّه جانى بن لشرف وجلس لى ، ووقّفت له بحرمته ويُسلّم ما عنده من سَلَب الحرمه الّذى تزتقر فيه الحرمه فى قواعد القبيله ، وإنّه منع يسلِّم . وقدنى عند اللّه وعندك يا مُنْصف الحقّ .

(٧)

(نقل) حكم بن عَوْزَر با عوظه

وجب فصـل بين بن لَشْرَف واهـل با تُراب . وجبت شـاهدَيْن على بن لشرف ، عَـدْلَيْن لا خُـصْمَـا ولا قُسْمَـا ، يُعَرَّضون على قائم ميفعه ، يشهدون لله وبين إيدات الله ، شَهاده جازِمـه لازمه ، أن سـالم بن حسين طرح عَدَل لبـا تراب فى حرمته فى ما تزتقر فيه الحرمـه ، والعَدَلى غريم ، وإنّ با تراب قفا ولا للحرمـه سلب باقى عنـد بن لشرف قارّ . ولا بلَّغ بن لشرف بالشّهود صاب . علّى ما فى سوَاس القبيله للحرمه شقَيّه كلّ يوم مِكْيالَيْن ونصّ حبّ ؛ وما شلّه على المَقْفِى ما فيه قافى . وإن لَغِب بالشّهود بن حسين لَشْرَف وجب على اهل با تراب

خَمْسه حَلَّافَه حَتَّامه، أوَّلهم دُمَيْدِم وتاليهم لَقْوَر، على با لَهْمَان، يحلفون بالله الرّحمان الرّحيم، مالى السّما برَحْمته، وراسك يا با لَهْمَان، يمين مَطْفِيَه النِّيَّار ومُخْلِيَه الدّيار، قاطعت الثَّرَا والثَّرِيَّه — لا طلّع لنا عَدَلِى غَرِيم فى ما تزدقر فيه حرمة بن حسين لشرف، وإنّ عنده من سَلَبْها لا حَدّ ما هُوه حدّ. ولا حلفوا خَراجوا، وإن لَغِبوا كلّهم مَرَدُّهم عندى. هاذا ما حكم به العاقل محمّد بن سَعيد بن عَوْزَر با عوظه. والله يعلم بالصَّوَاب.

(4) *A Document of Procedure*

Sālim bin Ḥusain Lashraf Bā 'Awḍah (1), and 'Alī bin Sālim Bā Turāb Dumaidim Bā 'Awḍah attended the court of Maifa'ah before me (2). They delivered over hostages into the hands of the qaim of Maifa'ah, Muḥammad bin Sa'īd al-Wāḥidī, as a guarantee of one (tribe) to the other, in the (matter of) the scrutiny (3) of the case, and the setting forth of claims (in the customary way of) the tribe of the Ahl Ḥamad bin Dhiyaib (4), according to their precedents (5) and laws. This (action took place) in (the case of) the wife of Sālim bin Ḥusain Bā 'Awḍah Lashraf and, over and above that, the theft of the sheep and the she-camel (6). I, the qaim of Maifa'ah bring (7) them the judges whom I choose from the Āl Bā 'Awḍah.

(5) *A Plaint*

Copy of the Plaint of Sālim bin Ḥusain :—

(I bring a plaint) before (8) God, and before you, oh Bin 'Awzar (9), that my wife ran away to her father's (house), and that I followed her at once, and deposited my pledge (10) for that on account of which my wife is with-held, according to the procedure of the tribe, but Bā Turāb refused any pledge, and did not produce my wife. So help me, and trouble me (11)! What I stole from Bā Turāb when he was refusing (12), does not cause me to incur any liability for a fine (13), according to that which (comes) within the custom of the Ahl Bā 'Awḍah.

(6) *A Defence*

Copy of the Defence of 'Alī bin Sālim Bā Turāb :—

My defence, oh Bin 'Awzar, is that my "honour" (14) came to me, being beaten, and not having received in full (the clothes and jewellery due to her (15)), and that Bin Lashraf came to me and sat in my house, and I agreed to return (16) him his wife if he would deliver (to her) the woman's clothing and jewellery he still owes her, (and) on account of which the woman is with-held, in accordance with the laws of the tribe ; but he refused to pay, and I am (therefore) before God, and before thee, oh (thou who) givest impartial justice (17).

(7) *A Judgment*

Copy of the Decision of Bin 'Awzar Bā 'Awḍah :—

A decision (in accordance with the circumstances (18)) between Bin Lashraf and the Ahl Bā Turāb is necessary. I have decided that two witnesses for Bin Lashraf, honourable persons, neither parties in opposition (to the other family) nor interested persons, should be produced to the qaim of Maifa'ah, to testify to God, and before the hands of God (19), an absolute and irrevocable testimony, that Sālim bin Ḥusain deposited a pledge for Bā Turāb, in respect of his wife, on account of that for which his wife is with-held, the pledge-holder being responsible (20) ; but that Bā Turāb refused, and that no clothing and jewellery due to the woman remain outstanding with Bin Lashraf. If Bin Lashraf produces the witnesses, according to the usages of the tribe, he will obtain damages for his wife, for each day (21) two measures (22) and a half of grain ; and for that which he took from the person refusing (23) he shall pay no fine.

If Bin Ḥusain Lashraf fails (to produce) witnesses, the Ahl Bā Turāb must (produce) five persons, each individual swearing a single oath (24) by (the saint) Bā Lahmān (25), the first of whom shall be Dumaidim (26) and the second Laḳwar, swearing by God the Merciful the Compassionate who fills the Heavens with his mercy (27), and your head, oh Bā Lahmān, an oath extinguishing fires, emptying houses, cutting off wealth and fortune (28), (that) he did not produce a responsible pledge-holder for us, in the matter of that on account of which the wife of Bin Ḥusain Lashraf is with-held, and that he (still) owes of her clothing and jewellery the following separately detailed items (29). If they swear, they are acquitted. If all fail (30) they should refer (the case) to me.

This is the decision which the headman Muḥammad bin Sa'īd bin 'Awzar Bā 'Awḍah gave. And God knows what is correct.

Notes

(1) Note the spelling 'Awḍah or 'Awẓah.

(2) I.e. Muḥ. b. Sa'īd.

(3) I was told that naḳd al-kalām meant scrutiny of the case to see whether it was a sharī'ah or 'ādah case, but I cannot think that was the intention here.

(4) One of the three sub-tribes of the Bā 'Awḍah, the Hal Yamanah, the Āl Biḥārah, and the Hal Dhiyaib. Landberg, *Arabica V*, op. cit., p. 231, names them the Āl Ḥusain b. 'Umar, the Āl 'Alī bin 'Umar, and the Hal Dhiyaib b. 'Umar. They are doubtless the same.

(5) The term sawālif seems to be of general use amongst Arab tribes, and is even found in the Sudan amongst the Beja (J. S. Trimingham, *Islam in the Sudan* (London, 1949), p. 180, footnote). The phrase above might also be rendered, " according to ancient custom and law."

(6) I.e. the theft of these animals by Lashraf from Bā Turāb as a sort of forcible compensation when the latter withheld Lashraf's wife. Lashraf, even if he had only paid over part of the agreed dowry, was nevertheless being deprived of services for which payment had been made.

(7) Note the change to the present tense, a not infrequent occurrence in narrative.

(8) As in the other plaint bi-'llāh is used, whereas in other places 'ind (at) is used. It might be better here to translate the phrase as " by God ".

(9) Bin 'Awzar is the muḳaddam (chief) of the Ba 'Awḍah, a stoutish man, light skinned, for a Wāḥidī tribesman.

(10) This pledge may be placed in the hands of any responsible person. Lashraf deposits a pledge for the unpaid portion of the dowry with a third party. He does not, of course, place it in the hands of his father-in-law, in the hope that the latter would return his wife.

(11) I.e. " to produce witnesses ", as in the previous set of documents.

(12) I.e. to return Bin Las͟hraf's wife. The sense is clear though the word is difficult.

(13) The term employed, ḳāfī, was explained to me as being the responsibility to return a stolen camel (and here, no doubt, the sheep also), and to pay a fine of five ḳurūs͟h (dollars) in addition. See note 12 to document 1.

(14) The term which has been translated as " honour " is actually the word ʿār, which is equivalent to the word ʿaib, a well-known term, which might perhaps be rendered as " impugnment of personal or tribal honour ". It is used here as a circumlocution for " my daughter ", as the tribesman dislikes reference to a female relative in the presence of others. It is, in fact, a term used to mean any female relative, because one's honour can be impugned in them. C. von Landberg, *Ḥaḍramoût* (Leiden, 1901), p. 173, gives the term maʿūrah from the same root, as " la femme parce qu'elle est le ʿār de l'homme, la chose qu'il doit défendre Le d͟jār = rabīʿ ou nazīl est aussi mon ʿār ", etc.

It is possible that a tribesman only cares about the sexual conduct of his womenfolk insofar as it reflects upon his own honour, though any tribesman here would impress on one, if questioned, the extreme measures he would take in the case of any sexual misdemeanour on the part of his womenfolk. In Dawʿan, however, I was informed of a type of tribal custom where, if a tribesman finds his wife in *flagrante delicto* with another, he demands payment with damages, to divorce the woman, who is then married by the adulterer. This is known as Irṭibāṭ, and is mentioned by ʿAlī bin Aḥmad bin Saʿīd Bā Ṣabrain in his D͟jumal min al-Muhimmāt al-Dīnīyah (written 1294 H.), a copy of which is described in *BSOAS*. (1951), op. cit. A Wāḥidī Sultan with a well-deserved reputation for gallantry, whispered to me that the sister of one of the individuals whose name figures in this collection had a reputation not free from reproach. I find it difficult, however, to believe that Wāḥidī tribeswomen can indulge in secret affairs of the heart, owing to the virtual impossibility of concealment. Ṭabarī, Tafsīr, v, 14, quotes Ibn ʿAbbās as saying of the Arabs of the D͟jāhilīya, " They used to forbid (ḥaram) such adultery (zinā) as appeared, but to allow (istaḥall) what was hidden, saying, ʿ concerning that which appears, it is disgrace (lu'm), but as for what is hidden, that does not matter.' " This reveals the essence of the tribesman's attitude to the subject.

In this connection, the gist of a conversation I had with the new Sultan Nāṣir may be quoted. The women of the sultans never leave the house, except perhaps two or three times in the year, for a funeral, feast, etc., when they may visit another house in 'Azzān.

A woman is then accompanied by her husband, leading the way, the woman following at a little distance. If the Sultan did not accompany his wife, the Bedouin meeting her, might cut off an ear or a lock of hair as an insult ('ār) to the Sultans. Their women do not laugh or talk much in the village of 'Azzān itself lest they be heard by Bedouin, who would say such conduct was unseemly. Should the Sultan's wife go to the window to look out on account of some noise in the street, he would reprimand her sharply and ask why she had done so.

Sultans usually, it seems, marry tribeswomen. Sultan Nāṣir himself was betrothed to a girl of the Āl Liswad, near Ḥabbān, and I was present at the betrothal visit and feast. Sultans can, of course, marry from all sections of the population except the Saiyids. In 'Azzān, the 'Askar al-Ṣulṭān (Soldiers of the Sultan), now mostly merchants owning a little land (ṭīn), and no longer regarded as tribesmen, seem to allow their women to come and go more freely than the Sultans. The 'abīd women move at their liberty, unveiled. In the tall dārs here, women live on the floor below the roof, and on the roof itself during the cooler portions of the day. Visiting a ma<u>sh</u>ā'i<u>kh</u> house in Ruḍūm, our host preceded us upstairs shouting " ṭarīḳ " as he went, to avert the women, as is common practice in South Arabia. In general, women of noble blood are much less restricted in Tarīm and Saiwūn than in Wāḥidī country, but wives of the <u>Sh</u>ibām merchants seem more closely confined, like women of the Wāḥidī towns.

(15) Lit. " shortage ", but it refers to what is known in Wāḥidī territory and elsewhere as ḳa<u>shsh</u> (see Landberg, *Gl. Dath.*), i.e. appurtenances of a woman, such as jewellery, clothing, and cosmetics, kept in a wooden box roughly painted in traditional style. These are agreed upon in the marriage settlement, but actually delivered later, or at least the full amount is usually delivered later. In Wāḥidī houses the woman, i.e. wife of the owner, has a little room of her own (<u>kh</u>alwah), sometimes used for more honoured

guests who may wish a little privacy, or where a few friends are entertained when the main reception room is not used. The woman is not, of course, present on these occasions. In this room she keeps her silver ornaments in the wooden box, and the walls are hung with a great variety of household gear, all this known as s̲h̲akkah ; there are basket containers of all sorts and sizes, gaily coloured palm-fibre trays (tafālah) for rice, etc., cloth or food stored in baskets, wooden bowls, incense burners, the cosmetic-pots, often old powder-horns of metal, or beaded glass bottles like African work, leather pillows, Japanese enamelled plates, and innumerable odds and ends, nearly all hung on the walls. The floor is covered with matting and the whole, when new, is pleasing.

(16) The sense of the context is clear, but the verb waḳḳaf is a little difficult. The reading is, no doubt, correct, as the texts were checked several times. One might otherwise have expected waffaḳt, but perhaps, by transposition, this dialect gives waḳḳaf the sense of waffaḳ.

(17) Bin 'Awzar is addressed here.

(18) This is how the term faṣl (lit. *separation*) was explained. It was also explained by the term ḥukm, which appears in the title of this document, but cf. vocabulary to the texts.

(19) This should not, I think, be regarded as an anthropomorphic phrase, but merely as Arabic idiom.

(20) Presumably to pay over the pledge, if required. Vide supra.

(21) I.e. for each day that his wife has been withheld by her father, the latter paying over the damages. Conversely, a woman who has fled to her people cannot re-marry or claim support from her husband (Landberg, *Ḥadramoût*, 163).

(22) I assume that a mikyāl is the same as a kailah. Wāḥidī cubic measures are as follows :—

2 kailahs (pl. akyāl)	1 mudd
2 mudds	1 mīzarah (maizaraḥ)
2 maizarahs	1 ṣā'
2 ṣā'	1 d̲h̲ahab (pl. d̲h̲ihāb)

According to Landberg, *Arabica V*, op. cit., p. 292, the d̲h̲ahab is equal to eight Aden bushels. My informants said it was equivalent to 12 muṣrās or 2 ḳahāwils.

(23) He must, of course, return the stolen animals.

(24) One individual ḥallāfah or oath-giver might take five separate

oaths, but five ḥallāfah ḥattāmahs will only take a single oath each, this, no doubt, being regarded as a more stringent oath than the former type. It is necessary to insert ḥattāmah to specify that five different persons shall take the oath.

(25) Bā Lahmān is the walī (saint) at Djōl al-Shaikh. The present manṣab there is Shaikh 'Alī b. Ḳāsim b. 'Abd al-Mānì', the latter being the family name of the Mashā'ikh there. Cf. Landberg, *Arabica V*, op. cit., p. 172, where it is noted that the manṣab of that time was a mubashshi', i.e. one able to perform trial by ordeal. For bishʻah see also 'Ārif al-'Ārif, *al-Ḳaḍā' bain al-Badw* (Jerusalem, 1933), p. 95, and Landberg, *Gl. Dath.* The 'Abd al-Mānì' have " spiritual influence " over the Bā 'Awḍah. Landberg's visit to Djōl al-Shaikh was remembered. The shaikh asked him for 200 riyāls as a gift for having entertained him.

(26) Dumaidim is the father of Bā Turāb, but I have not recorded who Laḳwar is, perhaps he may be the uncle of Bā Turāb.

(27) Raḥmah, which has also the sense of " rain ". In Ḥaḍramawt it is said : " Ṣulṭān Ḥaḍramawt al-raḥmah," i.e. " The sultan of Ḥaḍramawt is Rain ".

(28) Tharīyah, here translated as " fortune ", was explained to me as meaning " inheritance ". It seems to me that the phrase is really a jingle, but perhaps the word dhurrīyah offspring is also in the minds of the speakers. For types of oaths in North Arabia, see " 'Ārif al-'Ārif ", op. cit., pp. 72 ff.

(29) Lit. " to the limit of what is a limit ".

(30) I.e. if neither party is able to produce the required number of witnesses.

Summary

This case does not seem to me to be inconsistent with sharī'ah law, while in two important points it agrees exactly with principles enunciated in the fourteenth century *Aḥkām al-Man'ah* (cf. supra) which tends to bear out the contention of the author of that work, namely that Man'ah is not inconsistent with sharī'ah but an extension of it. On fol. 72*b* the author says that the plaintiff in all the Man'ah laws has the onus of the proof, and on him who denies the charge is the necessity for taking the oath to this effect. The Aḥkām al-Man'ah also states (fol. 57*b*) that " whosoever takes away his (relative-in-law's) wife from the house of his relative-in-law (ṣihr) without cause, and without fault on the part of the husband, has done wrong, and must pay restitution (niṣfah) to the extent of a ram worth ten dirhams ". Fines prescribed in special cases follow. Comparison may be made also with the section on Ḳasāmah in Bukhārī, Ṣaḥīḥ (trans. O. Houdas (Paris, 1914), iv, 414.

Appendix

The Appointment of a Manṣab of the Mashā'ikh

The manṣab in Southern Arabia is the ruler of the sacred enclaves known as Ḥawṭah, independent entities owing obedience to no temporal overlord. The Ḥawṭah is a centre for the tribes, neutral territory upon which they can meet to trade or settle disputes.[1] The manṣab is naturally a person of great importance in the country, and acts as impartial mediator between warring tribes. In turn, the tribes have some say in the election of a manṣab of Mashā'ikh, in the Wāḥidī area, but among the Sādah in Ḥaḍramawt the manṣabate seems usually to be hereditary. The notes upon which this appendix is based were taken from the Manṣab of Ṣa'īd himself, Shaikh 'Abdullāh bin Muḥammad Bā Ḳādir, of the Bā Ḳādir Mashā'ikh, descended from Ḳādir bin 'Abdullāh, who is buried at Ṣa'īd.

When a manṣab dies, a ḥawīk (khādim, servant) or ṣabī (of the non-Arab but Arabic-speaking submerged race known in this part of South Arabia as Ṣubyān) is sent with a note to all districts to inform the people. The ḳabā'il (tribes), ra'āyā (peasants and craftsmen, etc.), sultans, and ṣubyān collect at the village of the deceased. They recite the Koran over his grave, and are entertained to a feast known as walīmat al-naḳaḍ,[2] the expenses of which are borne by the brother or son of the late manṣab.

The chiefs of the land (ru'asā 'l-Arḍ) collect and select a new manṣab, that is to say the principal persons and the representatives of the various classes. The ra'āyā have no real head of their class, but they elect (istankhabū) one. Notables of all sections then, including the Mashā'ikh, collect in a circle in the open. All must consent to the election. The dawlah (sultans) are said to be present only for consultation, as the election is a matter for the people of the district, but I was informed that Sultan Ṣāliḥ bin Muḥsin of 'Azzān

[1] For the Ḥawṭah and the Ḥabaṭ, material from Landberg has been utilized in articles in the Encyl. of Islam. These might be consulted. Ṣa'īd is a Ḥabaṭ.

[2] naḳaḍ *to go away* (according to my informants). Gl. Dath. gives it the sense of *to annul, untie*.

was a supporter (ḥamīl) at the election of the Shaikh of Al-Rawḍah. I am not sure whether potential manṣabs would be present at the election, but I think they can hardly be present at the preliminary discussions.

Among the Bin 'Abd al-Māni', there are three branches (shu'ūb). and the manṣabate passes from one branch to another in rotation, The other Mashā'ikh have the office of manṣab confined to one house (dār) only.[1]

When the manṣab has been elected, one of the manṣab's own fakhīdhah (section) walks round the assembled circle several times, carrying a rosary, and then throws it over the head of the chosen person, saying: " This is our father " (Hādhā abū-nā). All present inform the newly elected shaikh that they wish him to be their manṣab. The tribesmen like a manṣab to be generous with the funds at his disposal, but for his functions, clearly he must be endowed with other qualities also.

After this, all go and visit the walī (saint) whose descendant the manṣab is, and the manṣab enters the ḳubbah (domed tomb) with all the people. They touch the ḳafaṣ (wooden or adobe ark-shaped canopy over the tomb), and go round the shawāhid (either the four corner-posts of the canopy, or the projecting upright stones on top of the tomb),[2] beat drums, and sing *mūkhadhs* (panegyrics of the saint), a sort of chant. From here all proceed to the manṣab's house and entertainment (ḍiyāfah) is prepared for them. They feast, and each individual gives the manṣab a present, every man according to his means (kullain bi-ḳadaruh), to help to defray the expenses of the occasion.

When he is appointed, conditions are made with a manṣab. Shaikh 'Abdullāh Bā Ḳādir showed me the agreement made at his own election, but I did not find it of sufficient interest to transcribe and examine in the limited time at my disposal. I did note its principal terms. The manṣab entertains all who come. He judges between the tribes and the ra'āyā. According to usual practice in South Arabia, the tribes must help the manṣab against a wrong-

[1] For the Mashā'ikh of the Wāḥidī area, see Landberg, *Arabica V*, op. cit., pp. 189 ff. The Mashā'ikh of Ṣa'īd, Djōl al-Shaikh, al-Ḥawṭah, and Al-Rawḍah, are all descended from a common ancestor, and they claim descent from 'Abd al-Ḳādir al-Djīlānī.

[2] For some notes and sketches of the shapes of tombs, see my *The Cemeteries of Tarīm* (Muséon, (Louvain, 1949)).

doer or pay a fine. The main part of the agreement was largely taken up with a list of fines for offences by tribesmen (ḳabā'il) against miskīns (peasants). If, for example, the ḳabīlī should steal an ox, he must return the ox and a sum equivalent to its value, half (nāṣifah) to the manṣab, and half to the robbed person (manhūb). If a ḳabīlī commits a misdemeanour, the usual procedure is to interdict him from the sūḳ (market), which in the case of Ḥawṭat al-Faḳīh 'Alī is an important sanctuary. The economic insufficiency of the tribesman is thus apparent, as he must have recourse to the market, and this is a powerful weapon in the hands of a manṣab.

Glossary to the Text

دُمَيْدِم dimin. of دُنْدُم *a sort of bird of the mountains.*

نَقَد الكَلَام نقد *scrutiny of a case.* Gl. Dath., نَقَد *avoir du jugement.* Lane, "suitableness of a judgment, and of what involves or implies a judgment."

حق *Setting forth of claims.*

يومها *At once, quickly.*

ازتقر *infra* ازدور *to be held firm, withheld.* Cf. Gl. Dath., for allied stems.

سَرَح *Bring forth, produce.* Cf. Gl. Dath.

تِبَب Note this type of Imperative common in Ḥaḍramawt, etc.

مَقَفِى Part. Act. Stem IV of قفا, u. Note the vowel of the preformative and compare مَظَفِيَة *infra.* Gl. Dath. اقفى *tourner le dos, s'en aller, partir.* Thence it must mean *to refuse.* Cf. قفا *supra.*

قافى Gl. Dath., gives قفا as *injurier,* and قَفِيَّة *injure,* and it may be from this sense that قافى is derived. It means here *a fine for the theft of an animal, paid as compensation to the owner.*

دَزِيعَة *Custom.* Cf. دَزِيم *an arbitrator* according to customary law. Cf. Djāḥiẓ, *Ḥayawān* (Cairo, 1356 H.), i, 167, where women are described as العار الاكبر.

عار *Female relative,* explained in notes to translation.

هَدَه *A beating.* Cf. Gl. Dath.

تَقْصُور Verbal N. Stem II, as frequently in dialect. One says, فلان قصّر فى فلان *A. has not fulfilled his duty by B.* Here it means *not having received the ḳashsh owed her.*

دنف See notes to translation.

سلب Usually *arms*, but here *women's appurtenances*, i.e. clothing, jewellery, ornaments, cosmetics. Syn. شن. For both words see Gl. Dath.

فصل Syn. حكم, *sentence, judgment.* Cf. Kor. LXXXVI. 13: "distinguishing between what is true and what is false."

عدل *A just person,* as in Class.

قسم pl. قسما *interested persons.* Cf. *supra.*

قاز *Outstanding.*

صاب i.e. اصاب.

شقية *Compensation for injury, damages.* Gl. Dath, *gages.*

لغب *To fail.* Gl. Dath., *être fatigué.*

خلافه Lane, *swearing, that swears much or often.*

خثاه Explained in notes to translation.

ثالي *Second.* Cf. Gl. Dath.

لقوز i.e. الأقوز *The obstinate.*

متطفيه Part. Act. أطفا.

ثرا Class. ثراء *wealth.*

ثريه Explained as *inheritance.* See notes to translation.

خراجوا i.e. خرجوا, the alif indicating a stressed penultimate syllable only, an error of orthography. *To emerge from a case, to be acquitted,* etc. This verb so used, is a technical term of tribal law, used also in other stems. Various forms of this root appear in several documents in my collection.

ADDENDA

P.34 Al-Aḥnaf b. Qays was addressed as Yā Bā (=Abū) Baḥr; he was a Tamīmī (al-Mufaḍḍal b. Salamah, *Mufākharah*, ed. C.A. Storey, Leyden, 1915, 242).

P.39 Major Jock Snell told me subsequently that Bin Laʿjam lost the case. The winners hired a man to construct another channel. Note 21 (p.44) does not apply as the case was over the actual channel.

P.40 ʿAlawī b. Ṭāhir al-Ḥaddād, *al-Shāmil*, 76, alludes to an ʿAwlaqī Sultan Ṣalāḥ b. Bā Ḳab at Yashbum in 959/1552, almost certainly this person. The spelling of Ḳab is uncertain. Al-Shillī's *al-Sanā' al-bāhir* (Mss.) alludes to a Sultan of Mayfaʿah, Ibn Sīdah, probably to be identified with Ibn Siddah of the Ḥaḍramī historian Bā Faqīh al-Shiḥrī.

P.44 Muḥ. b. Hāshim, *Tārīkh al-Dawlat al-Kathīriyyah*, 1367/1948, renders *withr* as *ʿahd*. *Bulgh* looks like a plural of *ablagh*, a colloquial usage?

P.46 *Yā* – I noted *Yā hū*, which one do you mean? said to me by a Yarīmī.

P.169 *Thariyyah*, cf. al-Jāḥiẓ, *al-Ḥayawān*, VI, 445 – *yamīn dhī thariyyah lam yakfur. Tharā* & *thariyyah* seem simply to mean moist soil, earth.

XIII

RECENT MARRIAGE LEGISLATION FROM AL-MUKALLĀ WITH NOTES ON MARRIAGE CUSTOMS

IN Ḥaḍramawt, it seems, there have been constantly reiterated attempts at creating effective sumptuary laws limiting expenditure at marriages and other social activities, especially in respect of the extravagant demands of women for dress and other forms of ostentation where their rivalry leads their male relatives into expenditure beyond their means. The sentiments of the Ḥaḍramī man are admirably expressed in a *qaṣīdah* by the shaikh Aḥmad Barakāt [1] of which one line may be quoted here :

Hātū wa-hātū mā lahin ghaira 'l-lifāt
hātū la-nā hātū la-nā

' Bring this, bring that—they're grasping all the time,
bring it to us, bring it to us ! '

It is to the insatiable demands of this rivalry that the Ḥaḍramī tends to attribute, at least in some degree, the tendency for the cost of marriages to rise, and as, of course, marriage is enjoined by Islam, it is morally right to make it reasonably inexpensive. I heard of an agreement concluded in 1313/1895–6 in Tarīm in which the various social orders of the community—the *saiyids*, *mashāyikh*, the people of the quarters (*ahl al-ḥuwaf*), agreed, each group within itself, as to what it should be permissible to spend on the customary usages (*'ādāt*), especially those relating to marriage, with a view to achieving economy (*iqtiṣād*), but though I tried to obtain a copy of this document I never succeeded, and I put this down to the fact that wherever anything touches on their womenfolk's affairs the Tarīmīs are unwilling to expose it to a stranger. A similar agreement was concluded in Shibām within the last ten years, but I was politely fobbed off when I inquired for a text of it. However, in the newspaper of al-Mukallā, *al-Ṭalī'ah* I, 6, 10 Muḥarram 1379/16 July 1959, I was delighted to see the publication of *Manshūr 'Āmm*, or Public Ordinance no. 10 (1959) containing provisions, probably similar to the sumptuary agreements of the Wādī Ḥaḍramawt which I am unlikely ever to be allowed to inspect. It was suggested to me that the Ordinance was issued at the instance of the elders of the town (*'uqqāl al-bilād*), and the religious committee (*lajnat al-shu'ūn al-dīnīyah*) of al-Mukallā, both regarded as conservative, and that the Qu'aiṭī government deferred to their pressure, and accepted their proposals. It is not thought, however, that its provisions are observed in practice at all, except that the *mushtariḥah* or female minstrel nowadays receives a fixed fee only,

[1] R. B. Serjeant, *Prose and poetry from Ḥaḍramawt*, London, 1951, Ar. text, p. 97.

without pickings and perquisites. It will at once be realized that the Ordinance contains provisions which cannot be enforced if the community is not prepared to co-operate with Government. In Ḥaḍramawt it has apparently swiftly been the lot of previous sumptuary agreements to fall into the dead letter category. The Ordinance also contains another type of provision, clauses aimed at abolishing customs which the *'ulamā'* would censure as *bid'ah*.

Although the possibility of a recurring economic factor linked to the appearance of these sumptuary agreements cannot be ruled out, possibly periods of rising prices and prosperity, I am inclined to look for social reasons giving rise to the decisions to limit expenditure and curb extravagance. Though its economic position must be quite different from that of al-Mukallā, the 'Awdhalī Sulṭanate, during the summer of 1961, has promulgated a law limiting and defining the traditional costs, fees, and perquisites of marriage, which Sulṭān Ṣāliḥ has recently communicated to me.[1] More recently similar legislation has appeared in Dathīnah.

In the Aden paper of 'Abd al-Raḥmān Girgirah, *al-Yaqẓah*,[2] a correspondence has been conducted on the difficulties confronting the young Adenese desirous of marrying. This has long been troubling the minds of the Adenese for I recall other newspaper articles on the same subject nearly ten years ago. In the case of Aden there has been a tremendous boom and rise in prices because of the heavy military expenditure of latter years.

One of *al-Yaqẓah's* correspondents sees the obstacles in the way of marriage as the excessive demands of the girl's family in dowries and the bride-price (*mughālāt ahl al-fatāh fi-'l-muhūr wa-'l-jihāz*), a phrase which might have been taken straight from al-Baiḥānī's *Ustādh al-mar'ah*,[3] and the way they regard marriage as a commercial transaction (*'amalīyat bai' wa-shirā'*). One young man goes so far as to declare, ' My social life is not guaranteed (*ḥayāti al-ijtimā'īyah ghair maḍmūnah*), so let me go to London where I can marry for nothing ', i.e. without the cost of dowry and bride-price ! [4] Others complain of the scarcity of housing, lack of furniture, the rise in the cost of living, the rise in dowries (*azmat al-masākin, azmat al-athāth, irtifā' al-ma'īshah, irtifā' al-muhūr*). A proposal is made that a committee be formed to study the problem and propose appropriate legislation. A contrary view holds that these are not the basic causes of the problem, but what he calls ' moral disintegration (*al-inḥilāl al-khulqī*) '.

While too much emphasis should not be laid on this so-called ' moral disintegration ', and what a conservative Muslim regards as falling within this

[1] *Fatāt al-Jazīrah* (Aden), XXII, no. 1697, 5 August 1961 ; *Ṣawt al-Janūb* (Aden), no. 21, 5 November 1961.

[2] *Al-Yaqẓah* (Aden), VI, 27 September 1961, p. 215.

[3] Muḥ. b. Sālim b. Ḥusain al-Kudādī al-Baiḥānī, *Ustādh al-mar'ah*, Aden, 1950, p. 55, *al-mughālāh fi-'l-muhūr wa-'l-j h zah* (error for *ajhizah* ?), *wa-hiya 'l-daf'*. I have discussed this work at greater length in a paper, ' Sex, birth and circumcision ', *Hermann v. Wissmann-Festschrift*, ed. A. Leidlmair, Tübingen, 1962, 193–208.

[4] The writer is clearly influenced by Western theories on social matters.

category is not likely to be exactly what would be considered moral disintegration in Europe, it must be pointed out that the coming of the oil refinery to Aden in 1952 has effected great social changes in the Asiatic communities, especially the Arabs, and not only in Aden but in the Western Aden Protectorate as I have already indicated.[1] ‘Abdullāh Muḥammad al-Maqṭarī with whom I discussed these statements, has put the matter into words, the following being the gist of them. The oil company provided its employees with furnished quarters at a time when home conditions were rather primitive in Aden, and the young women began to demand that their husbands, not employees of the company, should furnish them with the same material standards of comfort as their sisters whose husbands worked at Little Aden. Since, say, 1957 young women have been demanding that their husbands live with them in an establishment separate from that of the husband's parents. This results partly from female secondary education, partly from their closer acquaintance, through numerous media, with the social system of the West. Al-Maqṭarī was of the opinion that the bride-price (*daf‘*) was probably not a great obstacle to marriage since it could be adjusted, though families like to boast that their daughter was married for a *daf‘* of such and such a (high) figure. It is the practice as elsewhere that the dowry is named, but not paid, except in case of divorce, but customarily it bears a value proportionate to the *daf‘*, e.g. if the latter is 6,000 shillings, the *mahr* would be 600 shillings.

In the Aden paper *Ṣawt al-Janūb*[2] were printed recently the words of a new song entitled *Operette al-daf‘*, composed and set to music by two well-known Aden artistes. This satirical song is expressive of the sentiments of the young Adenese of the class corresponding in their way, to the ‘ effendi ’ of other Arab countries, and is stated to have been received with acclamation at its first performance.[3]

The theme is quite new, and though in diction it does not break away entirely from traditional Aden or South Arabian verse, it is a notable departure from it, on the lines of the free verse fashionable elsewhere. The language is a mixture of Adenese, with a diction partially Contemporary Arabic, partially Egyptian colloquial intermingled with its basic Adenese—as affected by some Adenese in such a context. For example *mā shāfat-sh* is not Aden usage, and I have never heard an Adenese say *maṣraf* when he means ‘ bank ’.

الشاب :

الجميلة الفاتنة بنت الاكابر	راح أبى لا عندَ أبوها،
اللى عين الشمس	لما شافت أمى أهلهْ،
ما شافتَنْش وَجْهِه يوم سَافِر	راغبين با يزوّجوها.

[1] In a paper, ‘ Social change in south-western Arabia ’, at the conference held by the Congress for Cultural Freedom in Khartoum in early 1961.

[2] No. 21, 5 November 1961.

[3] ibid., no. 22, 11 November 1961.

والد الشاب :
نحنا والله طالبين القُرْب منك
لابننا عبده ،
ونشتى بس اذنك.
عبده عمره تِسْعَطعشر ،
يشتغل كاتب
وعاده في خمسطعشر ،
ذا معاشه ستميه
غير «الأَوْفَرتِم» ،
وانت شوف بس رغبتك
يا حاج قاسم.

والد الفتاة :
قوللى ، طيب ،
ايش دفعك؟

والد العريس :
فى القِياس با ادفع لك الفَيْن —
وانت شَرْعك.

والد العروس :
ما يخارج شوف بصيره ،
والوليد عاده مشاهرته حقيره.
شى معه بيت أو رصيد فى البنك
وسياره وتيره؟
شى معه فوق المعاش رتبه كبيره؟

والد العريس :
نحنا والله يا أخي
فى سِتْرة الحال ،
ذا غِنا النفس عندنا
أغلى من المال ،
أنا دلّال فى الجلود
وابنى موظّف.

والد العروس :
بس قُلْلِى
ذا غنى النفس
يصطرف فى أى مصرف؟

نفس الشاب :
قلت لابي ونحنا نروح ،
بس لَيْش ليش بالعجل؟
الزواج مُو بس هارب ،
العجل فيبه ضَبَل.
قلْتها وانا أعزّى
قلبى فى جُرْحه الكبير
من مفاهيم ناس مساكين ،
اسكتوا صوت الضمير.

The youth. The lovely attractive girl, daughter of the notables, whose face [1] the eye of the sun never saw unveiled—my father went to her father after my mother had seen her family, wishing to marry her (i.e. to me).

The youth's father. Wallah, we should like to enter into relationship with you (by marriage) for our son 'Abduh [2] and want only your consent. 'Abduh is 19, working as a clerk when he was only 15; his salary is 600 (shillings),

[1] Note the feminine termination *wagh-ih* as later *ahl-ih*.

[2] So common is the name 'Abduh in Aden that the Adenese are dubbed in fun 'Ayāl 'Abduh, which might be rendered as ' the 'Abduh tribe '.

apart from ' overtime '.[1] So then you think what you want (as bride-price), Ḥājj Qāsim.

The girl's father. Good, tell me then, what is your bride-price ?

The groom's father. According to the usual rate I'll pay you 2,000 (shillings), but it's up to you.[2]

The bride's father. That won't do.[3] You think it over. The boy's salary is still nothing. Has he a house, or a bank account, or a nice car ? Apart from the salary, has he a good position ?

The groom's father. Wallah, my friend, we can just preserve appearances.[4] Enough for a person, in our view, is worthier than wealth. I am an auctioneer in hides, and my son is a salaried employee.

The bride's father. All right, but tell me, is that ' enough for a person ' cashable [5] at any bank ?

The youth himself. I said to my father as we left, ' Enough, why, why the hurry ? [6] Marriage can come any time. Haste brings trouble [7] with it '.

I said this, comforting my heart for the great wound in it at the ways of foolish folk.[8] Quieten the voice of conscience.

The Aden schoolboy of 15 or 16 used to marry at this age, but it looks as if material considerations which did not exist before the desire for a higher standard of living may be raising the age of marriage among the educated class.[9] For some time to come the transformation of Aden Arab Muslim society, in respect of relations between the sexes, to a more Westernized model as, say, in Egypt, is like to be confined to the educated classes. The process will undoubtedly cause considerable strain, dislocation, and maladjustment, of which the feeling against the *daf'* may be a symptom. The advantages the change brings in its train may not altogether outweigh the disadvantages. As in other Muslim countries, however, Westernization of the society has its strong protagonists and its strong conservative opposition, the latter not necessarily stemming from the *'ulamā'* who can on occasion show an extraordinary degree

[1] The English is transliterated but apparently there is a word which has become Arabic, *habartain*, i.e. ' overtime '.

[2] *Wa-anta shar'-ak* means *zai mā tishtī* ' whatever you want '. He means that he should say what he wants as bride-price.

[3] cf. E. V. Stace, *English–Arabic vocabulary*, London, 1893, 88, *khārag al-dain* ' pay a debt '. Perhaps one should render it as ' it doesn't meet the case '.

[4] The phrase *sitrat al-ḥāl* in this context means that though they may have to pinch and scrape or even go hungry they have enough to keep up a decent appearance to the outside world.

[5] *Iṣṭaraf* ' to be changed, cashable '.

[6] *Mū—mā hū.* There is an Aden saying, *yā shaikh hū mush hārib*, i.e. ' it won't fly away ', you can have it any time '.

[7] One says, *hū/hī ḍablah* ' he/she is a trouble through his/her perpetual demands, wishes, whims '. *Ḍabal* means something like trouble, bother on account of the responsibilities it brings.

[8] *Mafāhīm* was explained as ' what they hold to be the case ', *mawḍah*, or ' mode '.

[9] The Aden paper *Ṣawt al-Janūb*, I, no. 45, 29 April 1962, the organ of the Aden Protectorate chiefs, in an article, ' al-Zawāj al-mubkir jarīmah ', protests against marrying boys of 15 to 16 to women of 25 to 30. The boys' fathers apparently like this because these women will not ask the fathers for rights for themselves in *māl wa-aṭyān*, presumably cattle and land.

of broadmindedness. As long ago as twenty years back, some Aden writers were attacking the way in which Adenese treated the institution of marriage,[1] and these persons, mainly journalists, still form the advance-guard of the Westernization of local society though they would not call it by this name, preferring such terms as *al-iṣlāḥ al-ijtimāʿī* ' social reform ', and other popular catchwords derived from the West.

The new Quʿaiṭī state marriage decree : text, translation, commentary

For the proper understanding of the Ordinance promulgated in al-Mukallā, it is necessary to outline the sequence of the traditional practices to be observed from the time of the formal betrothal visit up to the entertainments that round off the actual consummation of the marriage. It is not claimed that the programme which follows is complete down to the last detail, and being derived from informants it lacks the quality of direct personal observation, but Doreen Ingrams [2] in presenting an account of a wedding she actually attended, it would appear, provides something of the colour and incident lacking here. I am indebted to Saiyids ʿAbdullāh al-Bīḍ and Muḥammad Saʿīd Midaiḥij, and more recently to Mr. J. Dofari of Aden who gave freely of their time to comment on the material constituting this short study.

The sequence of the wedding ceremonies

1. The *madād*

   i.e. the betrothal visit—*qahwah fī bait al-ʿarūsah.*

2. *Lailat al-rubūṭ*

   i.e. the night of the binding. Days, or months, or it could even sometimes perhaps be years after the *madād*, the women hold the *lailat al-rubūṭ*. They take a locally made *subāʿīyah* [3]—which is men's wear, not women's and cover the face and body of the bride-to-be, saying, *Antī marbūṭah li-fulān* ' You are

[1] Mukhaiyam Abi 'l-Ṭaiyib (Society), *Aqlām al-Mukhaiyam*, Aden, 1942, where Muḥ. ʿAlī Luqmān condemns plurality of wives, and ʿAbd al-Razzāq al-Fikrī, writing on married life in Aden, accuses the Adenese of not knowing the true meaning of marriage ! He makes the observation that the Aden girl blushes if marriage is mentioned to her and knows nothing about what has passed between her parents and her suitor's family until the last moment, when she has no option but to obey. I wonder how true this is in 1962 ?

The *Aqlām* might be contrasted with a book written some 15 years before it, Saiyid ʿAbdullāh b. Muḥ. b. Ḥāmid al-Saqqāf, *al-Tarbiyat al-nisāʾīyah*, Sourabaya, 1346, which is rather old-fashioned, but it nevertheless encourages women to learn to read and write. Old-fashioned custom, as in other countries, was to discourage this activity, cf. *BSOAS*, XXIV, 2, 1961, p. 395, col. 2. At the very time this article was going to press, the newspaper *al-Rāʾid* (al-Mukallā), II, no. 74, 2 April 1962, reported some opposition in Shibām town to the Quʿaiṭī government proposal to open a girls' school there, on account of the old tradition that the teaching of girls breeds difficulties and calamities.

[2] *A survey of social and economic conditions in the Aden Protectorate*, [Asmara, 1949]. F. M. Hunter, *Account of the British settlement of Aden in Arabia*, London, 1877, 448 seq., is good also. C. von Landberg, *Études . . . Daṯînah*, Leiden, 1905, 28–9, 192–5.

[3] This is a word remounting to medieval times, and it denotes a striped cloth usually used as a *fūṭah*. C. von Landberg, *Ḥaḍramoût*, Leiden, 1901, pp. 233–6, quotes and comments on a verse which alludes to the custom described, but seems to have been unaware of this custom which would explain his verse more satisfactorily. cf. Doreen Ingrams, *Survey*, 101.

becoming (lit. bound) the wife of so-and-so'. This is because she does not know about the marriage which has already been agreed, although among the Bedouin a girl does know she is going to be married even if she does not know when. A *nuqbah* (head-scarf) is sometimes used in place of a *subā'īyah.*

3. *Al-zawāj*, the marriage

(*a*) *Al-ḥinnā'* or *lailat al-ḥinnā'*, lit., 'the night of the henna', when the bride and groom are dressed up and decorated with henna, the men having their *makhdarah* [1] and the women theirs. In Ghail Bā Wazīr the *ḥinnā'* with all its preparations and including the *lailat al-'aqd*, lasts for eight days; but it varies from place to place, and in al-Mukallā it is only three days or so from the beginning of the wedding till the girl goes to her husband's house.

(*b*) *Lailat al-'aqd*, also called *lailat al-dukhūl*, or *al-dukhūl*, or *al-dukhlah*. The *'aqd* or contract comes a little before *al-dukhūl*. There is a wedding-feast (*wajbah*) at the bride's house, when the young man comes to claim her, and she goes to his house in the very early morning.

(*c*) *Al-ṣubḥah*,[2] i.e. the morning gift to the new wife, the maidenhead gift.

(*d*) The *wajbah* or *mūjibah*, the wedding breakfast, or lunch, a feast given by the bridegroom's family to return the hospitality of the bride's family.

4. *Naql thamān* or *al-nuqlah*

After eight days the bride visits her former home.

Language

It will be perceived that the Ordinance is not very far removed from the educated colloquial, and that many dialectal words are employed. Typical is the construction of *ammā* without the following *fa-*, often to be found in the writings of Ḥaḍramī *'ulamā'*.

منشور عام رقم (١٠) لعام ١٩٥٩ م.

بسم الله وبحمده.

أما بعد نظراً لِما هو واقع من الضرر دينياً واقتصادياً وخلقياً بسبب التنافس في مُؤَن وشئون الأعراس وتقاليدها من لباس وجِهاز وغيرهما من العوائد التقليدية الخارج كل ذلك عن حــدود الاعتدال إلى حد الإسراف قــرر مولانا صاحب العظمة السلطان في المجلس ما يلي وذلك كقرار مجلس الدولة رقم (١) تاريخ ١٠ شوّال ١٣٧٨ هـ. الموافق ١٨ ابريل ١٩٥٩ م.

[1] The *makhdarah* in Aden means both the ceremony and the wooden erection (put up nowadays there by contractors) in which it is held. See p. 489, n. 1, *infra* for further usages of this word.

[2] cf. Landberg, *Gloss. daṯ.*, 2113 ; al-Baiḥānī, op. cit., 216, for gifts of the bridegroom before marriage and on the *yawm al-ṣubḥīyah* ; W. Leslau, *Lexique soqoṭri*, Paris, 1938, 280, '*sábḥa*, trousseau, vêtements, voile, tablier que le mari apporte à la femme après la prière du soire'.

(١) المداد

حفلة المداد ممنوعة للرجال مطلقاً. أما حفلة النساء فتبقى كما هى العادة لما فيها من مساعدة.

(٢) الجهاز

البِكر لا يزيد جهازها على ستمائة شلن مقطوعة الصُبْحَه.
الثيّب لا يزيد جهازها على ثلثمائة شلن مقطوعة الصبحه.
ولا بأس أن يقدم الزوج هدية لزوجته بحيث لا تتجاوز قيمتها خمسين شلناً ولا يمكن أن تذهب الزوجة إلى بيت الزوج بأكثر ممّا يأتي — قعادة، فرش واحد، ثلاث مَدَاكِي، أربع وَسيد، صندوق، شنطة.

(٣) اللباس

الكُرَت والنقاب المراد استعمالها في الزواجات والمناسبات العامة يجب أن لا يزيد ثمن الكُرْته على ستين شلن والنُقْبه لا تزيد على عشرين شلن، وما عداه من الألبسة التى تزيد أثمانها على ما ذكر فممنوع مطلقاً في الزواجات والمناسبات العامة.

(٤) الوليمة

تكون وليمة الزواج يوماً واحد[1] فقط سواء كان في بيت الزوج أو الزوجة.

(٥) البَسْط

يمنع البسط نهائياً للمدعوين في بيت الزوج والزوجة.

(٦) الفَوْجه

ممنوعة مطلقاً.

(٧) المُحَايَاه

محايات الخالة لا تزيد على ثلاثين شلن فقط.

(٨) الباب

يمنع منعاً باتّاً ما يسمى الباب وكذلك الدفع الذي يعطى باسم الباب.

[1] Correctly *wāḥid-an*.

(٩) المَسْحَه

والمسحه بالكيفيـة الموجودة ممنوعة ويقتصر فيها على زيارة الزوج لأم زوجته، ولا بأس أن يذهب معه قريبا[1] له أو صديق، وأن لا يقدم له سوى القهوة كالعادة القديمة.

(١٠) المُشْتَرِحَه

أجرة المشترحه من أهل المُوجِبَه لا يزيد على ثلاثين شلن، ولا يتبعها أي شيء من هدايا أو تَقَادِيم أو غيرها.

(١١) الطرُوحَات

(أ) لا يزيد طَرْح أهل العَرُوس على عشرة شلن فقط.

(ب) طرح الزَفين شلن واحد فقط لمدة الشَرْح في بيت الزوجة، وشلن لمدة الشرح في بيت الزوج.

(ج) العروس التى تخرج لأول مرة يكون الطرح منها ثلاثة شلن فقط.

(د) أما طرح المَعْشَرَه الذي يعود لأهل الزواج لا مانع منه في الزواج الأول فقط.

(١٢) سَهَرَات الزواج

أقصاها للرجال والنساء إلى الساعة الواحدة.

(١٣) المَخْدَرَه

يسمح بالمخدره للرجال في الزواج الأول فقط ولكن لا يسمح بها للنساء مطلقاً.

(١٤) أجرة المُطْرِب

لا تزيد على خمسين شلناً.

(١٥) أُجرة المُشْتَرِح

لا تزيد على أربعين شلناً مقطوعة، أو عشرين شلن، وله أن يأخذ من الزفّانه والخيرة لصاحب المُوجِبَه.

[1] Correctly *qarīb-un*.

(١٦) زَفّاف العَروس

الزَفّة العلنية في الشوارع ممنوعة مطلقاً، ويجب أن يذهب بالعروس إلى بيت زوجها قبل الساعة الواحدة وأن تكون النقليه[1] داخل سِدّة أهل الزوج فقط.

(١٧) نَقْض العُقْده

ممنوع نهائياً ما يسمونه نقض العقده.

(١٨) النَقيلَه

ممنوع الدعوة العامة للنقيله ويقتصر على دعوة الأهل فقط بدون شَرْح ولا زَفين، ولا بأس بحفلة نساء في العصر تقدم فيها قهوة فقط.

(١٩) الشَوْف

ممنوع شوف النساء الفضوليات مطلقاً، ويقتصر الشوف لحفلات الأعراس للنساء المدعوات.

(٢٠) عوائد المَقادِمَة في الأعراس تستمر كما هي بحسب العادة الجارية.

(٢١) سَرَيان مفعول هذا القرار

(أ) يسري مفعول هذه الأوامر ويعمل بها من فاتحة محرم سنة ١٣٧٩ هـ.

(ب) وسوف تتولى الشرطة المدنية بالمكلّا تنفيذ هذه التعليمات.

(ج) وتقديم من يخالفها إلى محكمة نائب لواء[2] بالمكلا للمحاكمة.

(٢٢) العقاب

كل من خالف هذا النظام يعاقب بغرامة مالية تختلف باختلاف أحوال المخالفين على ألّا تقل الغرامة عن شلن ./١٠٠ (مائه شلن) ولا تزيد عن ./١٠٠٠ شلن (ألف شلن). وفيما بعد سترتب الحكومة دفع مبلغ الغرامة لصالح الحافه التى حصلت فيها المخالفة ومن عجز أو امتنع عن دفع الغرامة يسجن لمدة لا تتجاوز أسبوعين.

[1] Said to be an error for *al-naqīlah*.
[2] Read *al-liwā'* probably.

بأمر صاحب العظمة
وزير السلطنة
السكرتارية — المكلا
١١ شوال ١٣٧٨هـ.
الموافق ١٩ ابريل ١٩٥٩م.

Public Ordinance no. 10 of year 1959.

In the name of God, praise to Him.

In view of the ills, religious, economic, and moral, resulting from rivalry in the matters and affairs of marriages and the traditional practices thereof, in dress, bride-price, and other traditional customs, all exceeding the bounds of moderation to the extent of extravagance, our Lord, His Majesty the Sulṭān, resolved the following in Council, this by decree of the State Council no. 1, dated 10 Shawwāl 1378, corresponding to 18 April 1959.

1. The betrothal payment (*madād*)

For men the *madād* reception is absolutely prohibited, but the women's reception shall remain as is the custom, because of the presents thereat.

2. The bride-price (*jiḥāz*)

For a virgin the bride-price, as distinct from the wedding-present (*ṣubḥah*), shall not exceed 600 shillings.

For a woman previously married, the bride-price, as distinct from the wedding-present, shall not exceed 300 shillings.

There is no objection to a husband presenting a gift to his wife, provided its value does not exceed 50 shillings. It shall not be permissible for the wife to go to the husband's house with more than the following :

A bed, one (set of) bedding, three cushions, four pillows, a box, a case.

3. Clothes (*libās*)

Skirts and head-scarves intended for use at weddings and on public occasions—the price of a skirt must not exceed 60 shillings, and that of the head-scarf 20 shillings. Other apparel exceeding in price what has been mentioned is absolutely prohibited at weddings and public occasions.

4. The wedding breakfast (*walīmah*)

Whether it be at the husband's or wife's house, the wedding breakfast shall last for one day only.

5. The breakfast (*basṭ*)

The breakfast for invited guests at the husband's or wife's house is utterly prohibited.

6. The congratulatory gift (*fawjah*)

Absolutely prohibited.

7. The salutation-gift (*muḥāyāh*)

The salutation-gift for a mother-in-law (*k͟hālah*) shall not exceed 30 shillings only.

8. The door-fee (*bāb*)

What is known as the ' door-fee ' is categorically prohibited, as also is the payment given under the name of ' the door '.

9. The laying-on-of-the-hand fee (*masḥah*)

The *masḥah*, in its existing form, is prohibited. It shall be confined to the husband's visiting his wife's mother, though there is no objection to a relative or friend of his accompanying him, provided that only coffee be offered him in accordance with ancient custom.

10. The female minstrel (*mus͟htariḥah*)

The fee paid by the family giving the wedding breakfast to the *mus͟htariḥah* shall not exceed 30 shillings, nor shall anything in the way of presents, gratuities, etc., go along with it.

11. Gratuities (*ṭurūḥāt*)

(*a*) The gratuity of the bride's family shall not exceed 10 shillings only.

(*b*) The gratuity for the *zafīn*-dance in the wife's house is one shilling only, for the period of the *s͟harḥ* dance, and in the husband's house also one shilling for the period of the *s͟harḥ* dance.

(*c*) For the first occasion upon which the bride comes forth (to perform the dance), the gratuity (given) by her shall be 3 shillings only.

(*d*) At the first wedding only there is no objection to the gratuity of the ' tray ' which reverts to the family (giving) the wedding.

12. Evening festivities (*saharāt*)

In the case of both men and women the very latest of these shall be up to 1 o'clock.

13. The *mak͟hdarah* ceremony

The *mak͟hdarah* is permissible for men at the first wedding only, but it is not permissible for women at all.

14. The musician's (*muṭrib*) fee

This shall not exceed 50 shillings.

15. The minstrel's (*mus͟htariḥ*) fee

This shall not exceed 40 shillings in all, or (alternatively) 20 shillings along with permission for him to take (gratuities (*ṭarḥ*)) from the dancers (*zaffānah*), the choice being up to the person giving the wedding breakfast.

16. The bridal procession (*zafāf al-'arūs*)

Public procession through the streets is prohibited outright. The bride must be conducted to her husband's house before 1 o'clock (a.m.), the ' transference ' (*naqīlah*) to be inside the gate of the husband's family only.

17. Cutting of the lock (*naqḍ al-'uqdah*)
    What they call the 'cutting of the lock' is absolutely prohibited.

18. The 'transference' (*naqīlah*)
    General invitation to the *naqīlah* is prohibited. It shall be confined to inviting only the family without *sharḥ* dance or *zafīn* dance, but there is no objection to a women's party in the late afternoon at which only coffee is served.

19. The viewing (*shawf*)
    Viewing (of the bride) by intruding women is absolutely prohibited. The viewing shall be restricted to the women invited to the marriage ceremonies.

20. Customs of the headmen at marriages (*'awā'id al-maqādimah*)
    These shall continue as they are, in accordance with current custom.

21. Coming into effect of this resolution
    (*a*) These orders shall come into effect and be acted upon as from the beginning of Muḥarram 1379 (1959).
    (*b*) The civil police in al-Mukallā will have charge of putting these instructions into effect.
    (*c*) Any person disregarding them shall be brought for trial before the court of the Governor (*Nā'ib*) of the province (*liwā'*) at al-Mukallā.

22. Penalty (*'iqāb*)
    Any person disregarding this statute shall be punished by a monetary fine, varying according to the circumstances of the offenders, but the fine shall not be less than 100 shillings, nor exceed 1,000 shillings. Government shall subsequently apply the sum paid by way of fine to the benefit of the ward (*ḥāfah*) in which the offence took place. Anyone unable, or refusing to pay the fine, shall be imprisoned for a period not exceeding one fortnight.

By order of His Majesty.

The Minister to the Sulṭanate,

The Secretariat,

Al-Mukallā.

11 Shawwāl 1378, corresponding to 19 April 1959.

Commentary

1. The *madād*

The *madād* means the proceeding of the intending husband accompanied by his relations and friends, to the house of the wife (*zawjah*) to be, in order to announce the betrothal (*i'lān al-khuṭbah*), and pay over the betrothal money. The name *madād* applies both to the ceremony and the actual sum of money. It was described to me as 'coffee in the bride's house (*qahwah fī bait al-'arūsah*)'.

On another occasion it was stated that a boy's father calls upon the parents of the intended bride ; he may take his son with him, but usually does not. He is entertained to coffee and pays over the *madād*, thereby indicating that a sort of betrothal has been formalized. All this business is kept fairly secret from the girl herself. The *madād* used to be fixed at about 30 rupees (a statement which must refer to some ten or more years ago), but each person pays at rates varying according to his social class, his means, etc. The town council (*majlis baladī*), and that of Ghail Bā Wazīr was no doubt in the speaker's mind, might restrict the amount, and in older days still, a fixed sum might be imposed on the community by the decision of the headmen (*'uqqāl*) ; this they would even be able to dictate to such noble classes as the *sādah* themselves.

The women also have a kind of *madād* ceremony when the bride's mother is visited by womenfolk bringing presents, to say to her, '*Mabrūk* !' i.e. congratulations on the betrothal.

2. The *jihāz*

The *jihāz* was explained as the *daf'* or *dafī'ah*,[1] i.e. the bride-price. It is provided by the bridegroom's side, and delivered to the bride's father. He retains it to apply it to the expenses of the wedding, but presumably, as Doreen Ingrams [2] suggests, he does quite well financially out of the bride-price. In the Bādiyah, the Bedouin areas, the *dafī'ah* is thousands of *riyāls*, paid of course to the father of the bride or to her family. The Bedouin do not pay any of the *mahr* or dowry at all, but it remains a debt, unless of course the girl should be divorced, when it must be paid over to her. The *mahr* is for the girl herself, however, in contrast to the *dafī'ah*, which goes to her family.

The *ṣubḥah* is the gift made to the bride after intercourse is presumed to have taken place for the first time. Ansaldi [3] considers it is made in compensation for the loss of virginity and this has frequently been confirmed to me. In the present context nevertheless where the woman has already been married, it could hardly apply in this sense. In Ḥaḍramawt nowadays this gift is a large trunk, with clothes, perfumes, a watch even, and all manner of things.

The gift to the intended bride is made by the fiancé through his mother to her mother, and will include an expensive frock, soap, perfume, etc., no doubt very like the gift described by Doreen Ingrams.[4]

At the time of the *nuqlah* or transfer of the bride to her husband's house, she brings with her a bed (*qa'ādah*) and bedding, along with other furnishings (*athāth al-zīnah*) with which the *majlis* or room is to be decorated at the husband's family's house. The *midkāh* (pl. *madākī*) is a cushion.

[1] cf. Landberg, *Ḥaḍramoût*, 476. In Yāfi'ī country in 1954 a typical case would be a *daf'* payment of 100 riyāls, half of which would be silver for the bride, half to go to her father. The groom would have to purchase what was necessary for the marriage in the way of clothes, wedding gear (? *adāt al-zīnah*), and entertainment (*iṭ'ām*) of the guests. Her father would have to send cosmetics (? *dihān*), turmeric (*hurud*), and a veil (*ḥijāb*). I am not quite certain what is exactly covered by these terms, for local custom differs greatly from place to place.

[2] *Survey*, 44. [3] C. Ansaldi, *Il Yemen*, Roma, 1933, 210–14. [4] *Survey*, 44.

3. Clothes

In both Tarīm and Shibām I learned that the sumptuary laws had attempted to limit expenditure on women's frocks, but these regulations had always become a dead letter. The *kurtah* (pl. *kurat*) is a Persian word (via India) for a skirt ; the *nuqbah* (pl. *nuqab*) is a kind of head-scarf, and an example we purchased is of gauzy material with embroidery in gold and coloured threads, decorated with spangles (*ra'shah*). I was told that a bride wears, apart from jewellery, a *kurtah*, *nuqbah*, and a *gōgarah*, i.e. a petticoat worn under the skirt, at her wedding.[1]

4. The *walīmah* or wedding breakfast

This is also called *walīmat al-zawāj* or *walīmat al-'urs*, or it is known as *al-ḍīfah*. There are two meals given, the first in the bride's house on the *lailat al-'aqd*, the evening meal (*'ashā'*). This is returned by the groom's family with a large *wajbah* or lunch for all the bride's family and friends, as well as his family and friends after the *dukhūl* following on the *'aqd*. These invitations (*'azūmāt*) are then repeated between the groom's and the bride's families, but with a smaller number of guests (*ma'zūmīn*) than before.

5. The *basṭ* or breakfast

The *basṭ* is something like the *walīmah*, only with a smaller number of guests. It is the breakfast given by the family of the bridegroom on the *lailat al-dukhlah*. The girl comes to the groom's house, al-Bīḍ thought between 4 and 5 a.m., but Midaiḥij said, round about 1.30 a.m., accompanied by her relatives, and the bridegroom's house provides them with the *basṭ*, which would be *harīs* (savoury dough) [2] made with meat, though nowadays it is more likely to be meat and rice.

On the *lailat al-dukhlah* the bridegroom, according to al-Bīḍ, leaves the bride's house for that of his parents between 12 midnight and 2 a.m., the girl following him between 4 and 5 a.m. At this early hour the women accompanying her mostly go unveiled, and take *basṭ* in the groom's house.

6. The *fawjah*

This term is difficult to translate. There is, however, a sentence in the *Lisān al-'Arab*

من قولك مرّ بنا فائج وليمة فلان — أى فوج ممّن كان في طعامه.

A *fawj* also means, *al-jamā'ah min al-nās*. These phrases suggest a derivation for the word *fawjah*.

Midaiḥij thinks the word *fawjah* is not specially linked to marriage celebrations, but applies to visits on several types of festive occasion, and the gifts brought at such times, as for example a gift of eggs to a woman when she is visited after bearing a child.

[1] My wife insists that women wear a little Malayan or Indian type *ṣudairīyah* or jacket as well but says this only applies to the coast not to the Wādī Ḥaḍramawt. The *ṣudairīyah* was not, however, mentioned by my informants, possibly through oversight.

[2] Serjeant, *Prose and poetry*, Ar. text, p. 33.

Visiting the bride's mother (*umm al-'arūs*), guests bring gifts in accordance with their means, even if only a few bananas. At al-Shiḥr a congratulatory visit takes place before the wedding, but it can also be made during the marriage, especially on the *lailat al-ḥinnā'*, the ' night of the henna '.

7. The salutation-gift

The term *muḥāyāh* is derived from the verb *ḥāyā-(hā)* ' to kiss someone ', and Landberg [1] states that it means ' saluer quelqu'un, lui dire *ḥayyā bak* '. The latter is one of the commonest greetings in Ḥaḍramawt. In this case, however, it means to kiss with respect, whereas *shamm*, properly, and indeed actually, ' to sniff ', is used of kissing with affection or passion. One says, *ḥāyait-hā* ' I kissed her '. When you see the bride's mother (*al-khālah*), you go and kiss her on the forehead, dropping a gift of money in her lap. It is at the time of the *masḥah* (*infra*) that you first see the bride's mother, whom of course in Muslim society you could not properly have seen unveiled before, but of course marrying her daughter brings her within the prohibited degrees and you can therefore see her unveiled.

8. The door-fee

Al-bāb, literally ' the door ', is applied to the tip that you give to the tire-woman (*al-kawbarah*) at the door of the bride's room on the *lailat al-dukhlah* to let you enter, but this is probably no longer a general custom at al-Ghail and has perhaps not been so for the past fifteen years.

In Ghail Bā Wazīr you go to a room upstairs and the girl is brought in by the female minstrels (*mushtariḥāt*), and when she comes in you stand up, put your hand on her forehead, and kiss your hand. The women conduct her to the bed, and all depart except the *kawbarah*. The *kawbarah* will start to take off her *nuqbah*, and the *ḥulī* or ornaments of silver, but if you give the woman a *rubbīyah* before she takes them off you can do this yourself. Otherwise she will divest the girl of all her finery, leaving her in her skirt (*kurtah*) only.[2] The groom may now consummate the marriage—in the house of the girl's parents, but Midaiḥij said he thought that this step was far from general, and that only sometimes does consummation take place at this stage. Al-Bīḍ said that it applied to the classes not *'askar*, i.e. Yāfi'īs who are tribesmen of the military class.

9. The *masḥah*

I presume that this part of the ceremony as performed at Ghail Bā Wazīr takes the form of placing one's hand on the girl's head and kissing it, as described in the immediately preceding section.

Midaiḥij, however, whose experience of local custom is derived from al-Shiḥr and al-Mukallā, says that on the *lailat al-dukhlah* between 9 and 10 p.m., the groom proceeds to the bride's house accompanied by drums, etc., and

[1] *Gloss. daṯ.*, 541.

[2] With a *ṣudairīyah* also ?

after a time departs upstairs along with one of the bride's male relatives, carrying his rosary (*ṣubḥah*) in his hand. The said relative takes the bridegroom's hand holding the rosary, and moves the hand clasping the rosary over and around the head of the bride. It is about this time that he meets her mother.

After this the bridegroom returns to the sail (*shirā'*) which has been stretched over the street for the marriage festivities; it is a sort of reception room in front of the bride's house, and the groom's house has a sail set up in front of it in the same way.[1] The groom may linger a quarter of an hour sitting under the sail, then he returns home. Later he will come back to the bride's house for the *dukhūl* ceremony.

10. The *mushtariḥah*

The *mushtariḥah* is the woman minstrel, singing to the accompaniment of her drum. In al-Ghail she is described as the female drummer (*ṣāḥibat al-ṭabl*), but she is also called the *zaffānah*, because she *tuzaffin al-'arūs*, lit. 'makes the bride dance'. The *zafīn* seems to be applied to the *sharḥ* [2] or dance (*raqṣ*) of the women in the afternoon preceding, and that following, the *lailat al-dukhlah*. The bride usually dances first, along with her nearest relation. In al-Mukallā, at one time, the bride used to be conducted from her house to that of her new husband dancing, but nowadays she dances only from the door to the top of the house (where the women's quarters are).

In Ghail Bā Wazīr the *mushtariḥah* gets a special fee (*ujrah khāṣṣah*). When she arrives you bring in biscuits, sweets (*ḥalāwā*), and tea for her—this is called a *taqdūm* (pl. *taqādīm*). Again, when she leaves, she may be given a present of, for example, a tin of *ḥalwā* or of honey (*'asal*). In Ghail Bā Wazīr, the *mushtariḥāt* are slaves (*'abīd*) and *ḥujūr*; of the latter there are one or two families living at al-Ghail. They use the *ḥajīr* and *mirwās* drums.

11. The gratuities

The *ṭarḥah* (pl. *ṭurūḥāt*) is a gift to the female minstrels (*mushtariḥāt*) of five shillings, or the sums specified here. The *ṭarḥah*, according to Landberg [3] is 'ce qui contient la main', and 'arrhes, ce qu'on donne aux nouveaux mariés'. The second sub-clause refers to gratuities given by the dancers to the female minstrels, as explained at greater length in the commentary to clause 15.[4] The third sub-clause refers to the first dance by the bride either after or before *al-dukhūl*, it being immaterial whether she be a virgin bride or one who has already been married. The fourth clause was explained by al-Bīḍ to refer to

[1] I recollect something of this kind at a reception given us by Ḥaḍramīs in Mombasa, the street also being decorated with streamers or coloured cloth running from one side of the street to the other.

[2] The *sharḥ* includes the *sharḥ* of the men and that of the women.

[3] *Gloss. daṯ.*, 2200.

[4] See p. 490, and my 'The Ma'n "gypsies" of the West Aden Protectorate', *Anthropos*, LVI, 5–6, 1961, 740.

the *ṭarḥ al-ma'sharah*, the 'gratuity of the tray'. The *ma'sharah* is a sort of metal tray or bowl, but the word may also be applied to the *tifāl* which is of palm-frond (*khūṣ*), sometimes used for *al-ṭarḥ*. It seems this ceremony is only performed when a man or a woman is marrying for the first time. Al-Bīḍ stated that when a man of a poor family wishes to marry, but cannot afford to do so, the family resort to the following device. They shave his head and dance, and while the application of henna is going on so does the shaving (*ḥalāqah*) of the head. The *ma'sharah* is set in the middle of the room and people throw into it *riyāls* or other coins. He stated also that this practice is rare nowadays, but I wonder if this applies more particularly to his experience at Ghail Bā Wazīr. I was present at the betrothal of the Wāḥidī Sulṭān in 1947 when coins were flung by the company into a tray in the house of the girl's father.

12. Evening festivities

Dancing and singing are intended here.

13. The *makhdarah*

Basically the *makhdarah* is a hut or tent erected on the occasion of a marriage[1]; or, as has been seen, in the coastal parts of Ḥaḍramawt, a sail stretched over the street outside the house where the marriage ceremonies are taking place. The work of putting it up would be executed by the Quarter or Ward of the town or village which plays a part in weddings as I have already described.[2] Midaiḥij described the *makhdarah* as a high platform (*minaṣṣah 'āliyah*) near the groom's house, if not actually in it, decorated in various colours, and provided, nowadays, with an amplifier. Here the groom sits, and after music and festivities (*lahū wa-ṭarab*) the presents are made, all this usually taking place at night. Carpets are laid down before the *makhdarah* and/or chairs for the guests ranged before it also. In front of the bridegroom is placed a bowl (*ṣaḥn*), usually of copper, but nowadays often of aluminium, into which the presents of money to the bridegroom are tossed, the coins ringing (*taḥinn*) against its sides, this being why a metal bowl is preferred.

The *makhdarah* of the women is in the bride's house, and it is this that is prohibited by the Ordinance. It usually takes place before that of the men and lasts a longer time. It is, however, quite clear that, as 'Abdullāh Muḥammad al-Maqṭarī has confirmed to me, the term *makhdarah* has come to be applied to the money gift made on this occasion, as it is in Aden. It would also seem to apply to the ceremony itself.

In Aden the guest entering the door of the *makhdarah* would see the bridegroom opposite him, sitting on the right of the platform, his male relations near by him.

[1] See p. 478, n. 1, *supra*. E. V. Stace, op. cit., 186, mentions a Bedouin word *sībāṭ* as synonymous with *makhdarah*, but I have not yet had this confirmed.

[2] Serjeant, *Prose and poetry*, p. 27.

14. The musician (*muṭrib*)

At the *makhdarah* which also has the nature of a musical evening, and at weddings generally, people sit and listen to the musician who is a guitar-player (*muqambis*). The *muṭrib* is displacing the *mushtariḥ* or minstrel in more sophisticated Ḥaḍramī circles. It might be added here that, according to the Aden and Ḥaḍramī press, very considerable changes have been introduced into the music of southern Arabia, this having taken place more particularly during the last eight years or so.

15. The fee of the minstrel (*mushtariḥ*)

The term *mushtariḥ* embraces both the minstrel and the female minstrel, the one performing at the men's side of the marriage, and the other at the women's side. In the olden days, and even now, it used to be slaves who acted as *mushtariḥs* with drums and the flute (*madrūf*); the *ḥajīr* and *mirwās* drums being beaten by the *mushtariḥ* or *zaffān* as he is also called.

Among the women too, in the olden days, the *zaffānah* or *mushtariḥah* used to have money tossed in front of her by the women as each one danced, say 5 shillings a time, i.e. a Maria Theresa dollar, and the *mushtariḥah* might make up to 2,000 shillings a night. Now this has ceased, and whatever else of the provisions of this Ordinance may not, in actual practice, be observed, the limitation on her fee, as remarked, has become effective. The party giving the wedding (*ṣāḥib al-'urs*) may take this money nowadays for himself; each money gift is known as *ṭarḥ*.

Midaiḥij explained the function of the female minstrel as, *Al-mushtariḥah tuzaffin al-'arūs—tarquṣ ma'-hā fi-'l-waqt alladhī taḥḍur fīh al-'arūs li-'l-sharḥ* 'the female minstrel makes the bride dance, dancing with her when the bride comes in to dance'.

16. The bridal procession

The *zaffah* is the conducting of the bride to her husband's house by night, to the accompaniment of the singing of the *mushtariḥah*, the beating of the drums and *ḥajīr* drum, and ululations (*zaghārīd*); she is, of course, accompanied by the women from her father's house, her mother, sisters, and female relatives. The word *naqlīyah* was stated by Midaiḥij to be a misprint for *al-naqīlah* (*infra*), or *al-nuqlah*, i.e. the *intiqāl* or transfer of the bride from her father's house (or in the case of an orphan from the house of one of her relatives (*aqārib*)), to that of her husband. In the interior of Ḥaḍramawt she will usually still be conveyed on the back of an animal, but in al-Mukallā, by car. The *zaffah* takes place on the *lailat al-dukhūl*; this must, I suppose, be the case where the marriage is not consummated in the bride's house.

17. *Naqḍ al-'uqdah*

This is the loosening of the lock of hair or plait, the *'uqdah* being a lock of hair on a girl's forehead, or perhaps a fringe which was loosened or cut by the tire-woman (*kawbarah*) after the marriage, once she is no longer virgin. This custom is said to be rather rare nowadays.

18. The ' transference ' (*naqīlah*)

Apart from its application in article 18 the *naqīlah* also means the visit paid by the new bride, eight days after the wedding, to her father's house. Her husband will accompany her on this visit to her former home ; in both cases, however, the *naqīlah* is an expensive business. In al-Mukallā it is also called *naqḍ al-thamān* ; other names are *naql thamān*, and *al-nuqlah*. Generally there is a sail (*shirā'*) in the street near the house for the women's *sharḥ* dance.

19. The viewing (*shawf*)

In Ḥaḍramawt the young unmarried girls see little of married women and, being shy, avoid them also. *Al-shawf*, lit. ' the seeing ', i.e. the viewing of the bride, takes place at the marriage, on the *lailat al-zawāj*, i.e. the *lailat al-dukhlah*, but especially at the *nahār al-ṣubḥah*, lit. ' morning of the " trousseau " '. The women come to see what the girl looks like now that she is emerging into the society of married women, whether she is pretty, nice, and the like.

20. The customs of the headmen

These have already been described [1] by me in various places. The headmen are the elders of the quarter or ward of the town and very jealous of traditional rights and privileges. It is perhaps an indication of the power of the quarter organizations that despite press attacks on the quarters (*al-ḥuwaif*) of the Ḥaḍramī towns, it is here stipulated that their customs should remain unchanged. In brief either the young man's father, or the bride's father, or both, go, taking a little present to the headman, known as *qahwat al-'urs* ' the wedding coffee ', and the headman arranges for a sail to be put up as an awning to keep off the heat of the sun, and for all the slaughtering, cooking, etc. necessary to the wedding celebrations.

As an illustration of the influence of the quarter organization, it appears that in al-Ghail there is a tendency for families, nowadays, in different quarters, not to intermarry because of the unseemly disputes that may arise at times of marriage. For example, the bridegroom cannot cross into another quarter accompanied by the drums and singing with which he passes through his own quarter. When he comes to the boundary between the two quarters the festivities must stop, and he enters the other quarter silently. For him to try to enter another quarter with the ceremonial of his own quarter, is an infringement of the sovereignty and privilege of the other quarter which cannot be tolerated even if upholding of this privilege should lead to bloodshed.

Ḥaḍramawt of the interior : terms relating to marriage

The late Saiyid Muḥammad b. Hāshim generously placed at my disposal

[1] loc. cit., pp. 27, 47 ; ' The quarters of Tarīm ', *Le Muséon*, LXIII, 3–4, 1950, 277–84, and in my forthcoming study on fisher customs.

some years ago certain lists of colloquial Arabic words classified by subjects, among which were the terms listed *infra*, but I had no opportunity of discussing them with him. Midaiḥij, however, has offered explanations to the best of his ability, though, since he comes from the coast, and Saiyid b. Hāshim came from Tarīm, he cannot be absolutely certain as to their precise application. Nevertheless his comments have both value and validity.

Taḥḍīr (تحضير).[1] Explained as *ḍarb al-ṭabl.* Young boys beat the drum during the days of the marriage to summon all to come (*yuḥaḍḍir*) and enjoy the marriage festivities. The young girls do this among the women in their own part of the house.

Takhḍīr (تخضير).[1] The days of the wedding during which the girl, still in her father's house, prepares for the bridegroom with *ḥinnā'* and her hair is done into plaits (*'uqad*).

Takhāwīd (S, *takhwīd*) (تخاويد). The removal of a woman's *nuqbah* or head-scarf, be it at the marriage or on any other occasion. To say of a woman, *takhawwadat,* means she has nothing on her head. Midaiḥij thought the word was used in the interior of Ḥaḍramawt, and amongst Bedouins. I surmise that it is part of the procedure on the *lailat al-dukhūl.*

Ḥarāwah (حراوه). The party which accompanies the groom to the girl's house, and hence a general term for a marriage celebration. These men who accompany the groom are called *ḥarwīyīn* (حَرْوِيين), i.e. *ma'āzīm,* invited persons.

Khurush (خرش). Probably *qanāqin* which Midaiḥij described as a sort of ear-ring, and Landberg[2] as *grelot.* I am virtually certain that I have seen a series of small bells of silver attached to the outer rim of the ear, worn by little girls, but probably only from tribal areas.

Khaṭrah (خَطْره). At Tarīm this is a big entertainment (*ḍiyāfah*) a month after the marriage to which the wife's parents invite all the husband's relatives. A *shaḥḥādhah* is present who calls down blessings and prayers on those present.

Khaiba'ān (خيبعان). A song sung in the women's part of the ceremony, an example of which I have already published and described.[3]

Dihīnah (دهينه). A good meal, from *dihn* ' grease, fat, oil ', to be compared with *iddasam* which is also employed in Ḥaḍramawt[4] in a rather similar sense. It is possibly a term for one of the feasts given during the wedding.

Shawfah (شوفه). Probably the same as the coastal *shawf, supra.*

Ṣubḥah (صبحه). Present after the loss of maidenhead, as above.

Ḍīfah (ضيفه). Marriage feast, as above.

[1] It is not clear which of these words was meant by Saiyid Muḥammad b. Hāshim, but Midaiḥij thought either possible.

[2] *Ḥaḍramoût,* 697. [3] Serjeant, *Prose and poetry,* p. 168. [4] op. cit., p. 50, n. 99.

Ghussah (غسّة). A Badawī word, the leaves of the *sidr* tree. A circle is formed in the middle of which the groom is seated and his hair washed with the *ghussah*. Among the Bedu it is a woman who performs this office, since with them the sexes are not segregated to the same extent as in the towns, but women mix relatively freely with men as a rule. This *ghussah* (cf. *ghusl*) [1] is or was contained in a bowl (*qadaḥ* or *ṭust*) into which the guests used to throw Maria Theresa dollars. The *sidr* leaves are saponiferous. Nowadays, at any rate in the towns, *ghussah* is not employed, but a man has his head shaved.

Ẓallah (ظلّة). Lit. 'shade'. The invited guests rest in the shade of a large tree outside the village where the marriage is to take place. They fire off their rifles as a greeting, and to inform the villagers of their arrival. The villagers issue forth from their village to welcome the *ma'āzīm*, firing their rifles in reply, and escort them back into it.[2]

Qarīḍ al-sha'r (قريض الشعر). Synonyms *manaṣṣat al-sha'r* (منصّة الشعر), *quṣṣah* (this latter a Bedouin term), a fringe of the girl's hair. Some at least of this they cut off (*qaṣṣin quṣṣat-hā*). It has never been cut up to the time of the girl's marriage, but on the marriage day it is cut off by the *kawbarah* or tire-woman, as on the coast.[3]

Ku'dah (كعده). A coffee *dallah* or kettle. I do not know why so ordinary an object should be included in B. Hāshim's list, unless the term has been given some specific application in Ḥaḍramawt.

Kilān (كلان). The bridegroom,[4] مُعَرّس.

Mūjibah (موجبة). *Walīmah*, wedding feast.

Some general notes on marriage

Among the leisured upper classes of Tarīm, a girl, when she arrives at the age of maturity (*dakhalat fi-'l-sinn*), and is a young virgin (*'adhrā'*), goes into a sort of retreat; she is then described as *maḥjūbah*. For several years she will not go out of the house, and seems to remain on the top floor for the most part, avoiding the company of married women even. This apparently holds true of the coast also. On the other hand the lower classes in Tarīm are not in purdah, though I am unable to say where the dividing line comes, but it must be remembered that purdah is a sign of rank, and that it may

[1] cf. *Gloss. daṯ.*, *ghasl*, p. 2369, meaning *'ilb* and *sidr*.

[2] In one set of fragments of medieval tribal law placed at my disposal by the late Ettore Rossi it seems that small boys are allowed to stone those arriving with the husband, i.e. groom, at the *awwal fitnah* but after they have been welcomed (to the village) they may no longer be stoned. This appears like a relic of marriage by capture, and indeed from Upper 'Awlaqī country I recall the saying *khadhaw-nā bi-'l-bārūt yā bint al-masājid* 'they took me by gunpowder, you daughter of the mosques', the phrase implying that the girl was carried off and married. In the case here, however, I think there is only the normal greeting between two parties when they meet.

[3] cf. *supra*, pp. 490–1.

[4] cf. *Gloss. daṯ.*, 2582.

not be irksome to the majority of Arab women in the way that Westerners often imagine.[1]

In Tarīm I was told that a *saiyid* might see the daughter of a *miskīn* in the street and fall in love with her. He would ask whose daughter she is, inquiring about her and her temperament. If he wants to marry her he would send a *khaṭīb* to ask for her hand, but also he will send a *khaddāmah* or some female known to him, to ask about the girl. The difference in mental outlook between the Ḥaḍramī woman of the upper classes and the *miskīns*, though there do exist differences, would appear to be in no way comparable with conditions in Europe. The *miskīn* would be delighted should a *saiyid* desire to marry his daughter, and it does sometimes happen. The girl will never of course attain the social standing of a girl in whose veins the blood of the Prophet runs, but she will have risen in social standing, and her children will have the honourable strain of the Prophet's blood. *Kafā'ah*, of course, in the sense that a woman cannot marry beneath her, is strictly observed in Ḥaḍramawt.

There are appropriate and inappropriate times of the year for marriages to take place ; for example one does not marry between the two feasts (*bain al-ʻĪdain*) as it would be bad luck (*shaqābah*), hence Shaʻbān, immediately preceding Ramaḍān, is a good month in which to marry. Almanacs sometimes indicate suitable seasons for marriage.

Midaiḥij told me that among the Bedouin a cousin can put a stop to a marriage right up to the last moment, because of his prior right to the girl's hand, but as he remarked specially on this point I infer this is not at any rate a right that can be exercised in the towns. He added that the Bedouin have what is called *lailat al-tafannun*, an evening when the girl can wish of the groom whatever she likes, be it for herself or for her family, and he is bound to give it her.

In Tarīm a boy is told by his father, 'I am going to marry you'. The boy has no choice in the matter, nor can he say no. The father has probably already a girl in mind for his son, and in the Āl Kāf family he goes himself to ask for her hand, it being the rule among the Āl Kāfs that the first to ask for the girl's hand gets it. According to my informant (in 1947) he will say, *Baghait bint-ak* 'I want your daughter'. This statement does, however, seem a little stark to me. Among the Āl Kāfs a girl will get a *jihāz* of 500 rupees, not really a very large sum for those days (1947) and she receives a wedding present of clothes, etc.

On my first visit to the Wādī Ḥaḍramawt the expression *qud-hā fi-'l-tifāl* 'she is on the palm-leaf mat now' was quoted to me, meaning that the matter is already established fact. At marriage festivals at one time a girl, whether a *saiyidah* (*sharīfah*) or otherwise, used to be put to sit on a mat of this kind,

[1] There has, however, been some agitation in Aden for abandonment of purdah, probably mainly stirred up by certain journalists and female secondary school teachers. A booklet, *Thawrat al-mar'ah 'ala 'l-ḥijāb fī janūb al-Jazīrat al-ʻArabīyah*, ed. Muḥammad Shafīq, Aden, n.d., but *circa* 1960–1 perhaps, has appeared—vapid schoolgirl essays having no contact with reality.

probably at the henna-ing, or later. Even in 1947 this custom was said to be obsolete, except perhaps in some of the villages. The import of the phrase is that the relations on either side can no longer discuss or fight over her and refuse marriage at so late a stage.

It is shameful that a man should treat his virgin bride roughly on the first night of marriage. So his mother or eldest sister will instruct him beforehand about the procedure in the wedding. They do not consider it decent to talk openly about the defloration of the bride, but they will give him indications of what they mean. This statement was made to me for Ḥaḍramawt of the coast, but I think it would also apply to the interior. In Aden a much more primitive custom still obtains, though not of course among educated young men who would not tolerate it. There even to this day the tire-woman, *mukaddiyah*, the Ḥaḍramī *kawbarah*, sits below the marital bed which is of a type imported from India and called *nāmūsīyah*, standing quite high above the ground, while the marriage is actually in the process of consummation—in the case of a virgin bride—and gives instruction to the bride. When the action is completed the *mukaddiyah* takes the *manshafah* and displays it to the near relatives assembled in the bridegroom's house. She then ululates (*tughaṭrif*), and the neighbours know the groom has had his way of the bride. Next morning they come to congratulate him on his prowess.

Learning this recently I was astonished, never having heard of the custom in South Arabia before, though it is known in Cairo, in Morocco,[1] and other places, but it does seem to support an impression formed from reading and conversation that Aden town tends to be more conservative of ancient pagan customs and practices of a type repugnant to orthodox Islam, than Ḥaḍramawt. Among the educated Adenese, however, i.e. Adenese with a Westernized form of education, the *mukaddiyah* gives the bride instruction on sexual matters before the groom comes to her.

I have already had occasion to refer to the interesting book written by al-Baiḥānī, a leading Islamic divine in Aden, and entitled *Ustādh al-mar'ah*, or the ' Woman's preceptor ',[2] in which he attempts to lay down rules of conduct for the Muslim woman, adapted to present-day circumstances but in accordance with traditional Islamic principles. As exemplary of the *via media* he treads, while condemning out of hand walking in the streets with one's betrothed,[3] he goes on to state that it is a bad custom with the Adenese that a man cannot see his betrothed (*makhṭūbah*), knowing nothing of her, except on the night when she is conducted to him, relying for his knowledge of her on his mother or the *māshiṭah* (tire-woman), called with them the *mukaddiyah*, who is only concerned for her *masḥah* and what she gets from the spouses and their families.

The *mukaddiyah* acts as an intermediary, and knows all the wealthy families. The *masḥah* is a fee which the bridegroom has to pay her before he can meet his

[1] E. Westermarck, *Marriage ceremonies in Morocco*, London, 1914, 228. In general the ceremony described bears a very close resemblance to those of South Arabia.

[2] *supra*, p. 473, n. 3.

[3] *Ustādh al-mar'ah*, p. 149.

bride, say 20 to 30 shillings (1961). On this occasion his friends also throw, say, 5 shillings each, into a small dish (*ṣaḥfah ṣaghīrah*) which, too, is the perquisite of the *mukaddiyah.* The bridegroom can then stroke the bride's head (*yimsaḥ 'alai-hā*) and bolder spirits may lift the *maqramah* or head-veil which covers her, to look at her face. As we have seen, the same custom obtains in Ḥaḍramawt.

In Aden the corresponding name for the female minstrel, the *mushtariḥah* of Ḥaḍramawt, seems to be the *'alaqah,* and she not only sings and beats the drum at weddings and other festivities of women, but appears to be a sort of witch doctress in that she functions also at the *zār* ceremony which is illegal in Aden, but kept up in secret as I am told.[1]

Al-Baiḥānī also reproves what goes on at the man's side of the wedding festivities [2] in the way of play, excitement (*ṭarab*), dancing, wine, profligacy, and libertinage (*khalā'ah wa-mujūn*). It seems that at weddings there is dancing by the *makhānīth* (s. *makhnūth*), young men who walk with a womanish gait—this it appears is what al-Baiḥānī castigates so roundly, as also extravagance (*isrāf*) at the wedding breakfasts (*walā'im*) and the processions (*zafāf*) of both bride and bridegroom. As in Ḥaḍramawt the Adenese make gifts of money (*naqṭ* (class. *naqd* ?)) [3] at the *makhdarah* of the groom, and its equivalent, the *muk'us* of the bride. The type of song sung at the men's ceremony is,

يا عَلَى آمْحِنَّاء   يا على آمحنّـاء[4]
حَنُّوا لِآبْنَنَا   وَآبن سِيدنَا
سَعْد يـا مسعود   بَخِّرُوا بِآلعُود (*bis*)

Come to the henna-ing, come to the henna-ing.
Henna our son, and the son of our lord.
Sa'd, O Mas'ūd,[5] cense with aloes.

The polygamous family in Ḥaḍramawt

In Tarīm (1947) I made a few jottings on the subject of wives in a polygamous family. Where a *saiyid* marries more than one wife, to avoid trouble each wife has a separate house. Even in the *miskīn* class if a man marries a second wife, he will try to provide a separate house for each of them. He might not buy a house if unable to afford it but he would rent a house. I know of a case in another town where two wives were kept in the same house but public opinion was against it. A certain wealthy *saiyid* born in more spacious

[1] There is a brief reference to the activities of the *'alaqah* in Muḥ. 'Alī Luqmān, '*Adan taṭlub al-ḥukm al-dhātī*, Aden, n.d., 40.

[2] *Ustādh al-mar'ah*, p. 55.

[3] One says, *yanqaṭū luh* ' they make money presents to him '.

[4] The first and third lines are on the pattern *fā'ilātun mustaf'ilun*, but the second line does not fit into the pattern. If the *am* of the article is a relic of the *am* used in the Aden Protectorate in some districts, and not merely because it is easier to say, it is odd that it should have survived in these verses.

[5] A slave name.

days whom I used to know slightly, had had no fewer than seven wives in all, but this must be unusual ; these were :

(1) a *sharīfah*, by whom he had several offspring ;
(2) a *shaikhah*, a *qarawīyah* ;
(3) a *shaikhah* of the Bā Faḍl family ;
(4) a *saiyidah* (*sharīfah*) ;
(5) a *qarawīyah* of a family of *mashāyikh* ;
(6) a *sharīfah* ;
(7) a Chinese woman.

The *saiyid* in question had undoubtedly spent periods of time in the Far East, especially in Singapore. I withhold his name because it is displeasing to the *saiyids* to have information about their womenfolk made public, however innocuous it may be. Normally in a family the first wife to be married has the highest status, but were a man, i.e. a *saiyid*, to marry a *shaikhah* first, then a *sharīfah*, the latter would rank higher, and moreover her son would take precedence over the *shaikhah*'s son, even if the latter were older, and the *sharīfah*'s son it would be who would act in his father's place. On the other hand both sons would inherit equally from their father.

Cosmetics

It is interesting to examine al-Baiḥānī's attitude to cosmetics, traditional and modern,[1] which play an important role in the preparation of the bride. Islam, he states, commends proper *tajammul* and *tazaiyun*, i.e. ways of a woman in beautifying herself, but forbids what is excessive or contrary to custom, because of its resemblance to that of infidel women—he means probably European women in the particular context. There are various well-known Traditions current in South Arabia on this point—such as the Tradition that he who dresses like the infidels will be resurrected with them which Raḥaiyam used frequently to repeat to me in Tarīm. Tattooing, al-Baiḥānī says, is *ḥarām* and should be removed if this can be done without causing undue suffering. This is curious because my impression is that it is confined to Bedu, that is, to tribal women, and in Ḥaḍramawt it is laughed at by townswomen. Perhaps al-Baiḥānī is reiterating an anti-tribal prejudice. Also prohibited is painting and plucking of the eyebrows (*tanqīsh al-ḥājib wa-tarqīqu-hā*), and removing of the hair of the face with the thread (*khait*) to make it wider and clearer.[2]

A woman may use henna (*khiḍāb*) on her face, hands, and legs, and designs drawn with henna (*al-takhṭīṭ bi-'l-ḥinnā'*), *kurkum* ' curcuma ', *'uṣfur* ' saffron ', *wars* (the well-known yellow cosmetic of the Yemen), and powder for cheeks and lips. If grey-haired she may apply yellow and red (*ṣufrah wa-ḥumrah*) to her hair, providing her husband does not disapprove. A husband is bound

[1] op. cit., p. 82.
[2] This is unclear and has not been explained to me.

to supply *sidr* leaves required for washing the hair, sesame (*simsim*) oil, coconut oil, and the unguents known to-day, with or without perfumes, kohl, henna, and perfumes.[1]

At weddings undue expense and competition in ostentation (*mufākharah*) between women in respect of clothes and jewellery are forbidden.

The ladies of Aden of course treat the learned *'ālim*'s precepts in much the same way as women have always treated the attempts of divines to impose restraints upon them contrary to their inclinations. Western dress and beauty preparations are used by Aden women if they wish, to say nothing of European, Indian, and Malayan costume.

[1] op. cit., p. 84.

Addenda

P.492 *Takhāwīd* also means a gift of money to a bride – presumably – when the *nuqbah* is removed.

P.492. *Khayba'ān* is also a term used in the Hijaz.

P.495 The high standing bed (*qa'ādah*), mounted with the aid of steps, is also native to the Yemeni Tihāmah.

High marriage costs were deplored in the Aden press in 1962–63. These are itemized in the *Aden Chronicle* (28/vi/62). *Al-Ayyām* (2/vi/62) proposes limiting *daf'* to 3,000 shillings. *Al-Kifāḥ* (18/viii/63) says this is not a problem for youth – anyway it is only possible for the wealthy, because of the high costs. It blames companies for paying foreigners highly but paying little to native employees. Attempts to limit marriage costs seem no new topic and, for instance, I recall that al-Sālimī notes an attempt by an early Ibāḍī Imām in Oman to restrict such costs. On marriage in the Yemen see C. Ansaldi, *Il Yemen*, Rome, 1933, 210 seq.; E. Rossi, *L'Arabo parlato a Ṣan'ā'*, Rome, 1939, 95 seq. and many recent writers.

XIV

Sex, Birth, Circumcision: Some Notes from South-West Arabia

The content of this brief study is but »gleanings«; it does not even take account of all written already on this extensive subject. An investigation of the wide diversity of custom in different districts is necessary. Topics on some of which I expect to publish separate papers, have been deliberately omitted such as *tawrīd* the provision of a woman for the guest, *irtibāṭ* compensation for adultery, the temporary lover, gypsy prostitutes, bastard (*farkh̲* or in Wāḥidī country, *laflūf* (pl. *lafālīf*), and venereal diseases which appeared in the Yemen for the second time in 906 H. (1500 A. D.).

Sex

Tribespeople are not very prone to discussing matters of sex, but in the Wādī Ḥaḍramawt one forms the impression that both sexes, and all classes, particularly the leisured and well to do, are intensely interested in it. Many South Arabians would opine, no doubt, that this interest is at least no greater than in the west; it is true too, that distractions in Ḥaḍramawt are mainly limited to conversation and sex, though hagiologies often speak of men who consistently performed the morning prayer with the ablution of the previous night, and there are injunctions to have as little to do with one's womenfolk as possible. The well-known erotic work R u j ū ' a l - S̲ h̲ a i k̲ h̲ is said to be in the hands of young men of the leisured classes of the Ḥaḍrami towns, and I have reported an erotic *»K̲h̲uṭbah«* from Tarīm.

Arabic medical literature is full of specifics for aphrodisiacs[1]; these are also sought by Ḥaḍramīs, and when in 1947, I first took these notes, the more sophisticated young men were already purchasing European preparations, an Italian product being shown me on one occasion with a quizzical enquiry as to what it was. In the leisured classes some, through over-indulgence, may find their sexual powers diminishing early. A young Saiyid in the western part of Ḥaḍramawt confided in me that, on marrying, he maintained intercourse three times a day for the first year, at night, early morning, and after mid-day. This had diminished to once per day some six years later when I met him, he had divorced his first wife and was now taking aphrodisiacs. Because of his standing as a Saiyid a Bedouin had come to him for advice on a young girl whom he had recently married but with whom he was mal-adjusted sexually (*ya'd̲h̲ī-hā*).

[1] An aphrodisiac is *muqwī*, and sexual power is *quwwah*.

In certain leisured circles in Tarīm, especially those in contact with the outside world of Indonesia or Malaya contraception was felt desirable but distasteful (1947), but since then European practice has undoubtedly become more widely known. A view was also expressed that *qaṭʿ al-nasl* was forbidden by moralists[2]. A Tarīmī said he believed women practiced contraception, and used abortifacients, but they tell men nothing of this and it is kept secret among them, though they might quite freely discuss it with other women. The high infant mortality is an effectual check on population growth in the lower classes, but not so in the upper classes where it is a matter of concern. A reduction of the high infant mortality would be dangerous to the narrow economy of Ḥaḍramawt, yet the public health measures of the protecting power tend to diminish it. However a contrary factor is the vast exodus of adult males has produced a scarcity of labour, so one often sees in the fields half a dozen women working alongside one old man.

So many men being abroad, it is said that Lesbianism (*mufāqaḥah*) is common, a female lover being called *ṣāḥibah*. The emigration of young males is not new problem to Ḥaḍramawt; it was said a Ḥaḍramī would go off to Indonesia, leaving his young bride in his father's house, without returning for many years, yet not divorcing her. These cases (30 years separation has been mentioned), are perhaps exceptional and repugnant to some Ḥaḍramīs themselves. In the *fiqh*-books there is a formula for automatic divorce of a wife when her husband goes missing abroad. S̲h̲aik̲h̲ Muḥ. b. Sālim al-Kidādī al-Baiḥānī[3] attacks Lesbianism (*musāḥaqah*) in Aden amongst girls and unmarried women, in many houses, as making marriageable girls unfit for marriage, and if they do marry, unfit for pregnancy and childbearing.

Homosexuality[4] is said to be common, but it must, I think, be specially incident among soldiers stationed in the many forts of the country where local women are generally kept strictly apart from the soldiery, but if this is so one should qualify these cases as rather heterosexual. Thesiger denies the existence of homosexuality among the Bedouin, also by nature of their occupation away from their wives for long periods, and I think he is right. I surmise too that it is not very common among the labouring classes.

[2] J. David-Weill. Le Djâmiʿ d'Ibn Wahb, (Le Caire, 1939), I, p. 133, quotes Traditions against contraception and drinks for inducing it.
The question of contraception seems to be avoided by al-Baiḥānī (infra).

[3] Ustād̲h̲ al-Marʾah, (Aden, 1950), p. 98. The author is a prominent *ʿālim* of Aden, said to be at rivalry with the other well known *ʿālim*, Bā Ḥamīs̲h̲. Muslim women in Aden are reported to have reacted to this book with such remarks as, "What has that old blind man go to do with telling us how to behave?" Al-Baiḥānī is blind, but a good scholar and an able man, not really at all ultra-conservative.

[4] The technical vocabulary is *muk̲h̲annit̲h̲*, with *mak̲h̲nūt̲h̲* catamite, and *lūṭī* is also used.
The vulgar vocabulary of Ḥaḍramawt has an expressive range of indecent sexual opprobrium of which I have recorded the following:
Ṣuḥbat-ak ṣubḥat al-kaʿāl, Your company is like that of the testes. i. e. it is of no use.
Faṣʿah lak, A penis to you. *Faṣʿah lummak,* A penis to your mother.
Labūk sabaʿ kanāfir, Seven *kumfarahs* to your father. (The *kumfarah* is the head of the penis where *the circumcision takes place.)*
Lummak al-kanāfir fī ḥubbi-hā, May your mother have *kumfarahs* in her sexual organ.
S̲h̲arjah fī kaʿab zār ummak, An itching in the urethra of your mother. The *zār*, properly a palm, is said also to be the *zambūr* or clitoris.

Pudor

All Arabs are most careful not to expose the privy parts to their fellows; this is just as true among the tribes-who do not cover as much as from the navel to the knee, as it is amongst the Ḥaḍramīs who do. If a man is accidentally exposing the parts below his *mi'waz* (kilt) one might say in Ḥaḍramawt, »*Ustur al-bunduq*, cover the gun,« or »*S̲h̲uf al-rajul s̲h̲ārif*, Look the man is exposed«[5].

A mass of regulations governs the modesty of a Muslim woman; they can be read in al-Baiḥānī's book of precepts. Nevertheless a Muslim woman of high degree, a *sharīfah* will not bother to veil before a slave, he being too menial for there to be any possibility of misconduct. In 1947—49 hardly any woman would so outrage her modesty as to allow my wife to examine her privy parts at her clinics in Tarīm or al-Mukallā, though possibly things are altered now. In the following passage taken from al-Baiḥānī's book[6] the worthy *s̲h̲aik̲h̲* is taking a broad-minded moderate view for a South Arabian *'ālim* of this question, yet it seems absurdly pompous to a European physician.

»If, my lady, you are a doctor or a nurse in a hospital it is permitted you to look at the places to be treated and what must be looked at in a sick person. If you yourself should be the sick person, do not let a doctor enter your presence unless you have your husband or one of the persons within the prohibited degrees (*al-maḥārim*) by you, and do not display any of your pure body to him except the places of the disease and those where it is necessary to place the medicament. There is no harm in your taking an injection or giving it, in any part of the body whatsoever, even with childbirth (*tawlīd*) if necessity requires. The doctor may look at your place where the child is delivered, if there is no trained woman doctor there.«

Conservative as the Arab Muslims of Aden are a change is taking place in regard to woman. Their veils nowadays are almost transparent — which they certainly were not in 1940, and a group of young women recently made the attempt to appear in public unveiled, though this demonstration was greeted by some hostility, and not approved of by al-Baiḥānī and Bā Ḥamīs̲h̲.

A Love-Charm

When enquiring about the term *al-tiwal*, a love-charm, cited by Ibn Wahb[7] I was told the Ḥaḍramī equivalent is *al-ṣarf*[8] which is something written out. A woman obtains a *ṣarf* and places it under the threshold, or in bed, or in water which the man she wishes to incline to her will drink. As this object can be got rid of if its exact location be known, the *ṣarf* may be put in a bottle and thrown into the sea, so that nobody knows exactly where it is. Many Ḥaḍramīs come back from East Africa (1954) and seem mad and bewitched until they return there. The African name for this spell »*Ūgāngah*«[9] is quite well known in Ḥaḍramawt. After their return to East Africa these men become quite normal again.

[5] Syn. of *s̲h̲ārif is maks̲h̲ūf*. Cf. C. de Landberg, Études . . . Daṯînah, (Leiden, 1905–13), II, p. 942, *itmak̲h̲k̲h̲aṭ*, mouche-toi le nez, used in this sense. *Bunduq*, syn. *qaḍīb*.

[6] Op. cit., p. 28.

[7] Op. cit., p. 111.

[8] Because thereby you „*tiṣrif al-maḥabbah*, Turn love."

[9] The Swahili word meaning "medicine charm."

Conception and Pregnancy[10]

The ideas current in Ḥaḍramawt explained in this paragraph may not be held elsewhere, and even these were mostly collected in Tarīm. It is popular belief that nine tenths of desire is with women, and only one tenth with men, but that women are only restrained by their modesty. Inside the female genitalia it is thought that there is at the top of the vagina, a single hair, known as *al-s̲h̲aʿrah al-yatīmah*, and this is in fact mentioned in the erotic *maqāmah* or rather mock *K̲h̲uṭbah* from Tarīm copied from al-Nafzāwī[11]. It is held that both men and women have *nuṭfah* or semen. In the case of a fat woman it is believed that her being fat prevents the semen from entering the uterus. When women do not become pregnant, intercourse is carried on with the woman's hips on a cushion, so as to allow, they believe, the semen to flow downwards, the women then being as the Ḥaḍramīs say, *mankūsah*[12].

Fertility customs, the majority associated with the tombs of saints are countless and varied, and nowhere more so than in Aden. In a collection of essays, Muḥammad ʿAlī Luqmān[13] remarks that, »In many milieux in Aden, women and men, believe that the ʿAidarūs Saiyid[14] has a cat descended from the Jinn *(aṣlu-hā min al-Jinn)*, for which animal they leave eggs, sweet-meats and parched grain *(qalīyah*[15]), and they repair to the grave of the saint and from it they take out earth which they eat to cure barrenness *(ʿaqm)*[16].« Another Adenese told me that women come on a Sunday to put down *qalīyah*, almonds, and eggs for the famous cats of the ʿAidarūs mosque-these, he said, are *nus̲h̲ūḥ*[17], that you throw down to keep away the Jinn. Some say there is actually a S̲h̲aiṭān in the ʿAidarūs cats. If a pregnant woman evinces strong desire for sexual intercourse her child will be a girl, but if on the contrary she shows distaste and repugnance to it, then her child will be a boy. Another pointer to the sex of the child is that if the woman is pained by the withdrawal of the *d̲h̲akar*, then the child will be a boy, but if there be no pain then it is likely to be a girl. If the child faces outwards it will be a boy, if inwards, it will be a girl. Again if the man should ejaculate first the child will resemble him, and vice-versa, if the woman does then the child will take after her. Some women know the actual night upon which conception takes place. These are current ideas in the Wādī Ḥaḍramawt.

[10] Doreen Ingrams, Survey of Social and Economic Conditions in the Aden Protectorate (Asmara, 1949), pp. 98—100, deals with birth and childhood. While the bulk seems drawn from Landberg, there are some interesting details based on her personal experience.

[11] Al-Īḍāḥ fī ʿIlm al-Nikāḥ (Tunis, n. d.) Cf. Brockelmann, Gal, II, p. 257, Sup., II, p. 369, & Prose and Poetry from Ḥaḍramawt (London, 1951), p. 53.

[12] Cf. my Hūd and other Pre-Islamic Prophets of Ḥaḍramawt, Le Muséon (Louvain, 1954), LXVII, p. 164, et passim.

[13] ʿAdan taṭlub al-Ḥukm al-D̲h̲ātī (Aden, n. d., circa 1951), p. 41.

[14] The famous saint of Aden, and its only Manṣab.

[15] Star-Calendars and an Almanac from South-West Arabia, Anthropos (Posieux, 1954), XLIX, p. 457, *qawālī* means toasted foods such as locusts and maize-cobs.

[16] Dust is commonly taken out of the *ṭāqah* or little hole into the grave for numerous purposes, but always with the idea of *barakah*.

[17] *Nus̲h̲ūḥ* according to Lane, Lexicon, means a drink a little less than to satisfy.

The condition of *raz'*[18] has been described to me by Adenese, mentioned, en passant, by al-Baiḥānī[19] as *'amalīyat al-raz'*. He condemns it in the same breath as the *zār*[20] which its ritual seems to resemble. Colonel Jacob[21] states that the rite is usually performed by a woman who calls for a black sheep and a piece of iron, or asafoetida. She slaughters the animal and consecrates it to her Jinn, saying. »This is thy supper. Possess such an one, and let him no more rise from his bed.« The woman can likewise order her Jinn to release the victim. Apparently, too, Jacob knew a man who was a *razzā'* who used to call on Allāh to lay this spell on a person!

My sophisticated Aden informant rendered *raz'* by the word Voodoo. A woman might say, »*Yishtū yarza'ū-nī*, They wish to constrict the foetus inside me« (so that she will be unable to deliver it). A woman under this spell is called *marzū'ah*. I recall that on our first arrival in Ḥaḍramawt, it was suggested to my wife that she might examine a woman in Daw'an supposed to have been pregnant for five years, though no word was said to us of magic. A man can be affected in like fashion so that »*Yikhallūn-uh bi-lā ḥaqq al-raggāl*, They leave him without any of the thing a man has.« i. e. without sexual powers. The *fakk al-raz'*, or release, can be accomplished by all sorts of people, but not seemingly by special families. People even go to Bin 'Alwān at Yifrus, and to al-Sharq for the purpose of freeing themselves from this sad condition.

In 1941 a Baiḍānī remarked to me that when a woman is actually in labour, and has difficulty in delivering her baby and arrives a point when she seems entirely unable to do so, her husband comes in and throws down some piece of his own clothing beside her, and it must be his own, after which she delivers the child. Unfortunately I have no further details as to what is said on this occasion.

Disposal of the Placenta

On visiting with our friend, Saiyid 'Alī b. 'Aqīl, his house in Masīlat Āl al-Shaikh the evening after his child had been born in 1947, he gave an exclamation of impatience as he crossed the threshold, finding the earth at the door had been disturbed. His explanation of the circumstance started my inquiries into a practice of which he disapproved, considering it merest superstition. His mother, I later heard, was, somewhat to his discomfort, known as a practitioner, amongst women of course, of folk medicine, including, I should think, remedies involving spitting, for the spittle of holy personages, Saiyids and Shaikhs, enters into many curative practices.

The placenta of a woman who has given birth is buried at the main door of the house, often there is only one door, about two feet below the surface. The plac-

[18] My informant gave me the following senses of *raza'*, "to dash to the ground", as one says, "*shallait-uh wa-razza't-uh*, I took him and threw him on the ground." However this seems to me inappropriate here and the senses of tasser, empiler, serrer, given in the Gloss. Daṯ., obviously come closer to the root of the meaning.

[19] Ustādh al-Mar'ah, op. cit., p. 241.

[20] The *zār* is well known in both Aden and al-Mukallā. I have collected a series of notes on it from both places. It is forbidden in Aden but no doubt goes on secretly.

[21] H. F. Jacob, Perfumes of Araby, (London, 1915), p. 168—9, describing also other types of raz'.

enta, known as *lummāt,* is first placed in ashes *(ramād)*[22] and an iron nail, a *wada-'ah* or cowrie-shell, and a little cotton placed on top of the *lummāt.* A *miskīn* woman in 'Aidīd said however, that you place the *lummāt* in a *quffah* or round basket, and put ashes on it so as not to let the cat eat it, and she added that only cotton (*'uṭb*) and a nail (*mismār*) were buried with it. A passing injunction of al-Baiḥānī[23], »The bone (*'aẓm*), the cowrie, and the bead (*kharazah*)[24] do not avert the evil eye, nor repel the snare of Satan,« may give an indication why a cowrie should be used. It seems to be objectionable that anything untoward should befall the *lummāt,* for of an excited or hasty man, you say, *»kalat lummāt-ak al-hirr,* the cat has eaten your afterbirth.«[25]

If the child is a boy the *lummāt* are buried outside, about the door-step, but should it be a girl, inside the *mardam* or wooden base sill of the door-frame in the *ḍaiqah* or entrance passage from the door into the house — this passage generally has a simple earth floor. As the *lummāt* are buried, the phrase *Bismillāh al-Raḥmān al-Raḥīm* is uttered, and many stones are placed over it. A man buries the *lummāt,* the father, brother, or a servant. A second *lummāt* would be buried beside the first lot. The reason for burying the *lummāt* of a boy and girl in different places is because it is desired that the girl should remain at home, and not *»til'ab,* play«, i. e. commit *zināwah* (adultery), while you want the boy on the other hand to go out and earn his living (*yisraḥ ya'īsh*)[26]. For Ḥaḍramawt this has a great significance, since emigration on a large scale has taken place for centuries but especially in the last century, and of course today. When I questioned a member of a Saiyid family why Ḥaḍramī women never left Ḥaḍramawt, he simply stated that to do so would be *'aib,* i. e. shame, though of course of more recent years this has altered a little. I surmise that the lack of privacy on dhows, especially in regard to sanitation, may have something to do with this, whereas air travel is a different matter.

22 Al-Baiḥānī' loc. cit., inveighs against "lines of blood *(khuṭūṭ al-dam)* and ashes on the walls and ways", and although he does not explain these superstitions it is plain from the context that they are precautions against the Jinn, so perhaps that is intended also in Ḥaḍramawt. One sees ashes in the lanes of Tarīm where the "long drop" of the privy opens onto the path, and I infer this is for the same reason.

23 Op. cit., p. 243.

24 He means beads worn by children, generally as far I can recollect of red coral or amber, but I have not made special investigations into this. There is a yellow amber bead which comes from abroad used by children in Ḥaḍramawt, called *kahrab miskī,* and known as *al-ṣaddāq,* and is supposed to avert envy *(yidfa' al-ḥasad).* Light burns it *(taḥruq-uh al ḍaw').* It is opposed to another kind of amber, *kahrab ḥajarī,* called *al-kadhdhāb. Kahrab miskī* has a smell when you rub it but the other has not. Muḥammad 'Alī Luqmān, op. cit., p. 41 however speaks of the *kharazat al-Ḥakamī,* the latter a family of the lower Yemen, which is used to cure tuberculous glands.

25 Compare the Aden saying, *"Yākul laḥm daggāg,* He eats chicken flesh." i. e. he is hot-tempered.

26 Dr Mustafa Kariem has written me the following note from the Sudan. "In the Sudan they dispose of the afterbirth *(khalāṣ)* by giving it to a person, man or woman, who is merry, and laughs often, to bury it inside the house. Children are brought to see it and they are supposed to laugh during the operation of its burial, so that the child grows up to be a merry person. With it is buried a piece of sugar, a date, and a sweet. The umbilical cord *(al-ḥabl al-surrī)* is kept in a box *(ḥuqq)* after being dried and a piece of dry perfume *('iṭr)* is kept with it." Cf. J. S. Trimingham, Islam in the Sudan (Oxford, 1949), p. 142, & Abdulla el Tayib, The Changing Customs of the Riverain Sudan, Sudan Notes and Records (Khartoum, 1955), XXXVI, p. 6. W. S. Blackman, The Fellāḥīn of Upper Egypt, (London, 1927), p. 63–4 says, "The placenta is buried under the threshold of a house. It may be buried under the floor of a house to appease the *ukht* (sister) and *qarīnah* if children have died. But otherwise it is thrown into the Nile or into a canal by a woman. She must smile as she does so – so that the child will have a happy disposition."

The umbilical cord (*surr*) is preserved, being dried and stored in a bottle (*yaḍumm-uh fī gharsh̲ah*). When the child has colic (*magh̲ṣah*)[27], the umbilicus is steeped in water, and the water given the child to drink to stop the pain. After steeping it in milk they apply it to children's eyes (*yukaḥḥilūn bah al-'uyūn*), a similar usage being remarked upon by the mediaeval author al-Sh̲arjī[28]. One often says to accompany the action, *»Bismillāh al-Raḥmān al-Raḥīm, mā sh̲ā' Allāh, lā quwwah illā bi-'llāh.«* Or with such cures one may repeat normal Islamic formulae like, *»Bismillāh al-Raḥmān al-Raḥīm, nuṣallī 'alā saiyid-nā Muḥammed, ṭibb al-qulūb wa-adwā'-hā wa-nūr al-abṣār wa-aḍyā'-hā, wa-'āl-uh, wa-ṣaḥb-ih, wa-sallam,* »In the name of God, the Merciful, the Compassionate, we bless our Lord Muḥammad, elixir of hearts and their medicine, light of the eyes and their brightness, and his Family and Companions.« In general if one feels unwell or weak, one says, *»Yā Saiyidī, yā Ḥabībī, yā Rasūl Allāh, qillat ḥīlatī, adrik lanā bi-'l-shifā' wa-'l-'āfiyah,* »O my Lord, o my Ḥabīb[29], o Apostle of God, my strength is little, hasten to aid me with healing and heath.« The *miskīn* woman in 'Aidīd did not seem to know of any particular formulae used in conjunction with these practices.

Ceremonies following the Birth

When the child is born the women immediately go to the top of the house and utter the usual trills of joy so that one knows where a birth has taken place in the Quarter. The newly delivered woman is cleaned, and a good dress put on, and when the women in other houses have time to deck themselves out, they start arriving to visit the mother. In the case of our carpenter in Tarīm, a *miskīn*, about 200 women came to pay their respects to his wife on such an occasion, coming to kiss her head (lit. sniff *sh̲amm*), and to kiss or, properly, to sniff, the baby. The *sh̲ammah 'alā kawr* as the ceremony is called, lasts seven days, and our carpenter looked somewhat rueful at the heavy expense of the birth, for all these women would have to be given some refreshment. The woman purefies herself (*taṭahhar*) after a period of 40 days, known as *'awfah*, but al-Baiḥānī says [30] that the *nifās*, or state of impurity consequent on child-birth, is from 40 to 60 days.

After the woman has borne the child you let eggs fall from the hand and break in the *ḍaiqah* (Syn. *dihlīz)*, some in the place where the birth has taken place, some in the house in general, adding perhaps the phrase *Bismillāh*, In the name of God. Another woman said, *wāḥid fi 'l-ḍaiqah*, one in the passage, another in the *muqaddimah*, i. e. the place in front of the room, and another in the room itself *(manzil)*. This is so that the Jinn will eat them, and not bring harm to the child or the woman. One woman said she did not know why eggs were broken, but it was just to keep

[27] Also a class. Arabic word.

[28] Ṭabaqāt al-Kh̲awāṣṣ, (Cairo, 1903), p. 147.

[29] Title of Muḥammad and of the Saiyids.

[30] Op. cit., p. 117. In Aden sacrifices are made before a woman returns to normal life. C. de Landberg, Etudes . . . Daṯînah (Leiden, 1905–13), III, p. 1777 describes the *dh̲abīḥat al-nafās*, sacrifice de l'accouchement, which is called the *fadū* (lit. ransom), which he identifies with the *'aqīqah*. The child's head is rubbed with the blood of the animal, and then the *taḥnīk* is carried out, which in Daṯh̲īnah is rubbing the child's mouth with a holy man's saliva. (p. 1712), or he may rub it with oil, against Iblīs.

any harm away; an egg, she said, is placed by the child's head *(kawr)*, and after some days it is broken. I heard a mission nurse allude to this practice in the Shaikh 'Uthmān hospital — which she tried to stop — it seems they would be dropped by the door of the hospital by a relative before the child is born.

The Ṣukhmah

At one house in Tarīm we saw a newly-born child with aloes (*ṣabir*) on its umbilicus, while on its brow was traced in the same substance, *»Mā shā' Allāh,* What God wills.« This phrase as is well known, is used to avert the evil eye from some desirable object. Sometimes the child simply has a black spot daubed on the middle of its brow, but we also saw this black mark on the face of a little boy at Qasam, and over his nostrils, against the evil eye — it was roughly sketched. Many have it marked on the bridge of the nose. Baby boys and girls sometimes have a letter *wāw* in reverse drawn on their brow to guard them against the evil eye (*sawwū wāw maqlūb yaḥrusu-hum min al-ḥasad*). I can recall that in one case I saw a number on the brow, and was told that it was merely to keep count of how many days had elapsed since the birth, but this may have been an attempt to turn a superstitious custom into an innocuous Islamic one. On some occasions I was told, a child in arms is marked in this way but not one newly born. By way of comparison Professor Taiyib[31] reports that in the Sudan a cross is made with antimony on a child's forehead, and he thinks this may have a Christian origin, but in view of its existence in Arabia also I am inclined to think it is a custom older than either religion, possibly with something of the idea of »blackening the face«, but I have no evidence for such a supposition. This cross or other mark is called *ṣukhmah,* and elsewhere in Ḥaḍramawt it is sometimes called *samād*[32], as to take a case in point, in Ḥuraiḍah. In Egypt it is known as *daqq.* Drawn on a woman's brow after delivering a child, it is also against the evil eye (*ḍidd al-'ain,* or *tiqṣir al-'ain*); this however is only done in the case of a primapara, and mothers giving birth for the third and more times, do not have this done to them. Another form of *ṣukhmah* on women is a cross on the brow, yet another is a line across the eyebrows, down the nose, and under the chin. I saw a mother with simply a line across her brows and down the nose.

That this is a very ancient custom is shown by the Tradition reported in the *Jāmi'* of Ibn Wahb[33], and I believe there only and not in the canonical collections, to which of course it is anterior. Here it is stated that a woman brought a small child, a boy (*ṣabī*) to 'Ā'ishah to ask for *tabarruk,* usually rendered as »blessing« for him. The text runs, *Qad khaṭṭat baina 'ainai-hi aw fī jabhati-hi khaṭṭ aswad,* She had drawn between his eyes or on his brow, a black line.« 'Ā'ishah, we are

[31] Abdulla El Tayib, The Changing Customs of the Riverain Sudan, Sudan Notes and Records (Khartoum, 1955), XXXVI, p. 7.
Naturally there are many parallels in South Arabia to the Sudanese customs. For instance in al-Mukallā also a string is worn round a child's waist, though I have no information as to why this is done.

[32] *Samād* is a word meaning "dung". It is not impossible that this is what it means in this context in Ḥuraiḍah. It leads one to speculate that the *ṣukhmah* could originally have been of dung, but there is no evidence for this.

[33] J. David-Weill, Le Djâmi' d'Ibn Wahb, p. 112.

told, refused to bless the child until this mark had been removed. The Tradition is cast in a familiar pattern, but at least it expresses the disapproval of early Islām of a custom which has survived in Arabia up to our own time. The same volume[34] informs us that when 'Ā'ishah saw a child with two anklets (*khalkhāl*) on its feet, she indicated that she preferred silver anklets, which leads us to conclude that these anklets were of iron for some superstitious reason, repugnant also to the early Muslims. One may still see children in Ḥaḍramawt with similar iron anklets or bracelets, but I have recorded no precise instance in my field-notes, though a *miskīn* who used to come to our house in Tarīm wore iron toe-rings round his big toes, against, as he said, accidents or pain in the feet; these rings were obviously not for practical purposes but on account of some superstition.

Naming the Child

Saiyid 'Alī b. 'Aqīl said that in olden days the grandfather would chose a child's name in the case of a boy at least, but he personally was submitting three names on three separate pieces of paper for his wife to chose; this is done because women are mostly illiterate, though she is not. However what is generally done is that, when a boy or a girl is born, the son asks his father and mother what it is to be called, and also his wife. Should there be disagreement, as probably nearly always happens, then the three names are written separately on three bits of paper and placed in a basket which is brought to the mother. After reciting the *Fātiḥah* she puts in her hand and draws out the first slip she touches, and thus the name is decided. I was told that anyone may draw the slip from the basket, and some people prefer that a boy below age of puberty should do so.

In al-Mukallā if the father of a child happens to be absent at the birth of his child, his near relations will propose various names; the mother usually has a name to suggest, and the other relations might comprise the child's grandfather, his great-grandfathers, or the father's brother. The choice is made by lot (*raw'*, pl. *arwā'*); a stranger is asked to select the name from a number of slips of paper, placing the slip he choses on the child's brow. This may be done once, or, if they are not satisfied, three times, after which there is no further dissent.

Nothing illustrates the elaborate conventions regarding women in Southern Arabia better than the devious means employed by a woman to communicate the good news to her distant husband. An illiterate woman will write to her husband through the intermediary of an old man who is literate, and this man will mention in the letter that he and the neighbours greet you, but the letter will be written as if by the husband's son, even if the latter be still an infant, and it will have the form, »*Walad-ak ṭālib al-du'ā'*, Your son the seeker of blessing . . .« or if it be daughters only, »*Awlād-ak al-mamlūkīn ṭālibīn al-du'ā'*, Your children the possessed, seekers of blessing . . . « It will be noted that the Arabic of the last formula is in the masculine plural, though daughters are intended, a convention also that of poetry, to use the masculine when speaking of a girl. The prospective father will realise at once whether the expected birth has taken place for the letter will be addressed to him as »*Lā-yad al-wālid 'Abduh Ḥasan.* To the hand of the

[34] Op. cit., p. 12–3.

father ʿAbduh Ḥasan.«[35] Otherwise it will simply bear the superscription, »*Lā yad ʿAbduh Ḥasan.*« In the case of a second boy being born to the father, the letter might be in the name of *Muḥammad wa-akhū-h,* Muḥammad and his brother. In the event of a boy there is of course no secrecy — one says for instance, »*Al-dīk yiṣīḥ min wasaṭ al-baiḍah,* The cock crows from inside the egg.« But, if a daughter be born to the absent husband, this will not be mentioned directly, though an allusion will be made to the birth, as for example, *ʿāj aswad,* black ivory; I suppose that the underlying concept is that through a girl child a man's honour may be blackened[36]. Another way to hint at the birth of a girl is to enclose a piece of a woman's dress in the letter; in the Yemen a bit of the yellow *wars* cosmetic, or of indigo (*nīl*), could be smeared on the corner of the letter. The Arab attitude to girl children is well known, but this does not of course mean that an Arab father is any less fond of his little daughter than any other race.

Names can vary according to the class of the family[37] though certain Islāmic names are common to all; the *miskīns* and *ḍaʿīfs* have often very curious names such as Musaibilī[38] or Bulrush Millet, but Saʿīd and its variants is common among them; I have also a long list of names only given to slaves and slave-women. If the son of a *miskīn* is born on a Thursday he is called Khamīs (fem. Khamīsah), and a girl born on Friday may be called Jumʿah, while a boy born on a Wednesday it was said, may be called Rabīʿ or Rubaiyaʿ, though in parts of South Arabia this is counted an unlucky day. A child born in ʿArafah (Dhu ʾl-Ḥijjah) is called ʿArfān in Ḥaḍramawt, Wāḥidi territory, and perhaps elsewhere; children are also named after the months Rajab, Shaʿbān, Ramaḍān, and Rabīʿ, but not after Ṣafar which is regarded as unlucky.

Precautions against Harmful Influences

In Ḥaḍramawt where conditions are such that it is common enough for only two children out of ten live births to survive, great fear of supernatural influences unfavourable to the survival of the child is entertained by the common people. In al-Mukallā, and later on in other places I saw a small boy dressed as a girl to avoid the evil eye, just as has been reported by E. J. W. Lane for Egypt; the little boy, perhaps a year or two old, wore a kind of bonnet (*kummah*).[39]

In Tarīm sometimes, when people have lost two or three children, instead of putting the newly-born baby, boy or girl, on a *ṭabaq* or tray for winnowing grain, they set it on a *khubrah,* i. e. a sort of open basket for covering the date-clusters till they ripen, and ask God to preserve the child, making various prayers inside their hearts but saying nothing. The child is then called Khubrah, the name being given

[35] It was remarked that one addresses a letter to *al-ʿamm al-wālid,* or *al-khāl al-wālid,* the paternal or maternal uncle, the begettor", on account of their close relationship to oneself.

[36] As one calls a female relation *ʿārī,* lit., my disgrace, but perhaps it may simply be an allusion to the fact that Ḥaḍramī women usually wear black. In letters a woman is often spoken of as "*al-madlūl,* the person indicated."

[37] Cf., e. g. my Saiyids of Ḥaḍramawt, (London, 1951), p. 10.

[38] Jacob, op. cit., p. 161 mentions a child called "hedgehog" against the evil eye. Might this be the explanation of tribal names like Kalb, dog?

[39] The *kummah* is said to be worn in the cold season, it is ornamented with beads etc. I actually heard this word in Tarīm not in al-Mukallā.

to either a boy or a girl, until it is 8 years old, though of course it has a proper name of its own, but it is then called by its own name, for with marriage in the not so very distant future (about puberty) this would not be a suitable name. The name Khubrah or Khibrah is against envy (*ḥasad*), and if they call it so, then it will be safe (*In sammaw-h bi-Khibrah yislam*). I believe that in this custom is a trace of the worship of the palm, for the existence of which in Ḥaḍramawt, there are several indications.

Also in Tarīm, when your child is sickly and yet is always eating, and all other remedies that you have tried have failed, you may take him to the tomb of Sālim Bā Dann in the cemetery area (al-Turbah) of Tarīm, a saint described by a verse in *al-Mashra' al-Rawī*[40] as a Shāfi'ī, but stated by Raḥaiyam to have been one of the Mashāyikh before the time of the ancestor of the Saiyids, 'Īsā al-Muhājir[41]. The parents place the child by the tomb, stand back a little, and either say aloud or think in their minds, some prayer such as, »*Baghainā wiḥdah min al-'awāfī*, We wish one of the healths.« Probably addressing the shaikh with the phrase, «*Bi-ḥaqq-ak*, By your right.« The sense is — either take him or leave him, and if after this the child cries, they know that he will live.

Falling within a similar category is the case of the *mushtarā* or »purchased« child, described to me by an Adenese. A woman who loses children, both boys and girls, year after year, goes to a saint (*walī*), and tells the Imām (*maimūn al-walī*), and buys the child from the saint, vowing (*tindhūr*), each year for the first seven years of the child's life, on each Muḥarram she will dress him in green silk (*ḥarīr akhḍar*), and that every night she will go from house to house disguised as a beggar-woman asking people for alms, with such phrases as »*Yallah, yā karīm*.« The proceeds of her begging will go to the saint. At the same time the child must wear an earring (*wazarah*) and a leather amulet (*ḥirz*) on a bangle of silver or iron. She takes the child with her when she goes out disguised as a beggar, and is accompanied by an old woman *mushtariḥah*, a singing woman, usually of negroid descent, perhaps a Sawākinīyah[42]. Perhaps it is for this reason that the *mushtarā* boy is rather girlish in his ways (*al-mushtarā dā'im-an banātī*). The walī releases the boy after the seven years are over, but every year during the first seven days of Muḥarram they entertain their friends to some liquid refreshment.

It is not known what the woman pays to the saint. The most prominent *walī* in the Yemen is the celebrated Bin 'Alwān, even although the Imām of the Yemen has destroyed his shrine; another place al-Sharg in the Yemen is also famous.

Circumcision (Khitān)

A short text on circumcision amongst the Qarā tribe has been published by Landberg[43] and a description with some wealth of detail is given by Thomas[44]

[40] Muḥ. b. Abī Bakr al-Shillī, (Cairo, 1319), I, p. 148. At the time of the Wahhābī incursions into Ḥaḍramawt early last century Bā Dann protected Tarīm by a miracle from them, so that they are reported to have said, „*Lī qad dhā dannu-hum aish 'ād maṣabbu-hum*, If that is their little drinking vessel (goblet) what will their ablution jug be like?" It is a somewhat rueful pun on his name; but I do not suppose there is any truth in the story.

[41] This would then make him an Islamic saint prior to the 4th century H.

[42] Probably an African woman.

[43] Ḥaḍramoût, (Leiden, 1901), p. 487 seq.

[44] Bertram Thomas, Arabia Felix (London, 1938), p. 71 seq.

also; more recently this same type of circumcision has been remarked among the Rāshid by Thesiger[45]. This is a public ceremony with exposure of the member in public if I understand the two latter accounts correctly, though no positive statement is made to this effect. Thesiger also mentions for western Arabia, 'Asīr, the »flaying circumcision« where it seems certainly exposed; which may be compared with the analysis by Landberg[46] of several 19th century accounts of the same. In Islāmic Ḥaḍramawt of the towns and villages this would be regarded as gross indecency I am sure, and the ceremony there is quite different.

Al-Baiḥānī[47] states what must be the normal Shāfi'ī-procedure. »The first thing that is obligatory (to perform) for him according to law (*s̲h̲ar'*), is the circumcision, and a sacrificial animal (*'aqīqah*) is desirable, two sheep for a male, and one for a female, to be slaughtered on the 7th day, and their meat given away. The *ad̲h̲ān* is performed at its right ear, and the prayer at its left ear; an upright man rubs its palate and choses it a good name. When its head is shaved it is desirable to give (*taṣaddaqa*) in charity the weight of its hair in gold or silver«.

According to Raḥaiyam circumcision used to take place in ancient times in Tarīm on the 7th day after parturition (*fi 'l-yawm al-sābi' ba'd al-waḍ'*), but it now takes place mostly after 7 to 8 years[48]. The Bedu however, he added, only circumcise when a man is about to marry; the operation is performed with the *jambīyah*, dagger, and is painful. Raḥaiyam believed that circumcision increases lust. Major Ian Snell[49] says of the Ḥumūm, »They still delay circumcision until the boy is about to carry a rifle (about 14 years old) and then they carry out the operation as a ceremony, if possible several boys at once, and there is a great party«. I am inclined to see in the Qarā-Rās̲h̲id-Ḥumūm initiation ceremony, the older practice which has survived in Ḥaḍramawt.

In Tarīm the circumcision is performed by the Āl Bā Salmah, who are cuppers (*ḥajjāmīn*), and in Tāribah by the *mujabbir* (lit. bone-setter), the *ṭabīb* (doctor), one by the name of Muḥsin bin Ja'far bin al-K̲h̲amīs al-'Āmirī. The latter insists that the children come to him, but the Bā Salmah go to the house of the boy to be circumcised, always at a time when it is neither hot nor cold (*fī waqt ma'dūl*), and either on the It̲h̲nain (Monday) or K̲h̲amīs (Thursday). Bā Salmah comes secretly (*yijī Bā Salmah bi-k̲h̲ufyah*) in order not to terrify the child who is soothed and calmed always, so that the blood will not be made to gush forth when the operation actually takes place. This is practically the reverse of the drama enacted by the Qarā and others.

The penis is massaged gently so as to get the *ḥashafah* (glans) to come out, and is oiled with ghee (*saman*). The operator brings with him a circle of rubber (*qiṭṭaḥ madrūjah*), by which Raḥaiyim meant, I must suppose, a rubber band. The boy is gripped by two or three persons and the rubber is put round the penis to bring out a piece of skin that can be cut.

After the operation a substance like *'iṭr* (perfume) called by a name not Arabic,

[45] W. Thesiger, Arabian Sands, (London, 1959), p. 89 seq.

[46] Ḥaḍramoût, op. cit., p. 491 seq.

[47] Ustād̲h̲ al-Mar'ah, p. 126.

[48] Snouck Hurgronje, Mekka, trans. J. H. Monahan (Leiden, 1931), p. 113, "The not yet Mekkanised Ḥaḍramīs are accustomed to circumcise their children already on the 40th day."

[49] I. E. Snell, Brief Notes on . . . Tribes of the East Aden Protectorate (mimeographed) (al-Mukallā, 1st Oct., 1952) p. 7.

mayakafutay, is put on the cut to stop the flow of blood. The flies are kept off it. The boy returns to his mother. They say, »*Ṭahharnā-h*, We have purefied him.« Men and women now come to give the boy something as a present, and on the next day an entertainment is given.

It is to be remarked that the phrase »*kulli mak̲h̲tūn*, every circumcised one«, is used in the Quarters of Tarīm in their documents to signify every adult male.

In Aden, despite the view of al-Baiḥānī it seems that boys are generally circumcised at 6,7, or even at the age of 10. The circumcision used to be carried out by the *ḥallāq* or barber, but I am told that it is usually performed nowadays by the Ḥumrān family from Ibb of the Yemen. On these occasions the children of the street eat honey with the fingers (*yilḥas al-ʿasal*) from the little cups without handles used in South Arabia. In Aden special songs are sung at circumcisions. When a child is circumcised in his first year the mid-wife will stand with him in her arms und small children will run in a circle round her, and they will sing the following words

Midwife:	*Igrū warā-nā.*	Children:	*Yā ʿayāl.*
	Run after me.		O children.
	Gāhil maʿā-nā.		*Yā ʿayāl.*
	I have a boy.		O children.
	Gāhil agā-nā.		*Yā ʿayāl.*
	A boy has come to me.		O children.

Children: *Yā giddah qawlī qabaʿ qabaʿ.*
O midwife. say *qabaʿ qabaʿ*. (sense unknown)

Yā giddah rās-ik ṣa 'l-ṭabaq.
O midwife your head is like a tray (i. e. big)

Midwife:	*Igrū warā-nā.*	Children:	*Yā ʿayāl.*
	Bi - ʿl-k̲h̲awzarānah.		*Yā ʿayāl.*
	With the bamboo.		O children.
	Gāhil maʿā-nā.		*Yā ʿayāl.*

Etc.

Female Circumcision

To quote al-Baiḥānī[50] once more, »Scholars have held differing opinions concerning circumcision for a woman, but with the S̲h̲āfiʿīs it is obligatory — the least of it is the cutting of a bit of the skin growing at the top of the vulva (*farj*).« He alludes also to the references in books of *fiqh* concerning women's actions in piercing (*tak̲h̲rīm*) the ears and nose to suspend ornaments from them, »which is an ancient custom and still continues in many countries.« As will be seen these two operations are carried out at the same time. Notwithstanding al-Baiḥānī's clear dictum however, I am informed that girls in Aden are no longer circumcised, though admittedly my informant was an educated young man, but the midwife (*muwallidah*) used to

[50] Ustād̲h̲ al-Mar'ah, p. 80.

do this. In reply to a question from al-Tawwāhī, the Aden paper *al-Nahḍah* (1952), CXVI, says circumcision of girls is not obligatory, adding that it lessens desire in women, and pointing to the known objections to it, especially as practised in the Sudan.

In Tarīm girls are circumcised by a woman about the second day after birth, usually by a woman who knows this art, and not by any particular family. The woman is generally a slave-woman (*amah*) who knows how to brand for illnesses, or to massage a child's neck[51] (*raqqab, tarqīb*) after a fall or on account of some other sickness.[52] »She also pierces her ears for her and keeps the hole (open) with a thread impregnated with indigo (*takhshuf lahā wa-timsak al-khudrah bi-khaiṭ nīl*)«, three holes in each ear for suspending ornaments (*li-ta'lūq al-ḥilī*), ornaments for the ear being called *qurṭ* or *mithqāl*. The *khaṣhṣhāfah* woman comes and operates both on the ears and clitoris of the girl, but how the circumcision was performed was quite unknown to Raḥaiyam who, of course, had never actually seen it done. An expression he remarked, is »*Ukhshif idhnī lak*, I pierce my ear for you«, but it simply means, »I thank you.« Landberg[53] however gives a description of the operation which, though in itself not absolutely clear (in the Arabic), I have taken in conjunction with the handbook on Ḥisbah of Ibn al-Ukhuwwah[54], himself a Shāfi'ī writer, but an Egyptian. The latter quoting a Tradition of the Prophet says that the tip of the piece of skin (i. e. the clitoris) should be taken, but it should not be »extirpated«. Landberg places the circumcision of a girl eight days after the birth.

Describing the tribes of the Ẓufār region, Bertram Thomas[55] concurs that a girl is circumcised without ceremony on the day of her birth, but he avers that the tribes here, probably he means the Qarā, practice clitoridectomy- while the tribes of Oman merely incise the top of the clitoris. If Thomas is correct, and these things are not easy to ascertain, even for a woman doctor, then, on balance, it would seem that the non-Arabic speaking group differs from the Arabic speakers to the east and west of them, but this is a point that requires investigation.

The Hermaphrodite

In Aden the Arabic word is *khunthā*, which Landberg considers the usual word in Southern Arabia. I saw a man in 'Awdhalī country, probably a hermaphrodite who was allowed to mix freely with women. Muslim legists discuss the question of the circumcision of the hermaphrodite at some length, as much, I suspect, because it is a fascinating topic as because of its importance in law.

[51] Massage is a common remedy for a large range of afflictions in Southern Arabia.

[52] My notes mention also *al-rafī'*, which is "*ḥijāmah bidūn fashṭ*, blood-letting without making a slit", but unfortunately I do not seem to have recorded whether this is a remedy for the child's neck or, more likely, an art practiced by these women.

[53] Ḥaḍramoût, op. cit., p. 490.

[54] The Ma'ālim al-Qurba . . . of . . . Ibn al-Ukhuwwa, edit. R. Levy (Cambridge-London, 1938), p. 164 (Ar. text).

[55] Op. cit., p. 71.

Appendix

The following account is translated from a passage in the voluminous notes of Shaikh Raḥaiyam Bā Faḍl. He prefaces this passage by the statement that Tarīm has statutes and customs (*qawā'id wa-'awā'id*) in accordance with the *sharī'ah* and *sunnah* of the Prophet.

»Concerning what pertains to the affairs of a boy from the time of his delivery (*waḍ'*), i. e. his coming forth from his mother's belly, until the time of his circumcision, i. e. his purefication (*taṭhīr*). It is the practice of the people of Tarīm, when a woman bears a male or female child, for the men present of his relations, to say the *adhān* (call to prayer) in the ear of the boy or the girl who is brought into being, saying the *adhān* in the right ear, and the prayer (*yuqīm al-ṣalāh*) in his left ear. They rub (*ḥannak)* some dates[56] or sugar on his lips, and make him sniff civet (*yurawwiḥūn-uh al-zubād*) or other sweet-smelling perfumes, and they recite the Sūrat al-Qadr three times over the boy, for it preserves him from committing immoral deeds (*fawāḥish*). Likewise they recite over him the two Sūrahs al-Mu 'awwidhatān (i.e.the last two chapters of the Koran) because of the preservation (from harm) and guardianship (against the Jinn or the *ḥāsid*, envious person) they contain. When they sever the umbilical cord, *ṣurr* or *surr,* they turn the newly-born child (*yankusūn al-ḥādif*) upside down on his face, so as the remaining blood in it can come out, for this is a safeguard (*amān*) against colic (*qāliṣ*[57]) and stomachache (*maghṣ*), and they blow (*yan-fakhūn*) in his mouth[58]. The people of former times used to take a *maḥqab*[59] of coffee, when a male child was born to them, to one of the Koran-schools (*al-'ilam*[60]) known for the teaching of the Koran and give the teacher the good tidings of the newly-born boy, and he would perform a *Fātiḥah* and pray for the well-being (*salāmah*) of the newly born boy, along with pious blessings, and give the children leave to go immediately after their reciting the *Fātiḥah* aloud. After the delivery (*al-waḍ'*) they sent small children at once to inform their relatives, acquaintances, friends or neighbours (*lahum jīrah*), and when a number of women have collected they ululate (*yaḥjuran*), i. e. they trill trills of joy (*yaṣluqan ṣalīq faraḥ*) to give notice of the health and well-being of mother and child. It is their custom to present money to the woman who has given birth, each person in accordance with his means (*wa-min 'ādāt-hum yubashshirūn bi-darāhim li'l-waḍi'ah, kull-in 'alā qadr ḥāl-uh*). In return for this (*fī muqābil hādhā*) the family of the newborn child gives an entertainment for the near relations, especially of the wife's people, everybody in accordance with his circumstances.

Now, concerning the naming day (*yawm al-tasmiyah*), i. e. the 7th day after the birth they carry out the custom (*sunnah*) of the *'aqīqah*[61] laid down in the law (*fiqh*) books but they differ as to how it is done and when. Some there are who distribute meat (*yuqassim laḥamāt*[62]), some who give a feast (*walīmah*), and some who do both; there are some who

[56] They put a little on his lips *(yufaṭṭirūn-ah)* or put it on his nose. In Tarīm we saw babies only a few days old given dates in a piece of cloth to suck.

[57] *Qalṣah*, i. e. *„al-waja' fi 'l-baṭn qāliṣ,* pain in the stomach is (called) *qāliṣ*. This is no doubt the same word as *jalsah* with is part of the nickname of Fughmah, cf. Hūd and other Pre-Islamic Prophets, op. cit. p. 148.

[58] This is so that *"yakūn ṣaiyit,* he may have a loud voice". Usually a woman blows into the child's mouth. If a man has a low voice they say to him, *„Man dhī nafkhat lak,* Who blew into your mouth for you?"

[59] The *maḥqab* which contains sugar and *jifl* (coffe-bean) is made of palm-leaf *(ḥaṣīr),* and is cone-shaped with a leather thong at the top, but it is not used nowadays.

[60] Sing. *'ilmah.*

[61] Raḥaiyam said two sheep for a boy and one for a girl, which of course is orthodox – if it is actually practice and not mere theory. I do not think many *ḍa'īfs* could afford so much.

[62] I. e. raw meat. Presents of meat are not uncommon. Saiyid Muḥammad b. Hāshim informed me that he was entitled to a present of meat from a certain mosque *waqf*. I recall also seeing the soldiers of the Emir ot Sokoto in N. Nigeria taking a daily gift of meat from the palace to people in the town.

make a big thing of it, some who are perfunctory, and some who are altogether unable (to do anything) through inability or poverty. If it is a feast (*walīmah*), when those invited are met together they recite the Mawlid of the Prophet Muḥammad, God bless and honour him, and chose three names for the new-born child, burying them in earth (*ṭīn*) which they place in front of the mother, and they stand by whatever name she chances upon[63].

When the boy's hair gets long (*iḏhā ṭāl rās al-ṣabī*) they »Wednesday« him, (*yurabbi'ūn lah*), i. e. they clip the hair of his head on a Wednesday, each shaving (*ḥilāqah*) (sic)[64]. People in former times used to give the barber (*ḥallāq*) a measure of grain (*muṣrā ṭa'ām*) by way of fee for each shaving. They bring up (*yirabbūn*) the boy the best way (possible) until he reaches seven or eight years old, or even more, and if they have already circumcised him during the days following childbirth (*aiyām al-nufsah*), good and well (*yā ḥabbaḏhā*), but if not, then that will come at its appropriate place.«

[63] An *'ālim*, scholar, *walī*, saint, or grandfather, *jadd*, choses the names, and they put them to the mother – or this is done when the people in the house disagree.

[64] There are *arba'īn ḥilāqah*, forty shavings, performed each Wednesday until 40 have been completed, after which the shaving may take place any day. For each shaving a line (*khuṭṭ*) is drawn on the wall. This seems to differ from the Daṯhīnah custom described by Landberg, Études ... Daṯînah, op. cit., p. 1778, who mentions the ḏhabīḥat al-kandarah, sacrifice when they shave the hair – which is carried out 40 or less days after the birth, to do away with the "hair of the womb".

Addenda

P.200 Professor Yasir Sulayman writes: In Palestine the word *skhām* is used to refer to black substance sticking to kitchen utensils. In a ritual women conduct to ward off the evil eye, *skhām* is put on the child's forehead after reciting a set charm. The *skhām* comes from the ashes of a small piece of black cloth.

P.205/26 The *khawzāranah* is the fez-shaped bamboo cap of the Yemen, very pliable and expensive.

XV

MARITIME CUSTOMARY LAW OFF THE ARABIAN COASTS

Arabic and Islamic literature is not lacking in allusion to sea-fishing and maritime activities off the coasts of Arabia-which itself lies between two important sea-highways of the Indian trade-route. Where navigation is concerned the data to be found in the standard works has been assembled by George Hourani in his admirable little book, though he has drawn hardly at all on Ibn Mājid and other authors made available to us by Ferrand in his *Instructions Nautiques*. Gerald Tibbetts however has commenced upon the difficult task of interpreting the information afforded us by the *Instructions Nautiques*. Where commerce is concerned Goitein's researches into the Cairo Genizah documents have added notably to our knowledge, and no doubt the Turkish archives could be despoiled to supplement our information on the Indian Ocean from the XVIth century onwards. I have for instance seen in the Topkapu Serai an Arabic document relating to the revenues of Mocha under the Ottomans. In the voluminous literature of Arabic itself there no doubt remains a wealth of data especially in the collections of legal decisions (*fatāwā*), and I hope that the edition of the *Mulakhkhaṣ al-Fiṭan* of 1411-1412 which Professor Cahen and I have in preparation, will present also its detailed picture of the India trade as seen from Aden.

Apart from scattered allusions in Arabic literature there is however no detailed treatment — to the best of my knowledge anyway — of the fishing and maritime communities, though one could deduce by a careful assembly of pertinent *fatāwā* something of the structure and activities of the maritime communities on the seaboards of the Indian Ocean. Whereas however, in the case of Arabia anyway, the deep-sea mariners and merchants have much of an international character as a community, the fisher-folk tend to be extremely parochial and conservative.

At the present day there exists a highly complicated and sophisticated customary law that governs the working lives of both mariners and fishermen.

It is so well established that it can be assumed to have a long history of development, though there are variations in it from place to place as one would expect. Nevertheless the principles of this law are largely identical everywhere. In speaking of South-West Arabia generally, Ibn al-Mujāwir, writing in the XIIIth century, says that the law followed is not *sharī'ah* but ancient pre-Islamic law and this statement in the context would seem to cover the fishermen also. The very existence of a native maritime law is hardly known to us, and it is only in attempts to improve fishing that Europeans have come to realise that there is this complex local fishing law. While my own experience of maritime customary law is mainly South-West Arabian, I have collected data from the Trucial Coast, from al-Baḥrain, and Sawākin in the Red Sea, and I have reason to believe in what I have seen of the East African coast that close correspondences will be found there too with custom in the Arab lands.

Firstly, to glance at the people who engage as fishermen or mariners, one should recall that in Arabia the inhabitants of the seaboard are at the mercy of the hinterland tribes who exact tribute from them in one form or another. So they generally form a protected class, and engaging in a sort of craft, they are regarded by the rigid class system of Arabia as inferior to the arms-bearing tribes. So in many places fisherfolk are despised as of low class — for instance as far back as the time of al-Jāḥiẓ in southern Iraq, and at the present day in South Arabia from Oman westwards, though the politico-economic changes of recent years have seen some tribesmen on the Ḥaḍramī coast take to fishing. In al-Baḥrain however tribesfolk engage in fishing with no loss to their honour, and in Ḥaḍramawt all classes take part in deep-sea sailing, including for instance one of my most valuable informants, Badr al-Kasādī of the tribe of Yāfi', the present *Nā'ib* of al-Mukallā. The Qawāsimī pirates who gave the Government of India so much trouble round about 1800 were also tribesfolk.

Where an organised centralised state of sorts has been able to wrest the power from the tribes, the exactions of the latter would be transferred to the state as revenue in the more famous ports of the India route, such as Jeddah, Aden al-Shiḥr, Muscat, al-Baḥrain, and others, some now ruined and deserted, while the fisherfolk would probably pay the state in kind from their catch of fish. I use the term « state », but in fact the state would consist of a Sultan whose support derives from his tribe, so it really means payment to a centrally organised body rather than to individual protecting tribes. In either case the seaboard communities remain separately organised with their own laws enforced by their own headmen. The customary law of deep-sea voyaging and international trade of course must inevitably come more closely within the ambit of the central government and its law-courts. Where navigational law was concerned, the states of South-West Arabia had a special official in the ports called the Amīr al-Baḥr who would probably, I think, also deal with the fishing community, and a thousand and one technical matters arising from the various maritime pursuits. An official with this appellation was to be found, for example, at Mocha and Aden at the time of de la Rocque's voyages in the early XVIIIth century, and this office existed in the Yemen during the present century, perhaps up till the revolution.

In all these communities the various categories of workers were, and mostly still are, bound to those persons who have enough to finance ventures, by an elaborate system of loans and debts. These are similar in their way to share-cropping farming finance in the agricultural districts. I suspect, though I have not investigated this aspect of local commerce, that the merchant and capitalist classes financing fishing and navigation are bound to each other by an intricate mesh of credit and debt. Nowadays it is fashionable to criticise these classes, but, in my view, that they perform an essential function in Arabian society appears obvious. To finance sardine-fishing with the great *jarīf* trawl-net, in which forty men or more will be engaged there is the *rubbān al-barr,* or « captain of the shore » in Ḥaḍramawt — and I suppose this type of fishing on the Trucial Coast is operated in the same way. The fish-traps of al-Baḥrain which are often rented from Shīʿah trusts are hired out to « farmers » (*ḍāmin*) who themselves may be financed by a *jazzāf,* a sort of fish-merchant. The « Pearling Law of al-Baḥrain » which I have recently translated, although it has been modified in certain respects under British influence, yet contains customary law that is ancient, for al-Bīrūnī in his *Kitāb al-Jamāhīr* alludes, though vaguely, to the finance of pearling ventures by the merchants, not the diving-crews. The modern document is almost entirely concerned with regulations regarding the advances to the pearling crews, safeguards for the financiers and crew, and procedure for the transfer of services of crew under obligation through advances of money, from one *nawkhudhā* to another. The *nawkhudhās* themselves, i. e. the ship-captains, are in debt to the *ṭawwāsh* or pearl-merchant. I might say in passing that Persian Gulf pearl-merchants also come to Socotra Island where there is a small fishery. The period of service in most cases is fixed according to the star-calendar — in Southern Arabia they use the 28 star-periods — the Mansions, but the pearlers, though essentially the principle is the same, designate their pearling season by special names. We have also the Nairūz reckoning at sea, which commences, now-a days, about the 6th of August — one counts the days from it until the closure of the sea — i. e. after the two monsoons have ended. In the south end of the Persian Gulf they appear to count from Suhail, commencing from August 25th. On parts of the Trucial coast they use for navigation and fishing a calendar composed of 10-day periods, each known as *darr,* and this system was known to Ibn Mājid.

Navigation

It is only of quite recent years that the works of Ibn Mājid, Sulaimān al-Mahrī, and others have begun to be thoroughly investigated. With the publication of a translation a great deal of detailed information will become generally available, but the texts, being technical and written in conventional near-classical colloquial Arabic, are not always easy to interpret. When I worked through some of them with retired *nawkhudhās* at al-Ḥāmī E. of al-Shiḥr in 1964 I discovered that, as they said themselves, the art of navigation had declined among them and they were not acquainted with certain aspects of navigation of which he treats. The *nawkhudhhās* of al-Ḥāmī simply use Norie's nautical tables, and many of the nautical tables they compose themselves are based on these. Ibn Mājid of course speaks of the Portuguese and indicates that the Arabs had learned from them, and in Gulf Arabic Portuguese words for parts of the dhow are current to this day, but it was especially in the XIXth century that Arab knowledge of the art declined. I also found that the works of the well-known modern Kuwaiti *nawkhudhā*, al-Quṭāmī, were to be found in al-Ḥāmī. Sea-faring people on the coast know the name of Ibn Mājid as a great *nawkhudhā* but the only place I have seen any of his works was in al-Baḥrain. Ibn Mājid flourished around 1500, but the conventional form of his navigational poems indicates that the tradition is very much older, to be connected indeed with the genre that I have called « route-poems » by which travellers in Arabic remembered the sequence of villages and natural features between one point and another — these go back to the Xth century and no doubt much earlier. The tradition still holds, for Shaikh Muh 'Abd al-Qādir Bā Maṭraf produced for me two route-poems — one Saiḥūt-Zanzibar, the other Muscat-Mocha and we had these explained to us by *nawkhudhahs* in al-Mukallā. They may be 200 years old, the author being a certain Bā Ṭāyi'.

The *Nā'ib* of al-Mukallā told me that mariners consider there are three dangerous places in the Arabian sector of the Indian Ocean — Rās Fartak, Rās al-Kalb, and Rās Ḥāfūn, south of Cape Gardafui. If ships are voyaging together *sinjār* — in convoy — from, say Basrah, they may break convoy by mutual agreement and part company when they pass Fartak, for then dangers from the sea are considered past, and every ship is eager to be the first to arrive in port and to be able to give the news of the expected arrival of other vessels. Bā Ṭāyi's poem has a verse alluding to the celebrations that are customarily made when one has passed this point, and to this day sailors make what they call a *fawlah* — a festivity (*farḥah*) with drums, at which they sing *zāmils* opening with the words *yā fawlah, yā fawlah*. The sailors get themselves up in a sort of fancy-dress and engage in horse-play (*li'b*). The *nawkhudhah* gives them presents, and the passengers collect money among themselves to give to the sailors.

When the Basrah dhows arrive at al-Ḥāmī persons (often fishermen) will come out in canoes (hūrī) to meet them — the dhow gives these the news of the coast, the prices of dates, how many ships are still to come, and how many passengers there are and who they are. Often a runner (*mikattib*) will carry this news to al-Shiḥr by land. The canoe-man (Arabic *muwāfī*) may be given an ornament by a woman on shore to go out to an incoming vessel and bring back news — he returns the ornament to her and she gives him 2 or 3 shillings. When dhows are delayed women may perform the *tajlūb* ceremony, gathering outside their houses about 9-10 p. m. to sing *tajlūb* songs to the accompaniment of drums, and this may continue until the small hours of the morning. These songs are prayers to God to bring the dhows home safely — they start with the conventional phrase — *yā jalaib ya 'l-mujallib*.

On arrival at a large port like al-Shiḥr flags are unfurled, and guns are fired. From a log-book of my friend Bā Maṭraf's grandfather we discovered that in 1884 he stopped at Difaiqah to take on gun-powder (*bārūt*) to fire in al-Shiḥr *bandar.* Al-Shiḥr besides being a celebrated port on the old India trade-route is also a centre of local distribution and in fact the tribes do not call it al-Shiḥr but simply al-Sūq, the Market. It is also an important fishing centre and depot for the export of salted fish to the Far East.

To return passing to the *fawlah* festivity which sailors make after Rās Fartak, I must quote Ibn al-Mujāwir who states that when a vessel arrives opposite the town of Socotra this is called *fawlah* — presumably meaning as it does nowadays « deliverance from danger », an earthen pot is taken and a sail, rudder and ship's gear set upon it, and food is placed in it — a little coconut, salt and ashes, and it is thrown into the sea. I think that Ibn Mujāwir, good observer as he was and most unusual in his reportage, frequently misunderstood what he saw or reported it inaccurately, for Ḥaḍramīs told me what corresponds closely to his report but supplements it and shows its significance — when a vessel arrives at Rās Ḥāfūn, from Africa, they told me, the crew prepare a coconut for the Jinn and send out little model boats for the Jinn to pacify them — after this there is *fawlah,* i. e. *salāmah,* safety. Sometimes in return for a safe arrival they sacrifice an animal. At Rās ʿAṣīr or Gardafui the sailors place some food in a little box and throw it into the sea so as to ransom themselves from the wrath of the Jinn who inhabit the mountains of Gardafui; they do likewise when they pass by Rās al-Kalb or the islands of Salāmah and its Daughters in the Red Sea. Ashes are commonly used in Ḥaḍramawt where it is wished to exclude or drive away the Jinn.

In former times then there was much ceremony attached to voyaging, as also of course religious practices too, and even now the *nawkhudhah* is considered a man of a certain consequence. In olden days he used to wear fine clothes and the *ʿimāmah Dabwānī,* a turban of Indian weave with a red stripe along the edges.

Convoy-Sanjarah

Though I have not attempted to hunt out the references in Arabic literature, such as the geographies, to the travelling of vessels in company it seems self-evident that this custom is ancient. The mediaeval Arabic almanacs from South Arabia, which I hope some day to publish, give exact dates for the periods in which each trade-fleet arrives at Aden, be it from East Africa, India, or Egypt though it is not stated that they come in a company.

The technical term for travelling in company is *sanjarah,* and one speaks of a *safīnah sinjār,* a vessel travelling as a partner in convoy with another, the two vessels undertaking to render certain known obligations to each other. The word *sinjār* is also to be found in Swahili, and I suspect it derives ultimately from the Persian word *zinjīr,* a chain — Ferrand has shown that there are many words of Persian origin current in the technical vocabulary of Arab navigation, and *sinjār* could have been a term current even in mediaeval times though it is not to be found in the lexicons. The master of a vessel would ask for *sanjarah* from another vessel under four circumstances :

1. When voyaging on the high seas.

2. Voyaging at a season (*mūsim*) outside the customary season for sea-travel.

3. Sailing through parts of the ocean known to be infested by pirates.

4. At times when the vessel has some defect or damage to it and it would be dangerous for it to voyage alone.

If a vessel passes another ship at sea and one of them hails the other to ask for *sanjarah* it is obligatory for the latter to assent, or at least so said one informant. It is the seaman in charge of the fore-part of the vessel, who is usually also the chief of the sailors, who hails the other vessel with the demand for *sanjarah*. At the pitch of his voice he shouts, *Sinjar-nā bi 'l-salāmah ...salām!* To which the crew of the second vessel reply, « *Salām* » or rather « *saloowm* » as they pronounce it. The serangs of the vessels then take up the parley as they draw alongside, exchanging news, and explaining the causes that made the first vessel ask for *sanjarah*. If the crew of the second vessel did not reply with a « *salām* » to the first this would imply refusal to agree to sail in convoy with it, but I imagine that as a matter of honour the request could hardly be refused.

The *sanjarah* consists of the ships sailing in company in line formation — hence I suppose comes the idea of a chain — the Persian *zinjīr* — if I am right. Should any untoward happening befall one of the vessels then the other must stop in order to assist it. Its attitude was described to me as very similar to that of the *sa'īf* (classical Arabic *rafīq*) on land, the companion of the road or escort who is bound by customary obligations to look after his fellow. The faster vessel must keep the sail of the slower one in sight by day, and his lamp in sight by night. It must stop at the *'aṣr* part of the afternoon to allow the slower one to come up with it. One vessel must supply any help required by the other in the way of gear, such as ropes, etc., or provisions (*zuwād*) or drinking-water if these should be short. If at sea one ship catches fish but the other does not, then the fish are divided equally, a division from head to tail (*qismah min al-rās ila 'l-dhail*), but, if there are four ships sharing, you do not cut the fish up lengthwise after the first division.

Firearms are still carried on these vessels against pirates who still seem to carry on their predatory actions against traders off the northern coasts of the Yemen and in some of the Red Sea islands off the Yemeni coast. These firearms normally remain in charge of the *nawkhudhah*, to be issued to the trusted fighters among the sailors if a pirate attack threatens. When attacked by pirates the *nawkhudhah* and his crew are specially concerned to protect the helmsman (*al-sakūnī*) around whom they place wooden beams to avert the bullets. The *nawkhudhah* takes all the weapons from the passengers who come on the board ship and keeps them under his own charge in a safe place — for instance, I imagine, in older times, in the famous brass-bound chests of the Indian Ocean now so much sought by collectors. These chests are not used now but plain wooden boxes only and I have noticed that the *nawkhudhahs* always keep them locked.

If a captain wishes to terminate the agreement of *sanjarah* he must send a *ma'lūmīyah,* i. e. a notification to the other vessel, and if the latter refuses to end the arrangement the first captain cannot unilaterally abrogate it.

Sometimes a vessel will infringe the laws of *sanjarah,* or perhaps it is sea-law in general, by passing by its sister ship on the port (*jawsh*) side — so called from the tack-rope on that side — it is all right to pass on the starboard (*dimān*) side known as *dābirah* — passing on the port side is known technically as *murūr mākhirah.* It is an insult (*'aib*) to do this, and if another vessel passes by you in this way, you will be a laughing-stock to the shipping fraternity. There is a rather similar law where fishing vessels are concerned. When two vessels fall out and quarrel about anything, a third vessel will judge the case between them, or else they will go the port or *bandar* and take their case to the authority there. As one informant put it, « if you disobey the laws of the *sinjār* you go to the *bandar* and the judgement (*ḥukm*) is given by the Amīr al-Baḥr who consults with the *nawkhudhahs* on the issue and gives his judgement ». So then the Amīr al-Baḥr will doubtless act in accordance with the traditional customary law of the sea. Nowadays in Ḥaḍramawt, if the offending party does not accept the decision it passes to the local *qā'im* for him to enforce its execution.

The Ship's Company

From Arabic and Perso-Indian sources we already know something of the composition of the dhow-crew, besides which a number of Europeans like Henri de Monfreid, Alan Villiers and others have given us instructive accounts of life on a dhow. On the South Arabian coast the crew is called *al-jazwah.* The table which follows shows the crew with their functions in order of seniority — more or less — and the shares in the proceeds of the voyage to which they are entitled:

1. *Nawkhudhah,* the Captain : 3 shares;
2. The *Serang :* 2 shares;
3. *Sakūnī,* helmsman, in accordance with his capacity : 1 1/2 or 1 share;
3. *Qabḍī,* helmsman's assistant, in addition to his ordinary share as a seaman : 1/4 share;
4. *Baḥḥār,* seaman (12-24 in number) : 1 share.

But the *baḥḥār* who climbs the mast-head to watch for land, or dives into the sea when something has happened to the anchor, receives an additional quarter share;

5. *Ṣughaiyar darak,* the captain's cabinboy, according to his capacity : 1/8 or 3/4 share;
6. *Ṣughaiyar qurṣ,* i. e. the boy who gets his bread, who serves the crew, receives no share, but the *nawkhudhah* gives him some clothing, and gifts to his family ;
7. Store clerk (probably called *karrānī*) : 1 1/2 shares;
8. *Ṭaḥḥān,* boy who grinds grain for the crew : 1/2 to 3/4 share.

The navigator, known as *al-mu'allim* or *al-rubbān,* is employed on the ship by special contract to make the voyage from al-Shiḥr to India or other ports

— I do not think you find one on every dhow — his wage for a single return-voyage would be between 600 to 1,000 shillings. While on board ship the crew are fed free upon rice, millet, dates, coffee-berry, oil, salt, and spices; they take the fish they need from the sea. Sweet water is only carried by the vessel for drinking, coffee, and cooking. The sailors bring it from the shore, and in some places they have to pay for water — a place where one can put in to water is called *mamzar.* One curious piece of information given me was that all sailors take with them cloth for a shroud and other necessities for burial so that they can be properly consigned to the deep should death overtake them at sea.

After deducting the cost of the crew's food and other trifling expenses the profit for the year is divided as follows — firstly half to the owner, from which he deducts a share which he gives to the *nawkhuhdah.* Even if the owner and *nawkhudhah* are the same person he receives one share in addition to his three shares. Out of the owner's share comes all the cost of repairs and replacements. Thus reports Badr al-Kasādī, but there are slightly differing reports from many places — though Djibouti seems to have much this order of the crew. Advances (*taqādīm*) are of course deducted, and a percentage is taken toward the payment of a man's debt (*qarḍah*).

The crew are allowed to carry free of freight (*nawl*) charges for disposal on their own account :

1. From Basrah : 2 *qawṣarahs* (baskets) of dates;
2. From al-Sawāḥil : *kīs ṭa'ām,* a sack of grain (probably millet);
3. From Aden : *ṭa'ām,* grain, or half a sack of rice, or coffee (*qahwah*).

The *ṣughaiyar qurṣ*, a small boy, only brings water to the crew, and hot charcoals (*jamrah*) for the water-pipes. They shout to him for it and he replies, « *hawallah* ». At the end of the voyage he receives a shirt and 10 raṭls of dates. The *ṣughaiyar darak* is older and cooks the bread — 1 round (*lubbah*), called on land *kisrah,* for the night, and half a round for breakfast. This is very little so he cooks extra bread for his friends and hides it. The crew try to find it and appeal to higher authority but if the boy knows in time he throws it overboard — he hides it in the *mawfā* or oven — but if caught he is punished. His duty is that he bales (*yizlakh*). He does not grind the grain, this is done by the *ṭaḥḥān.* He also looks after the boat that takes the crew on shore and must fetch them from the shore. He will be about 15 years old, but he shares in the *suhūmīyah*, the sharing out of the annual profit.

Discipline

The *nawkhudhah* is respected by the crew though no obligations of one to the other appear to be specified. The *nawkhudhah* deals with disputes and offences on his ship and possesses authority over the sailors and passengers without interference from the land authorities even when his ship is in port. If he is unable to cope with affairs on account of sickness or absence the serang takes over after him, the *sakūnī* or helsman. Typical offences are fighting (*miḍrābah*), theft, or trouble with the passengers. Preparatory to settling the dispute, the two parties at loggerheads will be tied to the mast by the sakūnī, and the *nawkhudhah* will give his decision. The guilty party will be confined in the *bandūl*, i. e. the place where the bilge-water is collected. A member of the crew may be sentenced to beating (*raskh*) while tied to the mast, and each member of the crew may be required to give him a blow with the rope when going forward or himself be beaten. He may be fined, or his advances may be withheld, or if he refuses to obey orders he may be dismissed — in such case he is required to pay back loans or debts even if to do this he is obliged to sell his house or his women's ornaments.

There are two sorts of loan — the loan made to the sailor before the voyage commences and before the beginning of the maritime year — this is called *qarḍ(ah)*, and there are the advances made to the sailor during the actual voyage called *taqdūm* (plural *taqādīm*). The maritime year starts about the 20th of August (*Suhail* I suppose) and ends about May, after which comes the closure of the sea (*taghlīq al-baḥr*) on account of the stormy weather. If for any reason a sailor transfers his services to another vessel the owner of the second vessel will deduct 15 % from the man's share to repay the advances and loans made to him by the original owner with whom he engaged to serve. This is similar to the arrangements made by pearl-divers and their captains in al-Baḥrain and elsewhere in the Persian Gulf. If the *nawkhudhah* should dismiss a man — which he has of course the right to do — for any cause but refusal of orders, he cannot compel him to repay his advances and debt if the man has not earned enough to cover these sums. A sailor will not be accepted for another vessel if he does not produce a statement of what he owes and what is due to him — these statements are given at the close of the maritime year. This arrangement is identical with that of the pearl-divers in the Gulf.

The Broker, Dallāl

In Southern Arabia the *dallāl* or broker acts as an intermediary between the tribes and the market-folk and even between one tribe and another in quarrels that may take place between them. But he also acts as the intermediary between visiting dhows and their ports of call — so there are *dallāls* in every port on the routes, such as Basrah, Muscat, the Gulf and the Arabian coast, frequented by the South Arabian dhow-masters. I might say in passing that the *dallāls* are an interesting group and I have accumulated a considerable amount of information on how they operate. At the present day the people of each place (*baldah*) customarily have a known *dallāl* in each big port — the people of Ṣūr of Oman, the Mahrah, and the Yemenis each have one in ports like al-Mukallā, but if cause should arise there is nothing to stop them from going to a different *dallāl*. In Mogadisho or Barāwah on the Somali coast one can deal with any *dallāl* one likes. Ibn Baṭūṭah tells us that at Mogadisho young men come out with a dish of food which they present to a merchant on the incoming vessel. The merchant accepting such a gift stays with the giver who acts as his broker in all transactions of buying and selling. Now although Ibn Baṭūṭah does not mention the word *dallāl* the function and customs he describes are exactly what the South Arabian *dallāl* follows with the *nawkhudhah,* though if the latter knows a port well he may act as his own *dallāl.* It seems to me that in Ẓufār and the Mahrah ports they preserve the older custom described by Ibn Baṭūṭah, for when a *nawkhudhah* arrives there for the first time, after the usual exchange of news and information as to current prices, the local inhabitants will ask him, « *Man rabī'ak,* Who is your protector? ». The *nawkhudhah* will indicate the person he chooses and the latter then takes him to his house and acts as his *dallāl.* Should the *nawkhudhah* return to the port on a subsequent occasion he is obliged to use the services of the person who first « accorded him protection ». The functions of the *dallāl* include feeding the *nawkhudhah* and his companions in his own house — the expenses of which are added to the *dallāl's* commission. The *dallāl* sells his goods and collects the payment from the different local merchants who purchase them. He also tries to find a new cargo for the dhow. Any samples of goods given the *dallāl* by the *nawkhudhah* are his perquisite and are not returned. He presents his account to the *nawkhudhah* deducting his commission and expenses. At the time of the *mawāsim,* the *dallāl* takes a commission (*khidmah*) from each passenger embarking on the dhow. If the *dallāls* have a dispute with each other they resort to the Amīr al-Baḥr for a decision — he submits the case to advice from experienced *dallāls* or merchants or *nawkhudhahs* who decide it with his help. I should remark in passing that the office of Amīr al-Baḥr in Ḥaḍramawt sometimes passes from father to son.

There is of course a great deal of information in MS *-fatāwā* on commerce which will bring to light many curious practices. Dr 'Abdullāh Maqṭarī informed me of a strange form of raising money in Aden, called *hakbah* which I merely cite as an example of what is to be found. A *hakkābah* is a woman who approaches, say 10 persons, women, to persuade them to undertake to save a fixed sum per month which they deposit with her; every time an agreed sum has been saved one of the savers draws it out to spend, the *hakkābah* taking at each such payment a commission of 10 %.

The Cargo

The *qawṣarah,* which is a palm-leaf basket bag of dates of the type imported from Iraq — a very ancient word, being known to Jāḥiẓ — was formerly used to measure the tonnage of dhows. It is 180 lbs (*raṭl*) or 9 *farāsilahs.* Half a *qawṣarah* is termed *nuṣfīyah.* Nowadays they use the ton as a measure of the capacity of sailing vessels. Of too heavy a load for ships or vehicles one says *hadhā jawr.* Certain limits above which a vessel may not be loaded have been established in international maritime law of our times, but I wonder if this did not already exist in the dhow trade of the Indian Ocean? There are two lines on a dhow — the *zunnār al-shaḥm,* and the *zunnār al-shaḥnah* — the first of these « the girdle of the fat » is a line where the greasing of the hull with fat and lime (*nūrah*) ends — it projects from the ship's side — this prevents the growth of slime on the hull. Between this and the « girdle of loading » is one plank only, and no cargo must be taken on by the vessel after this line has touched the sea (*al-zunnār ṭabb al-baḥr*). Bills of lading — an

Indian word *satmī* is employed — are known as far back as 1412 and might perhaps be traced back much further.

Jettison

If a storm (*ḍarbah*) has continued for 12 or 24 hours, according to which rule is observed, all the sailors and the *nākhudhah* may agree to toss cargo overboard. Some *nākhudhahs* consider it a disgrace to do this and refuse until the crew tie them to the mast and jettison the goods in spite of them. Laws vary on jettison. In Ḥaḍramī vessels if the jettisoned goods bear the mark of the owner then the owner alone stands the loss, but if they bear the marks of a number of owners then the loss is distributed among them according to the number of shares they hold in the goods jettisoned. But the Ahl al-Sūr — i. e. the Omaniṣ, divide the loss among all the persons owning cargo even including the value of the slaves who form the crew and who are the property of the *nākhudhah*, and they do not take owners' marks into consideration. I might remark that when an Omani *nākhudhah* mans a vessel with his slaves he takes all the proceeds of the voyage, but he looks after his slaves like his children, feeds, clothes, and marries them, and they in return fight faithfully for him. In Basrah, Yemen and India, there is a sort of division made called *warār*. An estimate is made of the value of the goods and of the vessel (*sā'iyah*). The goods left are shared out, but the ship only seems to lose the passage-money (*nawl*) and freight-charges (*ḥumūl*) on the goods jettisoned.

Man Overboard

If a sailor or passenger should fall overboard in a stormy sea where it would be dangerous or difficult to save the man the *nawkhudhah* shouts as soon as he hears of the accident, «*al-fātiḥah*!». That is to say he asks the company to recite *Sūrat al-Fātiḥah* for the soul of the man, considering him as already dead, and the ship proceeds on its way. In other cases the vessel is required to make search, within reason, for the man, but if not found it continues on its way and no blame attaches to it.

Salvage

I have translated the South Arabian word *jadḥ* as salvage — and it may be given two categories — the salvage of goods thrown up on the shore, and salvage at sea. Where the land is concerned agreements concluded mainly by Britain or British India have imposed salvage laws on the coastal people, and it is uncertain whether they recognised any rights over goods cast upon the shore other than their own freedom to plunder them at will. Here I ought to interpolate that the word *jadḥ* is used also in a quite different sense. In the Wāḥidī Sultanate they used to *yijdaḥūn* the Somalis who arrived there from Africa — i. e. they used to take protection or escort money (*siyārah*) from them when they came ashore to sell their *Barbarī* sheep. The Somalis who come to collect incense (*lubān*) in the mountains behind the coastal ports of Ḥaḍramawt used to pay Gate tax (*'ushūr al-siddah*) at the port (*furḍah*) on this incense. In Raidat Āl ʻAbd al-Wadūd, the Thaʻyan tribe, the Āl Kathīr, and the al-Ḥamūm used to take one fish in 10 from the fishermen — this they called *judūḥ*. On the Faḍlī coast the Danākil divers for mother-of-pearl used to pay taxes to the Marāqishah of the Coast.

To return however to the question of salvage — it may be a relic of mediaeval custom that the *Nā'ib* of *al-Shiḥr* will order all the able-bodied males to turn out to salvage a ship wrecked on the coast. They go forth at a trot shouting, « *Yā darkaah, yā darkaah, fīnā gharīqah.* It is an *ʻār* or disgrace not to turn out on these occasions. This as I know from my other researches into the organisation of the city wards in Ḥaḍramawt is really fundamental to the functions of the *Ḥāfah* or city quarter which gives communal aid in case of fire, drowning, and collapse of wells or the mud house walls, to save the victims, human or animal. I was told by one informant that if you claim goods cast up on the coast there is no salvage to pay, only *khidmah*, fee to those who have collected it. This does not seem entirely consistent with other statements that the Wāḥidīs take one quarter of good salvaged, and the Quʻaiṭī state one tenth.

At sea the law of salvage seems to be very strict. If, for example, a canoe (*hūrī*) or any gear belonging to a vessel is lost and later salvaged by another vessel, then the latter is entitled to a feast consisting of a lamb and a quarter bag (*kīs*) of rice. If a vessel sees something of ship's gear floating on the sea, it is in duty bound to salvage it and return it to its owner. If the vessel neglects to salvage the gear, then the *nākhudhah* responsible for the negligence is responsible for repaying the value of it, provided of course that it is proven against him that he did this on purpose and that the sea was calm and the wind favourable.

Fisher Law

The customary law of the fishermen of the South Arabian coast does not appear to differ in principle, but only in detail, from one place to another, and then it will sometimes be only the variations imposed by different conditions. One finds however that the stretches of coast to which one particular set of laws and customs applies is distinguished relatively sharply as lying between certain fixed points. Each of these coastal stretches is, as far as fishing is concerned, under the jurisdiction of an *ʻāqil* (headman) or *ʻāqils* who settle fishers disputes.

It is known that the fish of the Arabian coasts have been an important item of commerce from remote times. To take one author among many, Ibn Ḥawqal mentions what one probably should read as *wuzif*, the dried sardines prepared from Ḥaḍramawt round to the Bāṭinah of Oman wherever shore conditions are suitable, to be used for animal fodder and the manufacture of fish-oil. This latter, known as *ṣīfah*, was used for oil-lamps. Dried shark is exported to the Far East and shark-fins to the Chinese market in Singapore and other places. Sardines and sharks are both subject to local taxes. In such towns as al-Shiḥr and al-Mukallā the fishermen sell to retailers *muʻaiyirīn* or *qaṭṭāʻīn*, and their dealings are regulated by local customary law. In al-

Shiḥr one may see what might almost be called a native fish-factory — the *ḥawsh* which I have studied in detail — these factories lie along the sea-front and in their yards fish are dried or smoked.

A very detailed customary law governs the lives of the fishermen but most of it is too technical to discuss here. In many respects their laws resemble those of the dhow-sailors, especially in regard to indebtedness. Certain types of fishing are prohibited at some seasons. Fishing is not permitted at all in some parts of the South at the time when the community should attend the Friday prayer. There seems to be no question of owning fishing-grounds, except for the actual hours of the day that a fishing boat is fishing over them, when certain rules come into force about how near other boats may come to a boat already fishing, and from what direction they may approach it. In al-Baḥrain there are customary laws which prohibit obstacles of any sort being placed in the way of the tide that carries the fish into the *ḥaḍrah* trap.

What I have told you is only selected from the mass of material I have collected, and what I have managed to collect is only a small part of what there is to know about the sea-faring communities of Arabia. The dhow trade will obviously disappear quite soon and with it much that will help us to understand the past — nor will the fishing communities be able to preserve their ancient ways. It does seem worth while to try to record what one can while it is still with us.

ADDENDA

P.195/13 The document is translated in our *Ṣanʿāʾ*, 75–76.

P.197/9 See my "Customary law among the fishermen of al-Shiḥr", *Middle East Studies and Libraries: Felicitation Volume for Professor J.D. Pearson*, ed. B.C. Bloomfield, London, 1980, 193–203.

P.198/17 See my "Ḥaḍramawt to Zanzibar: the pilot-poem of the Nākhudhā Saʿīd Bā Ṭāyiʿ, *From Zinj to Zanzibar: in honour of James Kirkman, Paideuma*, Wiesbaden, 1982, XXVIII, 109–27 & Muḥ. Bā Maṭraf, *al-Rafīq al-nāfiʿ ʿalā manẓūmāt al-mallāḥ Bā Ṭāyiʿ*, al-Mukallā, 1966.

XVI

Omani Naval Activities off the Southern Arabian Coast in the Late 11th/17th Century, from Yemeni Chronicles

INTRODUCTION

Oman and the Yemen during the 10th/16th century had been affected by the irruption of the Portuguese into the Indian Ocean and the development of their great maritime empire. Even earlier, the Yemen had been exposed to the Mamlūk expansion down the Red Sea coast in 1515 – this was swiftly followed by the Ottoman Turks who conquered it as part of their imperial venture, both attracted by the country's reputed riches[1] and to counter the Portuguese blockade of the trade-routes to India. Muscat was early occupied by the Portuguese and strongly fortified. It was an unhappy experience for the Arab population for Mamlūk, Turk and Portuguese were cruel, perfidious and rapacious.

The Zaydī Imāms of the Yemen succeeded finally in expelling the Ottomans from their coastal ports by 1045/1636. A few years later with the capture of al-Mīrānī[2] Fort, or Fort Capitan, by Sulṭān b. Sayf, Oman was able to assert its own authority in Muscat. The Omanis in fact went on to revenge themselves by carrying war into Portuguese possessions in India and East Africa, raiding Bombay, Diu and Mombasa. The impetus of these movements swept along these two dynasties on a wave of acquisition of territories formerly independent or semi-independent. It was almost inevitable they should come into collision.

The Omanis are a maritime as well as an agricultural and pastoral people and their strength lay in their sea-power, whereas the Zaydī Imāms derived their authority and support from their influence with the war-like tribes of the northern mountains – landsmen without a sea-coast. In this respect they differed from the Rasūlid Sulṭāns of Ta'izz of the 13th to mid-15th centuries who were able, through control of the sea, to exert their influence along the southern coast of Arabia to the extent of levying an annual tribute from the coastal ports, Ẓafār, al-Shiḥr and other smaller places, known collectively as Bilād al-Tafārīq (a term also known to later Ottoman documents), havens for the India trade fleet. They even maintained a naval force to combat pirates. The Zaydīs do not seem ever to have built up a navy. Local uprisings brought loss of their sea-ports and thereby loss of revenue, which in turn rendered them unable to pay subsidies and probably played a considerable part in their decline in the late 18th and early 19th centuries.

The clash between Oman and the Yemen first came over Ẓafār province that had been held by petty semi-independent dynasties such as the Ḥabūẓīs and Manjūwīs. But, as the Ḥaḍramī historian, Shanbal,[3] records under the year 807/1404–5, 'Āl Kathīr took Ẓafār and expelled the Sulṭān . . . and Ibn Aḥmad b. Jassār went up to them and they agreed that Ẓafār should be halves between [Sulṭan] Rāṣi' and Āl Kathīr.'

THE KATHĪRĪ SULṬĀNS

The Kathīrī tribe, belonging to the Ḍannah/Ẓannah, rose from historical obscurity, gradually extending their control over Wādī Ḥaḍramawt from Ẓafār. From about the last twenty years of the 8th/14th century they provided Ḥaḍramawt with Sulṭāns, but, following the universal pattern of ruling houses, they soon fell into dispute over the succession. This led to intervenion in their affairs by the great Zaydī Imām of the Yemen, al-Mutawakkil (1054–87/1644–76).

This started with the event recorded by the chronicle *Ṭabaq al-ḥalwā*[4] under the events of the year 1064/1653–4 which states that 'in it Badr b, 'UMAR,[5] Lord of Ḥaḍramawt, al-Shiḥr and Ẓafār, made the Friday address in the name of the Imām (*khaṭaba li-'l-Imām*) and his nephew, Badr b. 'ABDULLĀH,[5] arrested him and his chiefs of state (*kubarā' dawlati-hi*), deposed him from power and placed him in irons.'

This bold statement is amplified a little by a modern historian, Sayyid Muḥammad b. Hāshim.[6] Sulṭān Badr b. 'UMAR, he says, being plotted against by his nephew, tried to bolster up his position by friendly alliance with the Imāms of the Yemen. It was rumoured he had embraced the Zaydī rite and, in 1058/1648, Badr b. 'ABDULLĀH seized him and imprisoned him in Maryamah near Saywūn. At the same time he released his own brother, Ja'far, from prison and made him governor of Ẓafār.

There is a discrepancy of six years between the two accounts, but the date given by *Ṭabaq al-ḥalwā* seems to accord better with the circumstances.

When al-Mutawakkil heard of Badr b. 'UMAR's deposal he wrote in 1064/1653–4 to the usurper instructing him to release his uncle and give him the governorship of Ẓafār. Much correspondence[7] passed between them but Badr b. 'ABDULLĀH ultimately fell in with the Imām's command. Alarmed by al-Mutawakkil's success against the warrior Yāfi'ī tribes he notified the Imām of his submission, promised to give the Friday address in his name and pay the obligatory taxes (*al-zakawāt al-wājibāt*); he also paid him a tax on the revenue from the Indian trade-fleet at al-Shiḥr. A letter[8] from him to al-Mutawakkil dated about 1067/1656–7 contains some interesting details about Ẓafār – it is couched in obsequious terms.

'We own a well[9] in Ẓafār from the time of our father and it belongs to us. From a servant (*khādim*)[10] of ours who oversees it we have heard that Parent[11] Badr (*al-wālid* Badr [b. 'UMAR]), has entered into its (the well's) concern. The reply from us to the servant was that he should leave it to him even though it belongs to us.' He adds that the affair of the well is a small matter to him but Badr b. 'UMAR's place in his esteem is high, and both he and his uncle have properties there come down to them from their families. Badr b. 'UMAR's sons, he says, had left in anger by ship for Mahrah country because of this well and after their departure Sulṭān Badr b. 'UMAR sought protection (*rab'*)[12] from the soldiers (*'askar*) and Āl Kathīr [tribes] and they gave him protection (*rabba'ū-h*).[12] This he did, feeling insecure at the departure of his sons. Badr b. 'ABDULLĀH however emphasizes that he had given his uncle 'complete security'. He had handed over to him bandar Ẓafār, land and sea, plain and hill (*barr-an wa-baḥr-an, sahl-an wa-wa'r-an*),[13] with its high impregnable forts (*ḥuṣūnu-hu 'l-'āliyah al-manī'ah*), except for a few negligible forts,[14] and he had got witnesses to attest to his having done this.

'As you are aware,' runs Badr b. 'ABDULLĀH's letter, 'we send ships on voyage there for gain (*nawāl*)[15] and we purchase frankincense (*lubān*) like strangers,[16] but now, if Parent (Badr b. 'UMAR), God preserve him, wishes we should stop frequenting the bandar with our ships as strangers do we shall leave this off, seeking thereby your goodwill and his, but if he likes us to be among the various sorts of people there is no harm (in that).' . . . 'Our Lord, the Commander of the Faithful, God preserve him, knows that in Ẓafār there are copious running streams (*ghuyūl*)[17] and one fifth (*khamīs*) is collected by assessment[18] from the [land irrigated by] the streams, from which provision is supplied for those who work the incense (*ya'malūn al-lubān*) – this had gone to Parent (Badr b. 'UMAR) before his entering upon this well. It is correct that now Ẓafār in its entirety, the streams and the rest have passed to him.' Badr b. 'ABDULLĀH suggests in tactful terms that the Imām should look into this case.

The affair of Ẓafār was however not allowed to rest and events took a new turn. Badr b. 'ABDULLĀH told his brother Ja'far that since the Imām has snatched Ẓafār from us and handed it over to our uncle there is not sufficient of the country left to us to provide our customary dues (*'awā'id*).[19] This caused Ja'far to betake himself to the Imām's court in the Yemen but he appears to have obtained nothing there so he returned to Ḥaḍramawt and seems to have conspired with his brother to take Ẓafār from their uncle Badr b. 'UMAR, with whom however Sulṭān Badr b. 'ABDULLĀH remained outwardly friendly. Ja'far gave out that he was bound for India and Oman (*jihāt al-Nu'mān*)[20] but collected a number of scoundrels (*awbāsh*) with whose aid he managed by a ruse to enter Ẓafār and occupy its fortress. Badr b. 'UMAR took refuge with some of the Bedu, then moved to the coast where he took ship to Mahrah country and thence to Aden. Arriving at the Imām's court in 1069/1658–9, he was well received and al-Mutawakkil wrote to Sulṭān Badr b. 'ABDULLĀH saying that he was 'at the side of Sulṭān Badr b. 'UMAR and he is of us, so that whatever offences are committed against him are also committed against us.'[21]

THE ZAYDĪ EXPEDITION AGAINST THE KATHĪRĪS IN ḤAḌRAMAWT

Al-Mutawakkil now resolved on mounting an expedition against Ḥaḍramawt,[22] al-Shiḥr and Ẓafār, appointing as general his nephew, Ṣafiyy al-Islām Aḥmad b. al-Ḥasan. The Zaydī forces caried out a remarkable campaign across difficult and dangerous country through territories held by warlike tribes. They proceeded from Mārib and Bayḥān to Aḥwar on the southern coast and thence by Wādī Daw'an to Wādī Ḥaḍramawt, arriving in the western part of the wādī in Sha'bān 1070/about mid-April, 1660, from which they entered its towns one by one. Ṣafiyy al-Islām was accompanied by Badr b. 'UMAR and the latter's nephew Sulṭān Badr b. 'ABDULLĀH came in to tender his submission to the Zaydī and was sent to Ṣan'ā'.

Al-Jarmūzī[23] reports that Ṣafiyy al-Islām heard that the Lord of Ẓafār, *i.e.* Ja'far the Kathīrī, had called in the people of 'Ahl Nu'mān', 'their rite being that of the Khawārij[24] who dislike the People of the House (the Sayyids), on them be peace, but they also dislike the people of al-Shiḥr on account of their sinful actions (*ma'āṣī*),[25] and they overcame this afore-mentioned Ja'far over Ẓafār.' The modern author, al-Jirāfī,[26] confirms that Ja'far, in 1070/1660 had sent an invitation to the Omani Amīr Khalaf[27] to enter and take Ẓafār. Ja'far in fact seems to have conducted himself badly for he had confiscated goods belonging to merchants of al-Kunj or Kung, a little to the north east of Lingeh, which he tried to sell in the Yemen as his own property. In general it may be surmised from the tone of the histories that for a local ruler to defraud merchants in ports on the southern trade route would affect the interests of the lords of the other ports which derived revenue from the Indian trade fleet and shipping from the Gulf.

Ja'far's letter had provided a way out of a serious difficulty for the ruler of Oman. Letters from Sulṭān al-Hind and Sulṭān Fāris[28] had been despatched to Ṣāḥib al-Nu'mān, as the Yemeni historians call him, instructing him to attack Ja'far al-Kathīrī – or else you will be at war with us! While it was a grave matter to disobey those monarchs it was awkward for him to attack Ẓafār which had come, however remotely, under Zaydī suzerainty. Now the Omani ruler could claim justification for taking Ẓafār.

In Ḥaḍramawt, after setting things to rights, Ṣafiyy al-Islām found himself in an uncomfortable even dangerous plight. The produce of the country was inadequate to provision his troops.

The Imām moreover had instructed him to leave their customary dues (*'awā'id*) to the Ḥaḍramī sulṭāns and accept submission, outward obedience and adherence (*i'tizā'*) 'to this Muḥammadan state and 'Alawī group'. His horses, camels and money were nearly exhausted and he had long been awaiting supplies from the Imām but he realised that the latter was unable to send him adequate supplies because of his own preoccupations nearer home in the Yemen.

Al-Nu'mān[29] (*i.e.* the Omani Amīr) in Ẓafār, after ejecting Ja'far al-Kathīrī, wrote to Ṣafiyy al-Islām to the effect that Allah had empowered them over this misguided fellow. 'We have expelled him from this bandar and you have discretion (*taṣarruf*) over him and us.' The Omanis made a show of obedience, and Ṣafiyy al-Islām 'replied approving what they had done, (adding) that what was wanted was to clear the land of the like of such a nefarious character (*fāsiq*) as this – or whatever he actually did say'. 'Had he wished to attack them,' says al-Jarmūzī,[30] 'he would have been unable to do so on account of the great distance between Ḥaḍramawt and Ẓafār, for it is about eighteen days for the post (*barīd*) and it would be more than a month for baggage (*athqāl*) since these are deserts with little water'. He would also have needed supplies which would have had to be collected from Ṣan'ā'. So he accepted outward obedience from them. It was easy for al-Nu'mān to obtain supplies for his soldiers. After making arrangements in Ḥaḍramawt Ṣafiyy al-Islām returned from Saywūn to Ṣan'ā'.

Ja'far would of course have won the Imām's displeasure for displacing his uncle Badr b. 'UMAR, but, at the close of Ramaḍān, 1071/about the end of May, 1661, Badr b. 'UMAR and Ja'far came to an understanding and the latter asked his uncle to mediate in obtaining a safe-conduct from the Imām. Later in the same year we find Ja'far arriving with the Faḍlī Shaykh[31] at the Imām's court.

At the close of Rajab, 1073/about early March, 1663, the Amīr of Ẓafār, acting for the Omani ruler Sulṭān b. Sayf, is reported by *Ṭabaq al-ḥalwā*[32] to have been in a confused and disturbed situation, for 'That stronghold (*ma'qil*) continued to be (like) a gash in their throats and a black flag in their market because, in relation to Ḥaḍramawt and Oman it occupies the place of the centre (bead) in a pearl necklace and they [the Kathīrīs] were considering Khalaf (the Omani Amīr) to have intruded upon Ẓafār'.

They (the Kathīrīs?) made raids on Khalaf, killing about forty of his men whom he had sent to demand accession to (certain) demands. So Khalaf fled by sea, leaving only two cannon in Ẓafār. Sulṭān Muḥammad b. Ja'far the Kathīrī entered Ẓafār, changed its statutes[33] and laws and transferred the (Friday) address to be conducted in the name of the Zaydī Imām (*baddal qawānīnahā wa-'l-aḥkām, ḥawwal al-khuṭbah li-'l-Imām*).

The Omani (Sulṭān) was vexed at this news, saying that he had sent his Amīr to this 'wretched district' in response to the appeal of the Kathīrī only (*talbiyah li-dā'ī 'l-Kathīrī*) for 'with our ample dominion and victorious state (*dawlah*) we have no need of this country'. It may be that the author of *Ṭabaq al-ḥalwā* is here drawing on Sulṭān b. Sayf's letter, written several years later, to supply an appropriate reaction on his part to the bad news from Ẓafār.

At this point it is necessary to establish the identity of the Omani Sulṭān or Ibāḍī Imām who was responsible for the action against Ẓafār and subsequently the maritime actions against Zaydī ports. S. B. Miles[34] has indicated that 'there is much discrepancy concerning the date of the death of the Imām Sulṭān b. Sayf'. He cannot have died in 1059/1649 as some Omani historians maintain since the Yemeni *Ṭabaq al-ḥalwā*, unconscious of any controversy, dates his famous letter, translated below, to 1080/1669, and it might conceivably be as late as 1090/1679 as given by Sir Edward Ross.

Sulṭān b. Sayf, for reasons unstated, took no action for a number of years to recover Ẓafār and engaged in no hostilities against the Kathīrīs or their overlord the Zaydī Imām – very likely he was fully occupied with affairs elsewhere. Nor do the Yemeni chronicles consulted record any interest taken by the Zaydī Imāms in Ẓafār until, towards the end of Dhu 'l-Qa'dah 1079/early summer, 1669, al-Mutawakkil despatched the shaykh Zayd b. Khalīl to govern Ẓafār of

Ḥaḍramawt. He arrived in al-Shiḥr and sent his son there and, after that, his first lieutenant his *mawlā*, al-Ḥājj 'Uthmān b. Zayd arrived at the Imām's court.[35]

OMANI NAVAL ACTIVITIES OFF THE SOUTHERN COASTS

For over a decade the *Ṭabaq al-ḥalwā* now records Omani raiding along the southern coasts and into the Red Sea to Mocha. While the Omanis were animated in part by their hate of the Portuguese they also sought plunder. This was an age when the Indian Ocean swarmed with pirates. For the Yemenis security of the shipping using their ports seems to be more important than considerations of religion or race; as already stated, the Imāms had need of the revenues from the customs at Mocha and Aden.

'At the new moon of Dhu 'l-Ḥijjah, 1079/about May 3rd, 1669,[36] the Omanis appeared off the coast of Aden and Mocha to plunder. They accomplished their aim by attacking three large dhows (*jilāb*),[37] these being such belonging to the Furanj (Franks)[38] as had arrived at the Gate[39] of the Harbour (Bāb al-Furḍah). The Franks defended their property and a number of them perished, slain. The Nā'ib of Mocha was unable to repulse them on account of their numbers, for they arrived in seven large ships (*birāsh*),[40] although he had brought in voluntary help (*ghawā'ir*)[41] from Zabīd and elsewhere against them and petitioned a reinforcement of picked troops from the Imām, but they did not arrive until the (Omanis) had already gone, with such property as they happened (to take). The bandar became unsafe (*ḍa'ufa*) because of this sortie (*khārijah*)[42] and some of the vessels took themselves off to Juddah. . . . At the close of Dhu 'l-Ḥijjah/May news arrived that the Omanis, on their return journey had reached the borders of the coast of Mahrah country, then entered and plundered it. They laid waste (*'āthū*)[43] the island of Socotra, robbed it, seized its shaykh, brought their sharp swords to drink of his head and returned, may God disfigure them, to their country.'

'In 1080/about June, 1669, a group of those Omanis passed by (*ṭāsha*?)[44] to Jīzān on the track of the vessel of Bā Yazīd[45] because it had bypassed Mocha. So they followed it in expectation, on their part, that they would return with it, but it gave them the slip (by going on) to Juddah. The people of Jīzān fled from them when they put in (to it). Then they left it, what they supposed having proved false.'

A month or two later after this event news from Ḥaḍramawt arrived in the Yemen that twenty large vessels (*barshah*) of the Portuguese had raided to Oman in retaliation for the Omani assault on Diu the previous year – in which some Muslim merchants had lost their property.

THE LETTER[46] OF IMĀM SULTĀN B. SAYF TO IMĀM AL-MUTAWAKKIL OF THE YEMEN AND HIS REPLY

In Rabī' I, 1080/August, 1669, a letter from 'the king of Nu'mān', Sulṭān b. Sayf, arrived at al-Mutawakkil's court. While al-Sālimī merely prints the letter and the Zaydī Imām's reply without introduction, comment or date, the *Ṭabaq al-ḥalwā* places the letter in its historical context and also, incidentally, provides the evidence that Sulṭān b. Sayf was still flourishing at this date.

Couched in the rhymed prose and ornate epistolary style of the age the precise sense the writer wishes to convey is not always easy to determine, and on a number of points I am not quite certain of the translation. In its English rendering the style is inevitably sometimes clumsy. The texts differ only on minor points – the text followed is that of *Ṭabaq al-ḥalwā* but where al-Sālimī's readings have any significance they have been inserted between square brackets.

From the Imām of the Muslims, Sulṭān b. Sayf [b. Mālik], Head of the Arabs, the Ya'rubī, [the Arab, the 'Umānī] – to the Apogee, the August Majesty, the Heroic Noble Ismā'īl b. al-Qāsim, al-Qurashī, al-'Arabī.

To proceed –

[Here follow the customary introductory praises of God]

If, dear friend, you ask about us and desire to learn of us exactly how our condition is, we are, by God's grace, in a condition whereby a person affected (to us) will be rejoiced but the envious vexed.

Then, may you know, (Honoured King and Exalted Lord (Sayyid)) that, over a period of days already elapsed and months already pierced,[47] there reached us a man from Your Majesty averring that, by his hand, you sent sheets containing pearls consisting of your superlative words and speech, but he says that the vessel in which he came was rendered unseaworthy by wreck and foundered at sea, so that sentence of destruction befell the written sheets[48] there. However he has restored[49] them to us through what his tongue produced and, from his clear utterance and exposition, it has become plain to us that you reproach us and are angered with us because of the interception last year by our servants of the [ships of] the Polytheists [themselves][50] at your Gate (Bāb),[51] and because they seized their ships which were proceeding to Your Majesty.

By my life, we know that reproach between friends is the preface to sincere love and affection and increased genuine sincere amity and good faith, though this must be (accompanied) by avoiding the commission of offences and violation of the inviolable. For our part we have followed[52] no path to committing those things, nor do we find you have evidence to attach the commission of such things to us, seeing that we did not despatch our vessels and prepare our hooks[53]for a ship[54] of your subjects, nor to plunder people under your rule and authority, but despatched armies and soldiers and made ready keen cutting swords to destroy the idolaters[55] and foes of (God) the Conquering King, by way, on our part, of seeking the favour of the Lord of the Universe and revivifying the Sunnah of his Trusty Prophet, being desirous of obtaining the reward/virtue of those who endure, fighters of the Holy War.

Far be it from such as you to be angered at combatting idolaters and foes of God and Islam! Are you not of the stock of 'Alī b. Abī Ṭālib who gave the Polytheists poisoned potions to drink. You are aware of the bloodshed, the many violent assaults and the plundering of possessions and property, the one by the other, that took place formerly between us and them on the Oman coasts, as well as other places and countries. Indeed we seize them everywhere their vessels put in and to which they come, even of Kung and Gombroon[56] the Shah's two ports, without his evincing reproach or disapproval of us on this account.

Certainly, o King, we remind you, for reminding profits the Believers,[57] and 'we are of those who warn you'[58] and of those who warn you to take care, that when we took possession in those days of the town (*balad*) of Ẓafār, though it is remote from us by waterless and barren deserts, we saw no virtue in retaining possession of it for any thing that scrutiny on our part deemed essential and that sense and reflection could relate. So we abandoned it – not out of fear of a conquering force or clear unity[59] against us, vanquishing hands or robbing palm.

At the time when our governor, Khalaf, withdrew from it he left behind some cannon of the Muslims, through negligence on his part[60] to transport them at that time. When you took the nose-ring of its strong she-camel[61] and looked upon the shining of its full moon and sun you did not hand those cannon over to us – just as if they had no one behind them to ward off and defend (them). You must be aware, o King, that the husband is jealous, the lion crushes, and the free man is forbearing over anything but insult! He who warns is exonerated and whosoever gives warning is not acting treacherously!

Yet, notwithstanding, we seek to reconcile the difference between you and us, being desirous of preserving your friendship, extinguishing dissensions and chosing to suppress hatreds[62] between you and us. If you desire what we desire and want what we want, give them back, God bless you,[63] to us, and do not sip, through swiftness of aggression, the outburst of wrath (occasioned by) it.[64] If (on the contrary) you refuse aught but the course of appropriating them as a prize, and so to go lampless at night (thereby losing your way), freedom of action and power lie in seeking the help of God. Whosoever is with God, God is with him.[65] Peace upon you and the mercy of God.

The reply[66] of Imām al-Mutawakkil, or, as al-Sālimī calls him, the King of Ṣan'ā', follows.

From the Sun of the Lofty Heavens of the Caliphate and site whereon the pavilions of the Muḥammadan Sharī'ah are pitched – to the distant land[67] of the Ruling King, Sulṭān b. Sayf b. Mālik al-Ya'rubī, the Arab, the 'Umānī, may God show him the way of guidance[68] and let him avoid the road of error and deviation.

To proceed –

God's praise, blessing and peace be upon His Trusty Prophet and His Legatee, the Valley-filling Torrent, the Large-bellied[69] whose sword harvests the heads of heretics.[70]

Your letter which you have charged with thunderings and lightnings has arrived, and in which you have turned away from setting the reproach to rights to (enter into) rude declamation, from presumption on your part that your babble of threats and the buzzing of flies of your menaces would shake one solid rock of our might or stir one lofty mountain of our dignity. But how could that be (when)

Upon our swords, in all East and West,
Are dents from the clash with mailed men.

Where has your contentiousness taken (you) so that you demand the cannon from us with these false tales and *baqāqi'* (?).[71]

Things coveted only get men's heads cut off. Do you not know that the lion when excited against its prey is more violently audacious, bolder and more resolute? Certainly it is because your lands and ours are far distant and countries intervene between us that you have given free rein to your tongue and gone beyond your limit in low estimation (of us) and (because) you are segregated in your land that you seek to thrust and do battle alone.

O you who tread among the keen swords
and spears,
I sniff the smell of blood upon you.

So cut off the ties of your aspirations to these cannon for, if God will, they are the first booty from your remote province. You have summoned us to accept the decision of the edge of the sword and blade of the spear, (but)

Wait a little and battle/the she-camel on heat
will come up with the camel.

We belong to those people who, on the Day of Nahrawān,[72] gave your people to drink of the cups of death, and you are the successors of those who were made to drink. By what our ancestors started with your forbears we shall put a terminus to whomsoever remains. Peace.[73]

Commentary

The sectarian differences of the Ibāḍī and Zaydī schools of Islam are clearly reflected in the language of the letters. Both rulers are styled 'Imām' by their sects, yet neither addresses the other by this title. Sulṭān b. Sayf does not even address the Zaydī ruler by his adopted title, al-Mutawakkil, but simply as 'August Majesty'. He describes him as al-Qurashī al-'Arabī, but makes no allusion to his descent from the Prophet, though he does cite his ancestor 'Alī b. Abī Ṭālib as a worthy model for him. Both rulers use the title 'King' in addressing one another. They follow the Sunnah or the Sharī'ah.

Al-Mutawakkil is incensed at the violation of Mocha by Omani vessels attacking the Portuguese there. This Sulṭān b. Sayf rejects, pointing to the Omani policy of attacking the Portuguese wherever they find them. From other sources we know that this attitude did not extend to the Dutch and other Christian powers.

The *Ṭabaq al-ḥalwā* scorns Sulṭān b. Sayf's assertion that Khalaf left Ẓafār at his Lord's wish. If so he would not have left the cannon behind. In point of fact, he says, 'He only went out of Ẓafār through the unexpected attack upon him by the Kathīrī Sultan's army (*bi-mā dahima-hu min jaysh al-Sulṭān al-Kathīrī*).' He informs us that al-Mutawakkil ordered the two cannon to be released, but adds that the person in charge of the reply to Sulṭān b. Sayf was not really fitted to do so and he remarks snidely on the promotion that kings (unwisely) give to clerks (*kuttāb al-inshā'*). Probably for this reason he does not quote the text of the reply but it is given by an anonymous marginal commentator who thinks that the author of the *Ṭabaq* takes an extreme view of the writer who is, he adds, the very learned Qāḍī

Aḥmad b. Ṣāliḥ b. Abi 'l-Rijāl,[74] of the well-known family of scholars.

If Sulṭān b. Sayf's letter is outspoken and quick to rebut al-Mutawakkil's charges with vague threats it nevertheless offers the possibility of conciliation. Al-Mutawakkil's rejoinder on the other hand is couched in aggressive and, to an Ibāḍī, highly offensive terms with references to 'Alī's action to suppress the Khawārij in language reminiscent of such accounts of the latter one finds in early writers like al-Mubarrad.

THE DECLINE OF ZAYDĪ INFLUENCE IN HADRAMAWT: PORTUGUESE AND OMANIS IN THE GULF OF ADEN AND RED SEA

In Rajab, 1080/late November to December, 1669,[75] 'a violent sea battle fell about between the Omani and the Franks. In its initial stages the wind of victory was with the soldiers (*jund*) of the Omani, then the Frank rounded on them and killed about two hundred of them – the rest were routed. Then the Franks settled to making havoc (*ya'ūthūn*) for some days until such of them as did came out to Mocha'.

'This year the people of Ẓafār revolted, killing seventeen of the best of the Imām's men, and the Amīr of the state (*al-dawlah*),[76] the son of Shaykh Zayd b. Khalīl, was besieged but held possession of it. The Imām's consideration (of the situation) came down on the side of sending his slave, al-Ḥājj 'Uthmān b. Zayd, to Ḥaḍramawt for the lieutenancy (*li-'l-niyābah*) of it. Shaykh Zayd b. Khalīl recalled his son from Ẓafār and they came out together to the court. As for Ẓafār one of the Kathīrī Sulṭāns (al-Dawlat al-Kathīriyyah) gained mastery over it, relying ostensibly on the Exalted Court (*al-Ḥaḍrat al-'Aliyyah*). The Imām had offered the governorship of the country of Ḥaḍramawt with its appanages to his nephew Sharaf al-Islām al-Ḥusayn b. al-Ḥasan but he refused this on the advice of his brother Ṣafiyy al-Islām [Aḥmad b. al-Ḥasan], so he sent one of his officers (*muqaddam*),[77] but no objective of his was achieved.'

At the end of Dhu 'l-Ḥijjah, 1080/about May, 1670, 'the governors of Ẓafār and Ḥaḍramawt arrived at the Imām's court and he cast the dice (?*qara'a 'l-dast*)[78] in favour of the kings of it (Ḥaḍramawt), Āl Kathīr, and none of the Imām's governors remained except the faqīh Amīn al-Dīn al-Qurashī in al-Shiḥr, and when the Imām perceived that the age was not conducive for initiating an expedition (*takhrīj*) against those far regions he passed them over to the governorship of Sulṭān 'Alī b. Badr, making him the blaze on its [Ḥaḍramawt] brow, apparently conferring a benefit upon him, and pretended to forget it entirely'.

Of this Sulṭān, 'Alī b. Badr, Muḥammad b. Hāshim[79] tells us that the Qarā tribes were not in complete subjection to the power of Ẓafār and by their natures liked their freedom, so that the governors of Ẓafār had often to turn a blind eye to their rebelliousness (*tamarrud*) and had to take to wheedling them. 'Alī wanted to subdue and conquer them but in the end he had to make peace with them along the lines they wished and after that the Āl Kathīr governors had no firm footing in Ẓafār. Little by little the power of the Zaydī Imām in Ḥaḍramawt, al-Shiḥr and Ẓafār declined until all that remained to him was the address (*khuṭbah*) in his name in all the Jāmi' mosques.[80]

To return now to the Yemen, al-Jirāfī[81] says that 'in the year 1081/1670–1, a large body of the Christians of the Portuguese arrived at Bāb al-Mukhā and announced to the governor (*ḥākim*) Sayyid al-Ra'īs al-Ḥasan b. Muṭahhar al-Jarmūzī[82] that they intended to declare war on him because he had not defended them against the people of Oman in the past year so that they attacked them. Indeed a body of the Portuguese did advance from Qal'at al-Faḍlī which is now ruined, but the force from around the guardposts (*min ḥawl al-makhāfir*)[83] faced them and the Portuguese fell back on their ships and were compelled perforce to return to their country. Then at that time commenced the construction of the Mocha forts (*qilā'*) as a protection for the town against the recurrence in future of such an event'.

In 1082/1671 the *Ṭabaq al-ḥalwā*[84] reports that the Franks, presumably the Portuguese, entered Socotra of the Bilād al-Mahrah and (the Mahrah) made a truce with them through inability to fight them and they settled (*sakanū*) in a place of it called Qishn (on the Arabian mainland). The Imām intended to send the Shaykh Zayd al-Hamdānī on an expedition against them, but he heard of Muḥammad Shāwūsh's expedition from Egypt to Mecca and abandoned the idea.

In 1083/1672–3[85] news arrived of a truce between the Lord of Oman and the Portuguese (Burduqāl), and he found relief from their afflictions.

In 1084/1673–4,[86] 'letters arrived from the Mahrī, Lord of the island of Socotra and the Ḥaḍramī coast lying between al-Shiḥr and Ẓafār appealing for the Imām's regard (*yastad'ī 'īnat al-Imām*) and (stating) that he had already resolved upon taking him as Imām (?*al-i'timām*)[87] and that his reason for this seeking of a link with him was that, in the past, some of those men of the Omani who had come to the coast of Socotra island had plundered it'. He had fled to the coast of al-Shiḥr, 'and the Amīr of the Omani had entered his country but not managed to get hold of what he had hoped since he (the Socotri) had taken with him what he had and those with him'. He laid all that pertained to him before the Imām. But the Imām was advised to deal with more important matters, 'for the Mahrī has only made proposals to you in order to cure this ache!' The Imām in fact had plenty of his own troubles in the Yemen itself.

Possibly because of the settlement with the Portuguese the Omanis seem to have been free to raid the Yemen once more. During the last ten days of Dhu 'l-Qa'dah, 1084/9th March onwards of 1674,[88] 'news came to the Imām that the Sulṭān of Oman had despatched an expedition of large ships (*birāsh*) to Mocha and his mind became preoccupied with this along with trouble (*fitnah*) coming in that had taken place between Āl 'Ammār and Duhmah, as well as the disturbed state of the 'Awlaqī and his independence on his own'. This was followed by news coming to the Imām in Muḥarram, 1085/early April, 1674, that 'the Omani's men (*aṣḥāb al-'Umānī*) had newly acquired Socotra island this year, killing a group of its inhabitants in cold blood. These days the Oman people made havoc (*'āth*) at sea and their large ships followed the Bāniyān (Hindu vessels) to Bāb al-Mukhā and hastened to plunder them, tossing a number of them into the waves, but the people of Ṣīrah and Aden rose[89] against them and forthwith fired muskets and zebratanas at them. These scoundrels (*awbāsh*) were routed and the rest of the large ships joined up with the routed party until they (re-)assembled at Bāb al-Mandab with munitions and soldiers – after which they held up comers and goers. Ṣafiyy al-Islām's victorious[90] troops (*junūd manṣūrah*) fired at them and his son, al-'Izz, aided him with his victorious army[91] until God quenched their keen swords and exterminated them by the swords of the Angels to the last man. Praise is God's'.

'In Ṣafar, 1085/May–June, 1674,[92] the Imām despatched his slave the gallant (*fatā*) 'Uthmān [b. Zayd] to bilād al-Shiḥr of the coasts of the land of Ḥaḍramawt at the head of three hundred of the soldiery (*'askar*) and entrusted him with preserving the bandar from the Omani from apprehension of such (attacks) as had already come from them (the Omanis).' 'News arrived this year[93] of the wreck of a large Omani vessel (*barshah*) off the coast of Aḥwar as its crew were returning from the Aden coast. Most of its crew perished with its cargo – those who were saved came to the coast and the Aḥwar people robbed them and killed some of them.'

In Shawwāl, 1086/approximately late December, 1675,[94] 'news arrived that the Omani's large dhows (*jilāb*) had put to sea, containing soldiers (*'asākir*)'. Several events are recounted by *Ṭabaq al-ḥalwā* which then goes on to say, 'During this time the arrival of the Omanis at Bāb al-Mandab was confirmed so Ṣafiyy al-Islām Aḥmad b. al-Ḥasan hastened to despatch Sayyid al-Ḥasan b. al-Ḥurrah at the head of a body of able men (there ?) and to despatch Ibn Madhbūr to Jabal al-Faḍlī.'[95] This coincided with news of troubles with the 'Awlaqīs and Duhmah.

In al-Mutawakkil's last year (1087/1676) the vessels arrived at bandar Mocha with a present from the Emperor Awrangzib for the Imām and a gift (*ṣadaqah*) for the Ashrāf of the Yemen[96] – which is perhaps some indication of his standing. *Ṭabaq al-ḥalwā* also remarks, rather cryptically, that the Omanis, come to complain (*al-shākūn*)[97], left the Imām's court for their country in a cordial atmosphere (*'alā wajh jamīl*) but he did not accede to their actual demands. After the accession of his successor the Ḥaḍramī Sulṭān is recorded[98] to have sent a gift to the Imām and delivered his allegiance (*bay'ah*).

No troubles with Omani raids are mentioned by *Ṭabaq al-ḥalwā*[99] until the close of Rabī' I, 1090/about May 11th, 1679 when 'the first of the Indian vessels arrived at Mocha – the Omani's men had intercepted them at Bāb al-Mandab and tithed/taxed them (*'ashsharū-hum*) there'. This seems to imply a change in the policy of the Oman sea-rovers from piracy to the exaction of protection money – unless perhaps they were simply not in sufficient strength to attack them. A little later, in Jumādā I/June 10th to July 9th) of the same year,[100] 'news arrived from the governor (*'āmil*) of Aden, Shaykh Rājiḥ, in which he said that a vessel from Masulipatam (Māsh līf tān) had arrived off the Aden coasts and that its crew were afraid of the Omani's soldiers (*jund*), so they sent to him at dead of night to reinforce them with men and aid them with brave men (*abṭāl*). He did as they said, and when the vessel was fixed up with the Indians and those troops (*junūd*) aboard it they had scarcely time to think after daybreak before the Omani's soldiers pounced on them in astonishing guise and set to dragging the vessel with grapnels (*kalālīb*) – whereat disaster overwhelmed them for they did not realise that the affair has already been decided by night and that the bullets of destiny were skirmishing with them. "And they called out and it was not a time of flight." [Qur'ān, XXXVIII, 2]. This business of theirs resulted in the slaying of twenty-five men and rout of the rest. So when the Omanis realised their powerlessness and the Pleiades (al-Thurayyā) rose at dawn, they returned by choice and perforce to their country. God's is the praise'.

In the Mss. and printed books used I have found no further allusions to Omani naval action off the Yemeni coasts. Al-Mahdī Aḥmad b. al-Ḥasan was strong enough to send an expedition over the sea from Mocha to take Zayla' in 1107/1695–6 and must have had some control over the seas in this area, but it could be that the Omanis, being increasingly concerned with East Africa, lost interest in operations against Yemeni ports.

A *qaṣīdah* composed by Khalaf b. Sinān al-Ghāfirī on the conquests of Sulṭān b. Sayf is quoted in part by al-Sālimī.[101] These include Mocha on which the poet puns. 'So, too, in Mocha he sucked the marrow of their bones (*Ka-dhā fī Mukhā qad imtakhkha min-hum a'ẓuman*).' He turned away with a number of their ships (*aflāk*) which looked like mountains: at Bāb al-Mandam[102] much blood (shed by the Omanis) was unavenged, much property taken. 'There is history of these raids,' says al-Sālimī, 'which has not been collected in books (*dafātir*).' It would be interesting to have versions of the events described by the Yemeni chroniclers here, from Omani sources.

APPENDIX 1

The important issue of security for the Indian shipping using Yemeni ports may be appreciated from measures[103] taken by al-Ṣafiyy subsequent to Hubert Hugo's assault in 1078/1662 on vessels at Mocha as recounted in my *Portuguese* (122 seq). In this the Omanis were not involved.

When al-Ṣafiyy arrived in Aden the merchants of India came to him and he treated them with friendliness, giving them places of honour and precious gifts. During the two months he stayed in Aden two vessels put in there, one called al-Sawākinjī (margin, Kunh sawā ī), and the other al-Markab al-Ṣāḥibī, *i.e.* the Queen of Bijapur, Barī Ṣāḥibah's vessel. These were the largest that ever put in to Aden – each with a cargo of 400 bales (*bandalah*) and 1,500 persons.[104] So large was each bale that the Gate of the Harbour (Bāb al-Furḍah) was not wide enough to admit its passage and they could only be brought in by the Coast Gate (Bāb al-Sāḥil). The Indians prepared a feast for Ṣafiyy al-Islām and his entourage the like of which they had never experienced, but on discovering to their dismay that it was prepared by the Bāniyāns, the Barāhimah, they vomited it up! When the 'Īd arrived Ṣafiyy gave a splendid and varied banquet to his chiefs to which the notables of the Indians were also invited. He inspected the port (*al-bandar al-sa'īd*) and found much of it in poor state, so he collected builders (*'ammār*) from Yāfi', the Yemen and Ṣan'ā', and rebuilt the walls.[105] When this was completed he sent for the chief men of the Indians to whom he made presents, 'for each *nākhūdhah* a horse, and he wrote to the Sulṭān, the Lord of India, and sent one of his men along with them with five noble Arab horses and their trappings, gear ornamented with silver, and a gift similar to this to the ministers. Then he sent to the Lord of Barr al-'Ajam (the African coast), the Lord of Ẓafār, the Amharī and the Lord of Ḥaḍramawt, and established regulations (*qawā'id*) for the people of those countries to which they assented, and (confirmed?) demands which they named.'

Ṣafiyy al-Islām's actions may be interpreted as intending to conciliate the India merchants and to promote good relations. It would have been interesting to know what were the regulations that he established, and perhaps they may have been part of some generally recognised body of maritime customary law but this is an open question.

APPENDIX 2

To Mr St.John Armitage who knows Ẓafār/Dhufar as it was during the reign of Sultan Qaboos's father, very well indeed, I am indebted for the following valuable notes on the production and trade in frankincense and the part played in this by Āl Kathīr and Bayt Kathīr, (writer's transliteration retained).

'The main marketable frankincense production comes from Qara territory. In 1956 the Sultan told me that the best production of *luban Najdi* came from 'behind', to the north and north east of Taqa where Jabal Qara and Jabal Samhan meet. Except for some very poor incense near Raisut, all the incense grows at an altitude of 2,000–3,000 feet; there are poorer quality gums at lower altitudes.

Al Kathir in Dhufar are mainly settled cattle owners who have a kind of enclave in Qara territory in Wādī Girziz between Salalah and the Najd. They are assimilated into the mountain life and very distinguishable from Bait Kathir. They and the Qara own most of the incense groves. However frankincense also grows in Bait Kathīr (the nomads who, with the Rawashid are 'Aiyal Hamdan of Āl Kathīr) territory, mainly the higher reaches of the wadis on the northern slopes of Jabal Qara. The Bait Kathir tribes roam these wadis westward to Habarūt (except for Bait Musan of Bait Kathir who have the plains to Mugshin and sands to Ghanim).

Now:

(*a*) Some Bait Kathir also own and collect frankincense. Its sale used to be the bonus which would buy their rifles and other luxuries.

(*b*) Some Bait Kathir also rent groves from the Qara as do the Bait ash-Shaikh (the Mashayikh) – the rent used to be half the produce. The Baniyans from Salalah would purchase the Qara's portion, even by marked tree (a custom which may have ceased).

(*c*) Qara, Al Kathir (including Bait Kathir) and Mahrah (settled in Dhufar) gather incense. The owner of the tree gets ten per cent of the value of the crop. Also a few Rawashid (Al Kathir) used to come to Dhufar for the frankincense collection season, *i.e.*, the summer months before the monsoon.

(*d*) the Al 'Amr (as they call themselves) are an offshoot of the Bani 'Amr of Oman and hold sway from Murbat to Hasik. They are much involved in the incense trade from Murbat. The latter was of course always of importance as a trading port because of its proximity to the Qara/Samhan groves. (I think that people from Murbat used to participate in the collection.) The recent war put the emphasis on Murbat as the main incense centre at Salalah's cost.

So, whilst I feel sure that the Al Kathir have had a place in the market because they have the *luban Najdi* area of their own and access to the Qara's crop, they do not have a monopoly – unless times have changed of course.

The *ghuyul* are, or rather were, open running streams developed from the *'uyun* (springs) of Rizat Girziz, *etc.*, but, in living memory, only Rizat was used for irrigation – of Sa'id bin Taimur's gardens at al-Ma'amurah and now, I think, at the Royal Farm. However the scale upon which two of the *ghuyul* once irrigated land between the RAF camp and the hills can still be seen from the air.

Al-Hafah, the village in the west between Salalah and al-Balid, ruins, was probably an important anchorage. I have heard Taqa referred to as Bir Taqa and there is a Qara connection, Bait Ma'ashani, with incense.'

NOTES

[1] *Cf.* Salih Özberan, 'A Turkish report on the Red Sea and the Portuguese in the Indian Ocean (1525)', *Arabian studies*, London-Cambridge, 1978, 81–88. 'Should it be conquered it would be possible to master the lands of India and send every year a great amount of gold and jewels to Istanbul.'

[2] The other fort is al-Jalālī.

[3] Quoted from my unpublished edition of his *Tārīkh*, but see Ṣāliḥ b. 'Alī al-Ḥāmid al-'Alawī, *Tārīkh Ḥaḍramawt*, Juddah, 1388/1968, I, 684, quoting Shanbal. Rāṣi' b. Duways is of the Āl Yamānī Sulṭāns.

[4] *Ṭabaq al-ḥalwā wa-ṣiḥāf al-mann wa-'l-salwā*, of Sayyid 'Abdullāh b. 'Alī al-Wazīr, Chester Beatty Ms. no. 4097.27 b.

[5] Since the two Kathīrī Sultans are both called Badr capitals are employed for the father of each to make the distinction between them a little clearer.

[6] Sayyid Muḥammad b. Hāshim, *Ḥaḍramawt; tārīkh al-Dawlat al-Kathīriyyah*, Cairo, 1367/1948, 70. Only limited reliance can be placed on this history.

[7] The correspondence is reproduced *in extenso* by al-Jarmūzī, *al-Sīrat al-Mutawakkiliyyah*, Ms. in the Sulṭān's Library, al-Mukallā, for which see my *Portuguese off the South Arabian coast*, 2nd ed., Beirut, 1974, 112.

[8] *Ibid*, 213.

[9] A *bīr* in Ḥaḍramawt means the land attached to the actual well.

[10] In Ḥaḍramawt the *khaddām al-nakhl* is the labourer who looks after a palm plantation; perhaps this is what is meant here.

[11] *Al-wālid* is apparently used as a title of respect.

[12] *Rab'* in this sense is not attested in the lexicons, but in C. de Landberg, *Glossaire daṯînois*, Leiden, 1920–42, 1074, *rabba'a* = protéger, as also in Ḥaḍramawt.

[13] These are clichés of a type that figures in local legal documents.

[14] *Ḥuṣūn* are also used as dwellings.

[15] Dozy, *Supplément*, salaire, solde. Landberg, *Études Ḥaḍramoût*, Leiden, 1901, 728, ce qu' on reçoit, bénéfice.

[16] That is, presumably, without any special concessions.

[17] In the Yemen a *ghayl* is often an underground channel like the Persian *karīz*, *qanāt*. At Ghayl Bā Wazīr in Ḥadramawt there are also underground *ghayls* of this type.

[18] *Wa-ṣurra bi-'l-khurs*. *Cf.* Landberg, *Ḥaḍramoût*, *op. cit.*, 562, *yakhrus al-māl*, taxe, estime la récolte.

[19] Muḥammad b. Hāshim, *op. cit.*, 70.

[20] *Ibid*, 71. Yemeni chronicles frequently use al-Nu'mān for Oman. This is probably derived from the Nu'mān district of al-Barkā' where there is a castle, Bayt Nu'mān, built by Bil 'Arab the Bū Sa'rar, near the coast. *Cf.* S. B. Miles, *Countries and Tribes of the Persian Gulf*, London, 1919, under Naaman.

[21] *Ilā jānib al-Sulṭān Badr b. 'UMAR fa-huwa ilay-nā wa-inna 'l-wāqi'fī-hi min al-jināyāt 'alay-nā*.

[22] Al-Jarmūzī, *op. cit.*, 225 seq.

[23] *Ibid*, 258.

[24] *Ṭabaq al-ḥalwā*, 24 a, describes the Ibāḍīs as holding the tenet (*qawl*) that the imāmate has no specific rank/principle (*manṣib*) – on the contrary it is suitable (*ṣāliḥah*) for all people along with piety (*taqwā*) as Nashwān and the Khawārij hold. *Ibid*, 18 a–b, describes other tenets of the Khārijī-Ibāḍīs. Ibāḍīs reject the view that they are Khawārij. See Sālim b. Ḥammūd b. Shāmis al-Siyābī al-Samā'ilī, *Aṣdaq al-manāhij fī tamyīz al-Abāḍiyyah min al-Khawārij*, ed Sayyidah Ismā'īl Kāshif, Cairo, 1979, Ḥamīd b. Muḥ. b. Ruzayq, *Sīrat al-Sādah al-Bū Sa'īdiyyīn*, ed. 'Abd al-Mun'im 'Āmir and Muḥ. Mursī, Cairo, 1397/1977, 508, where it is stated to the Shāh of the time, 'We are not the Khawārij. The Khawārij are the extremists (*ghulāt*) of us in ancient time. We have separated from them in ancient and modern time.'

[25] These would include such as are mentioned by al-Jarmūzī, 257, the open sale of wines (*khumūr*) in al-Shiḥr *sūqs*, upon which the Kathīrī Sultan collects a tax (*qānūn*). He alludes also (216) to (musical) instruments, usury (*ribā*), which the Zaydīs attempted to abolish, and (256) the involvement of the Kathīrīs in Ḥaḍramawt with usury.

[26] 'Abdullāh b. 'Abd al-Karīm, *al-Muqtaṭaf min tārīkh al-Yaman*, Cairo, 1370/1951, 162.

[27] Al-Jarmūzī, 258, calls him 'Āmir b. Aḥmad.

[28] *Ibid*, *loc. cit.*, the Moghul Emperor and the Shah?

[29] *Ibid*, 259.

[30] *Loc. cit.*

[31] *Ṭabaq al-ḥalwā*, 45 b.

[32] *Ibid*, 49 a–b.

[33] *Qawānīn* might be 'duties/taxes' here rather than 'statutes'.

[34] *Op. cit.*, I, 214.

[35] *Ṭabaq*, 78 a.

[36] *Ibid*, 78 b.

[37] *Cf.* my *Portuguese*, *op. cit.*, 135, sing., *jalabah*, but perhaps this is too restricted a description.

[38] The vocalisation is that of the Ms. These are the Portuguese.

[39] See my *Portuguese*, 123, plate 7 showing Mocha Road about 1720. I am inclined to identify the Gate (Bāb) with the mooring place between the ends of the two capes. The plate does however show an actual Gate to the town. It has not been possible to identify it from E. Macro, 'The topography of Mocha', *Proceedings of the Seminar for Arabian Studies*, London, 1980, X, 55–66.

[40] *Cf. Portuguese*, 134. A *barshah* is a large ship, but it can also mean a galliot, long covered boat.

[41] It is suggested that this word means *ghārah*, syn., *najdah*. *Yā ghāratah* is the exclamation used in calling for help, and *ghawwar* means to call for help. *Cf. Ṣan'ā': an Arabian Islamic city*, London, 1983, 145.

[42] This sense has no lexical support.

[43] Or 'made havoc of'. *Tāj al-'arūs*, *afsada wa-akhadha bi-ghayr rifq*.

[44] *Ṭabaq*, 79 a, has *ṭāsa*, and Jīzān is restored from a word transcribed without diacritics.

[45] Bā Yazīd will be a Ḥaḍramī.

[46] *Ṭabaq*, 80 b seq.; E. Griffini, *Rivista degli studi orientali*, Roma, 1910, III, 912, no. 119, *Kitāb Ṣāḥib 'Umān ila'l-Imām al-Mutawakkil 'ala 'llāh Ismā'īl b. al-Qāsim, al-Imām Sulṭān b. Sayf*; printed in Nūr al-Dīn 'Abdullāh . . . al-Sālimī, *Tuḥfat al-a'yān bi-sīrat ahl 'Umān*, Cairo, 1347 H., II, 56 seq.

[47] *Takharramat*, used for the rhyme, a little difficult in the context.

[48] Reading the printed *al-ṭurūs* for *Ṭabaq*, *durūs*.

[49] Reading *afā'a-hu* for *afā-hu* of al-Sālimī.

[50] Perhaps to be translated as 'the Polytheist slaves', by way of insult to them.

[51] Bāb al-Furḍah ?

[52] Al-Sālimī has *naqṣid* for *nasluk*.

[53] *Reading nattakhidh* with al-Sālimī. By 'hooks' he probably means grapnels, but *makhālib* also means claws, talons.

[54] *Sayyārah*, a deep sea vessel. Al-Sālimī's *yasārah* appears corrupt.

[55] S. B. Miles, *op. cit.*, I, 214–5, alludes to the profusion of images looted or smashed when the Omanis entered the church at Diu.

[56] *Ṭabaq* has a word without diacritics which could be read as J m b rūh; this would agree with the Turkish *Jahân Numâ* which calls it 'Gumrû'. Al-Sālimī reads Jīrūn. G. Le Strange, *Lands of the Eastern Caliphate*, Cambridge, 1930, 319, Jirūn (*sic*) is an island near Old Hurmuz. Gombroon is modern Bandar 'Abbās.

[57] Qur'ānic diction though not Qur'ān.

[58] Qur'ān, XXVII, 92, *Inna-mā anā min al-munadhdhirīn*.

[59] This is to understand *kalimah* in the sense of *kalimah wāḥidah*; *ẓāhirah* rendered as 'clear' can mean 'victorious'.

[60] Al-Sālimī omits 'on his part'.

[61] Al-Sālimī reads *'īs*, tawny-white camels.

[62] Al-Sālimī reads *miḥan*, tribulations.

[63] Al-Sālimī omits the blessing.

[64] Reading with al-Sālimī, *lā taḥtasi*. He seems to mean the wrath that swiftness of agression would rouse in the Omani Sultan.

[65] Al-Sālimī adds, *Wa-ḥasbu-na 'llāh wa-ni'ma 'l-wakīl*.

[66] The text used is al-Sālimī, II, 85.

[67] *Qāṣiyat arḍ*.

[68] This phrase may convey a subtle insult for a Jew converted to Islam is known in Zaydī Yemen as *muhtadī*, guided, and of course al-Mutawakkil would regard Ibāḍīs as heretics.

[69] *Al-Baṭīn*, stout, is an epithet of 'Alī b. Abī Ṭālib in a complimentary sense.

[70] *Māriq*, heretic, as in Sunnī accounts of the Khawārij.

[71] This word has not been traced in the lexicons.

[72] The battle at which 'Alī defeated the Khawārij.

[73] The version on the margin of *Ṭabaq al-ḥalwā*, concludes with blessings on the Prophet, his Family and the Companions. The allusion to the Family, the Sayyids, would seem to have been distasteful to al-Sālimī, being an Ibāḍī, and to have therefore been omitted by him.

[74] Muḥammad al-Shawkānī, *al-Badr al-ṭāli'*, Cairo, 1348 H., I, 59–61, says he was born in al-Ahnūm in 1029/1620 and died in 1092/1681, a well-known scholar and author of a work on biographies of noted Zaydīs.

[75] *Ṭabaq al-ḥalwā*, 82 b.

[76] Local sulṭāns who broke away from the Zaydī Imāms come to be styled *dawlah*.

[77] In Ḥaḍramawt *muqaddam* means a chief.

[78] *Cf.* F. Rosenthal, *Gambling in Islam, Leiden*, 1975, 32–3, *qur'ah*, casting of lots to decide equal claims. *Dast* in Persian can mean 'dice'

[79] *Op. cit.*, 87. He died in 1107/1695–6. Perhaps it was he who had gained mastery over it in 1080/1669.

[80] *Ibid*, 88.

[81] *Op. cit.*, 164.

[82] Author of *al-Sīrat al-Mutawakkiliyyah*. His brother is in Muḥammad . . . Zabārah, *Nashr al-'arf*, Cairo, 1359–77 H., I, 505 seq. *Cf.* note 7 *supra*.

[83] See *makhfar* in Wehr's *Dictionary*. By the 12th century H. Mocha is recorded as having a *tarskhānah*, arsenal (*Nashr al-'arf*, I, 575).

[84] 91 b.

[85] *Ṭabaq*, 96 b.

[86] *Ibid*, 100 a.

[87] Lit., 'to take as a pattern', but the suggested sense seems appropriate here.

[88] *Ibid*, 100 b – 101 a.

[89] Reading *tanaqqaḍa*. Ṣīrah island is of course on the right of Aden Bay and has mediaeval fortifications.

[90] *Manṣūrah* is a conventional epithet for troops.

[91] *Jaysh al-manṣūrah*, incorrectly?

[92] *Ibid*, 102 a.

[93] *Ibid*, 102 b.

[94] *Ibid*, 106 b.

[95] Both these names lack diacritics, but see Qal'at al-Faḍlī *supra*.

[96] *Ibid*, 107 a.

[97] Reading dubious. Imām Sulṭān b. Sayf did however send to Ṣan'ā' for horses and arms for the Muslims though dates for this are not mentioned, and this may explain the presence of Omanis in the Yemen.

[98] *Ibid*, 112 a.

[99] *Ibid*, 122 a.

[100] *Ibid*, 122 b.

[101] *Ibid*, II, 61–2.

[102] A common variant for Mandab.

[103] Al-Jarmūzī, *op. cit.*, 318–9.

[104] Even allowing for the crowding on pilgrim ships this does seem an enormous number.

[105] Some important detail is given on the rebuilding of parts of Aden.

ADDENDUM

P.84/11 The printed *Ṭabaq al-ḥalwā*, Ṣan'ā', 1406/1983, 258, records the Imām's release of the cannon, but without comment.

XVII

NOTICES ON THE "FRANKISH CHANCRE" (SYPHILIS) IN YEMEN, EGYPT, AND PERSIA

It is well known to those who have studied Arabian medicine that there is no clinical description of either syphilis or gonorrhoea in early Arabic medical writings. H. P. J. Renaud and G. S. Colin in their careful study, *Documents marocains pour servir à l'histoire du "Mal Franc"*[1] have cited Dāwūd al-Anṭākī's statement in his *Nuzhah*[2] that syphilis was first seen in Arabia in 807 H. (A.D. 1404–5), but they do not concur with him that this could have been at so early a date, holding that 907 H. (A.D. 1501–2) should be substituted instead, and that his 807 H. is simply an error. Most, but not all of the evidence at my disposal tends to confirm their view. In Egypt, says Dāwūd al-Anṭākī, the "Frankish chancre" (*al-ḥabb al-Ifranjī*) is known as "*al-Mubārak*", "the blessed", or "the lucky"; amongst certain Arabs and in the Hejaz it is called "*al-Shajar*", "the tree". A special type is distinguished by the epithet "*al-Ḍānī*" but my own very clear MS of this treatise reads "*al-Ṣannānī*", perhaps incorrectly. It is a disease, he says, which was first known from the people of Firanjah from whom it was transmitted; people of latter days link it to the Persian Fire (*al-nār al-Fārisī*), but this is simply ignorance.

Ibn Īyās (to whom reference is made at second-hand by the two authors), after describing 903 H. (A.D. 1497–8) as a year of calamity and disaster, adds,[3]

And as if all of this were not enough, a disease called "*al-Ḥabb al-Ifranjī*" (the Frankish chancre), God preserve us from it, spread among the people, the physicians being unable to cope with it, nor had it ever before appeared in Egypt except in the opening (years) of this century, and through it perished an untold number of people.

So, it would seem, the disease, commencing about 900 H. (A.D. 1494–5), rose to epidemic proportions a few years later, though

[1] Institut des Hautes Études Marocaines (Paris, 1935), XXVII, 12.

[2] Cf. Brockelmann, *GAL*. II, 364, *Sup*. II, 491 f. A MS copy of his *Tadhkirah* is also to be found in the Āl Bin Sahl library in Tarīm.

[3] M. Sobernheim, P. Kahle and Muhammed Mustafa, *Die Chronik des Ibn Ijâs*, dritter Teil, Bibliotheca Islamica, V, C (Leipzig, 1936), 386.

nowadays, of course, syphilis would not, in itself, be considered a mortal disease.

Whether it spread to Arabia from Egypt or from some other quarter is not yet known, but only a few years later, in the entries for the year 909 H. (A.D. 1503–4) the Ḥaḍramī chronicler of *al-Nūr al-sāfir*,[1] as also his compatriot Bā Faqīh al-Shiḥrī,[2] records:

In this year the prayer on the *minbar* of the *khaṭīb* continued and his supplication was raised for the removal of the chancres known as the "Persian fire" which had afflicted people (*kashf mā ḥalla bi-'l-nās min al-ḥubūb al-ma'rūfah bi-'l-nār al-Fārisī*). This had been common (*kathura*) in the land of the Yemen, increased, left the people, returned, and continued with them until the first (part) of the year 906 H. (A.D. 1500–1), and subsequently, breasts thereby being straitened and spirits oppressed.

The same chronicle[3] further refers to pestilence at Zabīd in the same year, mostly in women and infants, though it is not precisely stated what sickness this was: again, in 908 H. (A.D. 1502–3) a sickness known as *al-sh m n d lah* manifested itself in Zabīd and Aden and their environs and in the mountains, but this mysterious, apparently foreign word, unknown to the lexicons I have consulted, does not, as far as can be judged, appear to indicate any known venereal disease. It is described as an ache (*rīḥ*) which takes grip of the joints and limbs, preventing any movement for three days, which may be accompanied by fever, then it goes away and one is all right.

The history of the "mal franc" in Egypt whence Egyptian troops or Red Sea merchants and mariners may have taken it to Arabia in the campaigns of the time, is carried a stage further in the section of Ibn Īyās's chronicle in which are recorded Mameluke preparations to capture the Yemen as part of the counter-attack they proposed to launch on the Portuguese who were probing their way around the South Arabian coast and up the Red Sea. Notices of their activities commence with the year 911 H. (A.D. 1505–6), and in 921 H. (A.D. 1515–16) Ibn Īyās says:[4]

On Tuesday the 20th of it (Jumādā I) the Sulṭān disbursed (*nafaqa*) subsistence money for the voyage (*nafaqat al-safar*) to the troops posted to

[1] Ibn al-'Aidarūs, *al-Nūr al-sāfir* (Baghdad, 1934), p. 52.

[2] Fol. 22*b* of my MS, Mukallā MS, p. 52. For this author cf. my *Portuguese off the South Arabian Coast* (Oxford, 1963), pp. 37 f.

[3] *Ibid.* pp. 44 and 51.

[4] Ed. Mohamed Mostafa, *Die Chronik des Ibn Ijâs*, vierter Teil, Bibl. Isl. v. d (Cairo, 1960), pp. 459 and 460.

India. He gave each Mamlūk 50 dīnārs, promising them that he would disburse 6 months' pay (*jāmakīyah*) to them in advance (*mu'ajjal*). It is said that from among them he exempted a number of the sons of (eminent) people (*awlād al-nās*)[1] on account of their complaining of physical debility, or those who had Frankish chancre. He began to make declaration to them publicly, saying, "Any man who is unable to make the voyage on the Salt Sea (*Baḥr al-Maliḥ/al-Milḥ*) should inform me of this and I shall exempt him from the voyage". This was accounted one of his good traits.

On Tuesday the 5th of it (Jumādā II) the Sulṭān disbursed four months' pay in advance to the troops posted to India. There were some of them who complained that they had the Frankish chancre (*al-ḥabb al-Ifranjī*) and were unable to make the voyage, so the Sulṭān exempted them from the voyage, saying to them, "Return the subsistence money (*nafaqah*) you have taken and do not make the voyage". Sometimes he bound (*rassam*) certain of the sons of (eminent) people[1] until they returned the 50 Ashrafīs which they had taken as subsistence money, saying to them, "Any man unable to make the voyage on account of his debility will return the subsistence money and not make the voyage". The total number of these troops enrolled (*kutiba*) for India was about 500 men, apart from the *Tarākimah*[2] sailors (*baḥḥārah*) of the Ra'īs Salmān's contingent (*jamā'ah*).

Something of the social problems created by the introduction of syphilis into Southern Arabia may be realized from a *fatwā* extracted from the collection of the Yemenite *faqīh*, Ibn Ja'mān (ob. 1034 H. (A.D. 1624–5)),[3] who flourished from towards the end of the tenth/sixteenth century well into that which followed. As will be seen below, the authorities he cites belong roughly to the first half of the tenth/sixteenth century.[4]

مسئلة : عن هذه العلّة الّتى ظهرت وانتشرت فى الدّيار اليمنيّة المسمّاة بالحبّ،
وعند قوم بالذِّرْب، وعند آخر بنار فارس، المشهورة بالاعدى[5]، ولو

[1] "Egyptian-born sons and grandsons of emirs" according to W. Popper, *Egypt and Syria under the Circassian Sultans*, Univ. of California Publications in Semitic Philology (Berkeley and Los Angeles, 1957), XVI, 115. *Ibn nās* also seems to be used in the Yemen in the sense of a person of good family at the present time.

[2] It has been proposed to me that *Turkmān* has sometimes the significance of "Ottomans" in Egyptian Arabic texts of this period, a sense that appears appropriate here.

[3] For this author cf. my *Portuguese*, index.

[4] My MS, fol. 270*a*. The *tashkīl*, in some cases the *tanqīṭ*, and the punctuation are mine.

[5] Properly الإعداء.

بعد البرا[1]، إذا وقع فى الزّوج ، وطلبت الزّوجة الفسخ ، هل تُجاب إلى ذالك وَيَسوَّغ لها ، قياسًا على الجذام والبَرَص ، أم بينهنّ فرق ؟ فإذا قلتم : تجاب إلى ذالك . وهل يجب للمدخول بها ، إذا طلبت الفسخ للنكاح بهذا العيب ، المهر المسمّى ، أم لا ؟

أجاب شيخنا رحمه اللّه تعالى : لا يثْبُت بالمرض فسخ النّكاح ، لا بحَضَارة[2] فى العيوب السّبعة ، ولا يلحق بها المرض المذكور ولا غيره . وبه أفتى شيخ مشايخنا العلّامة وجيه الدّين خاتمة المحقّقين عبد الرّحمن ابن زياد ، رحمه اللّه تعالى . وسئل عن ثبوت الخيار به أيضاً شيخنا العلّامة جمال الدّين محمّد بن أبى بكر الأشخر ، رحمه اللّه تعالى . فأجاب بما حاصله أنّ الحبّ الفارسىّ المعروف بالشحر[3] لا يثبت الخيار به فى النّكاح ؛ بل هو كالبَخَر والصُّنَان . ثمّ قال : قلت ذالك مع اطّلاعى على فتوى بعض العلماء بثبوت الخيار ، وهو غير مبنىّ على القواعد المذهبيّة رأسًا — حتّى لو حكم شافعىّ به نقض . (انتهى) وهو صريح فيما أجبت به . واللّه عزّ وجلّ أعلم .

Question: Concerning this malady which has appeared and spread abroad in Yemenite territory, called "*al-ḥabb*" (the chancre),[4] and by some people "*al-dhirb*" (the ganglion), and by others "Fire of Persia", notorious for its infection, even after the cure—when it occurs in the husband, and the wife demands annulment, is her petition complied with, and is it made lawful to her, by analogy with leprosy and white leprosy,[5] or is there a difference between them? Furthermore, if you say, "She is met with compliance in the matter", is a woman who has been penetrated due the dower named (in the marriage-contract) if she demand annulment of the marriage on account of this defect, or not?

The Response of our shaikh, God rest him, was: Annulment of

[1] For بُرْء or بَرَاء, though according to Lane the latter *maṣdar* is used in another sense.

[2] MS بحضاره.

[3] *Sic*, but read *al-shajar*.

[4] One is to understand here "*al-ḥabb al-Ifranjī*". The name *dhirb* may have been given it because the primary chancre is like a nodule.

[5] It is to be remarked that Dāwūd al-Anṭākī, *Nuzhah* (cf. Renaud and Colin, *op. cit.* p. 12) states that *al-ḥabb al-Ifranjī* should be placed after *judhām*, leprosy, perhaps considering that there is some resemblance of one to the other.

the marriage is not validated by sickness, nor by (its) being found in the (category of the) seven defects,[1] nor does the aforementioned disease or any other fall within their category. The shaikh of our shaikhs, the very learned, eminent in the faith, seal of those who have reached the knowledge of mighty verities,[2] 'Abd al-Raḥmān b. Ziyād, God rest him, issued a legal opinion in this sense. Moreover, our shaikh, the very learned Jamāl al-Dīn Muḥammad b. Abī Bakr al-Ashkhar was questioned on the validity of option in this matter (*sc.* annulment), and he gave a response, the gist of which is that option in marriage in the case of the Persian chancre known as "*al-shajar*" (the tree)[3] is invalid; indeed on the contrary, it resembles halitosis and fetor.[4] Then he said, "This statement I make, notwithstanding my having perused the legal opinion of one of the authorities that option is valid, for fundamentally it is not based on the tenets of the sect, so that even had Shāfi'ī (himself) given a decision in favour of its (validity) he would have been controverted" (concluded). It is explicit, in accordance with the response I have given—but God is most knowing.

Ibn Ziyād, cited by Ibn Ja'mān, was a celebrated *'ālim* and *ṣūfī* whose biography is to be found in very considerable detail and length in Ibn al-'Aidarūs, *al-Nūr al-sāfir*,[5] his name being 'Abd al-Raḥmān b. 'Abd al-Karīm...al-Ghaithī al-Muqṣirī (?) al-Zabīdī.[6] He is the author of many legal works as noticed by Brockelmann, and I have myself seen MSS of his legal treatises in Ḥaḍramī libraries.[7] Ibn Ziyād appears to have been at variance in legal questions and quibbles (*mukhālafat wa-mushāḥaḥāt fī masā'il*) with the even more famous Ibn Ḥajar al-Haitamī who flourished from 911 H. (A.D. 1505) to 973 H. (A.D. 1565) or later, while Ibn Ziyād lived from 900 H. (A.D. 1495) to 975 H. (A.D. 1568).

[1] See below.

[2] I have taken *muḥaqqiq* in the Ṣūfī sense cited by Dozy, *Supplément*, though it could presumably mean here one who verifies with precision and exactitude.

[3] The term quoted by Dāwūd al-Anṭākī above, and evidently used in Zabīd also. Al-Anṭākī spent his latter days in Mecca.

[4] Bakhar is the stench of the breath, *ṣunān* is the smell of the arm-pits and creases of the body, as, e.g. in Jāḥiẓ, *Ḥayawān* (Cairo, 1938–47), I, 226, *ṣunān 'araqi-hā* of young goats. Though unaesthetic these defects do not justify annulment of a marriage.

[5] *Op. cit.* pp. 305–14.

[6] Cf. Brock. *GAL.* II, 404, *Sup.* II, 555. 'Umar b. Yūsuf b. Rasūl, *Ṭurfat al-aṣḥāb* (Damascus, 1949) reads Muqaṣṣir/Muqaṣṣar.

[7] In the Āl Bin Sahl Library in Tarīm (cf. "Materials for South Arabian History", I, *B.S.O.A.S.* (1950), XIII, II, 286), I saw *Ḥall al-ma'qūd fī aḥkām al-mafqūd*, and *Fatḥ al-ṣamad 'alā Sharḥ al-zubad*.

Muḥammad b. Abī Bakr al-Ashkhar (ob. 991 H., A.D. 1583)[1] was a pupil both of Ibn Ziyād and Ibn Ḥajar al-Haitamī, the author also of a volume of *fatāwā*, an example of which I noted in 1954 in the *waqf* library of the late Sulṭān 'Alī b. Ṣalāḥ al-Qu'aiṭī in Qaṭn, the end portion being missing. I have speculated whether the allusion in his Response to a difference of opinion with another scholar might not refer to Ibn Ḥajar, but in such works of the latter as I have perused I have not lighted upon this topic.

Ibn Ziyād was of the Maqāṣirah tribe, a branch of 'Akk b. 'Adnān, born in Zabīd where he held office and ultimately died. Though syphilis would first have manifested itself in Zabīd when he was a small child, his *fatwā* itself would most likely have been issued nearer the height of his career when he had achieved rank and authority, and, of course, when the symptoms of the disease itself had become well recognized.

The seven defects which validate the annulment of a marriage are doubtless enumerated in certain of the Shāfi'ī legal manuals but in my MS of the *Mishkāt al-miṣbāḥ, sharḥ al-'Iddah wa-'l-silāḥ*[2] of 'Afīf al-Dīn 'Abdullāh b. 'Umar b. 'Abdullāh Makhramah al-Ḥaḍramī (ob. 972 H., A.D. 1564–5) it is stated that the *arkān al-nikāḥ* include freedom from the defects invalidating option to annul the marriage, these being white leprosy (*baraṣ*), *judhām* (leprosy) which are confirmed, insanity, and weakness of the faculties through the effect of disease (*ighmā'*). These defects in either sex are discussed with reference to the *Ḥadīth* in Ṣāliḥ b. Ghālib al-Qu'aiṭī al-Yāfi'ī's *Maṣādir al-aḥkām al-shar'īyah*,[3] but in Ḥaḍramī manuals on forms of plea,[4] however, only such defects as exist in a woman are cited, and the sole example of a plea which

[1] Cf. Brock. *Sup.* II, 548. His biography is given in *al-Nūr al-sāfir*, pp. 390–404.

[2] MS p. 73. The *K. al-'Iddah wa-'l-silāḥ fī aḥkām al-nikāḥ* is by Abū 'Abdullāh, Muḥ. b. Aḥmad b. 'Abdullāh b. Muḥ. b. 'Alī Abū Faḍl al-Ḥaḍramī, and is apparently unknown to Brockelmann. There is an example in the Āl Kāf Library in Tarīm (cf. *B.S.O.A.S. loc. cit.*). Apart from my own copy of the commentary by Bā Makhramah, there is an example in the Āl Kāf Library at Saiwūn. The author of the *K. al-'Iddah*, a Bā Faḍl shaikh describes himself in the Tarīm copy as being *al-Yamanī al-'Adanī mawṭin-an*. The title of his work is in the nature of an academic pleasantry—*The powder-horn and the gun concerning the laws of marriage*. Brock. *Sup.* II, 972 notes by 'A. b. 'A. al-Hijrānī al-'Adanī a work with the same title as the commentary, Ind. Off. 1724. For the commentary and its author see also *al-Sanā' al-bāhir* (B.M. MS), fols. 327*b* f.

[3] (Cairo, 1948–50), III, 178 f.

[4] Cf. my "Forms of plea, a Šāfi'ī manual from al-Šiḥr", *Rivista degli Studi Orientali* (Roma, 1955), XXX, I–II, 13.

a woman can prefer in favour of annulment is when her husband is unable to support her. Is one to infer that, in practice as opposed to theory, a woman will not seek annulment of her marriage for any other cause?

In Saiwūn about 1954 I purchased a Yemenite medical MS containing three treatises,[1] the first a handsome example of the *Nuzhah* of Dāwūd b. 'Umar al-Anṭākī,[2] the source already drawn upon by Renaud and Colin, the second an anonymous dictionary of medicaments, and the third, anonymous also, a treatise on *al-Nār al-Fārisī*, i.e. syphilis.[3]

The second treatise I have not identified; perhaps it might be an original Yemenite composition,[4] which I doubt, but the third treatise of sixteen folios was transcribed in 1170 H. (A.D. 1756–7), i.e. before the *Nuzhah* along with which it is bound. This latter treatise appears almost identical with the mid-sixteenth-century Persian work, *Risāla-i ātishak* of 'Imād al-Dīn Maḥmūd b. Mas'ūd b. Maḥmūd al-Ṭabīb which I have consulted in Dr Cyril Elgood's translation.[5] Even before the identification I had begun to suspect that my treatise must be a translation on account of the

[1] An annotation on the fly-leaf states that the MS was "nusikha bi-'ināyat mawlā-nā Amīr al-Mu'minīn...al-Mahdī li-Dīn Allāh...al-'Abbās b....al-Manṣūr bi-'llāh...al-Ḥusain b....al-Mutawakkil 'ala 'llāh". The Imām al-Mahdī li-Dīn Allāh flourished between the years 1131–1189 H. (A.D. 1718/19–1775/6). A marginal note on the title-page states that this volume came from the library of the Splendour of the Age, King of the province of the Yemen, the Commander of the Faithful, son of the Commander of the Faithful, al-Mahdī li-Dīn Allāh (*min khizānat bahjat al-zaman mālik quṭr al-Yaman*).

[2] The *Nuzhah* is copied in fine *naskh* hand on gold-sprinkled paper, with ruled margins in red and gold, rubrications, etc., but the two other treatises are written in a cruder South Arabian hand without ornament, apart from rubrications. The paper of all three treatises is similar, watermarked with a vertical line of three crescents. A note states that the MS was transcribed on the 29th Muharram 1173 H. (A.D. 1759–60). Its present fine if rather damaged binding case does not fit it and may have been taken from another MS.

[3] Though, as mentioned above, Dāwūd al-Anṭākī denies the correctness of this term as applied to syphilis.

[4] The anonymous author does however mention, for instance, treatment for "the remains of *ḥabb al-Ifranj* and *al-nār al-Fārisī* commonly known as *al-shajar*". The last being an Arabian term it may be an Arabian composition or adaptation. This stage of the disease is treated by raising the temperature to perspiration point and administering "Chinese wood".

[5] C. Elgood, "Translation of a Persian Monograph on Syphilis", *Annals of Medical History* (London, September 1931), III, no. 57, 405–86. The monograph in question is the *Risāla-i-ātishak* of 'Imād al-Dīn Maḥmūd b. Mas'ūd b. Maḥmūd al-Ṭabīb (B.M. MS Add. 19619).

bad Arabic in which it is couched, containing errors of a type not to be made by a native Arab, but rather by a foreigner imperfectly acquainted with the language. The MS commences:

الحمد لله العلى العظيم . . . وبعد هذه رساله وجيزه فى معرفه انواع النار الفارسى وحب الافرنج وحب الارمنى المسهور بالشحر عند العرب وبالفارسيه اتشك واسامه وطرق حدوثه وعلاماته واسبابه وعلاجاته .

Praise to God. . . . This is a brief treatise on the recognition of the various types of Persian fire and the Frankish chancre and the Armenian chancre known as *al-Shajar* by the Arabs and in Persian as *Ātishak* (lit. fire), its names, incidence, symptoms, causes, and treatment.

He goes on to state that the Persians,

on account of this burning (which accompanies the early stage of the disease) give (it) the name *ātishak*, and they call (it) the chancre of the Franks (*ḥabb al-Ifranj*) because the original place in which this disease appeared was from the land of the Franks, and they (the Persians) call it the chancre of the Armenian, because the Armenians are afflicted with this malady and it is common (*kathīrah*) in their country.

The use of the term "fire (*ātishak*)" may be compared with the slang word "fireship" of eighteenth-century England, but perhaps this was not the earliest term used in Persia. Up to the present it had been considered by writers on the subject that there were no references to syphilis in Persia prior to 'Imād al-Dīn, *c.* A.D. 1550, but Professor Minorsky's publication of a translation of the biography of a certain Sulṭān 'Alī, a celebrated calligrapher, radically alters the position, providing a significant early date for its existence in Persia under its Frankish name. Sulṭān 'Alī says in his poem,[1]

As a consequence of the grievous Frankish scourge
I was crippled by the hand of the pox
For several years without interruption
I was worn out with its complaint
With a broken heart and no trace of strength (in the body).

The poet composed his poem in 920 H. (A.D. 1514–15), at the age of 74 (he died, it appears, in 926 H. (A.D. 1520)). If we consider that his youth, during which he claims to have suffered from the

[1] V. Minorsky, *Calligraphers and Painters* (Washington, 1959), p. 124. I am indebted to Professor Minorsky for the Persian original of the essential passage,

که زدست بلای شوم فرنگ   شده بودم زدست آبله لنگ

pox, lay between the ages of 15 and 40 (though more likely 15 and 30), this gives a dating of 867 H. (A.D. 1462) to 892 H. (A.D. 1486). The importance of this dating, if it be reliable, is that it carries us back before 1493, the year in which Columbus returned from America, whence, according to one strongly supported theory, venereal syphilis is supposed to have been brought to Europe.

"Persian fire" (*nār Fāris* or *al-nār al-Fārisī(yah)*) is in itself no new term, being cited by Dozy[1] from the Glossary to the *Manṣūrī* of Rhazes, i.e. in the late third or early fourth century H., though, at this date, there is no reason to identify it with syphilis. A little later than this the *Mafātīḥ al-'ulūm*[2] defines it in the words, "the Persian fire is swellings[3] filled with serous fluid which come out after itching and inflammation (*al-nār al-Fārisīyah nuffākhāt mumtali'ah bi-mā' raqīq takhruj ba'd ḥikkah wa-lahīb*)". Perhaps then the Frankish chancre was mistaken at first for an ailment already known. Tha'ālibī,[4] who flourished during the latter part of the fourth/tenth century and early fifth/eleventh century, alludes to Persian fire and Balkh ulcers (*al-qurūḥ al-Balkhīyah*). In this last connexion one may speculate as to whether such non-venereal forms as yaws, if existing in the Islamic world at this period, may have been known to medical authors under such names as the Balkh ulcer. Yaws[5] is stated to be common at the present time in parts of Northern Yemen, and I saw what was said to be a bad case of this condition at al-Qārah (the headquarters of the Imām al-Badr at the time of writing); in this case the whole heel was raw flesh and the only cover was a rag and a little string of garlic onions worn round the ankle.

It will be remarked that in all these notices there is no mention of gonorrhoea. Of this strange omission I can offer no explanation, but the very lack of data requires exploration, and notices of it or descriptions would surely be interesting to discover.

[1] *Supplément*, s.v. *nār*, érésipèle, though I should like proof of the identification.

[2] G. van Vloten, *Liber mafâtîh al-olûm* (al-Khwārizmī) (Leiden, 1895), p. 158.

[3] Lane calls *nuffākhah* an inflation of a humour caused by a disease.

[4] De Jong, edit. *Laṭā'if al-ma'ārif* (Leiden, 1867), p. 132.

[5] P. W. R. Petrie and K. S. Seal, *A Medical Survey of the Western Aden Protectorate 1939–1940*, Colonial Office, Middle East no. 66, p. 95 have some notes on yaws in the Yemen and Aden Protectorate. A condition resembling yaws which a European physician described as "Zabīdī syphilis" is mentioned, possibly "Bejel", non-venereal syphilis. It attacks the nose sometimes leaving a gap where the nose was, generally in the second or third decade of life (R. Napier, letter, *British Medical Journal* (London, October 1936), p. 738.

NOTICES ON THE "FRANKISH CHANCRE" (SYPHILIS)

From the Yemen within very recent years, prior, it is true, to the revolution, though it might well survive it, is a strange piece of folk-medicine reported by Muḥammad 'Alī Luqmān.[1] There, he says, syphilis is spoken of as "Father" illness (*maraḍ ab*), its "father" being one of the saiyids in al-Mukhā (Mocha) or a place in the Yemen called Yakhtul. "All that the 'father' does is to buy the disease." He merely advises the sick man to confine himself to dry food (*al-'aish al-jāff*) and sesame-oil (*salīṭ*). This belief, he says, continues to be held, despite the proved efficacy of the treatment with penicillin and 606. Ulcers (*qurūḥ*) generally, he remarks, are cured by onion and garlic skin and *kāt* (*sic* for *qāt*?). My friend Saiyid Muḥammad 'Abduh Ghanem comments that one pays the "*abū*" and he buys the sickness, and that the selling of a disease is a common popular notion.

Stace[2] some sixty years ago refers to Balad al-Muḥibb as a place in the Yemen where syphilis is cured, but Saiyid M. A. Ghanem tells me that there is a *mabraz*, a sort of salon as it were, *mabraz al-Muḥibb*, the present Muḥibb being Saiyid Muḥammad al-Amīn, at Balaksah Street, about two streets south-west of the Za'farān Road in Aden, in the vicinity of the Bā Nuṣair Mosque. The Muḥibb is usually a Saiyid from Mocha who is believed to possess the ability to cure diseases common among fishermen, especially venereal disease. The treatment of the latter usually takes the form of a diet of dates and oil with sandbaths at Ḥuqqāt (Holkat Bay), though, with the recent construction there, that must be difficult nowadays. Saiyid M. A. Ghanem thinks that *Muḥibb* is a special title or surname assumed by the Saiyids from Mocha because they belong to a particular class or ancestry endowed with miraculous powers to cure certain ailments. The present *Muḥibb*, like many if not all of his predecessors, is a Shādhilī.[3]

In the Aden Protectorate syphilis is known as *al-Ṭair*, the bird, and gonorrhoea as *al-Raddah*, though what the origin of these two terms is I am entirely ignorant. Both diseases are very un-

[1] *'Adan taṭlub al-ḥukm al-dhātī* (Aden, n.d., but *c.* 1954–5), p. 41. Among various medical curiosities he describes, a person afflicted with boils urinates on them, and often sick persons drink their urine because in their view sickness is uncleanliness (*rijs*), and only uncleanliness like it can remove it. In cases of smallpox the urine of the afflicted person is poured on his eyes to prevent blindness. The author only speaks of these practices to inveigh against them.

[2] E. V. Stace, *English–Arabic Vocabulary* (London, 1893), p. 128.

[3] The Shādhilīs of Mocha, patron saints, as it were, of coffee (*qahwah Shādhilīyah*), are of course celebrated.

common in the country areas or, for instance, in the towns of Ḥaḍramawt of the interior; the same would not of course be true of the large ports. As I have noticed elsewhere,[1] when I asked if venereal diseases were found among and transmitted by the gypsy girls of Da<u>th</u>īnah my informant's answer was that they were not, since the country was clean and far from Aden. During the last ten years, with the vast development of travel and improvement of communications, coupled with the beginnings of disintegration of the older form of society, that happy condition may have to some extent altered, though as it has been accompanied also by a great increase in medical services in the territory, and as I think it would be *'aib* for a tribesman to return to his village so afflicted, the state of affairs may not have changed so very much.

On Socotra Island, according to a fairly recent report by Dr N. I. Corkhill, syphilis is still known as *Franjī*, which must surely be the old term of four and a half centuries ago still persisting. This it apparently also does in Oman, to judge from the Omani author al-Sālimī[2] who lived from 1869 to 1913, for in his long metrical compendium of Ibāḍī law,[3] discussing the causes which give a woman the option of annulment of her marriage (these being much the same as those adduced by the <u>Sh</u>āfi'ī authors already cited, except in the case of syphilis), he says

يقع الخيار بالافرنج　　إن كان فيه او بذات الغنج
وقيل لا خيار لكن يمنع　　من وطئها لضرر قد يقع

Option comes about through *al-Ifranj*
When present in him, or through a woman with lovely eyes.[4]
It is said also (according to another view) that (in such case) option does not exist, but it is prohibited
To have intercourse with her on account of ill that may occur.

The editor remarks that *al-Faranj/Firanj* is syphilis (*maraḍ al-zuharī*). From the data already presented I surmise that the

[1] "The Ma'n "Gypsies" of the West Aden Protectorate", *Anthropos* (Posieux–Fribourg, 1961), LVI, 743.

[2] Cf. Brock. *Sup.* II, 823, but this should be supplemented by the biography in the *Jawhar al-niẓām*.

[3] Muḥ. b. 'Abdullāh...al-Sālimī, *Jawhar al-niẓām* (Cairo, 1345 H.), I, 186, edit. of Cairo, 1381 H., p. 184.

[4] Al-<u>gh</u>unj according to the commentator means *malāḥat al-'ainain*. It also means, however, amorous gesture, voluptuous movements.

second view quoted by al-Sālimī was a species of compromise which preceded the more categorical first view that he offers. It is clear, however, that this question must have been discussed by the legists of the Omani Ibāḍīs, and when their hardly known legal literature is examined we can confidently expect to find some data on syphilis. The point of interest would be to discover whether they attribute its arrival in their country to the Portuguese or to some other visitors to their coast.

ADDENDA

P.241/12 M.C-F. Volney, *Travels . . .*, London 1787, I, 247, "Another very general distemper at Cairo is that which the vulgar there call the *blessed evil*, and which we also improperly term the *Neapolitan disorder*: one half of Cairo is infected with it". Cf. C.S. Sonnini, *Travels in Upper and Lower Egypt*, London, 1800, 260, 629, 673, speaking of whimsical names for the various venereal complaints, the general *embarek*, blessed, and the *goat disease* or *camel disease*. One treatment is to bury oneself in hot sand up to the neck for 20–30 days. Dr E.M. Sartain cites ʿAbd al-Qādir al-Shādhilī, *Bahjat al-ʿābidīn.*, Chester Beatty Ms. 4436, 48a, for a scholar "sick of the *ḥabb* (chancre) with which most of the people were afflicted", who died in 945/1539.

P.242/6 Ba 'l-Faqīh al-Shiḥrī has apparently copied this passage and that on *sh m n d lah* from Ibn al-Daybaʿ, *al-Faḍl al-mazīd*, ed. Y. Chelhod, Ṣanʿā', 1983, 282 & 277.

P.243/fn.1 Cf. Rossi, *L'Arabo parlato*, 175. My field notes also have *ibn al-nās* in this sense.

P.250/6 I visited Yakhtul, a small coastal fishing village, and al-Mitaynah of the Muḥibb Sayyids where they treat venereal disease. See my "Tihāmah notes" in the Professor A.F.L. Beeston Festschrift, Oxford, 1991.

XVIII

NOTES ON SOME ASPECTS OF ARAB BUSINESS PRACTICES IN ADEN

A little over ten years ago Dr ʿAbdullāh b. Muḥammad Maqṭarī [1] discussed with me how business was carried on in Aden among the Arab community, and the notes below are based on the information which he has generously permitted me to write up under my own name.

The practices described here had obviously been going on for a very long time but the circumstances of today must inevitably mean that some have disappeared, been modified, or are in abeyance. Under communist rule, it is reported, every business down to the single owner shop has been "nationalized", which, in effect, means the seizure from the owner without compensation while the latter has become an employee on the same basis as the rest of the staff. Many formerly prosperous Aden merchants, often Yemeni by birth, betook themselves to al-Ḥudaydah and Mocha, or other places in and outside the Yemen, when communist measures in Aden rendered commerce impossible for them. It is possible that similar customs still flourish in these Yemeni ports, for they must have a well developed local set of commercial practices, such as existed in Aden.

Though in Aden the century and a quarter of stable British government made possible the establishment of a considerable number of European firms and a small European business community, this was organized naturally on a different basis from that of the Arabs dealing with Arabs. European businessmen for the most part probably did not have a very intimate knowledge, with certain exceptions naturally, of how the Arabs carried on their business [2]. It would be interesting to study how the Parsee and Bāniyān communities, most of whom came to Aden after it was captured by the British (though Bāniyāns flourished there from at least mediaeval times [3]), managed their business affairs. A study of

[1] Author of "Water Rights and Irrigation Practices in Laḥj" (Cambridge 1971).

[2] Nevertheless F. M. Hunter, "An Account of the British Settlement of Aden" (London 1877 and reprint), has much of interesting data. South Arabian books on law (mainly in Ms.) contain much information on business practice.

[3] See my "Portuguese off the South Arabian Coast" (Oxford 1963: 32 s.).

Jewish business methods in Aden and their relations with the Arabs could probably be still made today though the community so long established there has left, probably to the last man. Many Indians were preparing to leave Aden before the British withdrawal in 1967, and since they will have been dispossessed, not to say robbed, by "nationalization" it is to be expected that most able to leave will already have done so. Very recently signs of a possible change of policy if not of heart, seem to have shown themselves in Aden under outside pressures. The collapse of Aden as a centre of commerce since 1967 is comparable to its fall under the first Ottoman occupation in 16–17th centuries when Turkish extortion so ruined the port that trading retreated to Mocha, and though it revived to some extent under the Zaydī Imāms, it had so far been ruined again by 1839 that its inhabitants numbered only about a thousand souls.

The *dallāl* and the *wakīl*

The *dallāl,* who can be described in Aden and Ṣan'ā' as a commission agent, is discussed in that branch of Islamic law known as *ḥisbah* which covers market law in general; but the *dallāl* in Ḥaḍramawt[4] has functions not to be found with the *dallāl* in these two cities.

There is a clear distinction between the professions of *dilālah* and *wakālah* in Aden, but a man may act as both a *dallāl* and a *wakīl* or agent. The task of a *dallāl* is simple – it is indeed explained by the meaning of the Arabic word (*dalla*) itself – he brings to the attention of merchants all goods, properties or other interests which may be potentially profitable. Once he succeeds in getting a merchant interested in certain goods or properties he is then asked to become a go-between, and when the deal is concluded he receives either a percentage or a service fee (*dilālah*). The good and well known *dallāls* will never accept anything but a percentage – which may lie somewhere between a half and two and a half per cent, depending on the amount involved – the larger the amount the less the percentage.

Of the *wakīls* the best known in Aden are the rent collectors who often deal with nothing else but real property – they are almost the same as estate agents in England. The practice in Aden is that they collect rents and deliver them monthly (which is rare), or every three months, or even once every six months – which is the practice common

---

[4] Cf. "le courtier" in C. de Landberg, "Etudes sur les dialectes de l'Arabie méridionale, Ḥaḍramoût" (Leiden 1901: 332 s.).

among those who manage vast numbers of properties. Rent collectors sometimes undertake repairs of property and often appear in the courts or in front of rent tribunals on behalf of their owners. In almost all cases the fee is 2% of the total amount of rent collected, beside the fact that some of them get the chance of investing some of the money that is kept in their custody, as well as collecting a portion of any "key-money" [5] which they may arrange to be delivered to the owner. In some cases, if the tenant of a premises agrees for a consideration, to vacate the premises and deliver it to another person, the *wakīl* would normally agree to obtain for him the consent of the property-owner, who normally grants it, again for a consideration. In such a case the *wakīl* would collect a service charge (*khidmah*) from both the owner and the original tenant.

Another type of *wakīl* is one who acts as an agent for persons working abroad. This category is usually to be found among merchants and shop-keepers. A man who leaves Aden or the Yemen for, say, East Africa, would ask some shop-keeper known to him to supply his family with food, provisions, clothes and maintenance money. The cost of providing these items as well as the money itself is considered an advance payment (*taqdimah*). The shop-keeper charges no service on this, but when the other party sends him money from abroad the shop-keeper will deduct service (*khidmah*) for saving the balance after he has deducted what is owing to him, besides any profit he makes on the rate of exchange from the foreign currency. For instance a man might send back from Sa'ūdī Arabia a sum of 500 *riyāls*, whether as notes enclosed with a letter, or with someone travelling back to Aden. The shop-keeper will refer to his account and see, perhaps, that he is owed 300 *riyāls* – which he will deduct from the 500 *riyāls* sent to him. He will retain the balance against the return of the man from abroad, but take service on the 200 *riyāls* for holding it on his behalf – how much exactly is uncertain but it would likely be two or two and a half per cent. This may be compared with a Ṣan'ānī practice where, till it was looted in 1948, people used to deposit money with the merchants of Samsarat Sīdī Muḥammad b. al-Ḥasan [6], who made a small charge for keeping it.

In the old days (i.e. before motor transport) communication between immigrants working in Aden and their families back in the villages of

---

[5] Called *ḥaqq al-miftāḥ*. It was frequently discussed in the Aden press during the housing shortages at the time of the tremendous expansion for about twenty years after World War II.

[6] This is discussed in our forth-coming study on Ṣan'ā' city.

the Yemen was via the Aden shop-keeper and the *gammāl*. This last was a camel-owner who always travelled at least once a month between Aden and a specific district in the Yemen – he was also called *al-ṭabal* [7] and acted as a sort of postman. Now these men no longer travel on camels but they are still known as *gammāl*. They come to Aden and collect all the *taṣādīr* (sing. *taṣdīr*), i.e. a parcel of goods, or an envelope containing money, etc. The sender would say, "*Ṣaddir-hā li-filān,* Take it to so and so." On the return journey the *gammāl* brings back with him all the *ta'ārīf* (sing. *ta'rīf*), i.e. acknowledgements of delivery, or receipts. In *Qānūn Ṣan'ā'* [8] a *taṣdūr* means a covering note accompanying goods to be delivered. The type of letter that the Yemeni would send back to his family – written by the professional letter-writer if he is not himself literate, would run, "*Ṣadar lak ṣudūr 'ishrīn riyāl/ ṭāqat bazz/ ḥawāyig,* There has been despatched to you twenty *riyāls*/ a roll of cloth/ spices." If letters are sent to a woman from abroad they would not be addressed to her but to a male child or other male relation, as in Ḥaḍramawt [9]. So Adenis, seeing a Yemeni reading a letter in a café, might poke fun at him with the conventional rhyming phrase, "*Ṣadar lak ṣadar maqramah wa-maṣar,* To you there has been despatched one shawl and one scarf."

The *hakkābah*

A very singular profession in Aden – where I am inclined to believe there were many strange customs not found or not preserved in most other south Arabian towns – was that of the *hakkābah* which may be rendered as "lady money saver". There are however also men who engage in *hakbah*. This word, in the sense in which it is used in Aden, is unknown to the Arabic lexicons consulted, but in Yemenite Ḥugariyyah the verb *hakab* means *confier, mettre en dépôt* [10]. The *hakkābah* is a well known institution in Aden and she acts as a sort of savings bank for the ladies of her neighbourhood (*ḥāfah*), but she might go round several *ḥāfahs* (*ḥāfah* in Aden nowadays just means a street), to get subscribers. Sometimes the *mukaddiyah,* i.e. the tire-woman of the bride,

---

[7] If the *gammāl* used a drum (*ṭabl*) to announce his arrival that might possibly be the origin of this name for him.

[8] To be published in translation in our forth-coming Ṣan'ā' book, note 395.

[9] Cf. my "Sex, Birth, Circumcision...". In: Festschrift HERMANN VON WISSMANN (Tübingen 1962: 201).

[10] LANDBERG, *Gloss. daṯ.*, 2875 (cf. note 4).

who has many functions, is also a *hakkābah,* but some *hakkābahs* do nothing else. There is a well known *hakkābah* in Shaykh 'Uthmān who makes a great deal of money out of this profession – she is said to keep the money in a box under her bed and never to go to sleep!

The customary way in which this form of money-saving operates is that the *hakkābah* will approach a number of persons (women) – but the converse is also true in that several women would take the initiative of approaching the *hakkābah* – to these women she will suggest a scheme for saving. She will find out how much each can save in one month, and will group them in accordance with the amount they wish to save. The amount to be saved is always in tens, twenties, thirties and so on, and is known as *farshah.* If, for instance, there are ten women willing to save ten shillings a month, the first *farshah* the *hakkābah* collects will amount to a hundred shillings.

The whole point of saving money in this way is that if a woman in a group contributing 100/– *per mensem* requires a sum of, say, 500/– immediately, she can receive it at once from the total sum already collected, i.e. she can raise a capital sum in a hurry, but of course she has to keep on paying into the fund. The *hakkābah* when delivering the sum saved to the person whose turn it is to collect will charge ten shillings in every hundred, 10 %, her fee being known as *hikābah.*

On the other hand the savers (*aṣḥāb al-hakbah*) may decide to make the final target of their savings 300/ – each, and if they pay 10/ – *per capita per mensem* then the first pay-out of 300/ – to the first individuel can be made only after three months of instalments have been paid. No doubt there are many ways in which the *hakbah* can be operated, but we did not record upon what principle priority is given for the first drawer to receive her instalment, be it by agreement, by lot, or some other method.

In 1965 the lady school-teachers wishing to spend a summer vacation in Cairo were saving money to do so in this way. Several of them put money together and perhaps one or two go to Cairo, next year one or two more, the persons in the ring saving the same amount each time – but they do this themselves and do not employ a *hakkābah* to do it for them!

Settlement of Disputes by Conciliation

Even in Aden the system of *ṣulḥ,* that is to say settlement outside the normal courts of justice, is very prevalent among the merchants – hence the well known dictum, "*Al-ṣulḥ khayr,* Conciliation is benefit/advantage." This is not a *Ḥadīth*-Tradition but *ṣulḥ* is recognized in

Islam and was certainly preferred by most Yemenis to the *sharīʿah* courts – indeed it can be confidently stated that it is the usual way of composing differences everywhere in Arabia outside the towns.

The result is that a great many disputes among the merchants never go to court, though it is now noticeable (1965) that this custom is diminishing. There are however two communities among the merchants of Aden whose members are known never to go to the courts unless they are involved with outsiders – these are the Ḥaḍramī Dawʿanīs (Ahl Dawʿan) and the Ḥabbānīs (Ahl Ḥabbān) – the Dawʿanīs are particularly well known as merchants both in Ḥaḍramawt and abroad. A member of the former community, a Bā Zarʿah man, told me[11] that he has never known a Dawʿanī merchant to take another Dawʿanī to the ordinary courts of justice. He stated that some Dawʿanīs even wait for years until they go back home, and then file their cases against their fellow countrymen in front of their elders. Muḥammad Aḥmad Bā Junayd (pronounced Gunayd, a Dawʿanī), a well known merchant in Aden who was previously established in Asmara, confirmed this, and told me of several persons in Asmara who waited for periods of over six years before they were able to go home and settle their disputes. He added that Dawʿanīs considered it an *ʿayb,* a shaming act, to disclose their disputes to strangers.

Mr Muḥammad ʿAlī Maqṭarī (my father), who has been a merchant for a long time and dealt with almost all the Ḥabbānīs in Shaykh ʿUthmān, confirmed that similar practices obtain among them. Most of the Ḥabbānī merchants in Shaykh ʿUthman are Sayyids. (The Sayyid families of Ḥabbān are Āl Fadʿaq and Āl Miḥḍār).

Neither community of course has organized courts, and their disputes are not always settled in the same manner, but there are certain men among them who are reputed to be *"aṣḥāb ʿaql wa-istiqāmah,* persons of sense and integrity." The decisions of these men who act as arbitrators is almost always accepted, but it may sometimes be refused on the grounds of lack of experience (*qillat fahm*) on the part of the arbitrator.

When the parties go to the sessions of arbitration they follow no rules of procedure, and sometimes both parties will be talking at the same time and friends will try to calm them. One way of calming people at these sessions is by saying, *"Ṣallī ʿalā Muḥammad,* Bless Muḥammad." Everyone would reply, *"Allāhummā ṣallī wa-sallim ʿalayh",* and the person asked to pronounce the formula of blessing would calm down. (This way of interrupting an argument could be heard in Dathīnah and prob-

---

[11] I. e. ʿAbdullāh Maqṭarī whose account is here reproduced verbatim.

bably in every customary law court in the former Aden Protectorates.) Oaths are sometimes taken, but often when the oath is taken it is decisive and final, concluding the arbitration. The arbitrator may demand it of one of the parties, but his demand will be ineffective if the opposing party refuses to accept the man's oath [12]. Sometimes it is demanded by or offered by one or other of the parties, but again both sides to the dispute must be willing to accept such an oath as valid testimony.

The above is evidence of how closely knit were the communities from the countryside settled in Aden.

---

[12] This seems to me based on the principle one finds also in customary law, namely that the plaintiff has the onus of the proof, and he who denies the charge must take the oath of denial. Cf. my "Two tribal law cases (Documents)". *Journal of the Royal Asiatic Society* (London, April and October, 1951, pt II, 165).

INDEX

In classifying entries no account is taken of the following words preceding proper names (although they may be included before them): the definite article al/am; Āl, Ahl, Hal, Hil, 'Iyāl (all meaning family, folk or people); Abū, Bū, Bā; Umm (mother, owner of); Ibn, Bin, Bir, B.; Bal; Banū, Banī; Dhū, Dhī; de and von. Titles such as Imām, Shaykh, Sultan are treated similarly except when proper names of individuals as may happen with Shaykh and Sultan.

Transliteration follows the *Encyl. of Islam* or *Arabian Studies* systems with minor modifications, but some continental systems employ ṯ for *thā'*, ǧ for *jīm*, š for *shīn*. Alternative transliterations for the diphthongs are au/aw and ai/ay. Hard g is employed for colloquial *jīm* in one article.

Some journals omit final *hā'* of the fem. termination; this has been restored between brackets for consistency. Aḥ. and Muḥ. stand for Aḥmad and Muḥammad respectively.